Master Z Bible – 2014 Edition

Rainer G. Haselier

Traktor 2 Bible
2014 Edition

Digital DJing with Traktor Pro 2 and Traktor Scratch Pro 2
English Edition edited by Karl Yates

English Edition edited by Karl Yates, Preston, United Kingdom
Section about Harmonics reviewed by Michael White, Washington D.C., United States
Cover Design: Rainer G. Haselier and Nick R. Lynch, Amsterdam, The Netherlands
Photos of the Author: Taco Smit, Amsterdam, The Netherlands
Layout and Typeset: Haselier IT-Services, Amsterdam, The Netherlands

ISBN-10: 1497314267
ISBN-13: 978-1497314269
Printed in the United States of America

Traktor Bible is a project of:

Traktor Bible Webshop, Rainer G. Haselier • Daimlerstraße 25 • 52531 Übach-Palenberg • Germany and Hits.Amsterdam, Vierwindenstraat 84 • 1013LA Amsterdam • The Netherlands
www.traktorbible.com

Contents at a Glance

Table of Contents

Table of Contents

Table of Contents

8   Staying in Sync – Beat-, Bar- and Phrase-Matching 271

Table of Contents

10 Using Loops 345

Table of Contents

Table of Contents

Table of Contents

Chapter 1

Introduction

The original idea to write the first edition of Traktor Bible (published in 2009) came about some years ago during my own first hand experiences with Traktor. At first glance one is faced with a feature-rich and complex piece of software. In the beginning it may be difficult to know where to start or how the different parts of the software and all the settings are related to each other. In addition to the, not always "transparent" software you are faced with numerous questions about the best hardware configuration to choose, which audio interface and MIDI controller to use and whether you wish to DJ with timecode or without.

Now we find ourselves in 2014, several new versions of the Traktor software have been released, Native Instruments has transformed Traktor from a mainly software focused product into a more hardware focused one, and the competition in the market for DJ software and hardware is more intense than ever.

Your Practical Guide

Not all things have changed though. As with the very first edition the 2014 Edition of Traktor 2 Bible has been written from a practical perspective. The main goal is to give you all information, tips, and techniques at hand that you need to have fun with Traktor and to get the most out of it.

It does not matter whether you are using a classic style DJ mixer with a soundcard and an add-on controller, or whether you use one of the many DJ controllers that are compatible with Traktor, or if you have one of the controllers made by Native Instruments. All possible setups are covered and explained in this book.

I have tried to put all information relevant to each topic into one chapter and explain the features from a practical perspective, including the related mapping commands. The chapters about cue points and loops for example describe how to create and save cue points and loops in the Traktor user interface. Furthermore the same chapters contain all the necessary information about the mapping commands available for cue points and loops.

This makes it much easier to map the desired functionality to the keyboard and to any MIDI or DJ controller. And this will also help if you wish to extend the functionality of your Native Instruments Traktor Kontrol controller.

You will find tutorials and HOW TO sections in several chapters. They explain some of the more complicated Traktor features by the use of exercises or they show how to implement advanced features in a mapping.

1.1 The Transformation of Traktor

There has been an incredible amount of change in the Traktor world since the first edition of Traktor Bible was published five years ago.

For a very long time Traktor was a software product, which was loved because of its feature-rich and open concept. Open meant that all features Traktor provided could be mapped to any controller, no matter whether it was a controller more designed for DJ usage, or whether it was a more general MIDI controller aimed at music production (the Akai APC 40 is a good example for this category).

The creation of mappings was not always easy. To help Traktor beginners, Traktor Bible created a mapping section on the website where Traktor users could upload the mappings they made for their controllers and share them with the Traktor community. Traktor Bible was the first DJ blog with a mapping portal. It was a ground breaking and unique concept which was later copied by other DJ websites on the net.

Everybody who made the effort necessary to create his own mapping ended up with a deep knowledge of Traktor and he finally had a controller that exactly fits to the personal workflow. Traktor features one uses regular were mapped and features that didn't fit to the individual needs, remained unused.

In the times when Traktor was a software-only product, Traktor users bought hardware controllers made by other, so called third party, manufacturers; naturally the earning went to them. At the same time the piracy rate of Traktor was very high, resulting in less profit for the makers of the Traktor software.

What would you do if you were in a leading position of such a company? Maybe you would simply produce the DJ controllers yourself? Or would you make it more difficult or even impossible for users to access certain software features with controllers that were not made by your company?

This has happened with Traktor in recent years.

Kontrol S4 – Sample Decks only for NI Controller

The first obvious sign of a paradigm change in the Traktor product strategy was Traktor Kontrol S4, the first four deck controller made by Native Instruments that hit the shop/street in November 2010. The DJ controller Traktor Kontrol S4, the version we now call MK1, shipped with a special Traktor flavor named Traktor Pro S4. This software variant was only available bundled with Kontrol S4.

One of the new software features of that S4 edition of Traktor were the sample decks, the ancestor of the remix decks. One sample deck contained four sample slots and all four samples could be played at the same time. In order to be able to use that software feature one had to buy a Kontrol S4 controller, simply because this was the only way to get your hands on that special Traktor S4 software.

In April 2011 Traktor Pro 2.0 was released; this version provided access to the sample decks for users of other controllers.

NI: The Move from a Technology to a Product Company

Roughly at the same time as Traktor Kontrol S4 arrived, German TV station Deutsche Welle broadcasted a feature about Native Instruments in their German Music Magazine PopXport. The feature gave a little insight into Native Instruments and it contains an interview with Daniel Haver (CEO of Native Instruments) and Mate Galic (CTO). It is worth watching: a link to the video is on *www.traktorbible.com/2014/links.aspx*.

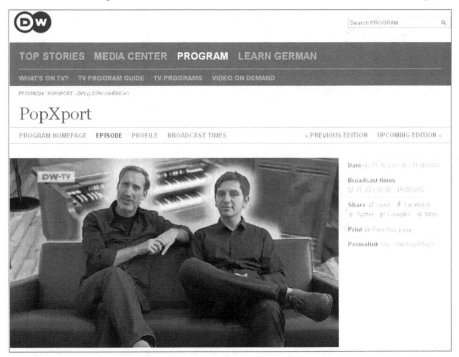

What we saw with the sample decks and Kontrol S4 on a physical level was mentioned by Daniel Haver in that interview on a more abstract level, namely that Native Instruments had successfully made the move from a technology company to a product company. For the Traktor software, that uses the technology from Native Instruments own

Reaktor, that meant making hardware products or integrated software/hardware DJ solutions. The good thing with hardware is that it cannot be illegally downloaded. And as Native Instruments has full control of the software and the features they integrate into their hardware, it also makes it much easier to be ahead of the other controllers. Manufacturers of other DJ controllers, that were partners for quite a long time, now became competitors.

Kontrol F1 – Remix Decks for NI Hardware first

What we saw with the sample decks and Kontrol S4 was repeated with the controller Traktor Kontrol F1 and Traktor software version 2.5, both released in May 2012. The main new feature of Traktor 2.5 were the remix decks, a clip matrix consisting of a grid with 64 cells, where the cells can be triggered and then played in the four sample slots one remix deck offers.

The Traktor software update to version 2.5 was available for free to all users owning an earlier version of Traktor Pro 2. The 64 sample cells could not be triggered by any controller, except for those that bought a Kontrol F1. With the remix decks the Kontrol F1 was used as a kind of dongle, because it was not possible to map the remix decks features to any other controllers. Even though the software update to Traktor 2.5 was free, you had to invest of $279/249 Euro (suggested retail price at launch) to be able to control the remix deck features. (You could and still can control the remix decks with mouse/keyboard actions; but this is quite cumbersome approach for a live performance.)

The integration between the software features of the remix decks and the Kontrol F1 was incredible and it offered DJs many stunning performance possibilities. Nevertheless a huge part of the Traktor community was angry as users felt that Native Instruments were almost forcing DJs that use the Traktor software to buy the F1. At the time I wrote a lengthy article on traktorbible.com citing why I did not see any technical reasons that could have prevented NI from making the most important features of the remix decks mappable by users for their personal choice of controller.

It took until Traktor 2.6.2, released in July 2013, for most of the remix deck features to become mappable to any other controller. We can only speculate about the motivation for this and there are many theories posted in the various DJ forums.

Who Should Read this Book

The changes in the Traktor world explained above are reflected in the new 2014 Edition of Traktor Bible. The book provides an excellent overview of all feature sets in Traktor and explains how to use them. If you are not sure whether Traktor is the right tool for you or if you are in the stage of making decisions about what hardware to buy, you will get information about the possible choices.

If you have one of the Native Instruments controllers Kontrol S2, Kontrol S4, Kontrol F1, Kontrol X1 or the controller/mixer Kontrol Z2, you will learn how to these controllers with their default settings. If the default configuration of the knobs, buttons, and faders is not exactly what you need, you will learn how to customize your controller.

If you prefer to use one of the many other controllers that are compatible with Traktor (made by companies like Pioneer, Vestax, Allen&Heath, Numark, Korg, Behringer, Hercules to name just a few), Traktor Bible will give you all the information you need to create your own mappings. Every chapter that explains one software area provides information about the commands you use to make this feature set accessible from the controller of your choice. Chapter 6 provides an in-deep coverage of the mapping architecture of Traktor. Several tutorials will help even beginners to find their way through the mapping world.

1.2 The different Traktor 2 Flavours

The Traktor 2 software exists in several flavours:

- **Traktor Pro 2** Feature wise Traktor Pro 2 is the most complete Traktor flavour. With Traktor Pro you can use four decks (each of the four decks can either be a track deck, a remix deck or it can be used for live input), you have more than 40 different effects which can be used in four FX units and you can save effect settings and recall them. Traktor Pro 2 offers different master clock modes to keep your tracks in sync and the support for MIDI and HID controllers has been improved. Traktor Pro is the flagship of the Traktor family.

- **Traktor Scratch Pro 2** Traktor Scratch Pro 2 offers the same feature set as Traktor Pro 2. Additionally you can control the playback of the Traktor decks with timecode vinyl or timecode CDs.

- **Traktor 2 Manufacturer Edition** The Traktor Manufacturer Edition is a custom mapped version of Traktor 2 and is bundled with a DJ controller. Compared to Traktor Pro, the manufacturer edition has a reduced feature set. The manufacturer Edition was available only with a few controllers. One controller was the Pioneer DDJ-T1 (meanwhile discontinued), another one the American Audio controllers from the VMS series (these controllers are currently shipped with Virtual DJ and not with Traktor anymore), and finally Numark 4Trak, which still is available with Traktor 2 Manufacturer Edition.

- **Traktor LE 2** Traktor LE 2 is kind of a "baby" in the Traktor family. Traktor LE 2 cannot be purchased as a stand-alone product and is available only bundled with other hardware. Traktor LE supports two decks only, but there are no remix decks available. Instead of six different effects you only get *Filter, Delay, Reverb* and *Flanger*. You can use only one effect for each deck instead of three as is possible in Traktor Pro. Also the loop and cue point features are reduced. For example you only can use the predefined standard loop lengths and neither loops nor cue points can be saved.

A more comprehensive comparison list describing the feature differences between the Traktor versions can be found on the Native Instruments website. You can open the page with the following short URL: *http://trktr.eu/s6WQo*

This book covers Traktor Pro and Traktor Scratch Pro, as the Manufacturer Edition and Traktor LE 2 no longer play such an important role.

All flavours – one executable file

All different flavours of Traktor actually live in the same bits. This means that the executable file of all Traktor versions is identical, no matter which flavour you own. In the process of activating Traktor and entering your serial number the software decides, which version and with which feature set is made available.

More information about changing the Traktor flavour without re-install the software can be found here: *http://kb.traktorbible.com/tp1002*

1.3 In this Book

The sequence of the chapters in this book tries to resemble the "relation history" you enter with Traktor. The second chapter therefore, explains the basic configuration of the software. Then, in chapter 3 it's time to load tracks and mix them. In chapter 4 you will find all the information you need to get Traktor Scratch Pro 2 with timecode control up and running. Chapters 5 and 6 finally answer all questions regarding MIDI and controller mapping. In chapter 5 you will find more technical information about MIDI protocol and its messages and chapter 6 explains all the practical things you need to know to create a customised keyboard and controller mapping.

The further chapters cover one main topic each and the sequence in which they are read is not quite as crucial as the previous chapters.

Several chapters of the book contain web links to blogs, articles, or videos that I recommend for further reading. A complete list with all the links can be found here: *www.traktorbible.com/2014/links.aspx*

1.4 Web Integrated Book

This book covers version 2.6.8 of Traktor Pro and Traktor Scratch Pro. Due to the high update frequency of Traktor the next update or bugfix will be available soon.

To keep you informed about all Traktor changes the Traktor 2 Bible and the Traktor Bible website are tightly integrated: You will find updates and information about software changes on the Traktor Bible website; updates are grouped by the chapters of this book and include information about bugs found by the Traktor community and if possible workarounds are explained.

You need to activate your Traktor Bible Plus Account to be able to access those updates pages. The Traktor Bible Plus Account is free for you as you bought the book and in that way supported my Traktor related work.

Follow these steps to get new and updated information:

1. Go to *www.traktorbible.com* and click in the main navigation on *Login*.
2. Click on *Create Account,* if you don't have an account yet, otherwise continue with step 3. Creating a new account is very easy. Once the account is created the website will send you an activation mail. Click the activation link contained in the mail to make your account active.
3. Once your account is created go to *www.traktorbible.com*, click on *Account* and log in.
4. Click in the main navigation on *Account* and then click in the *Plus Account* menu on *Activate*.
5. Select the edition of Traktor Bible that you own. Answer the two simple questions that verify that you own the book.
6. Once the verification has been successfully completed you will see the menu entry *Updates* in the *Plus Account* menu on your *Account* page. This menu gives you access to all available updates. You can sort the update articles by chapter, Traktor version number or by publishing date.

If you would like to be automatically informed about updates subscribe the "Traktor Bible Newsletter" on *www.traktorbible.com/newsletter*.

1.5 Thanks and Feedback

Some users of the Traktor user forum have "tested" several chapters of this book while they have been written. My special thanks go to those users who took the time to read and comment on samples from the book.

Whilst writing the book I visited the Traktor user forum frequently (I realise how often the deadline of the book has been changed, unfortunately maybe too often). As well as trying to be helpful I wanted to understand the main issues that new Traktor users are facing and to understand those questions and issues that even the more advanced user is confronted with. A lot of the questions being asked in the forum found their way into this book and had a lot of influence on the weighting of the topics. Therefore I offer a big thank you to all forum users for their questions.

The future editions of this book will continue to focus on the questions and needs of the Traktor user community. If you find errors in the book or have questions which need to be answered or if you wish to propose topics please feel free to send an email to *rainer@traktorbible.com* or use the contact form on the Traktor Bible website at *www.traktorbible.com/contact*. Of course if you wish to praise the book I would be very happy to hear that too.

Thanks to the team of the DJ Division from Native Instruments in Berlin for their support.

Please note that we use a mixture of British English and American English in this book. The text has been written in British English (that's why we use *behaviour* instead of *behavior*, for example). The text in the user interface of Traktor however, uses American English (that's why they use *behavior* instead of *behaviour*). This is nothing to worry about, we just wanted you to know.

A very special thank you goes to Karl Yates, from the Traktor user forum on the Native Instruments website better known as Moderator Karlos Santos. He has checked my English translation of the original German edition and has helped make the English version a more pleasurable read for native English speakers. All kudos goes to Karl, if there are still errors in the book please don't blame him.

Greetings from my "bedroom".
Have fun with the 2014 Edition of
Traktor 2 Bible!

Rainer G. Haselier
Amsterdam, March 2014

Chapter 2

First Steps

The first sections of this chapter explain how to get Traktor up and running very quickly. You will learn how to configure the various Native Instruments controllers, the many Traktor Ready controllers (controllers for which Traktor provides a mapping), for any other controller you may own and where you have downloaded a mapping from the website of the controllers' manufacturer. Another section explains how to configure the audio routing in Traktor and the differences between internal and external mixing mode.

Once the basic setup is done we will take a closer look at Traktors' user interface and how to adjust it so that it fits better to your personal needs.

2.1 Basic Configuration of Traktor

Before you can use Traktor two main areas need to be properly configured:

◻ **Audio Configuration**   With regard to the audio configuration Traktor provides two different operation modes: *internal mixing mode* and *external mixing mode*.

In internal mixing mode the audio from the Traktor decks is mixed internally inside the software. For internal mixing mode Traktor requires an audio interface with at least two stereo outputs. One stereo output is used for the master signal, the second one for the headphone signal. The headphone signal is used to pre-listen to tracks, before they are mixed into the master signal and then being audible to your audience.

In external mixing mode the audio from the Traktor decks you use is mixed inside an external hardware mixer. Traktor requires one stereo output for each Traktor deck you wish to use. If you wish to use all four Traktor decks you need an audio interface with four stereo outputs.

When you setup the audio configuration in Traktor you connect the "virtual" outputs of Traktor to the "real" outputs of your audio interface. This process is called routing.

◻ **Controller Configuration**   Before you can control Traktor with a DJ controller, Traktor needs a mapping. In a mapping the various controls of the controller are mapped to the functions of Traktor. For example: If you press the Play/Pause button on your controller, Traktor starts or stops the playback of a deck.

The following sections describe the steps you need to perform to configure your audio setup and your controller setup. Depending on which equipment you use the steps are slightly different:

◻ **Native Instruments Devices** Traktor detects the audio interfaces and controllers made by Native Instruments automatically and configures them when they are plugged in.

◻ **Pioneer Devices** Some – but not all – mixers, controllers and CDJ players made by Pioneer will be configured automatically when Traktor detects them. For the supported mixers and hybrid controllers (controllers with an integrated audio interface) Traktor configures the audio routing. For the supported CDJ players and hybrid controllers Traktor activates the mappings. More information about the configuration of the supported Pioneer devices can be found on page 30.

◻ **Traktor-Ready-Controller** Traktor provides many ready to use mappings for controllers made by other companies. These controllers are known as Traktor-Ready-Controllers. With the Traktor setup wizard it is quite easy to configure these controllers. If you wish you can load the mappings for the Traktor-Ready-Controllers at a later point without running the setup wizard again. Section "Traktor-Ready-Controllers" on page 31 explains the details.

◻ **All other Soundcards and Controllers** You can use any soundcard with Traktor as long as it has at least two stereo outputs (for internal mixing mode) or four stereo outputs (for using all four decks in external mixing mode). Once you understand the different usage scenarios Traktor is able to handle, the setup of an audio interface becomes very easy. Section 2.2, "Audio Setup" on page 37 and onwards will help. There the various configuration options are explained in details.

You can use any controller with Traktor, as long as it can send and receive MIDI data. Section "All other controllers" on page 35 explains where to find the appropriate mappings and how to import them into Traktor.

Soundcards and Controllers from NI: Automatic Configuration

The various NI controllers and audio interfaces are configured by Traktor automatically. Please ensure that the audio interface and/or controller is connected before you start Traktor.

On OS X there are no drivers needed for the newer models of the NI soundcards and controllers as they use the corresponding frameworks (Core Audio and CoreMIDI) provided by the operating system. However, on Windows drivers are required. The drivers are installed during the installation of Traktor, as long as the corresponding checkboxes are enabled in the Traktor setup program (see picture on the next page).

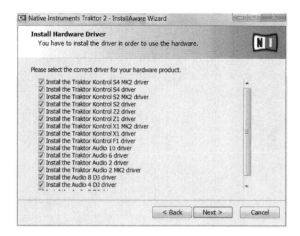

You can download updated Windows drivers from the Native Instruments website (*https://co.native-instruments.com/index.php?id=freeupdates*) for free. On the same webpage you can download the Device Updater. Use Device Updater to update the firmware of your NI devices. The most current version of Device Updater contains the most recent firmware version for all NI devices, i.e. you need to download Device Updater only once.

Back to auto configuration. Depending on whether you have a NI controller, a hybrid controller with integrated audio interface, Traktor performs the following actions when the device is detected:

◻ **Audio Interface** For the different NI audio interfaces (like Traktor Audio 8 DJ or Traktor Scratch A10) Traktor configures the audio setup. The "software" inputs and outputs are routed to the inputs and outputs of the soundcard. You can take a look at the settings Traktor made by opening the *Preferences* dialog (see page 37 for more information about the audio setup options provided in this dialog).

◻ **Controller** If you have one of the controller-only devices (like Kontrol X1/F1) Traktor activates the default mapping for the controller. With some controllers you need to perform additional steps on the controller itself. For example, if you are using two remix decks C and D and have one Kontrol F1 attached, you can select whether deck C or deck D shall be initially controlled with Kontrol F1 on the controller.

◻ **Hybrid Controller** If you have one of the hybrid controllers, like Kontrol S2 or Kontrol S4, Traktor will configure the audio setup and it will activate the mapping for the controller.

During the automatic configuration of the audio settings it may happen that Traktor shows the following dialog (of currently another soundcard is selected in Traktor). Click *Yes* to activate the soundcard that is shown in the dialog.

Pioneer Devices: Automatic Configuration

Traktor supports automatic configuration for some, but not for all Pioneer hardware. Supported are:

- ◻ **Mixer**   In regard to automatic configuration Traktor supports only those Pioneer mixers that are certified for Traktor Scratch. In Traktor version 2.6.7 these are the following mixers: DJM-850, DJM-900nexus and DJM-T1.

- ◻ **Hybrid Controller**   The following Pioneer hybrid controllers are automatically detected and configured by Traktor: DDJ-T1, DDJ-ERGO und MEP-7000.

- ◻ **CDJs**   The following Pioneer CDJ players can be used with Traktor in HID mode (these players are automatically configured): CDJ-400, CDJ-900, CDJ-2000 and CDJ-2000 nexus. Once the CDJ is connected and detected by Traktor you need to select which of the Traktor decks it shall control (see the following picture), this is done on the CDJ. Then you are ready to go

  Please note that CDJ-900nexus is currently – as of Traktor version 2.6.8 – not supported.

This video tutorial made by Pioneer contains more useful information about HID mode and Traktor 2.6: *http://youtu.be/nvdlIPPzhwA*.

Please not that all other Pioneer mixers and the other Pioneer DJ controllers can be sued with Traktor as well. You simply need to perform the configuration manually. The other sections in this chapter will provide you with the information you need to get this done

Traktor-Ready-Controllers

The next group of DJ controllers are the Traktor-Ready-Controllers. Traktor does not configure them completely automatically but you can set them up in an easy, semi-automatic way.

Traktor-Ready-Controllers are those controllers where Traktor already includes a configuration file and a mapping. A Traktor-Ready-Controller can either be a controller-only or a hybrid controller with an integrated audio interface.

To setup Traktor for a Traktor-Ready-Controller the Setup Wizard is used. The Setup Wizard configures the MIDI mapping, loads a mapping for your keyboard and configures the audio setup if applicable.

Configuration of Traktor-Ready-Controllers with the Setup-Wizard

The Setup Wizard is executed automatically when you start Traktor for the first time. However, you can start the Wizard any time you wish to change your configuration.

1. Open the *Help* menu and click on *Start Setup Wizard*.

The Setup Wizard creates a new Traktor configuration file by using the information about your setup that you provided in the subsequent dialog boxes. During this process a backup of your current configuration is created. You can use that backup to restore your old settings, if necessary. More information about how to restore your settings can be found below.

2. Click *Next*. If you use any kind of controller (this can either be a DJ controller, a CDJ player or a hybrid device, i.e. mixer and controller in one box), select *Yes* and click *Next*. Otherwise select *No* and click *Next*.

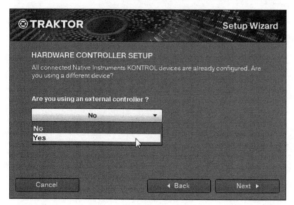

3. Use the page *Hardware Controller Selection* (which is only shown if you clicked *Yes* in step 2) to select the controller that you use. Open the upper list box, *Choose your manufacturer* to select the manufacturer of your controller. Then open the list box *Choose your model* to select your controller. Click *Next*.

4. Use the page *Deck Layout Selection* to select the number of decks and the deck modes that you wish to use.

   The options in list box *Select your setup* are slightly different for Traktor Pro and Traktor Scratch Pro. Open the list box and select the option that fits to your setup.

   If you cannot make up your mind: you can change the deck setup at a later point. Section 2.3 on page 46 and onwards explains how to configure the user interface of Traktor.

(Traktor Pro)

(Traktor Scratch Pro)

5. Click *Next* to see a summary of the settings you made. Click *Finish* to apply the choices you made.

Traktor should now be ready to use. It may be necessary to make small corrections to the audio setup and the audio routing (see page 37 and onwards for more information).

Loading Mappings of Traktor-Ready-Controllers manually

You can load the mappings of all Traktor-Ready-Controllers manually without using the Setup Wizard. Using the Setup Wizard is not always the best choice as it overwrites all settings and mappings that already have been made.

Perform the following steps to load a mapping of a Traktor-Ready-Controller manually:

1. Click on the *Preferences* button in the Traktor header *to open the Preferences window.*

2. Click in the category list at the left side on *Controller Manager*.

3. Click on *Add In* and point on *Import TSI.*

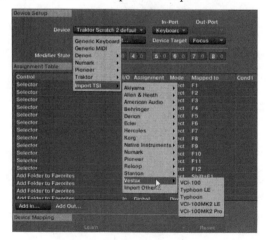

4. Point on the name of the manufacturer of your controller and then click on the controller you have. Traktor imports the mapping file.

5. Use the list boxes *In-Port* and *Out-Port* in the upper section of the window and select your controller there.

NOTE You cannot use the steps explained above to import the mapping for the automatic configured controllers. If you select one of these devices, nothing happens (at least in Traktor 2.6.8). However, you can import these mappings manually as explained in the next section.

You can find the mapping files for the automatically configured devices in the following folders: OS X: */Library/Application Support/Native Instruments/Traktor 2/Factory Settings/[2.x.x]/AutoConfig.* Windows: *C:\Users\All Users\Native Instruments\Traktor 2\Factory Settings\[2.x.x]\AutoConfig.* Replace *[2.x.x]* by the Traktor version you are using.

TIP The PDF files explaining the mappings of the Traktor-Ready-Controller and the supported Pioneer CDJ players can be found in the program folder of Traktor:

- **OS X** */Applications/Native Instruments/Traktor 2/Documentation/ Controller Mappings*

- **Windows** *C:\Program Files\Native Instruments\Traktor 2\Documentation\ Controller Mappings*

All other Controllers

If you have a controller that does not fit into any of the categories discussed above, do not worry. Almost all manufacturers of DJ controllers provide configuration files and mappings on their websites. The settings can be imported into Traktor with some simple steps. Doing a web search for the model of your controller plus the phrase "Traktor Mapping" to find mappings for your controller.

Or have a look at *traktorbible.com/freaks.* You can find many mappings for various controllers here which were created by other Traktor users.

Traktor mappings and configurations live in TSI files (TSI = Traktor Settings Information). TSI files can contain mappings only or additional configuration settings, like the audio setup, settings for the Traktor effects and settings regarding the layout of Traktor.

Once you have downloaded the TSI file for your controller perform the following steps to import the settings into Traktor:

1. Click in *Preferences* button in the Traktor header *to open the Preferences window.*

2. Click in the category list at the left side on *Controller Manager.*

3. Perform one of the following actions:

☐ If you want to import the controller mapping only click in the **upper area** of the window on *Add/Import TSI* and then on *Import other*. Change to the folder with the TSI file, select it and click *Open*.

This action imports the controller mapping only from the selected file (or multiple mappings if the TSI file contains more than one mapping. Mappings that already exist will not be removed.

☐ If you want to import the controller mapping(s) and other settings, click in the lower part of the *Preferences* dialog on Import. Change to the folder with the TSI file, select it and click *Open*. Traktor displays the *Select Categories to Import* dialog.

Activate the check boxes of all settings you wish to import and click *OK*. If you select *Controller Mappings* all mappings currently available in Traktor will be removed and replaced by the imported ones.

Sometimes you need to import additional settings for a mapping to work properly. One example is the mapping for the Pioneer controller DDJ-SX) (see web page with the soft links for this book). The Pioneer mapping provides several Instant FX buttons. Pressing one of these buttons activates different effect combinations. In order for these buttons to work, the FX units of Traktor need to be configured in a specific way. If you have already created or loaded other mappings, it is recommended to import this kind of TSI file in two steps as it ensures, that no mapping is overwritten:

☐ First use the *Import TSI* command in the upper section of the *Preferences* dialog to import the mapping only.

☐ Then use the *Import* button in the lower part and select the same TSI file again. When the *Select Categories to Import* is displayed, select all categories except for *Controller Mappings*, and click *OK*. This imports all the other settings needed by the mapping imported in the first step.

2.2 Audio Setup

If you use a soundcard, a hybrid controller or a mixer with an integrated audio interface that is neither configured automatically nor by the Setup Wizard, you need to
perform the audio setup manually. This is done on three pages of the *Preferences* dialog. Here you can

◻ Select the audio interface Traktor shall use and configure the latency setting

◻ Select a fallback device that Traktor shall use in case the standard audio interface
is not connected (Windows only)

◻ Configure the audio input routing and output routing

Selecting and Configuring your Audio Interface

Audio Device Use the category page *Audio Setup* in the *Preferences* dialog to select
the audio interface that Traktor shall use. For Windows the list *Audio Device* shows all
audio drivers installed on your computer, even when the audio interface is not connected currently. For OS X only the currently available audio devices are shown.
Choose the audio interface you wish to use in Traktor here.

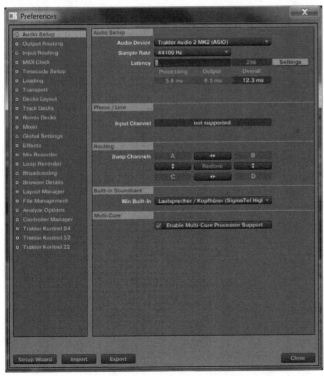

If you are running Windows and, if your audio interface has more than one driver type installed and if one of the drivers is using the ASIO protocol and the other one is using the WDM protocol (Windows Driver Model) or the Windows Audio Session API (WASAPI), then always select the ASIO driver. ASIO drivers generally offer better performance than WDM drivers (see sidebar on page 39).

Sample Rate   Use the list *Sample Rate* to specify the sampling rate that Traktor shall use for the audio data that it sends to your audio interface. The available options depend on the audio interface and its drivers. The default value for the sample rate is 44.1 kHz, which is the same sampling rate used by audio CDs. In most cases this default setting is acceptable. A higher sample rate may create a better sound but this is usually dependent on the particular audio interface and the individuals' sense of hearing. Fact is: a higher sample rate results in larger audio buffers that are used to process, manipulate and send the audio data to the audio interface. If for example the sample rate is doubled to 88.2 kHz then the size of the audio buffer doubles as well. Traktor therefore needs to transport more audio that in turn leads to a higher CPU load.

Audio Latency   The section *Audio Latency* shows the current latency time as a value (in milliseconds) and in a slider. The latency time is a measure of the time it takes until an action in Traktor (like activating an FX unit) is audible. Generally speaking a latency time between 5 and 15 milliseconds is considered an adequate and decent value.

Depending on the audio driver and on your operating system the latency time can sometimes be configured directly with the slider. If the slider is not moveable you will find the button *Settings* next to it. Click the button *Settings* to open the configuration tool of your audio interface and setup the latency time there.

Make sure that the buffer size is at least 128 samples (this is the minimum buffer size Traktor uses internally) and that it is a multiple of 128 (i.e. 128, 256, 512 or 1.024 samples).

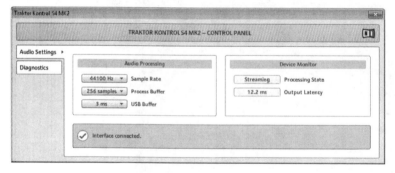

The picture above shows the Windows Control Panel for the integrated soundcard of Traktor Kontrol S4 MK2 (the control panels of the other NI soundcards look the same). You can change the audio latency by opening the list box *Process Buffer* and selecting another number of samples.

The following picture shows the *ASIO* tab of the settings tool for the Pioneer mixer DJM-900nexus. Here you can change the latency with the slider which in turn changes the buffer size (= number of samples).

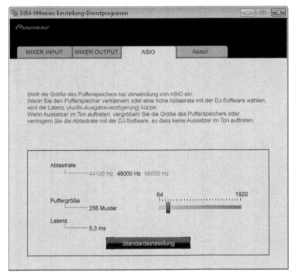

TIP If you hear clicks and pops in the audio output of Traktor or if the audio output is interrupted then in most cases the solution is to increase the latency time. Why this helps and the reasons for the distortions are explained in the following sidebar.

Sidebar: Latency Time, Buffer Size, ASIO

As a general rule the lower the latency time, the better. But: a low latency time can cause some issues. One is caused by the method by which the audio data is sent from the application (in our case Traktor) to the audio interface (to be more precise: to its digital-to-analogue converter, which transforms the audio data into audible sound).

To guarantee a continuous data stream the audio drivers provide a data buffer. Traktor writes the generated audio data into this buffer. The audio driver then transfers the received data to the audio interface hardware and the hardware makes the data audible. To achieve a lower latency the data buffer needs to be as small as possible. With a small buffer the amount of audio data is very small and Traktor needs to update the data buffers more often to make sure that the data stream is not interrupted.

After each action that is performed in Traktor, the buffers need to be refreshed very rapidly and the result of this action is audible because of the small size of the buffers.

However, the problem here is that Traktor needs to share the processor time with other applications and the operating system. If Traktor cannot update the data buffers quickly enough the data stream is interrupted. This can lead to either, disturbing clicks and popping noises or in the worst case to real "holes" in the audio signal. And: a smaller buffer results in a higher CPU load because Traktor needs to write data into the buffers more frequently.

When larger data buffers are used, the clicks and pops disappear; the disadvantage is that this increases the latency time as well. Because of the larger buffers, it takes more time for Traktor to write new audio data into the buffers (i.e. until the data in the buffers is "consumed"). This means that an action like activating an FX unit is more audible than if a shorter latency time with smaller data buffers is used.

The actual latency time is also dependant on the buffer size and the number of operating system layers the audio data needs to walk through until it reaches the audio interface hardware. Mac users do not need to worry about this. The Core Audio drivers are originally designed in a way that their latency time is quite small.

To overcome these latency and other issues with earlier Windows audio drivers (and as a way to improve sale of their own products) German company Steinberg developed the ASIO protocol (Audio Stream Input/Output), which in 1997 became an open standard, whereby other manufacturers could develop hardware and drivers who used this protocol. The main goals for the development of ASIO were to give applications direct access to the input and output functions of the audio interface and so to avoid the need for data to be transported via several layers in the operating system first. This results in a better data throughput and in a decrease in latency time. At the same time ASIO removed the previous restriction that only one stereo output and one stereo input could be used and made it possible to create and support audio interfaces with several inputs and outputs.

NOTE   Using more than one audio interface   In the list *Audio Device* only one audio interface can be selected, i.e. Traktor can use only one audio interface at a time. Another reason for this conceptual decision is to avoid problems which can arise if two different audio interfaces are controlled at the same time (different latency times etc.).

If you use Mac OS X the operating system itself provides a mechanism to aggregate several audio interfaces and to create a new main device. The client using this aggregated audio interface sees it as one sound card. A guide for audio aggregation can be found on the Apple website: *http://support.apple.com/kb/HT3956*.

Once several audio interfaces are aggregated into one device you can select the option *Aggregate Device* in the list *Audio Device* on the *Audio Setup* dialog.

It is possible to aggregate several audio interfaces in Windows as well; here you use the tool ASIO4ALL*(www.asio4all.com)*. Once the ASIO4ALL driver is installed open the list *Audio Device* and select *ASIO4ALL v2*. Then click the button *Settings* to open the control panel of ASIO4ALL. The control panel shows all installed audio interfaces for which a WDM driver is installed. Activate the audio interfaces you wish to use with Traktor. Return to the *Preferences* dialog and open the category *Audio Routing*. Now all selected channels are available as options for the output routing.

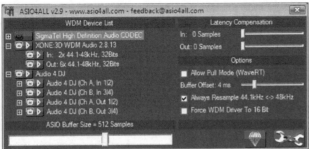

The latency time when using ASIO4ALL is always bigger than with a generic ASIO driver because the audio data from Traktor is first sent via the ASIO protocol to ASIO4ALL and then via the WDM protocol to the audio interface. For this reason using ASIO4ALL should be seen more as a workaround

Automatic Audio Interface Configuration and Fallback Device

As explained above one of the new Traktor 2 features was the automatic configuration and automatic activation of the Native Instruments audio interfaces and also for some third party soundcards. Additionally Traktor 2 activates a fallback device if the standard audio interface is not available. The activation/selection of the audio interface follows these rules:

◻ If the integrated audio device is currently selected and a Native Instruments audio interface is then connected, the Native Instruments audio interface will be activated without further enquiry.

◻   If an external audio interface is connected and selected and a Native Instruments audio interface is then connected, Traktor will display a message box and asks if the new audio interface should be activated.

◻   If the currently activated audio interface is connected and, if another Native Instruments audio interface is connected, it then is activated. In case there is no other Native Instruments audio interface connected, the integrated audio interface is activated.

On OS X Traktor always uses the integrated audio interface as fallback device. On Windows you need to select the device that shall be used as fallback device in the list box *Win Built-In* (see the figure on page 37).

> **TIP** The audio icon in the header is red if no audio interface has been selected or if the selected audio interface is currently not available (usually because it is unplugged). In this case Traktor will not react to incoming MIDI messages and it will also prevent audio playback. You can click the red icon to open the *Audio Setup* dialog. If this icon is blue, then the selected audio interface is available and Traktor can use it. The icon is orange if currently the fallback device is used.

Configuring Audio Routing

You can use the *Preferences/Output Routing* dialog to configure the signal path, i.e. here you select which audio data Traktor shall send to which outputs of your audio interface.

Internal Mixer

The first setting you need to make is to configure the mixing mode. This can be done in the *Mixing Mode* section of the dialog *Preferences/Output Routing*. Select *Internal* if the audio data of the decks is to be mixed by the internal Traktor mixer. Even if some of the hybrid controllers with an integrated audio interface do look like a mixer (including the various NI controllers), the audio is mixed inside the software and you need to set *Mixing Mode* to *Internal*. If you are using a controller-only plus an external audio interface (for example Traktor Audio 2), internal mixing mode is used as well.

Set *Mixing mode* to *External* only if you are using an external mixer.

The picture on the following pages shows the *Preferences/Output Routing* when Traktor Audio 2:

The following figure shows the signal path for internal mixing mode. Here Traktor Audio 2 is used as an example again. We could have used another soundcard here or one of the various hybrid-controllers with an integrated audio interface.

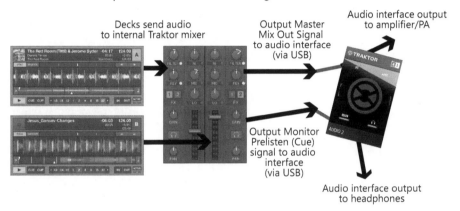

The audio data from the decks may have been altered by the FX units, the deck filter, the key knob, the pan settings or the equalizer.

▫ **Output Master**   The internal Traktor mixer then sends the mixed deck data (depending on the current settings of the channel faders or of the cross fader) to the audio interface. This signal is called *Mix Out Signal* or *Master Output*. Traktor uses the two outputs which have been configured in section *Output Master* of the *Output Routing* dialog. Connect these two outputs to your amplifier, your active speakers or to the club PA.

▫ **Output Monitor**   Using the Cue buttons of the decks (the buttons with the headphone icon) the audio signal of either deck can be sent to the second stereo output of the audio interface, independent from the current position of the channel fader and the cross fader. The two outputs of the audio interface which shall receive the pre listen signal are configured in the section *Output Monitor*.

If you use Traktor in internal mixing mode you must have an audio interface with two stereo outputs (four channels). One of the stereo outputs receives the master signal (mix out) and the other one receives the pre listen/cue signal.

External Mixer

When using an external mixer two different cases need to be distinguished: Either the mixer already has an integrated audio interface (like the Pioneer DJM-900nexus or the Allen&Heath mixer Xone:DB2 and DB4), or a "normal" DJ mixer (without an integrated soundcard) is used; in the latter case an additional audio interface is needed.

Since the entire mixing process is now done on the external mixer and not with the internal Traktor mixer, the channel faders and the cross fader in Traktor are disabled/hidden.

In external mixing mode you need one stereo channel for each Traktor deck that you wish to use. If you only intend to use two Traktor decks then an audio interface with two stereo channels (= 4 channels) is sufficient. In the event that you want to use all four available decks than you need an audio interface with four stereo channels (= eight channels).

Due to the different signal paths in the audio routing, configuration is also different if you use an external mixer. Here you assign each Traktor deck to one of the available stereo outputs of your audio interface.

The following figure shows an example of the signal path if an external mixer is used with an integrated audio interface. The audio interface of the Xone:DB4 shown here is equipped with four stereo outputs (eight channels).

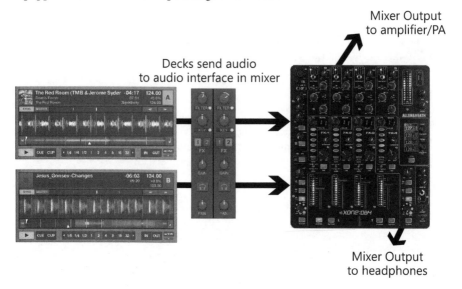

Mixer Output
to amplifier/PA

Decks send audio
to audio interface in mixer

Mixer Output
to headphones

In external mixing mode you can also use a mixer that does not have an integrated audio interface. In this case you need a multi-channel audio interface to which Traktor can send the audio signals. The audio interface needs one stereo channel for each Traktor deck that you wish to use (= two channels). The following figure shows one of the possible configurations; here the audio interface Traktor Audio 10 by Native Instruments is used. Traktor sends the audio data from the decks via USB to the audio interface. The audio outputs of the Traktor Audio 10 are connected with normal cinch (RCA) cables to the line inputs of the mixer.

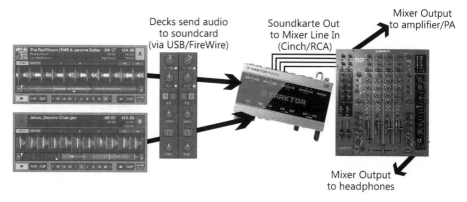

Decks send audio to soundcard (via USB/FireWire)

Soundkarte Out to Mixer Line In (Cinch/RCA)

Mixer Output to amplifier/PA

Mixer Output to headphones

The assignment between the four decks (Channel A to D) and the audio outputs looks like the following figure showing the *Preferences/Output Routing* dialog:

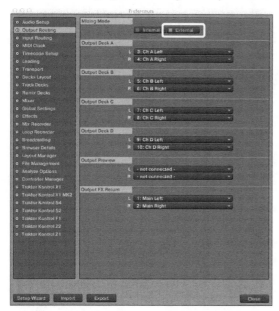

2.3 Overview of Traktors' User Interface

This section provides a rough overview of the Traktor user interface and its different functional groups. This information helps you become familiar with Traktor as quickly as possible and to become better acquainted with the Traktor terminology. In addition this knowledge is helpful if you use Traktor Pro and want to create and manage Traktor layouts with the layout manager.

Header

The header is at the top of the Traktor window. The middle part of the Traktor header is used to display some general system information. You can use the list box at the right side of the header to change the Traktor layout. One of the buttons opens the *Preferences* dialog and another one switches Traktor into full screen mode.

The following table contains short descriptions to the meaning and/or function of the different symbols and buttons in the header.

Icon/Button	Description
● CTRL	Lights up, if Traktor receives messages from the connected controllers. Traktor reacts only to incoming messages if the audio setup is functional.
▦	This icon is grey if no controller has been configured, it is blue if all configured controllers are connected and it is orange if only some of the configured controllers are connected.
◀ AUDIO	Lights up blue if the audio interface map selected in the Audio Setup dialog is found and working. This indicator is red if there is a problem with the selected audio interface.
▬ LOAD	Indicates how much of the CPU time reserved for the Traktor audio engine is currently used. A value larger than approximately 80% can lead to audio dropouts. This value is not identical to the CPU load of the application as a whole. For example, if Traktor is analysing a track, then the complete CPU load rises, however, the value shown here is not affected.
21:03	Shows the current time, depending on the current country settings either in 24 hour or in AM/PM format.
▬ MAIN	In internal mixing mode the level meter displays the signal strength of the master out signal. In external mixing mode the signal strength of the deck with the strongest signal is shown.

Icon/Button	Description
░ BAT	Lights up blue if the computer is running on external power. The icon is blinking red if the computer runs on batteries; in this case the icon shows the state of charge of the batteries.
● REC	Lights up red if Traktor is currently recording.
Essential ▼	Shows the name of the currently active layout. Click the arrow to open a list with the available layouts; then click a layout name to activate it.
🔍	Toggles the track browser size between normal and maximized view
⚙	Opens the Preferences dialog.
🎛	Activates/deactivates the AutoPlay mode (known as Cruise mode as well).
⛶	Toggles Traktor between full screen mode and the windowed mode.

Global Section

The Global Section consists of three elements: The middle part of the Global Section contains the Master Panel with the Loop Recorder, the knob to set the volume of the master out signal and two buttons to activate the Snap and Quantize mode.

On the left side of the Global Section either the first FX panel or the Traktor Master Clock is shown; on the right side either the second FX panel or the Audio Recorder is displayed. You can use the buttons at the outer left or right of the Global Section to select which panel shall be visible. Chapter 13 explains the FX units and contains a detailed description of the available effects. The Master Clock and all questions regarding beatgridding are covered in chapter 8. Chapter 14 explains of how to record your mixes with the integrated Mix Recorder.

Global Section in Traktor Pro showing the Master Clock, the Master Panel with Loop Recorder, and the FX Units 2 and 4

You can configure the Global Section in the *Preferences/Global Settings* dialog.

Activate the check box *Show Global Section* if the Global Section is currently hidden. Use the two list boxes *Left* and *Right* to select which element shall be shown at the left side/right side.

Decks, Mixer and Crossfader

The decks and the controls for the mixer occupy the largest space on your screen. Depending on your requirements you can either display two (deck A and B) or all four decks. The decks themselves can be setup for three different flavours and they offer five different sizes.

Deck Types (Deck Flavour)

The different deck types are:

- **Track Deck**   This deck is used for playback of audio files. In Traktor Pro/Scratch Pro all four decks can be uses as track decks.

- **Remix Deck**   One Remix Decks consists of four sample slots; each sample slot can be used to playback an audio file/sample. You can load a remix set into a remix deck. Each remix set can hold up to 64 samples. Remix sets are organized in a kind of table with four columns and sixteen rows. The samples of each column can be loaded and played in the sample slot above them. Each sample slot has its own volume fader and filter and you can change several other playback parameters of the samples (like sync mode, sample type, or reverse playback).

  Remix decks are covered in full length in chapter 11.

- **Live Input**   In Live Input mode an external audio signal (from a turntable, a CD player, an MP 3 player, a microphone, or from the audio interface of another computer) is routed into the deck. You can then use the effects, the equalizer or the deck filter of that deck to modify the audio signal as you would do with a track deck. In Traktor Pro/Scratch Pro all four decks can be set to Live Input.

There are two ways to switch between the different deck types:

- Click the deck letter of the deck you want to change and select the type you wish to use.

◻ Open the *Preferences* dialog and open the category *Decks Layout*. Use the list boxes in section Deck Flavor to change the deck type.

Deck Sizes (Deck Layout)

Traktor offers five different sizes/layouts for all deck types. The five deck sizes for track decks are:

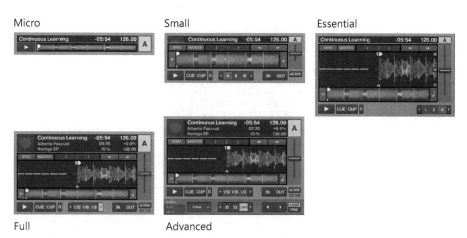

◻ **Micro** With this variant only the track name is visible in the deck header. The waveform of the track is not visible, but you can see and use the stripe and the Play button.

◻ **Small** Shows the largest version of the stripe. Next to the Play button the buttons CUE and CUP and the elements to control the loops are visible.

◻ **Essential** Shows the largest version of the stripe and the waveform. Only the title of the track is displayed in the deck header. To control playback the buttons Play, CUE and CUP are available, and a smaller version of the loop length selector.

◻ **Full** With this variant all track information is visible in the deck header and a mid-sized waveform and stripe are used. Additionally the buttons Play, CUE and CUP and the loop controls are visible. You can use the little button below the Active button (it is used to activate loops) to open the advanced deck panel.

◻ **Advanced** This variant is equal to the full version; additionally the Advanced Panel is shown in the lower part of the deck. The advanced panel offers three different modes. You can use the advanced panel to setup the beatgrid *(Grid* mode); to change the playback position or to move loops *(Move* mode); the third mode is used to create and edit cue points *(Cue* mode).

The same deck sizes are available for remix decks.

Micro   Small   Essential

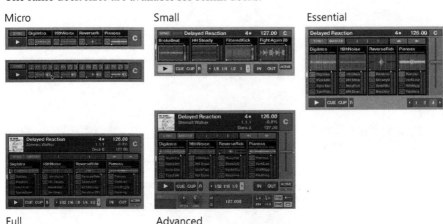

Full   Advanced

◻ **Micro** In size *Micro* you can only see the four sample slots and the waveform of the loaded samples. The small icon at the left side shows the sample type (loop, one-shot). It can be used to start/pause the sample.

◻ **Small** In size *Small* you can see the four slot players with the currently loaded samples of the remix set and the transport section with the buttons Play/Pause, CUE, CUP, and the loop size control.

◻ **Essential** When *Essential* is selected, Traktor will display almost the same information as in size Small. Additionally the waveforms of the samples loaded into the four slots are displayed. For the loop size control the smaller variant is used

◻ **Full** In contrast to *Essential* you will see the complete deck header with the cover art of the remix set (assuming this option is enabled and the remix set has a cover). However, the waveforms of the loaded samples are smaller than in size Essential.

◻ **Advanced** This option is equal to the full version; additionally the Advanced Panel is shown in the lower part of the deck. You can use this EDIT panel to change several playback parameters for the sample in the currently active cell.

You can change the deck size for the two adjacent decks. The quickest way to change the deck size is to double-click on the upper frame of the decks. For each double-click Traktor switches to the next available deck size. You can also open the *Preferences* dialog and switch to category *Decks Layout*. Here you can change the size with the list boxes in section *Deck Layout*.

Section *Deck Layout* additionally provides the check box *Enable C & D; activate it to make decks C and D visible.*

Mixer

The middle area between the decks contains an equalizer panel for each deck, the channel fader and a panel with the filter knob, the panning knob and the cue button which is used to feed the pre listen signal into the monitor output.

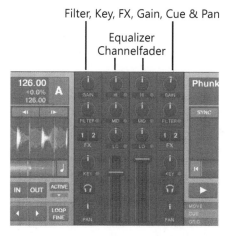

Filter, Key, FX, Gain, Cue & Pan

Equalizer
Channelfader

Use the section *Mixer Layout* of the *Preferences/Mixer* dialog to configure which options shall be visible. The topic mixing is covered in chapter 3 and the equalizer is described in more detail in chapter 12, together with information about harmonic mixing.

NOTES In external mixing mode you can display the *EQ+Fader* as well as the *Crossfader* panel, but only the functionality of the equalizer is enabled. If you use internal mixing and in case that the faders are not visible on the panels you may have had activated the external mixing mode by accident. Open the *Preferences* dialog and activate option *Internal* on the *Output Routing* page to solve this problem.

Crossfader

Below the decks you can see the crossfader (if it has been enabled), which corresponds to the crossfader on a "normal" DJ mixer. At the right side of the crossfader are two important knobs for internal mixing mode. The first knob controls the ratio between the master out and the cue signal that is sent to the headphones (the output configured as Output Monitor). The second knob is used to set the headphone volume.

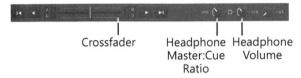

Crossfader   Headphone Headphone
                  Master:Cue Volume
                  Ratio

Browser

The lower part of the Traktor window contains the browser. You can use the browser to access your tracks and to manage your track collection and playlists. The following three elements are always visible in the browser.

- **Folderlist (Browser Tree)**   The folderlist contains all folders that can be used to access your tracks. With the *Explorer* node you can access all drives on your computer. You can use the iTunes node to open the iTunes library on your system, if iTunes is installed. The other nodes represent special Traktor folders like the Track Collection, all of your playlists and the playlist where Traktor saves your audio recordings. The folder list is always visible.

- **Tracklist**   The track list always shows the contents of the folder that is selected in the folder list or it shows the search results, if you have performed a track search. The track list is always visible.

- **Search Field**   You can use the *Search* field to find a track in the currently opened play list or in the complete track collection.

The browser contains five more elements, which you can switch on and off, as you need it (see page 55 for more information):

- **Preview Player**   In the upper left part of the browser is the preview player. The preview player acts like a fifth deck and you can use it to preview tracks without loading them into one of the "normal" decks.

- **Favourites/Shortcuts**   Above the track list the favourite bar is shown. You can drag and drop any folder or playlist from the folder list onto the favourites bar. You then can quickly open it by clicking one of the buttons in the favourites bar. You can also drop tracks onto a button that represents a play list to add this track to the corresponding playlist.

Preview Player
Search   Favourites/Shortcuts

Folderlist   Cover Art   Status Bar   Track Info   Tracklist

☐ **Cover Art**   If a track contains cover art Traktor displays it in this area. This feature is not available for tracks displayed in the iTunes node.

☐ **Status Bar**   The first part of the status bar is used to inform about currently active background tasks, like an ongoing track analysis. The same space is used to show warning and error messages. The second part of the bar is used to display the number of tracks and the approximate playing time and size of the tracks currently displayed in the track list.

☐ **Track Info**   This area is used to display the title and the artist of the currently selected track from the track list.

You can use the dialog page *Preferences/Browser Details* to select which elements are shown and which are not (see page 55 for more information). Chapter 7, "Organizing Tracks" explains how the browser works and how you can use it to get your tracks organized.

Using Traktor in Full Screen Mode

To make optimal use of the available screen space it is recommended to use Traktor in full screen mode. Use the button shown here to switch between full screen mode and window mode.

You can also activate a Traktor setting to get full screen mode automatically when starting Traktor. Open the *Preferences* dialog and select the category *Global Settings*. Then activate the check box *Switch to Fullscreen on Startup*.

The list *Fullscreen Resolution* shows all screen resolutions supported the current use graphics driver. The option *Desktop* corresponds with the currently used screen resolution. If you select one of the other resolutions Traktor switches to this screen resolution before the full screen mode becomes activated.

> **TIP** If you are just starting to use Traktor I recommend to activate the check box *Show Tooltips*. When tooltips are enabled Traktor opens a small window describing the function of a control when you hover over it.

2.4 Creating and Using Layouts

The Traktor user interface can be configured by using several options which are scattered on different pages of the *Preferences* dialog. Most of the options are saved in the layout definitions. So it is possible to change several settings simply by selecting a different layout. Only a smaller part of the options are global, i.e. they are always valid and do not depend on a particular layout.

All settings that are part of a layout definition are marked  with a small icon in the Preferences dialog.

☐ **Preferences/Layout Manager** Use this page to manage (i.e. add, rename and delete) layouts.

☐ **Preferences/Decks Layout** This page can be used to configure the decks. Use the check box *Show C&D* to decide if only two or if all four decks shall be visible. You can configure the deck size and the deck flavour here.

The section *Tempo Fader* can be used to switch on the Tempo Fader for each deck (functioning like the ones found on turntables/CD players).

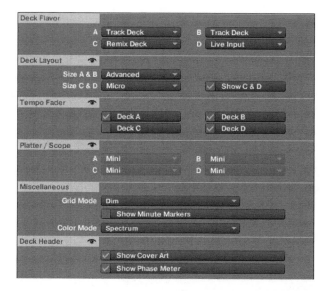

You can use section *Platter/Scope* to configure the size and the visibility of the scope panels; they display information that are useful if you use Traktor with timecode. The options in this section are only enabled in Traktor Scratch (more information about timecode can be found in chapter 4).

If the option Show *Cover Art* is checked and if the track or remix set contains a cover graphic it is shown at the left side of the deck. Use *Show Phase Meter* to activate the phase meter in the decks. The phase meter is helpful when synchronizing the playback of your tracks.

◻ **Preferences/Browser Details** Use this page to specify which of the optional elements of the browser shall be visible or nor (see figure on page 53). All five options are saved together with the definition of the current layout.

◻ **Preferences/Global Settings**   Here you find the options to make the Global Section visible and to configure which panel shall be shown at the left and at the right side of the Global Section (see page 47).

◻ **Preferences/Mixer**   Use this page to configure the mixer options. With regards to the layout, the options in the section *Mixer Layout* are important and they are available in all four flavours (see also the figure on page 51).

Changing a Layout Definition

All changes you make in the user interface settings and the layout-related settings and that are not global settings,

◻ always apply to the currently selected layout and

◻ are saved automatically when Traktor exits; this overwrites all previous settings for the currently selected layout.

If you have created and optimised different layouts and if you want to keep them, then you export the layout settings and import them if necessary. To do this proceed and follow as explained on page 62 and activate the check box *GUI Layout*.

Creating a New Layout

Follow these steps to create a new layout:

1. Open the dialog *Preferences/Layout Manager*.

2. Click on *Add* to open the menu with the layout templates. Then select the template that shall serve as base for your new configuration.

Traktor creates a new layout based on the selected template and adds it to the list *Personal Layouts*.

3. Select the new layout in the list *Personal Layouts*. Type a new name for the layout into the field *Change Name* and then click on *Rename*.

4. Configure the new layout either by using the options in the *Preferences* dialog or by making changes in the user interface itself.

Moving and Deleting Layouts

You can use the buttons *Move Up* and *Move Down* to change the order of the layouts. Changing the layouts order can be problematic if you use the mapping command *Layout | Layout Select* with the Interaction Mode *Direct*. This command internally uses the sequential number of the layouts based on the current order. If you change the layout order later Traktor will activate the wrong layout. To fix this you need to change the mapping of the command *Layout | Layout Select* and select the desired layout again in the list *Set to value*.

Use the button *Remove* to delete the selected layout. There must always be one layout available. If you click on *Remove* and try to delete the last available layout, Traktor will ignore your action.

Selecting a Layout in the User Interface

Traktors' layout definitions are written into your personal configuration file. Depending on the options you selected in the Setup Wizard Traktor adds some predefined layouts into this file. All available layouts are shown in the layout selector in the header and in the list of the *Preferences/Layout Manager* dialog (see page 54).

To select a different layout open the layout selector in the Traktor header and click on the name of the desired layout. Or open the dialog *Preferences/Layout Manager* and select the layout you wish to activate. The active layout is highlighted in the list. Additionally the column *Type* informs, if it is a 2 deck or a 4 deck layout.

Selecting a Layout with Kontrol S4 and Kontrol Z2

You can switch between different layouts directly from Traktor Kontrol S4 and Kontrol Z2.

▣ **Kontrol Z2**   Press the *Settings* button on the Z2 to activate settings mode. Turn the left *LOOP/SIZE* encoder until LAY is shown in the left 7 segment display.

Now turn the right *LOOP/SIZE* encoder to switch between the different layouts. The right 7 segment display shows the number of the currently selected layout. Press the *Settings* button again to leave settings mode.

◻ **Kontrol S4**   On Kontrol S4 you can use the deck focus buttons to switch between layouts: hold the *SHIFT* button and press *Deck C* or *Deck D* to activate the next layout.

If there are two layouts you need the most, you can assign these layouts directly to *SHIFT* plus *deck focus buttons*. First you need to make sure that these two layouts are at position 0 and 1 of the layout list of the *Layout Manager*. To do this, open *Preferences/Layout Manager* and move the two layouts to position 0 and 1 as explained on the previous page.

Then switch in *Preferences* dialog to category *Traktor Kontrol S4*. Open the list boxes *Layout Switch Left/Layout Switch Right* and select the two layouts you wish to activate directly. If you want to keep one button for browsing through all available layout keep option *Next Layout* in one of the two list boxes.

2.5 Configuring the Waveform and the Stripe

The section *Miscellaneous* on the *Preferences/Decks* Layout dialog offers several options to customize the waveform display in the decks and in the stripes.

The most visible feature is the colour of the waveform, which is called TruWave in Traktor marketing language. Traktor 2 provides four different colour modes that can be selected in the *Color Mode* list box:

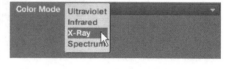

◻ **Ultraviolet**   colours the waveform and stripe blueish

◻ **Infrared**   colours the waveform and stripe yellowish/brownish

◻ **X-Ray**   colours the waveform and stripe in greyscale tones

◻ **Spectrum**   colours the waveform and stripe with multiple colours

No matter which colour mode you choose, the waveform colour you use defines the hue and the frequencies of the audio modulate the saturation. High frequencies (and white noise) appear white. Which colour mode you use is more or less a question of personal taste. However, you will no doubt see that you quickly learn which colour/saturation corresponds to which sound. And I am pretty sure that you will not want to lose the colours after using them for a couple days.

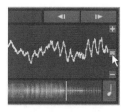

As well as the coloured waveforms there are four new options with which you can customize the beat grid. Choose your favourite in the list box *Grid Mode*.

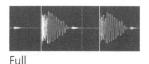
Full

Dim

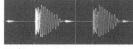
Ticks

The *Full* mode shows the beat grid as we know it from earlier Traktor *versions; Dim* shows horizontal lines in dark grey that are almost invisible against the even darker waveform background and option *Ticks* shows only small vertical lines at the top and the bottom of the waveform. Choosing *Invisible* makes the beat grid even more invisible as it already is when either *Dim* or *Ticks* is selected. If you are using the remix decks and wish to see the grid lines, I recommend setting the *Grid Mode* to either *Dim* or *Ticks* as option *Full* leads to the waveform becoming not so good visible anymore.

Option *Show Minute Markers* enables the minute markers for all decks.

If this option is activated the stripe shows a marker for each minute of a track.

What is really cool in Traktor 2 is the almost seamless zooming for the waveforms. This makes it much easier than with earlier Traktor versions to set cue points and beat markers exactly where you want them. Use the three buttons at the right side of the waveform (+, =, –) to zoom in, zoom out and to reset the waveform zoom to the default zoom factor. These three buttons become visible when the mouse pointer is on the waveform; otherwise these buttons are hidden. Traktor provides eight different zoom levels.

The default zoom factor can be set by moving the slider *Default Zoom* in section *Miscellaneous* on the *Preferences/Track Decks* dialog. Before you change the default zoom setting you want to make sure that at least one deck is set to the default zoom factor by clicking the = button. Then open *Preferences/Track Decks*, move the slider *Default Zoom* and use the deck that is set to default zoom as reference. My advice is to use a value of –0.5 or –0.4 as the default value. This allows you to see approximately 2 bars of a track with a BPM between 120 and 140.

2.6 The Traktor Configuration Files

Traktor is shipped with a set of predefined configuration files for several controllers and audio interfaces. All Traktor configuration files use the extension *.tsi*. During the Traktor installation the configuration files are copied into the following folders (where *x:* is the Windows system drive). Starting with Traktor 2 there will be a separate sub-folder for each released Traktor versions and the version number is uses as the folder name (2.6.5, 2.6.7, etc.). Replace the version number *2.x.y* in the following folder names by the Traktor version you have:

◻ **OS X** Macintosh HD/Library/Application Support/Native Instruments/
Traktor/Factory Settings/2.x.y

◻ **Windows 7/8** *x:*\ProgramData\Native Instruments\Traktor\Factory
Settings/2.x.y

This folder contains the following subfolders: The folder *AutoConfig* contains the mappings for all controllers that can be configured by Traktor automatically (Traktor detects the controller when it is connected and loads the appropriate mapping). The folder *Default Settings* contains more configuration files and controller mappings that are used by the Setup Wizard.

When Traktor is launched for the first time, the configuration files from the installation folder are copied to the home directory of the logged in user (~ for Mac OS X) or to the folder with the user documents (Windows) respectively. Traktor will create a new folder for each Traktor version you have installed/updated. Replace the version number *2.x.y* in the following folder names by the Traktor version you have:

◻ **OS X** ~/Documents/Native Instruments/Traktor 2.x.y/Settings/Default Settings

◻ **Windows 7/8** *x:*\Users*[Username]*\Documents\Native
Instruments\Traktor 2.x.y\Settings\Default Settings

The *Default Settings* folder contains the following subfolders:

◻ **Audio** Here are the configuration files the wizard uses to set up the timecode medium (vinyl, CD) and the mixing mode (internal, external).

- **Controller**   Here are (almost) all the mappings for those controllers that you see on page *Hardware Controller Selection* of the Setup Wizard. Each manufacturer has its own subfolder and there you find the controller mapping file and PDF files that document the mapping.

  Exceptions are those controllers that can be configured by Traktor in a Plug&Play manner. The mappings for those controllers remain in the *AutoConfig* folder.

- **Effects**   This folder contains the default settings for the macro effects.

- **Keyboard**   This folder contains the keyboard mappings for Traktor 2. There is one mapping for Traktor Pro and another one for Traktor Scratch Pro. Both mappings exist for a German keyboard layout (QWERTZ) as well as for an English keyboard layout (QWERTY).

- **Layout**   This folder contains the default layout definitions for the different Traktor flavours.

The Personal Configuration File Traktor Settings.tsi

Traktor uses the options that you chose in the Setup Wizard to create a personal configuration file named *Traktor Setttings.tsi*. This file is stored by default at the following location (Traktor will create a new settings folder for each released Traktor version. Replace 2.x.y by the version number of Traktor that you are using):

- **Mac OS X**   ~/Documents/Native Instruments/Traktor 2.x.y

- **Windows 7/8**   *x*:\Users\\[*Username*]\Documents\Native Instruments\ Traktor 2.x.y

This folder is also the default setting for the Traktor root directory. You can change the root directory by opening the dialog *Preferences/File Management* and clicking the browse button next to the *Root Dir* text box.

The file *Traktor Settings.tsi* contains **all** settings you can make in the *Preferences* dialog, i.e. also all keyboard mappings and controller mappings you created. Traktor creates a backup copy of the settings file when you exit Traktor. The settings file that was loaded as you launched Traktor will be copied into following folder:

- **OSX** ~/ Documents/Native Instruments/Traktor 2.x.y/Backup/Settings

- **Windows 7/8** *x:*\Users\[*Username*]\Documents\Native Instruments\ Traktor 2.x.y\Backup\Settings

The current version of the settings file will then be saved into your root directory.

If you plan to make extensive changes to your keyboard or controller mapping make sure that you have a backup copy available. You can create a new backup of your settings file by re-launching Traktor or by mapping the command *Global | Save Traktor Settings* to your keyboard, for example.

In the event of something going totally wrong you always have the option of replacing the corrupted file with the saved one or to re-import your old settings or mappings.

Importing and Exporting Settings

It is very easy to export the settings from your personal configuration file *Traktor Settings.tsi* into another .tsi file or to import settings from a .tsi file into your personal configuration file.

1. Open the *Preferences* dialog by clicking the corresponding button in the Traktor header.

2. Click the button *Import* in the lower part of the dialog. Browse to the folder containing the .tsi file with settings you want to import and select this file.

   Traktor opens the dialog *Select Categories to Import.*

   Only the check boxes for those categories found in the selected file can be activated.

3. Activate the checkboxes in front of all categories which settings shall be imported. Then click *OK.*

> **ATTENTION** Traktor **copies** all settings from the selected categories into the personal configuration files and **overwrites** all existing settings.

Exporting settings is easy as well. Open the *Preferences* dialog and then click on *Export*. Activate the check boxes of the settings you want to export. Then click on *OK* and select the folder and filename of the exported file.

Sidebar: The Traktor Folders

Traktor uses different folders and folder types respectively, to save files and to access particular kind of information.

- **Root Dir** The Traktor root directory contains two very important files. First, the file *Traktor Settings.tsi* contains all settings you have made in Traktor. Second, the file *Collection.nml* contains all information about the tracks you have added to the Traktor Collection and additionally all playlists you created. The root directory contains some additional folders. One folder is used to create backup files of your collection file automatically.

  Others contain additional data Traktor needs to perform its function, like thumbnails of the cover art and the stripes used in the decks. You can change the root directory in the dialog *Preferences/File Management*.

- **iTunes Music Library** This node is a virtual folder you can use to view the content of your iTunes library. Traktor automatically creates this node if it finds iTunes installed. You can change this folder by using the *Preferences/File Management* dialog and selecting the iTunes XML file Traktor should use. More information about the combination iTunes/Traktor can be found in chapter 7, "Organizing Tracks".

- **Music Folders** You can specify several folders on your hard drives as dedicated music folders. Traktor will automatically import all new files it finds in the music folders into the track collection on start-up. The Music Folders can be configured in section *Music Folders* of the dialog *Preferences File Management*.

- **Sample Dir** This is the folder where Traktor will save the samples that you copied from a track deck or from the loop recorder into a sample slot. You can change the folder location in the *Preferences/File Management* dialog.

- **Remix Sets Dir** Traktor will use this folder for all remix sets you import. You can change the folder location in the *Preferences/File Management* dialog. More information about remix decks and remix sets can be found in chapter 11.

- **Recording Folder** The last folder is the location where Traktor saves the wave files recorded with the audio recorder. You can configure the location for the recorded wave files in the dialog *Preferences/Mix Recorder*. For more information about recording with Traktor see chapter 13, "Recording".

2.7 Mapping Commands for this Chapter

Some of the actions described in this chapter can be performed with mapping commands and so can be mapped to the keyboard or to a controller. This section lists the mapping commands which are related to the different buttons of the Traktor header and the commands to change the deck size and the deck type.

Changing Deck Type and Deck Size

Deck Common | Deck Flavor Selector	Interaction Mode: Direct Set to value: Select deck type	Sets the deck to the deck type/deck flavour that is selected in list Set to value.
	Interaction Mode: Inc/Dec	Selects the next/previous deck type.
	Interaction Mode: Reset	Sets the deck to deck type Track Deck.
Deck Common | Deck Size Selector	Interaction Mode: Direct Set to value: Select deck size	Sets the selected decks to the size that is selected in list Set to value. This command changes the size for two adjacent decks.
	Interaction Mode: Inc/Dec	Selects the next/previous deck size.
	Interaction Mode: Reset	Sets the decks to deck size Small.

Selecting Layouts

Layout | Layout Selector	Interaction Mode: Inc/Dec	Switch to the next/previous layout in the list as displayed in the dialog box Preferences | Layout Manager. Inc and Dec perform a wraparound at the beginning respectively the end of the list.
	Interaction Mode: Hold Set to value: select layout	The layout selected in Set to value is activated as long as the button is hold.
	Interaction Mode: Direct Set to value: select the desired layout	Activates the layout selected in the list Set to value. Attention: Though the list Set to value shows the layout names, Traktor internally uses the number of the layout which is shown on the page Preferences | Layout Manager. That means that you need to reconfigure this command if you change the order of the layouts.
	Interaction Mode: Reset	Activates the layout at position 0 of the list Personal Layouts of the Layout Manager dialog.

> **TIP** Traktor offers no mapping commands to switch between the display of Master Clock/FX Panel 1 respectively the Audio Recorder/FX Panel 2. Currently this can only be done by clicking the corresponding buttons in the Global Section. But there is a workaround to accomplish this: define different layouts with different settings for the Global Section, for example one with the Master Clock and the Audio Recorder and another one showing both FX Panels. Then use the mapping command *Layout | Layout Selector* to switch between the different views of the Global Section.

Maximizing the Browser

Layout | Only Browser On	Interaction Mode: Toggle	Maximizes the track browser window or resets it to its normal size. This command behaves like a toggle.
	Interaction Mode: Direct Set to value: Browser Default/Browser Only	Tip: If you use the maximized track browser window to search for a track then assign this command to the same button you use to load a track. Use the Interaction Mode Direct and choose the option Browser Default in the list Set to value. In this way the track browser will return to its normal size after the track has been loaded.

Activating Tool Tips

Global | Tool Tips On	Interaction Mode: Hold/Toggle	Activates/deactivates the tool tips.
	Interaction Mode: Direct Set to value: 1=On/0=Off	

Activating Full Screen Mode

Layout | Fullscreen On	Interaction Mode: Hold/Toggle	Toggles Traktor between the full screen mode and the window mode.
	Interaction Mode: Direct Set to value: 1=On/0=Off	

Setting the Zoom Level of the Waveform

Track Deck | Wave-form Zoom Adjust	Type of Controller: Knob/Fader Interaction Mode: Direct	This combination allows setting the zoom level with a knob or a fader.
	Type of Controller: Button Interaction Mode: Reset	Set the selected deck to the default zoom factor. The default zoom factor can be configured on the dialog Preferences/Decks.
	Type of Controller: Button Interaction Mode: Inc/Dec	Selects the next/previous zoom level. Traktor provides eight zoom levels.

Traktor Settings File, save and create backup

Global | Save Traktor Settings	Interaction Mode: Trigger	Creates a backup copy of the lastly saved version of the configuration file *Traktor Settings.tsi* in the Backup folder; then the current settings are saved in the file *Traktor Settings.tsi* in your root directory.

Chapter 3

Loading and Mixing Tracks

So, the installation of Traktor has completed. The first thing we *should* do is organize our tracks in the Traktor collection so we can analyse them, set correct beatgrids and make ourselves familiar with the different master clock modes and the synchronisation features of Traktor. The crucial word here is "should". It is more likely (and I know this from my own experience) that you will want to get straight on with playing the tracks. For this reason the following chapter describes the Traktor features which are important when mixing.

> **IMPORTANT** Please read chapter 2 first before digging into this chapter. Chapter 2 explains both basic setups of Traktor (using the internal or an external mixer). And it contains important information about audio interfaces and how to connect everything. If an incorrect mixing mode is selected or if the cabling is wrong the procedures explained in this chapter will either only work in part or not at all.

3.1 Loading and Playing Tracks

You can use the browser in the lower part of the Traktor window to browse the tracks of your track collection, of the drives and folders on your computer and the tracks and playlists managed by iTunes. When you open a playlist or folder on the left side of the browser the track browser at the right side shows its content.

> **NOTE** The Traktor track collection is covered in greater detail in chapter 7. There you will learn how to import tracks into the collection and how to organize your tracks. The easiest way to load some tracks while you try the steps explained in this chapter is using one of music folders on your hard disk. Go to the folder tree at the left side of the Traktor browser. Double-click on the Explorer node to open it. Then navigate to one of the folders where your tracks are located. Once this folder is selected in the folder tree Traktor will show all tracks from this folder in the track list on the right side of the Traktor browser. You can load your tracks from there.

To load a track, select it in the track browser and perform one of the following actions:

- Drag the track onto the deck you wish to load and drop it there.  Drag & Drop always works even when the track is not yet in the collection. If the loaded track isn't in the collection Traktor will analyse it first and then add it to the collection. It will then take a moment until the waveform and the stripe are visible.

- Right-click the track to open its context/action menu. Then 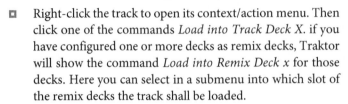 click one of the commands *Load into Track Deck X.* if you have configured one or more decks as remix decks, Traktor will show the command *Load into Remix Deck x* for those decks. Here you can select in a submenu into which slot of the remix decks the track shall be loaded.

  These commands are only available if one of the following nodes is opened: *Track Collection, Playlists, Explorer* or *Audio Recording*. You cannot use these commands in the nodes *iTunes* and *History*.

- If you used the Setup Wizard (see chapter 2), the wizard will install a default keyboard mapping. You can then use Ctrl+Left to load the track into deck A and Ctrl+Right to load it into deck B.

- Use one of the mapping commands for loading tracks and map the desired command to your keyboard or controller. These commands are explained further down in this chapter.

Loading Tracks with Timecode

If you use timecode records or timecode CDs you can use special areas on the timecode medium to scroll the track browser and to load tracks. The last two segments of the timecode record and track 3 of the timecode CD are the so called scrolling zones. When you playback the scrolling zone and turn the record or the jogwheel of your CD player backward and forward to scroll in the currently opened playlist/folder. Once you have stopped the record or the jogwheel Traktor will load the currently selected track into the deck that has the input focus.

> **NOTE Deck Focus**   Several actions and mapping commands can be configured in a way that they affect the deck that has the input focus. Traktor highlights the deck letter of the deck with the input focus if the option *Deck Focus* on the dialog box *Preferences/Global Settings* is set to *Software*. I recommend enabling this option if it is not already set. You can change the deck focus by clicking the deck letter. Or you can use the mapping command *Layout | Deck Focus Selector*. Please note that you have to select the target deck in the list *Set to value* (Interaction Mode: *Direct)* and not in the list *Assignment*.

The option *Hardware* allows two decks to have the focus if the controller layout offers controls to control two decks at the same time. Currently this option works with Traktor Kontrol S4 only and it would have been better to name this option *S4* instead of *Hardware* to avoid confusion.

Options for Loading Tracks

There are several options related to the loading of tracks that can be configured on the *Preferences/Loading* dialog.

- ◻ **Loading only into stopped deck** This option assures that a track can only be loaded into a stopped deck. I recommend enabling this option. If it is enabled the attempt to load a track into a running deck causes Traktor to display a warning message. This warning message can be a lifesaver and is better than having a new track loaded in your current main deck very abruptly, especially in the late hours after a few drinks!

- ◻ **Stop playback at end of track** This option stops the playback when the end of the track is reached. If this setting is disabled you need to stop playback manually with the *Play/Stop* button.

- ◻ **Duplicate deck when loading same track** This checkbox activates a Traktor feature that is called "Instant Doubles". When you load a track that has already been loaded in another deck the track will not be loaded again; instead Traktor will create a duplicate of the loaded track. The action performed is the same as with duplicating, i.e. the playback position and a possibly active loop are copied as well.

- ◻ **Loading next at end of track** You can use this option to automate the track loading process. If this setting is enabled Traktor will load the next track from the playlist automatically when the current one ends. It is important to know that the first two options both affect the loading process. If you use the option *Loading only into stopped deck* you need to enable *Stop playback at end of track* as well, otherwise automated loading will fail.

HOW TO: Loading Tracks with Mapping Commands

Traktor offers several mapping commands to load tracks (more information about controller and keyboard mapping can be found in chapter 6). The following table shows all commands that are available:

Loading Tracks		
Deck Common | Load Selected	Interaction Mode: Trigger Assignment: Deck A – Deck D or Device Target	Loads the selected track into the deck selected in the list Assignment.
Deck Common | Unload	Interaction Mode: Trigger Assignment: Deck A – Deck D, or Device Target	Unloads the track currently loaded in the deck selected in the list Assignment.
Deck Common | Load Next	Interaction Mode: Trigger Assignment: Deck A – Deck D or Device Target	This command behaves similar to the Next button of a CDJ player.
		Pressing the button once: Sets the playback marker to the beginning of the track.
		Pressing the button twice ("double-pressing" the same as double-clicking): Loads the next track from the tracklist into the deck selected in the list Assignment.
Deck Common | Load Previous	Interaction Mode: Trigger Assignment: Deck A – Deck D or Device Target	This command behaves similar to the Prev button of a CDJ player:
		Pressing the button once: Sets the playback marker to the beginning of the track.
		Pressing the button twice ("double-pressing" the same as double-clicking): Loads the previous track from the tracklist into the deck selected in the list Assignment.

Traktor provides more *Load* commands in the submenu *Remix Decks* of the controller manager which allow you to load a remix set into a remix deck and to load individual samples into one of the sample slots of the remix decks. These commands are explained in chapter 11, "Remix Decks". There is an additional load command, *Track Deck | Load, Loop, and Play* which will loop the track automatically once it is loaded. This command is covered in chapter 10, "Loops".

Starting and Stopping a Deck

Once a track is loaded you can start the playback with the *Play* button in the deck. If you use timecode the playback starts when you drop the needle in segment 2 of the timecode record or when you play track 2 of the timecode CD. This area of the time-code media is called playback zone.

The red line in the middle of the waveform is the playback marker. This marks the position in the track currently being played back or – if the deck is stopped – the position where playback will start. (You can move the line indicating the playback marker by setting a new value with the slider *PlayMarker Position* on the dialog box *Preferences/Track Decks)*. The right side of the waveform contains three small buttons (+, = and –) which you can use to set the zoom factor of the waveform.

Three buttons in the transport section and the stripe in the decks will look slightly different depending on whether you use timecode or not.

Deck without Timecode Control (Internal Playback)

Deck with Timecode Control (Scratch Control)

If you are not using timecode control the function of the first buttons is to start/stop the deck. The buttons 2 and 3 offer slightly different CUE functionalities which are explained in chapter 9.

If you are using timecode control then the three buttons are used to switch between the different timecode modes, called timecode tracking modes. The *Play* button switches the deck into internal mode. If a deck is in internal mode you can playback a track even when the deck isn't receiving any timecode signal. The second button (record without a pickup arm) sets the deck to relative mode. When in relative mode the current position in the playback zone doesn't matter. However, for the deck to be played it must receive the timecode signal. The third button (record with a pickup arm) switches to absolute mode. In absolute mode the position in the playback zone that is currently playing exactly matches the position in the track in deck that is playing. More information about the different timecode tracking modes can be found in chapter 4, "Traktor Scratch Pro 2 and Timecode Control".

The differences between relative and absolute mode are the reason why the stripe contains one blue and one red line when in timecode control. As you can see in the previous figure (right deck) the deck is currently in relative mode. The second button is highlighted.

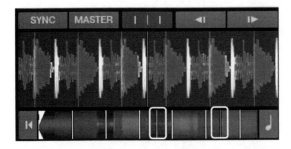

The first vertical line (blue) displays the current position of the timecode medium. The second vertical line (red, after the dark part of the stripe) displays the current playback position of the track. If you use the absolute mode only one vertical line is shown; then the playback position in the track and the current position in the timecode medium are identical.

> **NOTE Deck Mode**   There is a small, important and often over-looked menu below the deck letter. If you click the deck letter the menu offers three choices to select the deck mode (which is different from the timecode tracking mode). The command *Internal Playback* switches to internal deck mode (i.e. deck without time-code control) and the option *Scratch Control* switches the deck to timecode control. The look and the functionality of the three buttons differ depending on the current deck mode.

Click the *Play/Pause* button a second time to stop the deck. In timecode control lift the needle or stop the CDJ player. The *Play/Pause* button corresponds to the following mapping command:

Starting/Stopping a Deck

Deck Common | Play/Pause	The Interaction Mode Toggle is possibly the most used one. It matches the functionality of the Play/Pause button. Additionally you can use the modes Hold and Direct (Set to value: 1=On/ 0=Off).	Starts the deck or stops it.

The mapping commands for selecting deck mode and timecode tracking mode are covered in chapter 4, "Traktor Scratch Pro 2 and Timecode Control".

Moving in the Track

No matter if the track is playing or not you can still move the playback marker by clicking the waveform or the stripe.

The behaviour of Traktor after clicking the waveform differs depending on the setting made for mouse control in the dialog box *Preferences/Transport*.

- **Vinyl Mode** Clicking the waveform and holding the mouse button stops the playback and the waveform can be dragged to any position. If the deck was playing before the waveform was clicked playback will continue from the new position.

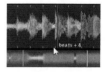

- **Snap Mode** If the waveform is clicked whilst the deck is playing, the click triggers a beatjump. The length of the beatjump is shown at the mouse pointer and it is identical to the distance between the playback marker and the mouse pointer. If the deck is paused the waveform snaps to the gridline or cue point closest to the click position.

Clicking the waveform is the preferred way to move the playback marker if the new playback position is visible in the waveform. If the new position doesn't show up then click the stripe. A single click in the stripe moves the playback marker to the clicked position.

Using the Beatjump Feature in the Decks to jump in a Track

Each deck contains an *Advanced Deck Panel* that offers three different views; each view provides different features. Click the button *Open/Close Advanced Panel* to show the advanced panel. This button is at the right side of the transport section (below the button *Loop Active*).

This is how to jump in a track with the beatjump feature:

1. Open the Advanced Panel if it isn't visible.

2. Set the Advanced Panel to *Move* view.

3. Open the list box at the left side of the panel and select *BeatJump* if another *Move* mode is currently selected.

4th Use the length-selector in the middle of the panel to select the jump length. The selected length is marked with a double arrow.

5. Use the buttons *Move Backwards* and *Move Forward* to jump either towards the beginning or end of the track.

> **NOTE** Please note that the phase of the deck is no longer in sync with the tempo master if you select a jump length shorter than 1 beat and if you choose *TempoSync* as synchronisation mode. In synchronisation mode *BeatSync* jumps with a jump length smaller than 1 beat are always quantized. Chapter 8 contains more information about the sync features of Traktor.

Create a Mapping to Move through a track

Traktor offers several methods to move the playback marker in a track. One of them is to use the advanced Move panel, described in the previous section. Chapter 6 contains two examples of how to jump in a track with a mapping. The section "Example of a Macro with three Mapping Commands: Beatjump" shows how to map a beatjump to a key or button. Section "Looping and Beatjumping" in the same chapter shows how to select the jump length with an endless encoder and how to map buttons for forward and backwards jumping.

There are two other mapping commands that can both be mapped either to an encoder or a knob. Turning the encoder will move the playback marker. The first command, *Seek Position,* has been available for some time. As useful as the In-Command *Seek Position* is, the Out-Command is just as useful. It allows to output the current playback position to an iPad, Lemur or similar controller.

The second command, *Beatjump,* allows you to perform a beat jump by a particular length with a single mapping command. Before the command Beatjump was available one needed to map several commands that match the actions you perform in the advanced Move panel. If you have already mapped a knob/encoder to set the loop length it makes sense to use the *Set to value* option *Loop* of the *Beatjump* command. This mapping triggers a beatjump by the currently selected loop length. In this setup you do not need a separate knob to set the *Beatjump* length.

Moving the Playback Marker

Deck Common | Seek Position	Interaction Mode: Direct Type of Controller: Fader, Knob, Encoder Assignment: Deck A – Deck D or Device Target	Moves the playback marker in the selected deck. Use the controller type Fader/Knob to map the command to a knob or fader with a defined start and end point. Or use the controller type Encoder to map the command to a jog wheel or an endless encoder. In this case use the slider Rotary Sensitivity to configure the seek speed.
	Interaction Mode: Inc, Dec Type of Controller: Button Assignment: Select deck Resolution: Min = ± 0,4% Fine = ± 1,5625% Default = ± 6,25% Coarse = ±12,5% Switch = ±50%	Use the interaction modes Inc and Dec to seek stepwise through a track. The step size can be set in the field Resolution. Because the selected option represents a percentage value the step size in seconds is always a relative value depending on the track length.
	Interaction Mode: Reset	Sets the playback marker to the beginning of the track.
Deck Common | Move | Beatjump	Interaction Mode: Direct Type of Controller: Button Set to value: Select jump length	Trigger a beatjump by the length that is selected in Set to value. Use this combination if you wish to map the command ton a button or the keyboard. Please note, that you can either select a negative jump length for a backwards jump or a positive jump length for a forward jump.
	Interaction Mode: Direct Type of Controller: Encoder	Use this combination if you want to map the Beatjump command to an endless encoder or a jogwheel.

HOW TO: Map the Deck Button Jump to Track Start

The button *Jump to Track Start* at the right side of the deck does not have an equivalent mapping command. You can emulate this button by using the command *Deck Common | Seek Position.*

◨   One variation is to use the interaction mode *Reset* which moves the playback marker to the beginning of the track.

◨   You can also use the interaction mode *Direct* with controller type *Button*. When using this combination you should enter a value between 0 and 1 into the field *Set to value* for keyboard mapping and for MIDI mapping. 0 represents the beginning of the track, 1 the end and 0.5 the middle of the track.

3.2 Channel Fader, Cross Fader, Pre-listen

This section covers the channel faders (up faders), the cross fader and the pre-listen button (cue). All three elements/panels can be made visible in internal mode as well as in external mixing mode (see chapter 2 for more information about these two mixing modes). When using external mixing mode the channel faders and the crossfader are not visible, only their panels can be seen. If you use an external mixer the blending technique is the same, but here you would use the faders and the cue button on your mixer.

There are two main techniques for making a transition. In variation 1 the cross fader is permanently set to its middle position (the volume of the decks assigned to both sides of the cross fader is the same). To blend two tracks the channel fader of the new track is opened and the channel fader for the current track becomes closed. The moment before the transition will look like the following figure.

In the second variation the cross fader is used for blending and the channel faders of the tracks are always open. The position of the cross fader controls the volume of the different decks (but only when the channel faders are completely opened). If the cross fader is at the outer left the signal from the decks which are assigned to the left side of the cross fader is sent to the output. The same is also true for the right side of the cross fader. In this scenario the moment shortly before the transition should look like this:

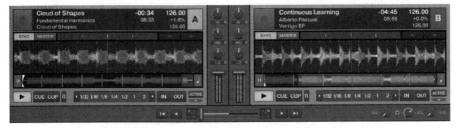

The method that is best suited depends on your personal mixing style and also on whether you scratch a lot or not at all. The fast blends performed while scratching cannot be done without using the cross fader. It is worth considering only using the channel faders and to hiding the cross fader from the screen. This saves screen space.

Another good reason not to use the cross fader is if you regularly use more than two decks. Blending with the channel faders means that you do not need to control the cross fader or pay any attention to the cross faders assignment. You can switch the cross fader on and off on the dialog box *Preferences/Mixer/Mixer Layout.*

Assigning the Cross Fader to the Decks

Immediately to the left and the right of the cross fader, there are little buttons showing the four deck letters. By clicking a letter you assign a deck to a side of the cross fader. The buttons behave like on/off-switches. You do not have to assign a deck to a cross fader side; doing this means that the deck volume can only be set with the channel fader.

> **NOTE No Sound?**   An incorrect assignment between decks and cross fader or an incorrect cross fader position (especially if the cross fader is hidden) is very often the cause of the "no sound"-problem. If you are using internal mixing mode and if you hear no sound then it is a good idea to check the cross fader settings.

The Buttons on the Cross Fader Panel

At the outer left and the right side of the cross fader there are four buttons. You can use the two outer buttons to start the automatic cross fading. The cross fader will then move in the selected direction. If you click the same button a second time the automatic cross fading is cancelled. You can configure the duration of the automatic cross fading (see next section).

If you click one of the inner buttons the cross fader moves stepwise in the selected direction. To move the cross fader from its middle position to one of the outer positions eight clicks are needed.

Configuring the Cross Fader

You can configure two different settings in the section *Crossfader* in the dialog box *Preferences/Mixer.* The slider *Auto Crossfade Time* defines the duration the cross fader needs during auto crossfade to move from the middle position to either the outer left or outer right position. A complete blend takes twice as long as the duration configured here.

With the lower slider you can change the cross fader curve. If the slider is positioned more towards *Smooth* then the blend between the audio signals of the decks is slower; if the slider is closer towards *Sharp* then the audio signal of the new deck is fed very quickly at its maximum value into the master out signal.

Crossfader and Kontrol S4 and Kontrol Z2

If you own the Kontrol S4 you can use the button combination SHIFT+FX-ASSIGN to change the assignment between the left/right side of the crossfader and the decks. On Kontrol Z2 the left side of the crossfader is by default to decks A and C and the right side is assigned to decks B and D. You cannot change the assignment directly from the controller but you need to use the assignment buttons in the Traktor user interface.

On the front panel of Kontrol Z2 there is a little knob that can be used to change the crossfader curve. If you use any other controller and want to be able to change the crossfader curve from your hardware, you can use the mapping command *Curve Adjust* (see following table).

Controlling the Cross Fader via Mapping

Of course, the cross fader can be completely mapped to the keyboard or to a controller. The following table shows the commands Traktor provides.

Cross Fading		
Mixer | X-Fader | Auto X-Fade Left	Interaction Mode: Trigger	Starts the automatic cross fading. After fading the fader is at the left side.
		Note: The duration of the fading can be configured in the dialog box Preferences | Mixer, option Auto Crossfade Time. The value is the time the cross fader needs to move from the middle position to the left or to the right.
Mixer | X-Fader | Auto X-Fade Right	Interaction Mode: Trigger	Starts the automatic cross fader; after fading the cross fader is at the outer right position. See also the tip for Auto X-Fade Left.
Mixer | X-Fader | Position	Interaction Mode: Dec Type of Controller: Button Resolution: Min = 256 steps Fine = 64 steps Default = 16 steps Coarse = 8 steps Switch = 2 steps	Moves the cross fader stepwise to the left. Use the list Resolution to select the number of steps it takes to move the cross fader from the middle position to one of the outer positions.

Cross Fading

	Interaction Mode: Inc Type of Controller: Button Resolution as for Dec	Moves the cross fader stepwise to the right.
	Interaction Mode: Reset Type of Controller: Button	Moves the cross fader to its middle position.
	Interaction Mode: Direct Type of Controller: Fader/Knob	The Interaction Mode Direct is the best option if you want to map the command to a fader or a knob.
Mixer | X-Fader | Assign Left	Interaction Mode Hold Assigns the deck selected in the list Assignment to the left side of the cross fader as long as the button is pressed. Interaction Mode Toggle Assigns the deck selected in the list Assignment removes the assignment. Interaction Mode Direct Assigns the deck selected in the list Assignment (Set to value: 1= On) or removes the assignment (Set to value: 0= Off).	Selects which deck/s is/are assigned to the left side of the cross fader. Tip: If you assign the mapping command X-Fader Assign Left to the same button as the mapping command X-Fader Assign Right and select in the list Assignment the same deck, you create a toggle button assigning the deck alternating to the left and the right side of the cross fader.
Mixer | X-Fader | Assign Right	Identical to X-Fader Assign Left	Selects which deck/s is/are assigned to the right side of the cross fader.
Mixer | X-Fader | Crossfader Curve	Interaction Mode: Direct Type of Controller: Fader/Knob	Allows you to change the crossfader curve by moving the slider from Preferences/Mixer/Crossfader with a fader knob on your controller.

Controlling the Channel Fader via Mapping

The channel fader can be controlled in a mapping also. The command needed is *Mixer | Volume Adjust.*

Setting the Deck Volume

Mixer | Volume Adjust	Interaction Mode: Direct Type of Controller: Fader, Knob, Encoder Assignment: select deck or Device Target	Sets the volume of the deck selected in the list Assignment.

Setting the Deck Volume

Interaction Mode: Inc, Dec Type of Controller: Button Assignment: select deck or Device Target Resolution: Min: ca. ±0,4% Fine: ca. ±1,3% Default: ca. ±6,25% Coarse: ca. ±12,5% Switch: ca. ±50	You can use the interaction modes Inc and Dec to change the deck volume stepwise. Use the list Resolution to configure the step size.
Interaction Mode: Reset Assignment: select deck or Device Target	Opens the Channel Fader.

HOW TO: Emulating the Punch-In Feature from Traktor DJ Studio 3

Traktor DJ Studio 3 (the Traktor version from 2006 before the software was renamed to Traktor Pro) provided a Punch-In feature which was removed in Traktor Pro. The punch button in Traktor 3 worked like this: the deck signal was fed into the master out signal as long as the punch button was pressed. This feature allowed short elements of other tracks to be quickly blended in.

If you wish to have a punch-in function you can achieve with by some clever mapping. This section explains two approaches. The first one can be used either with a keyboard or a controller mapping and the second one can only be mapped to a controller.

Option one is to use a modifier and map a button or key that creates a toggle function. When the button is pressed for the first time the channel fader is opened; when it is pressed for the second time the channel fader is closed again. The complete implementation needs four mapping commands. The modifier used here is just an example; you can use any other available modifier. All four commands are mapped to the same button.

Pressing the button for the first time activates the Punch-In; two commands are needed:

◻ Modifier #7, Interaction Mode: Direct, Set to value: 1, Modifier Conditions: M7=0

◻ Mixer | Volume Fader, Interaction Mode: Direct, Set to value: 1.000, Modifier Conditions: M7=0

Then the channel fader is open. The second button press closes the fader. Now two more commands are needed:

▢ Modifier #7, Interaction Mode: Direct, Set to value: 0, Modifier Conditions: M7=1

▢ Mixer | Volume Fader, Interaction Mode: Direct, Set to value: 0.000, Modifier Conditions: M7=1

The second option is to create a button that works in hold mode: if you press the button the channel fader shall be opened; if you release the button the channel fader shall be closed. The only problem is that the mapping command *Volume Adjust* does not offer interaction mode *Hold* if you select *Button* as *Type of Controller*.

You can still make it work by using a little trick. Add the command *Volume Adjust* to your mapping and active the Learn feature to assign this command to a button of your controller. Traktor proposes Fader/Knob for the Type of Controller option. Change the type to *Encoder*, set *Interaction Mode* to *Relative* and select *3Fh/41h* in list *Encoder Mode*. Now you can use the slider *Rotary Sensitivity* to configure the position of the channel fader. If you use 100% the channel fader is opened half way; if you use 200% it is opened completely.

Why does this work? When a MIDI button is pressed it normally sends a value of 127; when the button is released it sends a value 0. The controller type *Relative Encoder* reacts to two different values: one value to increase the parameter and another one to decrease it. When the physical MIDI button is pressed this causes an increase of the value inside of the *Relative Encoder*. This increase is configured with the slider *Rotary* Sensitivity. In our example this opens the channel fader. When the physical MIDI button is released this causes a decrease of the value. In our example the value of the rotary encoder is reset to 0%; this closes the channel fader.

If you wish to map the Punch-In feature to a MIDI button, the second approach is much better because it is easier to implement. However, if you wish to use a keyboard key instead then you need to use first approach, because the controller type *Rotary Encoder* isn't available for keyboard mapping.

More information about the controller types and about the MIDI protocol in general can be found in chapter 5, "MIDI Background" and in chapter 6, "Controller, Mappings, Modifier, Hotkeys, and Macros".

HOW TO: Setting the Deck Focus with the Cross Fader

If you map one of the deck-related commands, like *Load* or *Play/Pause*, you need to set the target for the command in the list *Assignment*. Here you can either choose one of the decks or you can use the option *Focus*. In the latter case the command is sent to the deck that is set to deck focus.

You can change the deck focus either by clicking the deck letter or by using the command *Layout | Deck Focus Selector*. This command can, for example be mapped to four different buttons where each button sets the focus to one of the decks. To map this use interaction mode *Direct,* controller type *Button* and select the deck in the list *Set to value* (not in list Assignment).

If you use an external mixer with a cross fader that is capable of sending MIDI messages, or a DJ controller with a cross fader and if you do not use the cross fader for mixing, you can map the focus switch to the cross fader by using the controller type *Fader/Knob* and interaction mode *Direct.* If the cross fader is in its outer left position the focus is set to deck A, if it is at the outer right then deck D has the focus. If you only use two decks in Traktor Pro and wish to perform a focus change between deck A and B only, then select controller type *Fader/Knob* and interaction mode *Relative.* Then set the *Rotary Sensitivity* to 5% and the *Rotary Acceleration* to 0%. You need to make sure that the cross fader curve on the MIDI controller/mixer is set to smooth.

Pre-listening (Cueing)

One important feature has yet to be mentioned: pre-listening. If you are using an external mixer then you can use its cue buttons. In internal mixing mode you can use the Cue button that is situated in the panel *Filter+Key+Gain+Cue+Balance* (this panel can be switched on and off in dialog box *Preferences/Layout Manager*).

When the Cue button is pressed the audio signal of the corresponding deck is sent to the headphone output (which is configured in section *Output Monitor* in dialog *Preferences/Output Routing*). The Cross Fader Panel panel contains two volume knobs: one to set the headphone volume and another to set the ratio between the master out signal and the monitor signal that is sent to the headphones (see next section).

Monitoring

Mixer | Monitor Cue On	Interaction Mode: Toggle Assignment: Select deck or Device Target	Sends the deck signal into the audio channels selected in the section Output Monitor of the page Output Routing (internal mixer mode). If you use Traktor in external mixer mode the cue function is needed to make the tick audible.
	Interaction Mode: Hold Assignment: Select deck or Device Target	Activates the monitor function as long as the button is pressed
	Interaction Mode: Direct Set to value: 1=On/0=Off Assignment: Select deck or Device Target	Can be used to switch the monitor function on and off directly.

The Volume Knobs on the Master Panel and on the Cross Fader Panel

The Master Panel of the Global Section has one knob and the cross fader panel has two knobs to control different volume setting. The *MAIN* knob controls the volume of the Master Out signal. The *VOL* knob is used to set the volume of the headphone (Output Monitor signal) and *MIX* sets the ratio of the Master Out and the Cue/Monitor signal that is sent to the headphones. Use the *AUX* knob to control the volume of the signal that is configured in section *Input Aux* on the *Preferences/Input Routing* dialog.

Global Section   Cross Fader Section

The *MAIN* button is also active when external mixing mode is selected. Then it controls the volume of all decks. The three knobs on the cross fader panel are only useful when you use the internal mixing mode.

Setting Volume for Mix Out, Pre-listen and Aux (Microphone)

Mixer | Master Volume Adjust	Interaction Mode: Direct Type of Controller: Fader, Knob	Sets the volume of the Master Output signal.
	Interaction Mode: Dec, Inc Type of Controller: Button Resolution (dB): Min = ± ca. 0,15 Fine = ± ca. 0,625 Default = ± 2,5 Coarse = ± 5,0 Switch = ± 50	Use the interaction modes Inc and Dec to set the volume of the master out signal stepwise.
Mixer | Monitor Mix Adjust	Interaction Mode: Direct Type of Controller: Fader/Knob	Sets the ratio between master out and cue signal. 0.5 equals to the middle position (=50%). The decimal value needs to be entered in American format, i.e. the point has to be used as a decimal separator.
	Interaction Mode: Direct Type of Controller: Button Set to value: decimal value in the range between 0.000 (equals 0) and 1.000 (equals100).	This command is disabled in external mixing mode.
Mixer | Monitor Volume Adjust	Interaction Mode: Direct Type of Controller: Fader/Knob, Encoder	Sets the headphone volume, i.e. the volume of the outputs configured in section Output Monitor of dialog box Preferences | Output Routing. This command is disabled in external mixing mode.

Setting Volume for Mix Out, Pre-listen and Aux (Microphone)

	Interaction Mode: Direct Type of Controller: Button Set to value: decimal value in the range be- tween 0.000 (= –0,80 dB) and 1.000 (= 10 dB). 0.75 equals to 0 dB.	Sets the headphone volume to the value config- ured in list Set to value
Mixer | Microphone Gain Adjust	Interaction Mode: Direct Type of Controller: Fader/ Knob	Sets the Aux/Microphone volume. This is the volume of the signal routed into Input Aux (Pref- erences/Audio Routing). In fact this input is only available in internal mixing mode and was intro-
	Interaction Mode: Direct Type of Controller: Button Set to value: decimal value in the range be- tween 0.000 (equals 0) and 1.000 (equals100).	duced with Traktor Pro S4 to support the Mic in- put on the Kontrol S4 controller. This command is disabled in external mixing mode.

Master Limiter

Traktors' audio engine is equipped with a limiter that makes sure that the level of the audio signal never exceeds a particular value to  avoid clipping (this is indicated by the red bars in the Master Level meter in the header).

To give you better control over the levels, the level meter in the Traktor header uses three different colours: it will be blue up to a level of –6dB and is orange in the range of –6dB to –1dB. The red clipping indicator will light up if the level is more than –1dB (Traktor limiter disabled) or if the limiter kicks in (Traktor limiter enabled).

The limiter can be switched on by activating the check box *Enable Limiter* on the *Preferences/Mixer* dialog.

> **TIP** If you hear a phase shift similar to the Flanger effect when using the Loop Recorder or in your headphones when using internal mixing mode, then switch the limiter off. This could help to solve the problem.

The limiter can be switched on and off with a mapping command.

Switching Master Limiter On and Off

Mixer | Limiter On	Interaction Mode: Hold	Activates the limiter as long as the mapped key/button is pressed.
	Interaction Mode: Toggle	Toggles the activation status of the limiter.
	Interaction Mode: Direct Set to value: 1=On/0=Off	Use Interaction Mode Direct to either switch the limiter on or off.

Mixer Headroom

The *Preferences/Mixer* dialog contains another option that affects the output level, the list box Headroom shown in the following figure.

What does this setting do? It reduces the signal level on all outputs and on the input for external recording by the specified decibel value without the need to change the Main Level knob on the Traktor user interface. The goal of the Headroom setting is to avoid clipping and giving you some headroom when unexpected peaks appear in the audio signal while leaving the Main Level knob in the Traktor user interface at 0.00dB.

If you are used to an analogue mixer like an Allen&Heath Xone:92 for example, then the normal operating range should be between –5db and +5dB and the average should be around 0dB. With this mixer the signal level must reach +20dB before clipping and distortion occurs, and the actual meters go to +10dB. Even if the level meters are completely red you still have an additional 10dB of room before clipping occurs.

With digital DJ gear things are a bit different: the maximum level that can be achieved is 0dBFS "„decibel full scale"; if the level is stronger the sound will clip and you will get unwanted distortion.

If you are using internal mixer mode the Master Output, the Headphone output and the signal sent to the internal mix recorder becomes attenuated. Please note that if you are using Kontrol Z2 a default headroom setting of –9dB is used and that this value cannot be changed.

If you are using external mixer mode the Headroom setting is hidden; Traktor will use a default setting of –3dB which cannot be changed. The outputs of the individual Traktor decks and the external input coming in for the internal mix recorder becomes attenuated. Reducing the internal levels has no effect on the audio quality; having the Traktor level meter constantly in the red does affect the audio quality and you should avoid this.

If you select option *None* Traktor will behave exactly as in earlier versions.

Gain Control: Channel Gain and Autogain

The *Filter+Key+Gain+Cue+Balance* panel has a gain knob which has the same function as the corresponding button found on hardware mixers. You use the gain knob to compensate volume differences between tracks. The volume of slightly quieter tracks (which is often the case with older tracks) can be increased; the volume of noisier tracks can de decreased. The target is two get the gain set in a way that when the channel faders of all the decks are completely open, the volume of the tracks is almost identical.

Autogain disabled	Autogain enabled	Autogain enabled	Autogain enabled
No button	Button blue	Button orange	Button orange
Gain Value	Gain Value	Autogain Value	Track is locked

If you add a track into the track collection Traktor analyses the volume of the track and it remembers at what decibel the signal strength needs to be raised or lowered. This value is called Autogain value. If next to the Gain knob a little blue button is shown, then the Autogain feature of Traktor is enabled. You can activate/deactivate *Autogain* on the *Preferences/Mixer* dialog in section *Level*.

While Autogain is enabled Traktor sets the Autogain value automatically to the value determined during the track analysis when that track is loaded. You can still change the channel fader Gain setting by using the *Gain* knob while the button is blue. The total gain that is applied is the sum of the Autogain value and the Gain value.

You can see the Autogain value analysed by Traktor by clicking the small blue button. Now the button becomes orange and the Autogain value is shown. You can also see the Autogain value by right-clicking a track in the track-browser and selecting *Edit*. The analysed values are shown in field *Autogain*.

> **TIP** You can display the total gain value (the sum of channel gain and autogain of the currently loaded track) in the deck header of the track decks. Open *Preferences/Track Decks* and choose option *Total Gain* for one of the info fields that the deck header provides (see figures on the next page).

If the loaded track is not locked by the Analysis Lock feature of Traktor you can change the Autogain value by turning the knob. Changes made to the Autogain value will be automatically saved with the track. If Analysis Lock is on, you can only see the Autogain value but you cannot change it (picture to the right in the figure on the previous page).

NOTE More information about Analysis Lock can be found in the section covering beatgridding in chapter 8.

Both gain values can be controlled in a mapping. Furthermore you can switch the Gain knob view between Channelfader Gain and Autogain.

Setting the Gain Level

Mixer | Gain Adjust	Interaction Mode: Direct Type of Controller: Fader/ Knob, Encoder Assignment: Select deck or Device Target	Increases or decreases the gain level for the selected deck.
	Interaction Mode: Dec, Inc Type of Controller: Button Assignment: Select deck or Device Target	Increases or decreases the gain level for the selected deck stepwise.
Mixer | Auto-Gain Adjust	See Gain Adjust	Increases or decreases the Autogain value of the loaded track. The Autogain value can only be changed if the track is not locked. Additionally the Autogain feature must be enabled on Preferences/Mixer/Level.
Mixer | Auto-Gain View On	Interaction Mode: Hold	Switches the view of the Gain knob to Autogain while the mapped button is pressed. The Autogain feature needs to be enabled. Hold is a good interaction mode that can be mapped to a SHIFT button.
	Interaction Mode: Toggle	Toggles the view of the Gain knob between Channelfader Gain and Autogain.
	Interaction Mode: Direct Set to value: 1=Autogain/0=Channelfader Gain	Allows it to switch directly to Channelfader Gain view or Autogain view.

Setting the Balance (Pan)

Finally at very bottom of the *Filter+Key+Gain+Cue+Balance* we have the balance knob (Pan), which is only visible if the Advanced Panel for the deck is switched on. This knob sets the volume ratio between the left and the right stereo channel.

Panning		
Mixer | Balance Adjust	Interaction Mode: Direct Type of Controller: Fader, Knob, Encoder Assignment: Select deck or Device Target	Sets the balance of the selected deck.
	Interaction Mode: Dec, Inc Type of Controller: Button Assignment: Select deck or Device Target	Sets the ratio between the left and the right channel stepwise. Dec emphases the left channel and Inc the right channel.
	Interaction Mode: Reset Type of Controller: Button Assignment: Select deck or Device Target	Resets the Pan knob its middle position.

3.3 Duplicating Decks

Not only is it possible to load a track from the track browser but also you can create a duplicate of a loaded track in another deck as well. When duplicating a deck Traktor copies the track and the current position of the playback marker. If a loop is active in the original deck, then it will be active in the duplicate as well.

Being able to duplicate decks opens a range of possibilities. One is to manually create the Flanger effect (which is also available as FX). After duplicating the deck move the phase in the duplicate up and down by using the *Tempo Bend* buttons.

Or you can use the duplicated deck to prelisten to the Traktor effects. Set the *D/W* knob in the duplicated deck to 100 so that only the effect signal can be heard. Once the effect parameters are as they should be, feed the effect signal into the mix by opening either the channel fader or the cross fader.

This is how to duplicate a deck with the mouse: Click the deck header in the original deck and drag the header onto the target deck and drop it there. Traktor provides the following mapping commands to duplicate a deck:

Duplicating Decks

Track Deck | Duplicate Track Deck A	Interaction Mode: Trigger Assignment: Select deck or use option Device Target	Creates a copy of deck A in the deck selected in the list Assignment.
Track Deck | Duplicate Track Deck B	See above	Creates a copy of deck B in the deck selected in the list Assignment
Track Deck | Duplicate Track Deck C	See above	Creates a copy of deck C in the deck selected in the list Assignment
Track Deck | Duplicate Track Deck D	See above	Creates a copy of deck D in the deck selected in the list Assignment

3.4 The Preview Player

As well as the four "normal" decks the trackbrowser offers a preview deck with which you can use to pre-listen to tracks without first loading them into the other decks

You can display the preview player by opening *Preferences/Browser Details* and activating the check box *Show Preview Player*. The audio signal of the preview player is sent to the same output that has been configured in *Preferences/Output Routing*. If you are using internal mixing mode you set the output in section *Output Monitor*. The volume can be set in the Master Panel with the volume knob for the headphone signal. If you are using an external mixer you select the outputs in section *Output Preview*. Then the volume is controlled with the fader on your mixer.

As with the other decks you can drag a track onto the preview player to load it. Or you can turn the column *Prelisten* in the trackbrowser on. Right-click the column heading; then click *Prelisten* in the menu, you can also drag the column *Prelisten* to the

desired position. The column will display a small headphone icon; when you click this icon the track is loaded into the preview player.

The preview player has a start/pause button and it shows a smaller version of the stripe; use the stripe to seek through the track.

The mapping commands for the preview player are shown in the following table.

Prelistening Tracks in the Preview Deck

Preview Player | Load Selected	Interaction Mode: Trigger	Loads the selected track into the preview player.
Preview Player | Unload	Interaction Mode: Trigger Assignment: Preview Deck	Unloads the track from the preview player.
Preview Player | Play/Pause	Interaction Mode: Hold/Toggle Interaction Mode: Direct Set to value: 1=On/0=Off	Starts/stops playback of the track currently loaded in the preview player
Preview Player| Seek Position	Interaction Mode: Direct Type of Controller: Fader, Knob, Encoder	Moves the playback marker in the preview player. The interaction mode Direct is best suited to seek quickly through the track if you want to map the command to a jog wheel.
	Interaction Mode: Inc, Dec Resolution: Min = ± 0,4% Fine = ± 1,5625% Default = ± 6,25% Coarse = ± 12,5% Switch = ± 50%	If you want to map the command to a button or if you want to create a hotkey use the interaction modes Inc and Dec to change the playback position stepwise. The selected resolution in seconds depends of the actual length of the track.

Chapter 4

Traktor Scratch Pro 2 and Timecode Control

Traktor 2 exists in two flavours: Traktor Pro 2 and Traktor Scratch Pro 2. Feature wise, both flavours are almost identical: The scratch flavour contain all of the features available in the non-scratch flavour, i.e. support of four/two decks, FX section to name just a few. Additionally Traktor Scratch Pro 2 allows you to control the software with timecode vinyl or timecode CDs. The physical bits of the executable files for all flavours are identical. Your serial number in conjunction with the product activation process determines, whether the scratch features are available or not.

This means that all Traktor features described in the other chapters of this book are available in Traktor Scratch Pro 2. This chapter specifically covers the additional timecode features that are only available in Traktor Scratch Pro 2.

4.1 Overview of Traktor Scratch Pro 2

To be able to use Traktor Scratch Pro 2 you need, of course, turntables/CD players and the following components:

◻ Traktor Scratch Pro 2 software **and**

◻ Timecode Vinyl or Timecode CDs **and**

◻ a soundcard, a controller, or a mixer which is supported by Traktor Scratch Pro. At present you can use:

  ◻ one of the following Native Instruments audio interfaces: Audio 4DJ, Audio 8 DJ, Traktor Audio 6, Traktor Audio 10, Traktor Scratch A6, or Traktor Scratch A10. In this setup you need additionally an external DJ mixer.

  ◻ the native Instruments controller Traktor Kontrol S4 (either MK1 or MK2)

  ◻ the native Instruments controller/mixer Traktor Kontrol Z2

  ◻ one of the mixers with an integrated audio interface that has been certified by Native Instruments for use with Traktor Scratch Pro (see also page 98)

Timecode Version 1 and Timecode MK2

Up to Traktor version 2.1.0 Traktor Scratch was shipped with a timecode decoder, timecode-vinyls and CDs which are now known as "timecode version 1". The use of this timecode version was licensed in April 2008 by Native Instruments from N2IT, a Dutch company holding patents for timecode controlled digital music playback. This agreement ended a lawsuit that was filed by N2IT against Native Instruments, alleging that the defendants' Traktor Scratch product infringes N2IT's patent on the technology. (The website with links for this book – see chapter 1 – contains several links to additional information.)

Starting with Traktor 2.1.1, which was released in September 2011, Native Instruments integrated its own timecode technology into Traktor Scratch. The new timecode technology is marketed as "Timecode MK2" and "Native Scratch Technology". Timecode MK2 allows for tighter and more precise control of the decks controlled by timecode media. This means that there is no longer a requirement to pay license fees to N2IT. The first Traktor Scratch versions with timecode MK2 contained some teething problems which were solved bit by bit in later updates. Since Traktor 2.6.2 (released in July 2013), and after a public beta test and after various improvements the new timecode versions seem to work more reliably and more stable.

Native Instruments made the switch to timecode MK2 very smooth and flexible. All Traktor Scratch users who bought a package that contained the "old" timecode media can continue to use timecode version 1. The same users can, once they updated the software to version 2.1.1 or later, use either timecode version 1 or timecode MK2. The old timecode media are still available.

All Traktor Scratch users who bought a package that contained the new timecode MK2 media, can only use timecode MK2.

> **TIP** There is some interesting information about the invention of the timecode architecture on the internet. One worth reading article can be found here: *www.who-invented-digital-vinyl.co.uk/*

Timecode Vinyl and Timecode CDs

The Traktor Scratch packages (Traktor Kontrol Z2, Traktor Scratch A6/A10, and the Traktor Scratch Pro 2 Software & Timecode Kit) contain a set of timecode vinyl as well as a set of timecode CDs. The default colour of the records is black; red, blue, and white vinyl and sometimes special editions of timecode vinyl are also available (must be purchased separately).

Timecode Vinyl MK2

Both timecode vinyl and timecode CDs contain an pilot signal constructed from two sinus waves, plus a binary coded signal. Depending on the media and the timecode version you are using the following frequencies are used for the pilot signal:

- for timecode version 1 (Vinyl and CD) the frequency is 2 kHz,
- for timecode vinyl MK2 the frequency is 2.5 kHz
- for timecode CD MK2 the frequency is 3 kHz

The Traktor timecode decoder extracts two different types of information from the incoming pilot signal:

- Playback speed of the timecode vinyl or timecode CD, respectively, and
- Playback direction (forward, backwards)
- Current playback position of the timecode vinyl or of the timecode CD

The detection of the current playback speed isn't very complicated because the timecode decoder knows the original frequency of the timecode signal. If the playback speed is slower, then the frequency of the incoming timecode signal is lower than the original frequency. If the rotation speed of the turntables or CD player is higher than 100%, then the frequency increases. The timecode decoder analyses the frequency of the incoming signal and uses the difference between the original and the detected frequency to calculate the current tempo. Traktor can then adjust the playback speed of the deck to the playback speed of the timecode medium.

Because Traktor uses the frequency to calculate the speed you must **never** activate the Master Tempo feature available on many CDJ players, because the Master Tempo function corrects the tone pitch. This is unwanted when using timecode.

If you are using turntables, that always flutter, the BPM display on a timecode controlled deck is never stable; this reflects the flutter of the turntables.

For forward playback the frequency information is sufficient but it is not enough to determine whether the timecode medium is moving forward or backwards. This information is absolutely necessary when scratching or manual beat matching. To detect the playback direction, the timecode signal is constructed from two sinus waves, one for the left and another one for the right channel. The phases of both waves are slightly shifted. This can be seen in the following figure which simulates this (let's assume the upper wave is for the left and the lower one for the right channel).

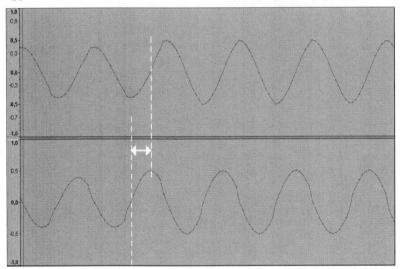

Because of the phase shifting the right channel is slightly ahead of the left channel. When the right channel meets the zero line, the values of the amplitude of the left channel are negative. When the playback direction is reversed and the right channel reaches the zero line, the values of the amplitude of the left channel are positive. Simply put, this is the trick by which the timecode decoder can detect the playback direction.

This is also the reason why Traktor always requires the timecode signal of the left and the right channel to be functioning properly. If one channel is missing (maybe because one cable is not connected or because the contacts of the cartridge are black or dirty) only forward playback will be possible. This mode is called emergency mode. More practical information about the left/right channel topic can be found further down in this chapter when timecode configuration and the timecode scope are covered.

This brings us to the third and final question, how does Traktor recognise the current playback position. Here timestamps are used, which are binary coded into the timecode signal. The frequency of the binary coded signal is below the frequency of the pilot signal. The following figure shows the frequency spectrum of a MK2 timecode

CD. You can see the peak at 3 kHz representing the pilot signal. The audio signal to the left of the 3 kHz peak contains the timestamp data.

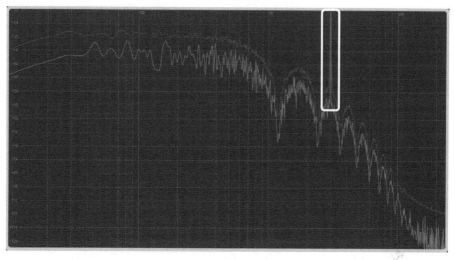

The position detection is the most enhanced part of using timecode, and it is error-prone so this is why all digital vinyl systems use some kind of error detection and correction. However, the better and clearer the timecode signal is, the more accurately the current position can be detected. Dusty or worn needles, dirty vinyl or an unclean audio signal resulting from ground hum, defect cabling between the turntable/CDJ and the audio interface or between the pick-up and cartridge all have an impact on the timecode signal received by the timecode decoder inside Traktor. In order to be able to use timecode properly not only should you make sure that all settings in Traktor are correct, but also that your "physical tools" are in good condition.

Admittedly, the description above is greatly simplified. The goal was not to cover the complex timecode processing in Traktor, but rather to provide some technical background about how a Digital Vinyl System (DVS) works in general, what is going on before the initial sound comes out of the speakers and to provide some helpful knowledge for troubleshooting purposes.

Audio 4 DJ/8 DJ, Traktor Audio 6/10, and Traktor Kontrol S4/Z2

The only external audio interfaces that can be used with Traktor Scratch Pro are the older soundcards Audio 4 DJ/Audio 8 DJ and the new audio interfaces Traktor Audio 6/10 and their successors Traktor Scratch A6/A10. All audio interfaces are made by Native Instruments. All four audio interfaces can be connected to any mixer.

> **NOTE** When describing features where there is no functional difference between the older Traktor Audio 6 and Traktor Audio 10 and the newer Traktor Scratch A6 and Traktor Scratch A10, we will refer to all four audio interfaces as Traktor Scratch A6/10.

Currently the only hybrid devices (audio interface/controller) that can be used with Traktor Scratch are Native Instruments' Traktor Kontrol S4/S4 MK2 and Traktor Kontrol Z2 (which can be also be used as a stand-alone mixer).

Due to the Traktor product policy of Native Instruments (focussing on the sale of NI made hardware) the chance is very small that we will see controllers or soundcards by other manufacturers that are compatible with Traktor Scratch. It is more likely that we will see a larger four deck version of Kontrol Z2.

The main features of these audio interfaces are listed in the following table:

Audio Interface	USB Audio Channels	MIDI Port	Other
Audio 4 DJ	4 Inputs (2 x Stereo, both Phono/Line switchable) 4 Outputs (2 x Stereo)	–	USB 2.0 Headphone Connector
Audio 8 DJ	8 Inputs (4 x Stereo, 2 ports Phono/Line switchable) 8 Outputs (4 x Stereo)	MIDI IN MIDI OUT	USB 2.0 Headphone Connector Microphone Input
Traktor Audio 6 Traktor Scratch A6	6 Inputs (3 x Stereo, 2 ports Phono/Line/Thru switchable) 6 Outputs (3 x Stereo)	–	USB 2.0 Headphone Connector
Traktor Audio 10 Traktor Scratch A10	10 Inputs (5 x Stereo, 4 ports Phono/Line/Thru switchable) 10 Outputs (5 x Stereo)	MIDI IN MIDI OUT	USB 2.0 Headphone Connector Microphone Input
Traktor Kontrol S4	4 External Inputs (2 x Stereo, both Phono/Line switchable) 4 External Outputs (one for Master Output, one for Monitor Output)	MIDI IN MIDI OUT	USB 2.0, Headphone Connector Microphone Input
Traktor Kontrol Z2	6 External Inputs (3 x Stereo, 2 x Phono/Line switchable, 1 x Mic/Aux input) 4 External Outputs (one for Master Output, one for Monitor Output)	No MIDI port but integrated USB hub	USB 2.0 Headphone Connector Microphone Input Separate Booth Control

IMPORTANT The most critical feature is the number of channels. As explained in chapter 2 you need one stereo channel for each deck that you wish to use with time-code control. This means that when using Audio 4 DJ/Traktor Audio 6/Kontrol S4, and Kontrol Z2 you can only use two timecode decks but with Audio 8 DJ/Traktor Audio 10 you can use four decks with timecode control.

If you already own a DJ mixer then a good choice is one of the packages containing either Traktor Scratch A6 or Traktor Scratch A10 (see the Native Instruments website for more information).

All audio interfaces are connected to your computer via USB. Only Traktor Audio 10 needs external power; all other Native Instruments audio interface, also the "MK2 version Traktor Scratch A10, receive the necessary power via the USB connection. (Traktor Audio 6/10 and Traktor Scratch A6/A10 have an external power connector, which must be used if you use the audio device in Thru mode.)

Traktor Audio 10/Traktor Scratch A10 are equipped with ten audio outputs and ten audio inputs, one MIDI IN and one MIDI OUT port. Additionally, the front side of has a microphone input and a headphone output. The following photo shows the rear side of the Traktor Audio 10.

Connectors at the rear side of Traktor Audio 10/Traktor Scratch A10

Traktor Audio 6 and Traktor Scratch A6 are equipped with six audio inputs and six audio outputs. They do not provide a MIDI port or a microphone socket. The head-phone socket can be found at the front side of Traktor Audio 6/Traktor Scratch A6.

Connectors at the rear side of Traktor Audio 6/Traktor Scratch A6

Certified Mixer

At the end of 2007 Native Instruments launched a certification program called "Traktor Scratch Certified". Within the scope of this program several external DJ mixers have been certified for use with Traktor Scratch. The mixer is used as a dongle: if Traktor detects that one of the certified mixers is connected and selected as the audio device in Traktor, Traktor activates the timecode functionality. (The audio interfaces by Native Instruments are being used as dongle in the same way.)

Whether this certification is necessary due to technical reasons may is questionable. It is certainly true that certified mixers are more easily setup. But – similar to the major competitor Serato Scratch Live – it is more likely that the main goal of the certification is to sell more hardware made by Native Instruments (or mixers made by chummy partners). There are other DVS systems, like MixVibes Cross, that do not use a soundcard or hybrid-mixer as a dongle and that can be used with any mixer or soundcard.

As of today (February 2014) the following mixers are certified for Traktor Scratch: Allen&Heath Xone:4D, Denon DN-X 1600 and DN-X 1700, and Pioneer DJM-900 nexus. Now that Native Instruments has brought out its individual own controller/mixers, the Traktor Kontrol Z2, to the market, I don't think that we will see any new Traktor Scratch certified mixers made by other companies, only those made by NI. Currently the Native Instruments webpage still has some general information about certified mixers; however, I couldn't find a detailed list. This looks as though Native Instruments is keeping other DJ hardware manufacturers out of the picture.

The main advantage of using a certified mixer is that you only need one piece of hardware because all certified mixers have an audio interface integrated. On the other hand, the advantage of Traktor Audio 6/10 is that the box is very small which makes it easy to carry and you can connect the audio interface to any DJ mixer that is installed where you may be DJing. The following table contains a feature overview of the different certified mixers:

Mixer	Channels	MIDI/HID	Interface	Website	Street Price[1]
Allen & Heath Xone:4D	Mixer: 8 (4 Stereo) Soundcard In: 8 Soundcard Out: 8 plus SPDIF in/out, coaxial and optical	Yes/No	USB 2.0	www.xone.co.uk	1,900 Euro 2,400 USD 1,000 GBP
Denon DN-X 1600	Mixer: 8 (4 Stereo) Soundcard In: 8 Soundcard Out: 8	Yes/Yes	USB 2.0	www.denondj.com	1,000 Euro 1,000 USD 840 GBP
Denon DN-X 1700	Mixer: 8 (4 Stereo) Soundcard In: 8 Soundcard Out: 8	Yes/Yes	USB 2.0	www.denondj.com	1,700 Euro 1,600 USD 1,400 GBP

Mixer	Channels	MIDI/HID	Interface	Website	Street Price[1]
Pioneer DJM-900 nexus	Mixer: 8 (4 Stereo) Soundcard In: 8 Soundcard Out: 8	Yes/Yes	USB 2.0	www.pioneer.eu	1,800 Euro 2,000 USD 1,600 GBP

[1] As of February 2014

More information about these mixers can be found on the manufacturers' websites. But because paper (even in an electronic format) does not always tell the whole story, I recommend checking the user forums on the Native Instruments website and to look out for what experiences other Traktor users have really had with a particular piece of hardware.

The following discontinued mixers can be also be used with timecode: Ecler Evo 5, Korg Zero 4 and Zero 8, Mackie d2.Pro and d4.Pro. Finally we have the Pioneer DJM-T1, which was developed as a 2-channel-mixer for Traktor Scratch. This mixer has since been discontinued.

4.2 Connecting the Hardware

Once all necessary hardware and software is in place it is time to connect the individual pieces together. This section explains the signal path when using timecode and it shows how to connect the separate components.

Signal Path and Connecting for Timecode and External Mixer

The following figure illustrates the signal path of the timecode and the audio signal when Traktor is configured for timecode use.

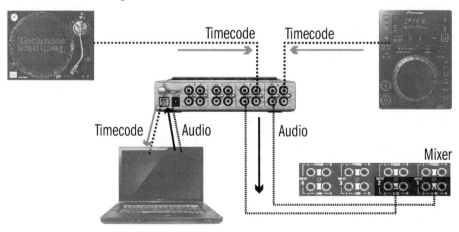

In this setup the signal flows through the following four stages:

▣   The turntable and the CD player in the figure send timecode data to the connected audio interface. Both devices are connected to the inputs of the audio interface. The input of the audio interface needs to be set to Phono for the turntable
and to Line for the CD player.

▣   The incoming timecode data is sent via the USB connection to Traktor and inside
Traktor to the decks that are set to Scratch Control/timecode usage.

▣   Traktor's timecode decoder modifies the deck's audio signal according to the
tempo and direction and position of the timecode data. The resulting audio signal
is sent via the USB connection to the outputs of the audio interface.

▣   The outputs of the audio interface are connected to the inputs of the mixer where
the audio signal is received. For both timecode vinyl and timecode CDs the outputs of the audio interface need to be connected to the Line inputs of the mixer.

This means for cabling:

▣   Connect the turntable/CDJ player to the inputs of your audio interface.

▣   Connect the outputs of the audio interface with the Line inputs of your mixer
even if you are using turntables/timecode vinyl.

Using the Direct Thru Mode of Traktor Scratch A6/A10

Traktor Scratch packages for Traktor Scratch 1.x contained multi core cables that
made switching between timecode control and using normal vinyl/CDs easy: switching between the two modes can be done by switching the input of your mixer between
Phono/Line or Line/Line. With Traktor Scratch A6/10 multicore cables are no longer
necessary. All four audio interfaces provide a THRU mode. In THRU mode the signal
from an input port is sent directly to the output port. A line level signal is "copied"
unaltered; when the input mode of that port is set to *Phono*, the incoming signal is
amplified and a line level signal is sent to the two outputs of that port.

Proceed as follows to use Direct Thru:

▣   Connect your turntable or your CDJ player to the L/R sockets of the input channel of your Traktor Scratch A6/10 that you wish to use.

▣   Connect the L/R sockets of the respective output of Traktor Scratch A6/10 to the
Line inputs of your mixer. You need to use the Line inputs even when you are
connecting a turntable.

▣   Start the control panel of Traktor Scratch A6/10 respectively.

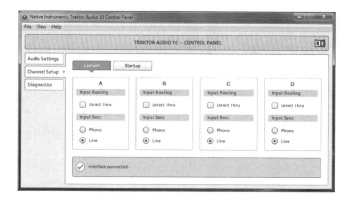

□ If you wish to use normal vinyl or audio CDs activate the input port (A to D) where the turntable/CDJ player is connected, option *Direct Thru*. If you wish to use timecode you need to make sure that *Direct Thru* is disabled.

□ Set the input mode in section *Input Sends* to *Phono* if you use a turntable or set it to *Line* if you use a CDJ player.

You can activate/deactivate Direct Thru mode from inside Traktor as well if the mixing mode is set to External. If in *Preferences/Audio Setup* either Traktor Scratch 6 or Traktor Scratch 10 is selected, clicking the deck letter opens the menu shown in the following figure. Use the *Direct Thru* command to set the channels that are routed into that deck to Thru mode. Traktor opens a confirmation dialog and asks if you really wish to switch to Direct Thru.

A deck set to Direct Thru looks as shown in the following figure. To disable Direct Thru for the input port routed into that deck click on *THRU* and then on *Enable Deck* or simply click the *Enable* button.

A slight problem with the Direct Thru mode is that it can only be activated/deactivated with the control panel application for Traktor Scratch A6/A10. Let's assume the worst case scenario that you spin with timecode and that your computer crashes during a gig. A crashed computer means that you cannot launch the control panel to activate Direct Thru and then use normal vinyl/CDs as fallback until your computer reboots. You can solve this by disconnecting the power adapter and/or the USB cable. On re-boot the startup configuration of Traktor Scratch A6/A10 will be loaded. If Direct Thru is enabled for the input ports that the turntable/CDJ player is connected to, you can use vinyl and audio CDs immediately.

Direct Thru Mode and Traktor Kontrol Z2

Traktor Kontrol Z2 supports Direct Thru as well. Here you can enable/disable Direct Thru directly on the controller by using the button with the Traktor logo (next to the input switches). While the button is lit the deck is controlled by Traktor or timecode. If the button is off Direct Thru is used and the audio from the connected turntable/CDJ stays inside the mixer. In Traktor the deck that is set to Direct Thru looks as shown in the following figure.

Connecting and Configuring Certified Mixers

There is no standard procedure for connecting the turntables/CDJ players to the Traktor Scratch certified mixers. The configuration is also mixer dependent. Traktor Scratch certified mixers normally detect if a timecode signal is fed into one of the inputs; they then send the timecode signal to Traktor and in turn Traktor sends the audio signal back to the mixer. The following paragraphs contain some mixer specific information.

If you are using an Allen & Heath mixer Xone:4D connect the turntables to the *Phono* inputs and CDJ players to the *Line* inputs. The hardware configuration is then done by using the buttons to select the input source. If you are using turntables set the upper button to *Phono* (LED is green); if you use a CD player set it to line (LED is red). This sends the timecode signal to the mixer and the 4D can then transmit it to Traktor. Additionally you need to switch the lower button to On (LED is red); that way the signal from the audio interface is fed into the mixer (this is the signal Traktor uses to send the audio back to the 4D).

Timecode with Traktor Kontrol S4 and Kontrol Z2

Currently Traktor Kontrol S4 and Kontrol Z2 are the only hybrid devices (controller, audio interface) that allow timecode use in internal mixing mode.

For Kontrol S4 MK1 turntables and CD players are connected to the input channels C and D at the rear of controller. Set the input switch *Phono/Line* to *Phono* if you are using timecode vinyl and to *Line* if you are using timecode CDs/CDJ players. Make sure that the *THRU/USB* switch for Channel D is set to *USB*, to make sure that the signal arriving at that input are routed via USB to Traktor and that it is not mixed into Master Out signal.

For Kontrol S4 MK2 the procedure is identical to S4 MK1, however the inputs are labelled different. Furthermore, there is no THRU/USB switch you need to worry about:

Traktor Kontrol Z2 provides four pairs of stereo connectors at the rear of the device, two pairs for phono level and two for line level signals. This allows you to connect two turntables and CDJ players at the same time. From each group A and B only one pair can be active. You use the input selector switch on the top of the Z2 to decide which input shall be used.

When using Kontrol S4 or Kontrol Z2 for timecode the signal path is slightly different than with an external mixer. In this configuration the timecode data is sent from the two inputs to the Traktor timecode decoder. The decoder analyses the timecode signal and sends the modified audio signal to the deck assigned to inputs (on *Preferences/Input Routing*).

In this setup the audio signal of the decks is not sent to the outside world, but it remains in the internal Traktor mixer. It leaves the internal mixer via the outputs configured as Output Master if the channel fader of the respective deck is open.

4.3 Configuring Traktor for Timecode

Once everything is correctly connected continue with the timecode configuration of Traktor. The Setup Wizard takes care of the basic configuration; nevertheless it is useful to know what has been configured and where. Configuring Traktor for timecode is especially confusing for beginners because there are several locations where timecode settings can be made. These locations are:

▣   *Preferences/Audio Setup* dialog: Section *Phono/Line* is used to check the input mode (Phono/Vinyl and CD/Line) for the Native Instruments audio interfaces. If you use either Audio 4 DJ or Audio 8 DJ you can change the input mode here. If you are using either Traktor Scratch A6/A10 can click the *Settings* button to open the Control Panel for your audio interface and change the Input Mode there.

▣   *Preferences/Input Routing* dialog: This page of the *Preferences* dialog is used to assign the timecode inputs, i.e. the input ports of your audio interface, to the decks. This assignment controls which of the decks can be controlled via timecode.

▣   *Preferences/Decks Layout* dialog: Use the section *Platter/Scope* to show/hide the scratch panels.

▣   *Preferences/Track Decks* dialog: Use option *Stripe View Fit* in section *Miscellaneous* to configure the stripe view when using timecode control. The stripe can either be scaled to the length of the currently loaded track or to the length of the current timecode control medium.

▣   *Preferences/Timecode Setup* dialog: This page contains additional timecode options; they are explained further down in this chapter.

▣   Each deck contains a deck mode menu. To open the deck mode menu click the arrow below the deck letter. You can use this menu to set the **deck mode**. For Traktor Scratch Pro the following deck modes are important: *Internal Playback* und *Scratch Control*.

◻ Finally we have the transport section of the deck (where the Play button resides). If a deck is set to deck mode *Scratch Control* you can use the buttons in the transport section to set the **timecode tracking mode**. Traktor offers three different modes of timecode control: internal mode, absolute mode and relative mode.

This ends the general overview. Let's have a closer look at these options.

Setting the Input Mode of your Audio Interface

All Native Instruments audio interfaces support either Phono or Line as input mode. If you use Audio 4 DJ, Audio 8 DJ, Kontrol S4, Kontrol Z2, Traktor Audio 6 or Traktor Scratch A10 you can switch two of the inputs between Phono and Line. Traktor Audio 10 and Traktor Scratch A10 have four switchable inputs. Switching the input between Phono, Timecode Vinyl and Line/Control CD can either be done on the hardware only (Kontrol S4/Kontrol Z2), with the control panel of the audio interface (Traktor Scratch 6/10) or directly on the *Preferences/Audio Setup* dialog.

The options that are available in section *Phono/Line* of the *Preferences/Audio Setup* dialog vary slightly for the different Native Instruments audio interfaces.

Audio 4 DJ

Audio 8 DJ

If you use one of the "old" audio interfaces Audio 4 DJ/Audio 8 DJ you can set the input mode for input ports A and B directly in section *Phono/Line*. The input mode for input ports C and D of Audio 8 DJ is always set to *Timecode CD/Line* and cannot be changed.

◻ Select Option *Timecode Vinyl* if you are spinning with turntables and Timecode.

◻ Select *Timecode CD/Line* if you use timecode CDs as well as you wish to use the inputs without scratch control (possibly for Live Input).

◻ Select *Phono* if you wish to record and digitize your vinyl with Audio 4 DJ/Audio 8 DJ.

◻ If you are using Audio 8 DJ and if you also wish to use timecode vinyl as well as timecode CDs use input ports A and B for vinyl and inputs C and D for timecode CDs.

Traktor Audio 6
Traktor
Scratch A6

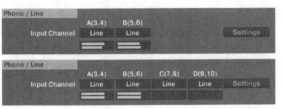

Traktor Audio
10, Traktor
Scratch A10

If you use Traktor Scratch A6/A10 the input mode for all inputs ports is shown in section *Phono/Line*. You cannot change the mode here. However, you can click the *Settings* button to open the Control Panel of your audio interface and change the input mode there.

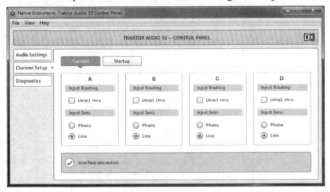

Open the *Channel Setup* tab and set the *Input Sens* to *Phono* if you are using timecode vinyl. Set *Input Sens* to *Line* if you are using timecode CDs. Make sure that for all inputs that are used with timecode the check box *Direct Thru* is **not** activated.

LEDs on the top plate of Traktor Scratch A6/A10 show the current configuration of the inputs (Phono/Line and Input Thru).

Kontrol S4
MK2,
Kontrol Z2

For Kontrol S4 MK2 and Kontrol Z2 section Phono/Line looks the same as for Traktor Scratch A6- However, for Kontrol Z2 the inputs are numbered 3–6 (inputs 1 and 2 on the Z2 are assigned to the Mic/Aux input.

Please note that you can click the *Settings* button on OS X, but it does not start the control panel as it is neither available nor necessary on Mac.

Other audio
interfaces

This message is shown for all soundcards not made by Native
Instruments.

Input Routing of the Timecode Signal

The *Preferences/Input Routing* dialog is used to assign the inputs of your audio interface to the decks you wish to use with timecode.

Let's assume you use the Audio 4 DJ and want to control decks A and B with timecode.
One turntable is connected to input port A and the second one to input port B. For
this configuration the *Preferences/Audio Setup* dialog would look like this:

Another scenario: The two external ports of Kontrol S4 MK2 are named input A and
B. If you wish to control decks A and B with timecode the *Preferences/Audio Setup*
dialog would look like this:

In Traktor 2 it is possible to assign the same input port to more than one deck. This
allows you to control two (or even more) decks with one turntable or one CDJ player.
This comes in handy if one of the turntable fails during a gig, or if you only own one
turntable or one CDJ player. This setup is configured like this on the *Preferences/Input
Routing* dialog:

More information about this feature can be found in section 4.5 „Timecode and one Turntable/CD Player" on page 120.

Swapping the Input Port/Deck Assignment

You can use section *Routing* of the *Preferences/Audio Setup* dialog to swap the input and output ports that are assigned to the decks. Clicking one of the buttons between two deck letters triggers the swapping. You can use the button *Restore* to restore the default routing for the Native Instruments audio interfaces.

Deck Mode

Once the timecode signal has been routed into the desired deck, the deck mode must be set to *Scratch Control*. Only then the timecode signal is sent to the Traktor internal timecode decoder, which will analyse the signal and use it to control the decks.

Click the little arrow below the deck letter to open the deck mode popup menu and then click on *Scratch Control*. Use deck mode *Internal Playback* if you do not use timecode control.

Switching the deck mode between *Internal Playback* and *Scratch Control* will change the buttons in the transport section of the deck. This way you can recognise which deck mode is currently active from the look of the buttons without opening the menu. The effects of the mode switch and what you can do with the buttons in deck mode *Scratch Control* are explained in the next section.

Timecode Tracking Modes

Once you have set the deck mode to *Scratch Control* the buttons in the transport section of the deck – this is where the Play button resides – change. In deck mode *Internal Playback* Traktor displays the buttons *Play/Pause, CUE* and *CUP* (upper part of the following figure). In deck mode *Scratch Control* Traktor displays three buttons that can be used to set the timecode tracking mode of the deck (lower part of the figure).

What is the difference between the timecode tracking modes?

◻ **Internal Mode**   In internal mode the deck behaves the same as in deck mode Internal Playback but the buttons CUE and CUP are not shown. In this mode the connection between the timecode signal and the deck control is broken, i.e. all actions on the turntable or CDJ player do not effect the deck.

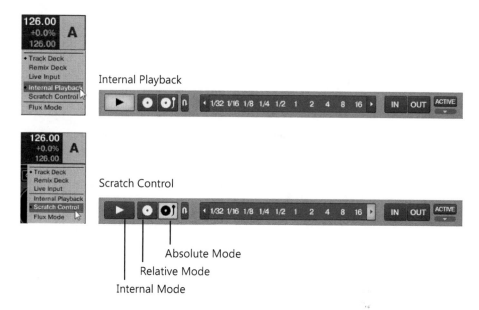

- □ **Relative Mode** In relative mode the timecode decoder only detects the playback speed and the playback direction, not the position information. If you lift the needle, the deck stops. If you then drop the needle at another location playback resumes from the same position where the needle was lifted. It does not matter, where you drop the needle.

- □ **Absolute Mode** In absolute mode the timecode decoder does detect the current position of the needle/the laser. So if you lift the needle and drop it one minute further towards the end of the deck, the track will be played back from the new position. Absolute mode is only active if the timecode position and the position of the decks' playback marker are the same. All actions you perform in the Traktor deck always lead to a mode switch from absolute to relative mode. These actions are: activating a loop, jump to a cue point, clicking the *Sync* button, etc.

  If you cannot switch to absolute mode it is most likely that the deck is not calibrated or there was a problem during calibration. See the sections from page 110 onwards for more information about calibration and the scratch panels.

Timecode and Tempo Faders in the Deck If a deck is set to relative or absolute timecode mode, the tempo fader in the deck is disabled. This is a useful feature as you use the pitch fader of your turntable/CDJ to change the playback speed. Furthermore, the deck tempo fader shows the tempo changes done with the pitch fader with a short delay. This is because the decks' tempo fader is bound to the stable tempo of the deck. (For more information see also section "Show the Stable Tempo in the Deck Header" on page 116).

As well as to these "normal" timecode modes there are two special modes which are activated automatically if one of the special conditions are met:

- ◻ **Emergency Mode**   In absolute mode the timecode decoder does detect the current position of the needle/the laser. So if you lift the needle and drop it one minute further towards the end of the deck, the track will be played back from the new position.

- ◻ **Locked Lead-Out Groove Mode**   In Traktor Scratch 1 when the needle was in the lead-out groove, you needed to switch to internal mode first before you could pick up the needle and drop it in the playback area of the groove. This is no longer necessary anymore, as Traktor Scratch 2 provides the so called locked lead-out groove mode. This is how this mode works:

   When the timecode decoder detects that the needle is in the lead-out groove, the locked lead-out groove mode is activated automatically. The deck tempo is locked to the last stable BPM. You can lift the needle and playback will continue. As soon as you drop the needle in the normal timecode area of the vinyl, Traktor reactivates the relative or absolute mode (depending on which mode was active before the locked lead-out groove mode was engaged). If you drop the needle in the lead-in area, playback restarts at the begin of the track. Traktor switches to absolute mode, if the timecode option *Switch to Absolute Mode in lead-in* is activated.

   As long as locked lead-out groove mode is active, the buttons *Relative Mode* and *Absolute Mode* are disabled. However, you can switch to internal mode.

Switching between Timecode Tracking Modes

You can switch between the timecode tracking modes as often as you wish. Switching from internal mode to relative mode is always seamless, i.e. there are no audible jumps. But when you switch from to absolute mode while the deck is playing Traktor determines the current timecode position and moves the playback marker in the deck to this point. This of course causes an audible jump.

Scratch Panels

If you are spinning with timecode it is good practice to have the scratch panels visible. Open the *Preferences/Decks* dialog and select in section *Platter*/Scope for the decks that you wish to control with timecode one of the following options *Minimized, Platter* or *Scope*.

 The Scratch panels offer three different views: the *minimized* view, the *vinyl mode* (platter mode) and the *scope mode*. In minimized view only the timecode meter is visible (the orange bar at the right side of the deck). The timecode meter informs you of the quality of the incoming timecode signal and the quality of the received timecode position information. Traktor must receive information about the current playback position of the timecode medium; otherwise the absolute timecode tracking mode will not work. The bar needs to be filled completely. If it is not filled completely or if the "fill level" of the bar constantly changes you should check for something going wrong. When bar is empty you can use Traktor Scratch in relative timecode tracking mode only.

Click the little arrow above the timecode meter to switch between minimized and normal view.

 In *platter mode* (vinyl view) the scratch panel looks like the adjoining figure. Vinyl mode shows a "virtual" vinyl or compact disc: the disc rotates if the deck is receiving timecode signals form the turntable or CD player. The direction and speed that the "virtual" vinyl is rotating corresponds to the direction and speed that the timecode vinyl or timecode CD is turning.

Click the scratch panel to switch between vinyl view and scope view. In scope mode the scratch panel displays information about the signal that the timecode decoder receives from the turntable or CDJ player. The level meter in the lower right shows the level of the incoming stereo signal. Please note that the value depends on the current Headroom settings (Preferences/Mixer, section Level) as show in the following figure:

And: Scope mode displays the most important button when using timecode: the *Calibrate* button. Clicking the *Calibrate* button calibrates the deck. More information about calibrating can be found in the next section.

The scope mode is an important source of information for detecting, analysing and solving problems with timecode control. The following overview shows how the scope mode can look like and explains what you can do to solve possible problems.

> **NOTE** If parts of the following overview look familiar to you: I have developed the concept of a visual guide to the scope views originally for a troubleshooting tutorial that was first published in September 2009 on the Traktor Bible website. Apparently Native Instruments liked this idea and used it in the newer version of the Traktor manual.

Firstly, here are some scopes that are identical in both timecode versions:

MK1/MK2	Description
	Message "Off" An audio interface that is compatible with Traktor Scratch Pro is in Audio Setup, but the timecode functionality has not been used yet and the deck has not been calibrated.
	Message "Waiting" Traktor is waiting for the timecode signal. This is a normal message and we don't need to be worried. This scope is shown, for example if the needle is lifted from the vinyl. Please note that the buttons for relative mode and absolute mode are deactivated until the deck is calibrated.
	Message "Scratch Disabled" The scratch functionality is deactivated. Reason is in 99% of all cases that in Audio Setup an audio interface has been selected, which is incompatible with Traktor Scratch. Solution: Open dialog Preferences/Audio Setup and select an audio interface that is allowed for use with Traktor Scratch.

The following table covers the scope views where the same timecode status is displayed differently depending on the timecode version. We will start with the scopes where everything is okay.

Scope MK1	Scope MK2	Description
		This is how the calibration circle looks with timecode vinyl if everything is okay. Traktor displays information about the detected medium in the lower part of the panel (here the 10 minute side of the vinyl). Please note in the scope for MK 1 the spot where the two circles cross each other. This is in the upper left of the circles and this is the correct place.
 		This is how the calibration circle looks with timecode CD if everything is okay. Traktor displays information about the detected medium in the lower part of the panel (here CD and CD MK2). Please note the spot in the scope of MK1 where the two circles cross each other. You can see it in the upper left of the circles and this is the correct place. In the lower image of timecode MK1 the two circles cross in the lower right. This is an indication that the left and right channels are swapped. You will see the same for timecode vinyl MK1. If the left and right channel are swapped when using timecode MK2 the blue circle turns clockwise; otherwise it turns anti-clockwise. Traktor detects the channel swap and corrects this automatically inside the timecode decoder.
		Depending on the playback speed of the timecode CD the circles may look slightly more jagged. There is no reason to worry if they do. If the circles look like this it is easy to see that they turn anti-clockwise (left/right are correctly connected) or clockwise (left/right connections are swapped).
		Traktor receives a timecode signal from timecode vinyl, but the input mode for your audio interface is set to CD-Control/Line. You can see a very small circle in the middle of the scope. It can be larger than in this figure if the cartridge has a high output level. The input signal is low because the phono preamp is off- Solution: Set the input mode of your audio interface Timecode Vinyl, Vinyl Control or Phono.
		Traktor receives a timecode signal from a timecode CD, but the input mode of your audio interface is set to Timecode Vinyl/Phono. The input signal is high because the phono preamp is on. Solution: Set the input mode of your audio interface to Timecode CD/Line or CD Control.

Scope MK1	Scope MK2	Description
		If the scope looks like this Traktor has detected the wrong timecode version for timecode CDs. In the left image the signal comes from timecode MK2 and Traktor identifies it as MK1. In the right image the signal is coming from a timecode version 1 CD but Traktor interprets it as CD MK2. Please note that in both images the quality meter is empty. Solve this issue by clicking on Calibrate.
		If the scope looks like this Traktor has detected the wrong timecode version for timecode vinyl. In the left image the signal comes from timecode MK2 and Traktor identifies it as MK1. In the right image the signal is coming from a timecode version 1 vinyl but Traktor interprets it as Vinyl MK2. Please note that in both images the quality meter is empty. Solve this issue by clicking on Calibrate.
		Traktor has detected the control medium (CD), but in this figure the right channel is missing. Solution: Check the cabling and check the cartridge connections if you are using a turntable.
		Traktor has detected the control medium (vinyl, 15 minutes side), but it only receives the right channel; the left channel is missing. Solution: Check the cabling and check the cartridge connections if you are using a turntable.
		If you see a diagonal line then in most cases the same left or right channel of the timecode is routed as left and right signal into the deck. Solution: Open Preferences/Input Routing and make sure that each timecode controlled deck receives a left and a right signal.
		This is how the scope view looks if a deck receives a normal audio signal and not a timecode signal.

Scope MK1	Scope MK2	Description
		Traktor has detected the timecode medium (here vinyl), but the medium is skipping. If you are using vinyl check if the needle needs cleaning or if the vinyl is worn out. Another reason can be heavy vibrations (maybe a bass speaker) that affect your turntable. The exact reason can only be found by trying different scenarios and isolating the source for the message.
		If Traktor shows a red grounding symbol in the middle of the scope the timecode engine is receiving a hum. This can be due to defective cables. Or the grounding cable of the turntable is not connected to the grounding screw of your mixer or audio interface.

Calibrating

When you drop the needle on your timecode vinyl or start playback of your CDJ player with a timecode CD inserted Traktor will automatically calibrate your deck. Nevertheless you can and should trigger the calibration manually by clicking the *Calibrate* button that is visible when the scratch panel is in Scope mode. You should manually trigger the calibration every time there is a timecode related problem and check how the scope looks by using the previous overview.

When a deck is calibrated Traktor analyses the incoming timecode signal. It detects the medium type (vinyl, CD) and whether both the left and right channels are connected. To repeat: You **should** calibrate **every** timecode deck **every time** you start up Traktor (if you wish to use timecode control). This helps in detecting potential problems early. Additionally you cannot switch to absolute tracking mode if the decks are not calibrated.

This is how to calibrate:

1. Open the scratch panel and switch to scope mode.
2. Set the pitch fader of your turntable or CDJ player to a neutral position
3. Drop the needle onto the timecode vinyl or start playback of the timecode CD.
4. Click the *Calibrate* button. The calibration process only takes a few seconds. During the calibration the yellow bar at the right side of the scope view raises.
5. Check if the calibration circle is okay. Also check if Traktor is displaying an error or warning message in the lower part of the scope view. In this case use the table on the previous pages to solve this issue.

Stripe Scaling and Minute Markers

Traktor provides two scaling options for the stripe view. Those can be configured with the option *Stripe View Fit* of dialog *Preferences/Track Decks* in section *Miscellaneous*.

- ◘ If the option *Track* is selected the stripe view is scaled in a way that the currently loaded track completely fills the stripe area.

- ◘ If the option *Record* is selected the width of the stripe and the number of minutes shown in the stripe corresponds to the length of the timecode medium. If the track is shorter the stripe does will not use all the space.

Additionally this dialog contains the option *Show Minute Markers*. If this option is activated white vertical lines are shown in the stripes, each line represents one minute.

Show the Stable Tempo in the Deck Header

Traktor 2 provides two new data fields that can be shown in the deck header. Both fields are useful if you use timecode.

The data field *BPM* always shows the current BPM value of the deck and the field *Tempo* informs you about the percentage deviation of the tempo compared to the original tempo of the track. If you use timecode both values will constantly fluctuate which is caused by the wow and flutter of the turntable and CDJ player. To see more stable values you can use the data fields *Stable BPM* and *Stable Tempo*. The values shown in these fields are normalized by Traktor and they do not react to fast tempo changes caused by scratching. Even when you change the deck tempo with the pitch fader or by nudging, the tempo change is not immediately shown. The new tempo will be shown if it stays stable for approximately three seconds.

More Timecode Options

In the lower part of dialog *Preferences/Timecode Setup* are more options to configure additional timecode settings.

◻ **Track Start Position** Use this list box to move the start position of the timecode record towards the end of the groove. This is useful when the beginning of the timecode vinyl is slightly worn out or if you wish to add a lead in sticker to the vinyl.

◻ **Turntable Speed 45 rpm** If you prefer 45 rpm instead of 33 rpm on your turntables you need to activate this check box in order for Traktor being able to interpret the timecode signal properly.

> **ATTENTION** If you use 45 rpm the minute segments on the vinyl represent approximate 45 seconds only.

◻ **Tracking Alert** If this option is activated and problems with timecode occur (maybe a bad signal caused by a dusty needle or if one of the stereo channels disappears and the deck is running in emergency mode) then both buttons *Absolute Mode* and *Relative Mode* are highlighted red.

◻ **Load next track when flipping record** If this option is enabled Traktor will load the next track from the collection/playlist when you flip the vinyl.

◻ **Use playlist scrolling zone** Both the timecode vinyl and the timecode CD contain a so called scrolling zone that you can use to scroll in the track collection or currently opened playlist. The scrolling zone resides in the last two segments of the timecode record and in track 3 of the timecode CD. If you leave the scrolling zone the currently selected track is loaded.

◻ **Switch to Absolute Mode in lead-in**   If this option is enabled Traktor will activate absolute timecode tracking mode when the needle is in the lead in area of the
record or if you playback the first track of your timecode CD. If Traktor does not
switch to absolute mode even though this option is enabled, check your timecode
configuration as explained on the previous pages.

◻ **Switch to Absolute Mode when loading**   If this option is enabled Traktor
switches to absolute mode after you have loaded a track. If Traktor does not
switch to absolute mode even though this option is enabled, check your timecode
configuration as explained on the previous pages.

◻ **Skip to start in lead-in**   This option is useful if you use mainly relative tracking
mode. Picking up the needle and dropping it does not change the playback position of the track. If you want to be able to "jump" quickly to the beginning of the
track without activating absolute tracking mode, enable this option. If you then
put the needle in the lead-in of the timecode vinyl the playmarker is set to the
begin of the track (as if absolute mode is active for a short moment); however, the
deck will stay in relative tracking mode,

Checklist

Admittedly, that was a lot of stuff. And Traktor doesn't make timecode configuration
very easy, especially for a newbie. A lot of interrelated and interdependent settings are
scattered throughout the software. This short check list contains the most important
things you should pay attention too.

◻ Did you select a Traktor Scratch compatible audio interface on *Preferences/Audio
Setup*?

◻ Are all cables connected correctly?

◻ Is the input mode on the audio interface or the Kontrol S4 correctly set?

◻ Did you configure the certified mixer for timecode mode?

◻ Did you assign the correct audio inputs to the desired decks on *Preferences/Inout
Routing*?

◻ Did you set the deck mode to *Scratch Control*?

◻ Is the needle okay? Is the timecode vinyl clean enough and not too worn out?

◻ Can you calibrate the deck without problems? If not, does the timecode decoder
display an error message? What does the scope look like?

◻ Is the master tempo feature of your CDJ player deactivated?

> **TIP** Traktor DJ Darrien has created another very useful checklist with troubleshooting tips and Best Practices. You can download his checklist from *www.traktorbible.com/checklist.*

4.4 Timecode Configuration via Mapping

The most important timecode actions can also be performed via mapping. The following tables show what's possible.

Setting Deck Mode and Scratch Panel View, Calibrate

Deck Common | Timecode | Scratch Control On	Interaction Mode: Direct Set to value: Internal Playback, Scratch Control	Sets the operation mode for the selected deck. This command corresponds to the little menu that opens by clicking the deck letter.
	Interaction Mode: Inc/Dec: selects the next/previous deck mode	Attention: This mapping command has wrapa-round functionality, i.e. if the last/first deck mode is reached the first/last mode is selected.
Deck Common | Timecode | Platter/Scope View Selector	Interaction Mode: Hold, Direct Set to value: Off, Mini-mized, Platter, Scope Assignment: select deck or use Device Target	Switches the Scratch Panel of the selected deck to the view selected in list Set to value.
	Interaction Mode: Inc/Dec Assignment: select Deck or use Device Target	Use these modes to select the next/previous style of the scratch panel. As both modes support a wraparound it is sufficient to map either Inc or Dec.
Deck Common | Timecode | Calibrate	Interaction Mode: Trigger Assignment: select deck or Device Target	Calibrates the timecode signal for the deck selected in list Assignment. This command corresponds to the Calibrate button in scope mode of the scratch panels.
Deck Common | Timecode | Reset Tempo Offset	Interaction Mode: Trigger Assignment: select deck or Device Target	Resets the relative pitch fader. This command is only available in relative timecode tracking mode.

Setting Timecode Tracking Mode

Deck Common | Timecode | Playback Mode Int/Rel/Abs	Interaction Mode: Direct Set to value: Internal Mode Assignment: Select deck or Device Target	Sets the deck selected in list Assignment to internal mode.

Setting Timecode Tracking Mode

Interaction Mode: Direct Set to value: Relative Mode Assignment: Select deck or Device Target	Sets the deck selected in list Assignment to relative mode.
Interaction Mode: Direct Set to value: Absolute Mode Assignment: Select deck Device Target	Sets the deck selected in list Assignment to absolute mode.
Interaction Mode: Inc/Dec Assignment: Select deck or Device Target	Activates the next or previous timecode tracking mode for the selected track. It is rather confusing that the order used here is not identical to the order of the buttons in the deck. Inc activates the modes in the following sequence: Absolute, Relative, Internal and Previous activates them in reversed order. Both interaction modes perform a wraparound, i.e. when the last/first tracking mode is reached the first/last of the three modes is selected.
Interaction Mode: Reset	Sets the deck selected in list Assignment to internal mode.

TIP Maybe the most important mapping command from the previous tables is *Deck Common | Timecode | Playback Mode Int/Rel/Abs,* Interaction Mode *Direct,* Set to value: *Internal Mode.* I recommend mapping this command to a key or button for each deck on which you use timecode control. Then, in the case that something goes wrong with the timecode processing (which could be a dusty needle that causes the track to play backwards), you can very quickly change the tracking mode to Internal Mode and save your set.

4.5 Timecode and one Turntable/CD Player

Even if you only own one turntable/CD player (or if during a gig one of your turntables/CD players dies) it is possible to spin with timecode. The reasons that this can work are:

◻   You can assign the timecode signal of one audio input to two decks.

◻   If two decks share one timecode signal only one of the two decks can be in absolute time tracking mode.

◻ If you activate absolute mode for one of the two decks then Traktor switches the other deck automatically to internal mode

Form a practical perspective this opens up the following usage scenarios.

Variation 1: Switching automatically to Absolute Mode when Loading a Track

Let's assume the timecode signal from the turntable/CDJ player is connected *Input Port A* of your audio interface and that you want to use deck A and B for timecode. In this variant you need to configure two settings:

◻ Use dialog *Preferences/Audio Setup* and route the two channels of *Input Port A* as well into Deck A as into Deck B.

◻ Use dialog *Preferences/Timecode Setup* and activate the option *Switch to Absolute Mode when loading*.

With these settings Traktor behaves as follows:

1. Load a track into deck A. Because the option *Switch to Absolute Mode when loading* is enabled Traktor sets deck A to absolute mode.

2. Play the track in deck A.

3. Load a track into deck B. Because the option *Switch to Absolute Mode when loading* is enabled Traktor sets deck B to absolute mode. Because **two** decks are sharing **one** timecode signal, and because only one of the decks can be in absolute mode, Traktor switches deck A from absolute, to internal mode. Now you can use your turntable/CDJ player to pitch the track in deck B and make the transition.

4. Once the channel fader of deck A is completely closed, load the next track into deck A. Traktor sets deck A to absolute mode and deck B to internal mode.

5. And so on.

Variation 2: Switching manually to Absolute Mode

Variation number 2 is based on the same principle as varation1 but in variation 2 you switch manually to absolute mode. The initial configuration is identical to the one from variation 1 (the signal from the turntable/CDJ player is fed into input port A and deck A and deck B are used for timecode). To use this variation you need to do three things:

◻ Use dialog *Preferences/Audio Setup* and route the two channels of *Input Port A* as well into Deck A as into Deck B.

◻ Create a hotkey mapping to switch deck A to absolute mode (Deck Common | Timecode | Playback Mode Int/Rel/Abs, Interaction Mode: Direct, Assignment: Deck A, Set to value: Absolute, maybe use key A for this mapping).

◻ Create a second hotkey mapping to switch deck B to absolute mode (Deck Common | Timecode | Playback Mode Int/Rel/Abs, Interaction Mode: Direct, Assignment: Deck B, Set to value: Absolute, maybe use key B for this mapping).

Both hotkeys set the deck selected in the list *Assignment* to absolute mode. Traktor switches other decks that are currently in absolute mode automatically to internal mode when one of these hotkeys is pressed.

4.6 Four Decks with Timecode

Although this chapter implicitly assumes that two decks are normally used with time-code control, it is possible to use all four decks and to create any combination of turn-tables/CDJ player setups. The requirements are that you have a four channel mixer and that your audio interface supports four inputs and that the inputs can be set to the input mode (Phono/Line) that you need. Then the following setups are possible:

◻ Controlling 4 decks with 4 turntables

◻ Controlling 4 decks with 4 CD players

◻ Controlling 2 decks with 2 turntables and 2 other decks with 2 CD players

◻ Controlling 4 decks with 2 turntables

◻ Controlling 4 decks with 2 CD players

The configuration for these scenarios is similar to a two deck setup. First you need to assign the inputs of your audio interface to the decks that shall be controlled by time-code. This is done in the dialog box *Preferences/Input Routing*. For the first three set-ups one input port is assigned to one deck.

For the two last setups you assign each of the two available input ports to two decks. For example, if the timecode signal for turntable 1/CD player 1 is fed into input port A and if you wish to control deck A and C with channel A you need to route *input port A* into *deck A* and *deck C*. And if in the same setup turntable 2/CD player 2 is fed into input port B and if you wish to control deck B and D with channel B then you route *input port B* into *deck B* and *deck D*.

The real art is to make the proper cable connections. How to proceed here depends on the audio interface you are using (Audio 8 DJ or a certified mixer) and whether you are using turntables or CDJ players.

Four Decks with two Turntables or two CD Players

This usage scenario is almost identical to the approach explained in section "4.5 Time-code and one Turntable/CD Player" on page 120 and further. Use the dialog box *Preferences/Input Routing* to assign each of the two input ports to two decks. To switch the two decks between internal and absolute tracking mode either use the automatic mode switching when a track is loaded or create a button/hotkey mapping to switch into absolute mode manually.

Four Decks and Certified Mixers

If you are using one of the certified mixers the configuration of four decks is the same as for two. The only problem here could be that not all four channels of the mixer are equipped with a phono-preamp (like the Xone:4D that has four channels; three of them can be switched between Phono and Line, and the fourth one can be switched between Line and Line only).

Chapter 5

MIDI Background

MIDI is the abbreviation of *Musical Instrument Digital Interface*, an interface definition from the early 80s. It has been developed as a standard for exchanging control data between instruments and PCs. The MIDI specification is maintained by the *MIDI Manufacturers Association (MMA)*. The MIDI protocol is one of the components of the MIDI specification and defines the structure and content of communication between a MIDI sender (master) and a MIDI receiver (slave).

The MIDI specification (see *www.midi.org)* is quite extensive. With regards to Traktor only a small amount of the specified MIDI messages are of interest, especially those that are used to control Traktor with a MIDI controller.

5.1 Controlling Traktor with MIDI Controllers

Before we take a closer look on the structure and the content of MIDI messages, this section explains the various steps that happen when a MIDI controller communicates with Traktor and vice versa.

The figure on the following page shows a simplified diagram of the steps that occur when a button on a MIDI controller is pressed and released. The example assumes that the button marked with an arrow is mapped to the mapping command *Deck Common | Play/Pause*. This command is used to start or pause the playback of a deck. In addition we assume that the button is an LED button. The LED will be on while the deck is playing and it will be off when the deck is paused. The figure shows an Allen&Heath Xone:K2; however, the concept shown is valid for any other controller.

Let's have a closer look at the numbered steps.

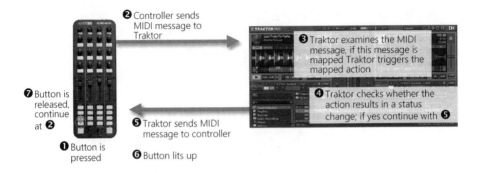

❶ In the first step the button on the controller is **pressed**. This button shall start playback of deck A.

❷ The logic board inside the controller detects the button press. It **creates a MIDI message** that contains data about which control was used and in which way. This message is sent to Traktor.

❸ Traktor analyzes the incoming MIDI message and checks, whether this message is mapped to an incoming mapping command. If Traktor can find that link the corresponding mapping command is executed. In our example the playback of deck A will be started.

❹ The action triggered in step 3 results in a change of the internal status of Traktor. Before step 1 deck A was paused and now it is playing. Traktor checks whether there is an outgoing command mapped to that status change.

❺ If Traktor can find an assigned outgoing mapping command for the status change, Traktor will package the information about the new status into a MIDI message and send it to the controller.

❻ The logic board in the controller analyzes the incoming MIDI message and switches the LED button to the state as desired. In our example the LED should be lit, indicating that deck A is now playing.

❼ The button is released. This new user action again triggers the creation of a MIDI message that is sent to Traktor. As there is now a command mapped to the release of the button, the other steps are not executed.

From the outlined steps you can detect that MIDI messages which are sent from the controller to Traktor, or which are sent from Traktor to the controller, need to contain two different pieces of data. First, the message needs to indicate which control (button, fader, etc.) was used or should be changed. Secondly, the message needs to contain data about the status of the control (pressed/released, position of fader, LED on/off or which colour).

There are some tools that allow you to inspect the MIDI messages being sent between a controller and a piece of software. The next section introduces two great tools: one for OS X and another one for Windows.

5.2 Inspecting Raw MIDI Data

You can use the Mac app *MIDI Monitor* and the Windows tool *MIDI-OX* to inspect and then analyze the raw MIDI data that your controller is sending.

> **MIDI Mode and Native Instruments' Controllers** By default all Native Instruments Traktor controllers use a proprietary protocol named NHL (more about that protocol can be found in the next chapter). As NHL is a proprietary protocol neither MIDI Monitor nor MIDI-OX are able to display the data that is sent via that protocol.
>
> However, all NI controllers can be switched to MIDI mode. Depending on the controller you have use one of the following button combinations:
>
> - **KONTROL S2 MK1/MK2**: Both SHIFT Buttons. In order for this to work you first need to open the Traktor dialog *Preferences/Kontrol S2*. Then go to section *MIDI Mode* and activate *Enable MIDI Mode via SHIFT + SHIFT*
> - **KONTROL S4 MK1**: SHIFT + BROWSE
> - **KONTROL S4 MK2**: SHIFT + PREVIEW
> - **KONTROL X1 MK1**: SHIFT + HOTCUE
> - **KONTROL X1 MK2**: SHIFT + LOAD LEFT + LOAD RIGHT
> - **KONTROL F1**: SHIFT + BROWSE. In order for this to work you need to select option *MIDI Mode* for *MIDI Mode Type* in the *Preferences/Traktor Kontrol F1* dialog.
> - **KONTROL Z2**: SHIFT + Settings (⚙)

OS X: Using MIDI Monitor

MIDI Monitor is freeware and you can download it from the author's website at *http://www.snoize.com/MIDIMonitor*. Kurt Revis, author of MIDI Monitor, has written a good tutorial on how to use MIDI Monitor; it can be found here: *http://www.snoize.com/MIDIMonitor/docs.html*.

The most important steps for using MIDI Monitor are:

1. Open section *Sources* and select the checkboxes of all MIDI ports, whose data you wish to see.

2. Open section *Filter*. Here you can select which messages the tool should show. By default all message types are selected. For Traktor you generally only need the messages from the groups *Voice Messages* and *Real Time*.

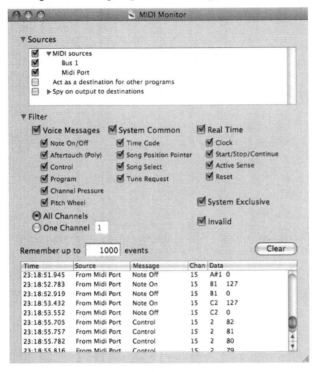

3. Open the *Preferences* window and then the *Display* tab. Use this page to setup the output format of the MIDI data.

The sections *Note format, Controller format* and *Data format* are important because you can configure whether the notes or their values are shown. For Control Change Messages either the default name of the controller or its value (in either decimal or hexadecimal format) can be shown. Additionally you can select the number format of the data.

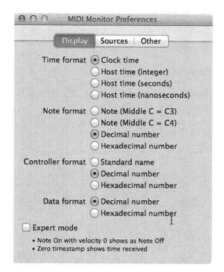

The received MIDI data is shown in the lower part of the window. The *Message* column shows the type of the MIDI message as text. The MIDI protocol defines several **types of MIDI messages**. The two most important ones are Note On/Note off messages (they are mostly used by buttons) and Control Change messages (abbreviated as Control in column *Message*, they are mostly used by faders, knobs, encoders).

In column *Chan(nel)* the **MIDI channel** of the message is shown. What MIDI channels are used for will become clearer in the next section of this chapter where we take a closer look at the structure of the MIDI message.

Finally the window with the incoming messages contains the *Data* column. Here the **data (two numbers)** contained in the message are shown. The first number identifies the control that triggered the message. The second number contains information about the current status of the control: Was a button pressed or released? What is the current position of a fader or a knob?

What exactly the data contains becomes more obvious when looking at the data of the Note On/Note Off messages in the picture on the previous page. The first number shows the note that is assigned to the button. The second data has a value of 127 for Note On (=button pressed) and a 0 for Note Off (=button released). These corresponds to the two messages from the example of section "5.1, Controlling Traktor with MIDI controllers.

Control Change messages are normally used by faders, knobs, or endless encoders. As with Note messages the first number of a Control Change message identifies the control that triggered the message. The second number contains the new value of the control, for example the new position of a fader. For example, the last four messages in the monitor window could have been sent by a knob that has been turned to the left.

Windows: Using MIDI-OX

The Windows tool to display the MIDI data, MIDI-OX, can be found on the website *www.midiox.com.*

> **IMPORTANT**   Because only one application can open a MIDI input port exclusively you need to exit Traktor before using MIDI-OX.

Run the setup and then follow these steps to explore the MIDI data with MIDI-OX.

1. Choose the command *Options/MIDI Devices* or click the corresponding button in the tool bar.

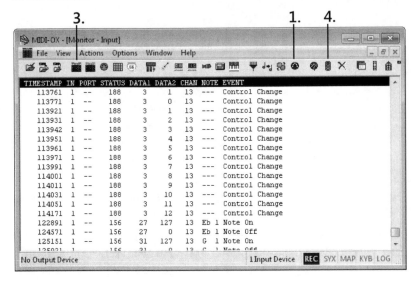

2. Click in the list *MIDI Inputs* to select the desired devices. The selected devices are shown in the *Port Map Objects* and are selected in the list *MIDI Inputs.* Click *OK.*

3. If the window *Monitor – Input* isn't visible choose *View/Input Monitor* or click the corresponding button in the toolbar.

4. Choose the menu command *Actions/Start Display* or click the corresponding button in the toolbar, to start the display of the incoming MIDI data.

For now only the columns *STATUS, DATA1,* and *DATA2* are of interest. Column DATA shows a value that contains the MIDI channel number as well as the type of message. The same information is also shown in columns *CHAN(NEL)* and *EVENT,* whereat *EVENT* contains the event type/message type as text.

For all messages displayed, column *DATA1* shows the control that triggered the event. Column DATA2 shows number that represents the current status of the control:

◻ The Control Change messages have been triggered by a fader or knob that has ID 3. Based on the increasing values in DATA2 we can assume, that a fader was moved upwards or that a knob was turned to the right.

◻ The Note On/Note Off messages in the lower part of the MIDI OX window were triggered by two different buttons. You can see this from the values in column *DATA1.* The first Note On/Note Off message pair was triggered by a button with the ID 27 (equates to note Eb1) and the second pair was triggered by the button with the ID 31 (equates to note G1).

Using the Monitoring Tools for Troubleshooting

If you are completely new to the MIDI protocol concept, I recommend downloading one of the tools and playing around with them. Try to find out which MIDI messages your controller is using and which data the messages contain. The next section explains the important Traktor related MIDI messages in more detail.

Furthermore, both tools are excellent for troubleshooting purposes. Let's assume that your controller isn't functioning properly in Traktor. You can then use the MIDI monitor tools to check, whether the problem is caused by Traktor or your mapping, whether it is caused by some drivers and/or the operating system, or whether your hardware is faulty. For example, if your controller is working fine with the monitoring tools, the problem is most likely caused in the mapping.

5.3 MIDI Messages in More Detail

It can be helpful to know a little bit about the basics of the MIDI protocol if you use a MIDI controller with Traktor. Some controllers allow changing the MIDI parameters for the individual controls (see section 5.4, Configuring MIDI Setting of Your Controller") for more details.

Furthermore some MIDI background knowledge is useful if you create your own mappings in Traktor. It will be easier to understand why Traktor supports different types of controllers in the list *Type of Controller* and the *Encoder modes* that you see on the *Preferences/Controller Manager* dialog.

Last but not least it is useful to know how MIDI messages are composed so that you can find errors in your MIDI mapping. The tools outlined in the previous section allow the inspection of the raw MIDI data a MIDI controller sends; this data can only be understood if you know something about the structure and the content of MIDI messages. This section will provide all that information in great detail.

MIDI Messages

MIDI messages can be roughly divided into two categories/groups (a complete list can be found on *www.midi.org/techspecs/midimessages.php*):

◻ System Messages

◻ Channel Messages

System Messages

System messages are used by the system as a whole, they are not related to a particular MIDI channel and their length is always one byte. From the system messages group Traktor uses the MIDI clock messages to synchronise two Traktor systems or Traktor with other software or MIDI controllers. (The practical aspects are explained in detail in chapter 6.) Another system message group are the exclusive system messages, which are defined by the manufacturer of the MIDI controller. Those messages are device dependent and are not used in Traktor.

Channel Related Messages

As the name implies channel related messages are always related to a particular channel. What channel means in this context becomes clear if we look more closely at the inner structure of a channel related message. A channel related message consists of three data packages (bytes) where each byte contains distinct information about the message.

MIDI Message

Package 1: Status Byte	Package 2: Data Byte	Package 3: Data Byte
Type of Message Channel Number	MIDI Control	Value

Status Byte

The first byte of a channel related MIDI message is called the status byte. The status byte contains the message type (button has been pressed or released, value of a fader or potentiometer that has been changed) and the channel that this message has been sent on. The second and the third bytes are the so called data bytes. The first data byte contains the information *which* MIDI control on the controller has been used and the second byte contains the value of this MIDI control (what is the current position of a knob, how far and in which direction a jog wheel been moved, what was the velocity of a pad on a pad controller that has been pressed).

> **NOTE** In the MIDI message itself the channel number has a value between 0 and 15, but software shows the channel number in the range from 1 to 16.

Each channel related MIDI message is connected to a particular channel. This for example makes it possible to control *two* Traktor decks with *one* controller, even when the same buttons on the controller are used. The Denon player DN-HS5500 uses this method and contains one shift button to select either deck 1 or deck 2. If deck 1 is active and if the play button is pressed the MIDI message is sent via channel 1. If deck 2 has been made active with the shift button the message is sent via channel 2. The MIDI messages are identical except for the channel number. Traktor can be configured in a way that the play-command sent on channel 1 will be assigned to deck A and that the same message is sent on channel 2 if the command is assigned to deck B.

The Korg controller nanoPAD offers another practical use. The twelve buttons can be assigned to four different scenes so that you can map in total up to 48 Traktor commands to those twelve buttons. The easiest way to implement this is using the Korg Kontrol Editor and assigning a different MIDI channel to each scene. You can then use the same midi control number in all scenes and distinguish the messages in Traktor by the channel number on which they are sent.

In MIDI mode the default configuration of the Kontrol S4 also uses multiple MIDI channels. Here the status of the deck focus button (button *Deck C* on the left side and button *Deck D* on the right side) affect the MIDI channel. When the left side of the S4 is set to deck A the deck related controls use MIDI channel 1; when it is set to deck C the controls use MIDI channel 3. The same applies to the right side; however here MIDI channel 2 is used for deck B and channel 4 for deck C. The effect section at the top of the controller uses MIDI channel 5.

Another application for multiple MIDI channels: You can use the channel numbers if you wish to use two identical MIDI controllers (let's say two two Allen&Heath Xone:K2 MIDI controllers). Each controller can then be configured in a way that it sends its messages on a different channel number so that you can assign the different channels in Traktor to the desired decks.

> **ATTENTION**   To be able to use the channel number when creating your MIDI mappings the controller must allow the channel number to be configured, either on the controllers hardware or by using a configuration tool. Take a look at the controllers' manual (if it is available as a download). You should do this before buying. Some examples of how the controllers' MIDI parameters can be changed can be found in section 5.4 on page 142 and onwards.

Data Bytes

The second and the third package of a midi message contain the data bytes. The first data byte contains information about which midi controller (button, fader etc.) has sent the message and the second data byte will carry the current value of this controller.

The receiver of a MIDI message needs to distinguish between the status byte and the data bytes. To achieve this, the following convention is used: the value of the status byte is always equal to or greater than 128 (technically speaking: the highest bit of the status byte is always set); and the value of a data byte is always smaller than 128 (the highest bit of a data byte is never set).

The following sections explain the MIDI messages that are used in Traktor:

◻ MIDI Clock Messages; these are used to synchronise several systems

◻ Note On/Note Off Messages; these are used to signal the press and release of a button

◻ Control Change Message; these are used to signal that the value of a MIDI control (fader, encoder, knob) has been changed

◻ Pitch Bend Messages; these messages are sent by the sliders of the Denon controllers DN-HS5500 and DN-HD2500 and they can also be used by the Korg nanoSERIES controllers.

MIDI Clock Messages

MIDI Clock Messages belong to the group of system wide messages, i.e. they are always related to the complete system and not to one particular MIDI device. Each MIDI clock message is one byte in length, they all contain the status byte and this clock message is used to synchronise several MIDI devices.

The MIDI protocol defines the following MIDI clock messages:

Message	Value	Description
Tick	0xF8 (248)	The tick signal. This message is sent 24 times each quarter note. The MIDI clock tick message does not contain time information and is always relative to the current playback tempo.
Start	0xFA (250)	MIDI Clock Start Message. This message was originally used to start the playback of a MIDI device.
Stop	0x FC (252)	MIDI Clock Stop Message. This message was originally used to stop the playback of a MIDI device.

Chapter 8 contains several examples of how MIDI clock messages are used for synchronisation purposes in Traktor.

Note On/Note Off Messages

The Note On/Note Off messages have been part of the MIDI specification since the early days. The reason is that MIDI was originally used to send information about pressing a button of a MIDI keyboard to the PC. Like on a normal keyboard the On and Off messages can be used to distinguish if a button has been pressed or released.

The Note On/Note Off message sent by a MIDI controller can either be two or three bytes long. Whether the message length is two or three bytes is dependent on if the button sending the message can only differentiate between the states "pressed" and "released" (in this case the message is two bytes long), or if the button is able to recognise which velocity was used to press it (then the message consists of three bytes). The buttons of specialised MIDI DJ controllers sometimes only send two byte messages; MIDI keyboards or pad controllers like Korg's nanoPAD or Trigger Finger from M-Audio send messages which are three bytes long.

The following figure shows the structure of the Note On/Note Off messages:

Note On Message

Package 1: Status Byte		Package 2: Data Byte	Package 3: Data Byte
0x9	Channel (0 - 15)	Button Number (0 - 127)	Velocity (0 - 127)

Note Off Message

Package 1: Status Byte		Package 2: Data Byte	Package 3: Data Byte
0x8	Channel (0 - 15)	Button Number (0 - 127)	Velocity (mostly 0)

The first data byte contains the information about which button has been pressed or released. Because the most upper bit of a data byte is always 0 the other 7 bits can be used to encode which button has been pressed/released. This means that 128 different values can be used (in the range from 0 to 127). If the MIDI controller transmits information about the velocity this is available in the second data byte of the Note On message. Because this byte has a value of 0 for the upper most bit, 128 different velocity values can also be used.

For a Note Off message the second data byte can contain information about the release velocity, but usually this byte has a value of 0. If your MIDI controller is sending information about the press velocity and the release velocity – as with a MIDI keyboard, or Trigger Finger from M-Audio or Korg's nanoPAD – then Traktor simply ignores this information.

Let's have a look at the status byte. The first nibble of the status byte for the Note On message contains the value 0x9 (binary 1001) and for a Note Off message it is 0x8 (binary 1000). This nibble indicates the message type. The second nibble contains the channel number. The channel number is used to distinguish which MIDI controller has sent the message. The receiver of the MIDI message, here Traktor, can be configured in such a way that if it receives the Note On message with note C on channel 1 it executes command A and if it receives the Note On message with Note C on channel 2 it executes command B. Using this principle it is possible to use two identical MIDI controllers with Traktor (or CD players with MIDI features) letting each controller use its own channel. This way one of the controllers can control deck A and the other deck B.

Sidebar: Decimal, Hexadecimal, Binary, Byte and Nibble

This sidebar contains a short and simple introduction into different number systems and it explains the terms byte and nibble. This information should help users to understand the following explanations about MIDI messages, the restrictions of the MIDI protocol and the impact they have on the MIDI functionality in Traktor.

Instead of the decimal number system that is traditionally used and that uses 10 as a base and the ten digits 0 to 9, in computer maths, either the hexadecimal or the binary numeral system is used.

When the binary numeral system is used then 2 is base and the digits 0 and 1 are used. The value of one position is the power of two of its position and the last digit has the position 0. Knowing this one can convert a binary number into a decimal number using the following scheme:

Binary 0110 is equal to $0 \times 2^3 + 1 \times 2^2 + 1 \times 2^1 + 0 \times 2^0 = 0 + 4 + 2 + 0 = 6$. The value of the different positions of a four-digits binary number is (back to front) 1, 2, 4, 8. This means that a four-digits binary number can represent 16 different values (0 to 15).

The hexadecimal numbering system is based on the value 16 and it uses the digits 0 to 9 and A, B, C, D, E, F. The hexadecimal number has a value of 10, B a value of 11 etc. and the digit F correspondents to the value 15. A single-digit hexadecimal number can be used to express the same values as with a four-digits binary number.

One byte consists of eight bits, i.e. it can be represented as a binary number with eight digits, as in 01011101. To make a binary value more easily read the different places are commonly combined in groups of four digits, as in 0101 1101. Such a group of four binary digits is called a nibble. One nibble can be expressed as one hexadecimal digit. And one binary number with eight digits can thus be represented as a hexadecimal number with two digits. The binary number 0101 1101 is thus the same as the hexadecimal number 0x5D (hexadecimal numbers use 0x as prefix or the letter H as a suffix). One byte can be used to represent 256 values, i.e. the value range of one byte is 0 to 255.

Control Change Messages, 7 Bit

The next important message used in Traktor is the so called Control Change Message. This message is sent from continuous controllers (i.e. those controllers that have more states than only On/Off), like faders, knobs or jog wheels.

> **NOTE Buttons and Control Change Messages**   Some of the newer DJ MIDI con-
> trollers – like the TRAKTOR Kontrol family – also use Control Change message for
> the buttons. Because the buttons still know On/Off states (pressed/not pressed),
> these controls send a value of 0 for not pressed and a value of 127 for pressed in the
> second data byte by default.

The following figure shows the structure of Control Change Messages:

Control Change Message, 7 Bit

Package 1: Status Byte		Package 2: Data Byte	Package 3: Data Byte
0xB	Channel (0 - 15)	Controller Number (0 - 127)	Value (0 - 127)

The first nibble of the first byte always contains the value 0xB. The second nibble of
the first byte contains (as with the Note On/Note Off messages) the channel number.
The second byte (i.e. the first data byte) is used to transmit the controller number. The
controller number is an ID that uniquely indicates the control of the MIDI controller
sending this message. Due to the MIDI specification for Control Change Messages
only the controller numbers in the range from 0 to 110 shall be used; the values from
120 to 127 are reserved for channel mode messages, like all controllers off, all notes off
etc. Most DJ MIDI controllers ignore this guideline and Traktor treats the reserved
controller numbers like normal controllers.

Absolute Values

The value of the control is transmitted in the second data byte (the third byte). Even
though all MIDI controls can only send values in the range from 0 to 127, the meaning
of the value depends on which type of MIDI control is sending it. Fader, slider and
potentiometers, which have defined start and end points, send absolute values between
0 and the maximum value (which is normally 127). The send value then indicates the
current position of the knob, fader etc.

Relative Values

Endless potentiometers (Rotary Encoder) however do not have a defined start and end
value. They can only convey in which direction they have been turned and how great
the value change is. That's why they transmit relative values and not absolute ones. In
other words: endless potentiometers can be used to increase or to decrease a value.
Depending on the mode used by the endless potentiometer the transmitted values have
the following meaning:

❑ **Mode 3Fh/41h** In this mode the encoder sends the value 0x3F (equal to decimal 63) if the value has been decreased (normally by turning the encoder anticlockwise) and the value 0x41 (equal to decimal 65) if the value has been increased (normally initiated by a turning the encoder clockwise). The value of 64 symbolises the current position and 0x3F and 0x41F increase/decrease the current value by 1. Some encoders can also detect the speed by which the encoder has been turned. In this case they will send values greater than 1 to indicate a higher turning speed. If the encoder sends the value 0x3D for example (decimal 61), then the current position has been decreased by 3; if the encoders send 0x42 (decimal 66) then the value has been increased by 2.

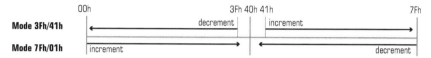

❑ **Mode 7Fh/01h** In this mode the encoder sends 0x7F (decimal 127), if the values have been decreased by 1 and 0x01 if the values have been increased by 1. This mode also allows greater value changes: 0x03 increases the value by 3 and 0x7C (decimal 124) decreases it by 4.

To find out which mode a potentiometer actually uses it can sometimes be helpful to have a look in the controller manual (unfortunately the quality of the manual is often quite poor). To be on the safe side you can use one of the tools described on page 127 and onward to examine which data the controller sends.

NOTE When you select the *Type of Controller* option *Encoder* in the dialog *Preferences/Controller Manager* you can choose the encoder mode in the list box *Enc.-Mode*. You need to make sure that the correct encoder mode is selected; otherwise Traktor cannot analyse the incoming MIDI messages correctly.

NOTE It is not necessarily so that an endless potentiometer always sends Control Change Messages. For examples the Allen&Heath controllers Xone:1D to 4D can be configured in a way that the upper most row of encoders can send either Control Change Messages in Mode 7Fh/01h or different Note On messages for a left and a right turn.

> **NOTE** Traktor offers both controller types in the list *Type of Controller* in the *MIDI Mapping* dialog. You have to choose the correct controller type here; otherwise Traktor cannot interpret the MIDI messages correctly.

Control Change Messages, 14 Bit

As explained above a data byte can transport in the 7 bits that are reserved for the data a value in the range of 0 to 127. This resolution is good enough if you wish to use knobs to change the panning or to set the loop length. If you use a jog wheel for scratching or to change the playback position in very small units this resolution is probably not good enough. That's the reason why several MIDI controllers like the Vestax VCI-300, Reloop Digital Jockey, EKS Otus, Numark NS7 to name only a few use so called high resolution MIDI messages. Hi-res MIDI messages are mostly used for the jog wheel, a pitch fader or a slider.

There are several ways a MIDI controller can be used to transmit more than 128 values for the current value of a control. One technique is to use message pairs. The MIDI specification states that for Control Change messages the controller numbers in the range from 32 to 63 are reserved to transmit a second data byte for the controls with the controller numbers 0 to 31- The following figure illustrates this for the controller numbers 19 (hexadecimal 0x13) and 51 (hexadecimal 0x33). The MIDI specification defines these controllers as "General Purpose #4, MSB" and "General Purpose #4, LSB". (These controllers are used by the pitch fader of the MIDI-Controller Vestax VCI-300.)

Control Change Message, 14 Bit

Package 1: Status Byte		Package 2: Data Byte	Package 3: Data Byte
0xB	Channel (0 - 15)	0x13 (Controller Number)	0x3F (Value, MSB)

Package 1: Status Byte		Package 2: Data Byte	Package 3: Data Byte
0xB	Channel (0 - 15)	0x33 (Controller Number)	0x20 (Value, LSB)

Data byte 2 of the first message contains the most significant byte (MSB) and data byte 2 of the second message contains the least significant byte (LSB). The seven bits of the most significant byte form the upper seven bits of the 14 bit value and the seventh bit of the last significant byte form the lower seven bits of the value. This way we have 14 bits that can be used to encode 16,384 different values.

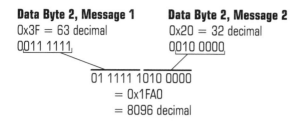

The problem with these message pairs is that they *can* be a pair of related messages, but they do not necessarily belong to each other. The only way Traktor can know this, is to analyse the incoming message in MIDI learn mode. If Traktor receives two messages at a certain time whilst in MIDI learn mode then it assumes, that this is a 14 bit message. In this case Traktor fills in the received controller numbers and the MIDI channels in the appropriate field of the dialog MIDI mapping. This can cause problems if you wish to MIDI learn the message coming in from a touchpad like the one on the Korg nanoPAD. These pads actually send two independent messages, one for the x-axis and the other one for the y-axis. This confuses Traktor because it interprets the two independent messages as one 14 bit MIDI message. To avoid this and to be able to map the x- and y-axis independently you need to use the controller configuration tool and disable the axis you currently do not wish to map in MIDI learn mode.

Pitch Bend Messages

The last MIDI message that Traktor can process is the Pitch Bend Message. This message was originally used to change the tone pitch and is used for example by the pitch bend wheel of the Akai MKP 49 keyboard. The DJ controllers/DCJ players Denon DN-HS5000 and HD2500 also send this message type if the pitch bend slider of the controller is moved.

The Pitch Bend Message would actually be the perfect solution for several of the incompatibility issues found with 14 bit MIDI. This message is standardised, it is a message type of its own, it is channel related (so 16 different MIDI controls could use it) and because the message contains two data bytes it can transmit a 14 bit value in just one message. The following figure shows the structure of the Pitch Bend Message.

Pitch Bend Message

Package 1: Status Byte		Package 2: Data Byte	Package 3: Data Byte
0xE	Channel (0 - 15)	MSB Value (0 - 127)	LSB Value (0 - 127)

> **HD MIDI** The *MIDI Manufacturers Association (MMA)* – the organisation manag-
> ing the MIDI specification – established a project group in 2005 which is working
> on the creation of a High Definition MIDI Protocol Standard. The main goal for
> High Definition MIDI is to adapt the outdated MIDI protocol to modern require-
> ments so that one single message can contain more channels, more controller num-
> bers and even higher data values. A release date for High Definition MIDI has not
> yet been published and I assume that it will be some more time before this new
> standard has been passed and we will see bug free implementations provided by the
> different hardware and software manufacturers.

MIDI Messages in Both Directions

The MIDI messages explained in this section can be sent in both directions (see also
section 5.1 on page 125 and onwards). Messages that are sent from a controller to
Traktor trigger an action in Traktor. Messages that are sent from Traktor to a controller control the status of an LED. For the modular interfaces Lemur and touchOSC (the
two most important touch surfaces for iOS (and in the case of touchOSC for Android
also), incoming MIDI messages can completely change the interface, like hiding and
showing panels, and so on.

5.4 Configuring MIDI Settings of Your Controller

With regard to how customizable the MIDI parameters are, the DJ MIDI controllers
can be classified in three groups:

◻ **Completely customizable** The MIDI messages and the MIDI channel can be
customized for all controls of the controller; to set the controller up to use a software provided by the controller manufacturer.

◻ **Partial customizable**   The MIDI messages used by the controls cannot be
changed. However, you can change the MIDI channel that the controller shall
use. For controllers that support several mapping layers (like the Allen&Heath
Xone:K2), you can configure the operation mode of the controller. In this regard
the operation mode affects which MIDI messages are sent or can be received. To
change the MIDI channel or the operation mode you will use a dedicated setup
mode and make your changes directly on the hardware, by using particular buttons or encoders.

◻ **Not customizable** The MIDI messages and the MIDI channel are hard wired
into the controller. You need a MIDI configuration map for the controller to see
which MIDI messages it uses. This information is important for the mappings
you create in Traktor. For example you must know, which values light up a button in the desired colour.

MIDI Messages/Channel completely customizable: nanoSeries

One example of controllers that can be completely customized is the nanoSERIES family made by KORG (www.korg.com/nanoseries2). The following picture shows a screenshot of the Korg Kontrol Editor; this is the tool used to change the MIDI parameters of these controllers.

The picture shows the configuration of a nanoPAD2 controller. The first pad currently uses Note messages and it is set to note C#2; this is shown on the label of the pad. If you select a pad by clicking it, you can change the MIDI parameters in the lower part of the window.

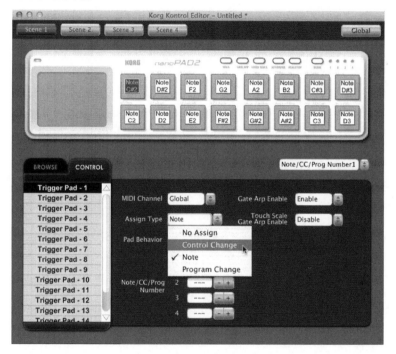

Use the *MIDI Channel* list to change the MIDI channel of the pad. Currently the list is set to *Global,* i.e. the pad is using the global setting that is valid for the complete controller. To change the global MIDI channel setting, click on *Global* in the upper right of the window.

In list *Assign Type* the MIDI message type can be selected. Currently the pad is set to *Note*; open the list to select another message type, like *Control Change* for example.

For pads and buttons the *Pad Behavior* setting is very important. Kontrol Editor provides the two options *Momentary* and *Toggle*. What do they mean?

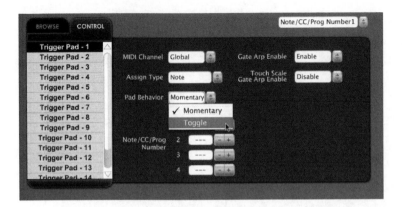

The *Pad Behavior* setting controls together with *Assign Type* **when** the controller is sending a MIDI message. There are four possible combinations:

☐ **Assign Type: Note/Pad Behavior: Momentary** When the pad is pressed Note On is sent and when the pad is released Note Off is sent.

☐ **Assign Type: Note/Pad Behavior: Toggle** When the pad is pressed a Note On message is sent and when the pad is released no message will be sent. On the next press of the button a Note Off message is sent and when the pad is released no message is sent. This means that in Toggle mode the pad remembers its pressed state.

☐ **Assign Type: Control Change/Pad Behavior: Momentary** When the pad is pressed a Control Change message is sent where the second data byte contains the value 127 and when the pad is released a second Control Change message with a 0 in the second data byte is sent.

☐ **Assign Type: Note/Pad Behavior: Toggle** When the pad is pressed the controller sends a Control Change message with a value of 127 and when the pad is released no message is sent. On the next press of the button a Control Change message with a value of 0 is sent and when the pad is released no message is sent. Using *Toggle* causes the controller to remember the status of the pad between presses.

If setting *Pad Behavior* is not properly configured, most often this means that *Toggle* is used instead of *Momentary,* you need to press a button twice to activate/deactivate a particular action in Traktor.

The NI controllers provide similar setting options for the behavior of pads and buttons; these are explained in the next section.

In section *Note/CC/Prog Number* you can configure the note or the controller number that the control shall use. It is important that each note or controller number is only used once for that particular controller.

MIDI Messages/Channel completely customizable: NI Controllers

The NI controllers of the Traktor Kontrol family can also be customized with a dedicated tool, the so called Controller Editor. In case the Controller Editor has not automatically been installed, you can download it from the NI website (www.native-instruments.com/?id=freeupdates).

Before you can use Controller Editor to change the MIDI parameters of the NI controllers, you first need to switch the controller to MIDI mode (see page 127). Then start Controller Editor. If there is more than one NI controller connected, use the menu in the header and select the controller you wish to customize. All controllers currently connected are marked with a small dot next to the controller name. Make sure that the *Connect* icon in the header has a coloured frame. Only then changes made to the configuration of the controller can be stored in the controller.

Mapping Pages

The large area at the left side of the window shows a graphic of the controller. Some of the framed sections of the controllers have a small menu; use the menu to switch between the different mapping pages. Mapping pages are used to assign several features to one control. The primary feature of the control is active while no other button is pressed at the same time. The secondary feature is active if a second button, for example the SHIFT button, is pressed while the control is used. In order to make sure that the MIDI messages transferred between the controller and the software are unique, you can configure the MIDI parameters for each mapping page.

Alternatively you can use the *Pages* tab at the right side of Controller Editor to switch between the mapping pages. Use the *Shift Mode* list on the *Pages* tab to select, when the MIDI parameters of the *Shift* page shall be active: In *Gate* Mode the shifted page will be active as long as the SHIFT button on the controller is held. In *Toggle* mode the first press of SHIFT will activate the shifted page; the next press of SHIFT will switch back to the *Basic*, i.e. non shifted, page

SHIFT and Deck Focus Buttons

As well as the SHIFT buttons the Kontrol S4 provides two more buttons to switch between mapping pages. These are the two deck focus buttons, labeled *DECK C* and *DECK D*. By using the deck focus buttons combined with the SHIFT buttons it is possible to create four mapping layers for the deck related section of the S4. The *Pages* tab in the following picture shows the four layers.

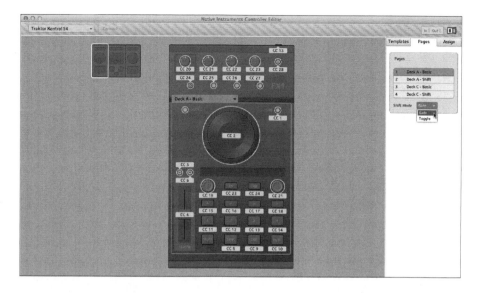

In its default configuration Kontrol S4 uses different CC numbers for the non-shifted and the shifted layer. Depending on the status of the deck focus buttons S4 uses different MIDI channels; the CC numbers of the individual controls remain unchanged. When deck A is in focus on the left side of the controller, MIDI channel 1 is used and for deck C the S4 uses MIDI channel 3. When deck B is in focus on the right side, the controls use MIDI channel 2 and for deck D MIDI channel 4.

> **SHIFT and Deck Focus Buttons are not customizable** As the SHIFT buttons and the deck focus buttons switch between the different MIDI pages (which is a feature of the controller firmware), those buttons cannot be customized with Controller Editor.

In most cases it will not be necessary to change the MIDI channel or the message type. However, it is important, that the behaviour of the pads and buttons is correctly configured. Furthermore, you need Controller Editor to setup the colours of the multi-coloured pads and buttons.

Configuring MIDI Parameters of Traktor Kontrol Controllers

Perform the following steps to change the MIDI parameters of a control of am NI Traktor controller:

1. Switch your controller into MIDI mode. Start Controller Editor and make sure that your controller is connected.

2. Select the mapping page you wish to edit.

3. Double-click on the control you wish to customize on the controller image. Controller Editor puts a frame around the selected control. At the right side of the window the *Assign* tab is opened.

4. Open the list *Type* and change the message to the type that the control shall use. Now you will see the message types *Note, Control Change,* and *Pitchbend* which are explained in section 5.3 of this chapter.

5. Use the fields *Channel* and *Number* or *Note* to change the MIDI channel and the Controller Number (for Control Change messages) or the Note (for Note On/Note Off messages).

6. Use the *Mode* list to change the behavior of the pads and buttons. This setting is actually the same as it is used by Korg Kontrol Editor. Select one of the following options:

   □ **Gate** If you selected *Note* as message type, the pad/button will send a Note On message when pressed and a Note Off message when released.

   If you selected *Control Change* as message type, the pad/button will send a Control Change message when pressed. The second data byte of the message contains the value specified in the field *Value on* (by default 127). Releasing the pad/button creates a second Control Change message where the value from field *Value off* (default value is 0) is used in the second data byte.

   □ **Toggle** In this mode the pad/button remembers its pressed state.

   If message type *Note* is used, on press a Note On message is sent and no message on release. When the button is pressed the next time, a Note Off message is sent and again no message is created when the pad/button is released.

   For message type *Control Change* the pad/buttons sends a Control Change message and uses the value from *Value on* (by default 127) in the second data byte when it is pressed and it sends no message on release. When the pad/button is pressed next, it sends another Control Change message and uses the value from *Value off* (by default 0) in the second data byte; again no message is sent on release.

   When *Toggle* mode is active, you can use option *Action on* to select whether the message is send on press (option *Down)* or on release (option *Up)*. Please note that for option *Up* the messages explained above are sent when the pad/button is released and not when it is pressed.

◻ **Trigger** This mode is only available if *Control Change* has been selected as message type. In this mode the pad/button only sends one message and it uses the value specified in the *Value* field.

You can use option *Action on* to select, whether the message is sent on press *(Down)* or on release *(Up)* of the button.

7. Buttons and pads with an LED are configured with the options in the lower part of the *Assign* tab. Option *LED on* is always available. Use *For MIDI In* if you want to control the LED from „the outside world", for example by a Traktor mapping.

If you use *For MIDI Out* the controller will take care of switching the LEDs on and off. This happens every time when a pad/button is pressed/released and when an outgoing MIDI message is created.

8. For coloured LED buttons use the *Color Mode* list to configure the colour mode.

◻ **Single** In *Single* mode you can use the colour picker *Color Value* to select the colour for the active state of the pad. If the pad/button is not active, the LED is off.

◻ **Dual** In *Dual* mode you can select one colour for the active state and another one for the inactive state. Use the *Color On* and *Color Off* pickers to select one of the default colours.

◻ **HSB** In order to use this mode you have to select *For MIDI In* in list *LED on.*

In HSB mode the colour of the buttons can be controlled completely by the software and you are not restricted to the 16 default colours provided by the colour pickers. In HSB mode the colour of the pads is defined by three parameters: hue, saturation, and brightness. You need to send three MIDI messages to the pad to set it to the desired colour. Always use the assigned message type and controller number/note. Then, for the first connected F1 use channel 1 for the hue value, channel 2 for the saturation, and channel 3 for the brightness. For the second connected F1 use channels 4 to 6, etc.

Show selected colours while customizing If you wish to see the colours selected with the colour pickers while you customize the controller, set option *LED On* temporary to *For MIDI Out* and press the pads/button. Once you are done set *LED On* back to *For MIDI In* if you wish to control the colours from a Traktor mapping.

MIDI Messages/Channel partially customizable

One example of a controller that can be customized directly from the hardware is the Xone:K2 by Allen&Heath. You can configure the MIDI channel, whether the K2 supports mapping layers, and you can select which section of the controller shall be layered.

To switch the K2 into setup mode press and hold the encoder labelled with Power On Setup, while you connect it to the USB port of your computer or to the X:Link port of the Allen&Heath Xone:DB2/Xone:DB4 mixer. The controller blinks three times to indicate that it is in setup mode. Pressing the Power On Setup encoder (from now on abbreviated as Setup encoder), activates the MIDI channel select mode.

Xone:K2: Configuring the MIDI Channel

Once the K2 is started in Power On Setup mode, the number of buttons that are on corresponds to the number of the currently selected MID channel. Turn the setup encoder to change the MIDI channel and press the encoder to save this setting. Changing the MIDI channel for the K2 is necessary if you use two K2 controllers with a Xone:DB2 or Xone:DB4. Because the MIDI message parameters of the K2 cannot be changed, you need to use different MIDI channels for the controllers: this makes the MIDI messages unique.

Xone:K2: Configuring the Mapping Layers (Latching Layers)

One special feature of the Xone:K2 is the latching layers system. It allows you to define the blocks of the controller that stay the same when you switch layers and that should act differently. The K2 provides different modes and this mode defines the behaviour of the different blocks. For example, you can configure the 16 buttons in the lower part of the controller in a way that they use one layer only, and activate multiple layer support for upper part of the K2. In total five different latching layers modes are available (see picture on the following page).

The layers mode can be configured on the controller; no software is needed. By turning and finally pressing the setup encoder the latching layers mode is selected and stored.

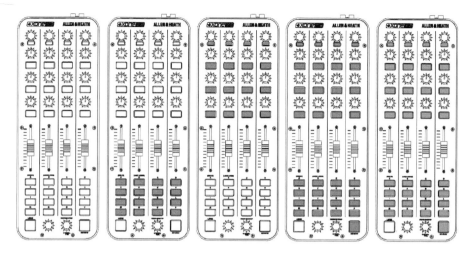

The manual for the Xone:K2 contains detailed information about the notes and controller numbers that are used by the various controls in a particular latching layers mode.

All buttons of the Xone:K2 are equipped with LEDs. All LEDs can light up in three different colours: red, amber, and green. Even when you do not use the latching layers system, i.e. you are using one layer only, you can use the different colours. To do so check the K2 manual: it shows the notes that you need to use in Note On/Note Off messages. The following figure is an excerpt from the K2 documentation, showing the upper four LEDs of the controller. The first row indicates the notes that light up the LED in red, the second row shows the values for amber, and the third row finally the values for green.

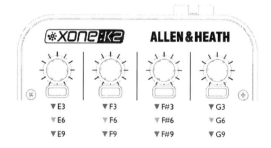

MIDI Messages/Channel Hard Wired

One example of a controller where MIDI channel and MIDI messages are hard wired into the controller is the CMD-LC1 from Behringer.

> **MIDI Channel can be changed**   It is not completely true that the MIDI channel of
> the CMD-LC1 is hard wired and that it cannot be changed. You can change the
> MIDI channel of the controller by using a (not documented) system exclusive mes-
> sage (SYSEX). One of the values in the SYSEX message defines the MIDI channel
> that the LC1 shall use. We won't dig any deeper here as the use of SYSEX messages
> is beyond the scope of this chapter. At the same time we did not want to spread
> incorrect information; that's why we added this note.

However, the CMD LC-1 is another example of how good documentation of the MIDI
messages a controller uses should look like. You will need this information to change
the colours and the blink state of the buttons and to control the LED rings of the encoders in the upper part of the controller.

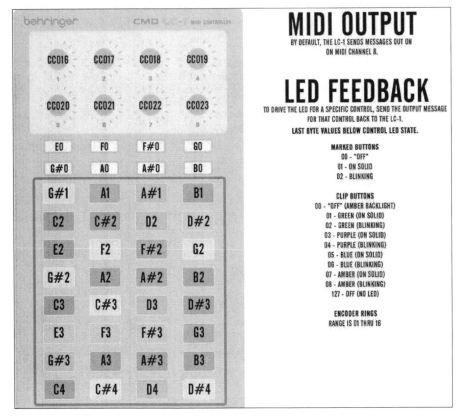

The figure above shows an excerpt from the MIDI map documentation of the LC-1.
The two upper rows of the controller provide four encoders each, which are equipped
with LED rings. To control the value that the LED rings show, you send a Control

Change message to the control. The documentation shows the value range that you can send to the control (the range is 1 to 16). Use one of the values from that range to indicate which of the LEDs of the ring shall be on.

To ensure that the range of a particular outgoing MIDI command in Traktor is correctly mapped to the range of a control on the controller, you need to enter the range that your MIDI controller accepts into the field *LED Options/Midi Range* of Traktors Controller Managers. An example for the LED rings of the CMD-LC1 shows the following figure. The outgoing command Slot Filter Adjust for the remix decks has a value range from 0.0 to 1.0. Traktor shows this value when you create a mapping for that command. As the value range for the LED rings is 1 to 16, we entered theses values into the *Midi Range* fields.

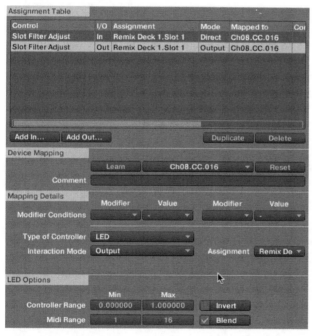

The clip buttons of the CMD-LC1 are controlled in a similar way. These buttons provide several colours; additionally the buttons can blink. Furthermore the buttons support two different off states. If a button receives the value 127, it will be completely off. If you send the value 0 to the button, it will light up with an amber backlight. As you can see from the MIDI map documentation all buttons use Note messages. However, specifying the *Midi Range* works in the same way for Note messages as it works for Control Change messages. To set the clip buttons to a particular colour, you will enter that colour into the Midi Range fields.

All practical questions are covered in greater detail in chapter 6 where creating your own mappings is explained. For the moment it is important to understand, that you will need a good documentation of the MIDI map that your controller uses. Sometimes you can find that information in the printed manual; sometimes you can download that information from the website of the controller manufacturer.

5.5 MIDI Ports

MIDI devices can be connected to themselves or to a PC in different ways.

◻ **USB/FireWire MIDI Ports**   Most of the MIDI DJ controllers, CD players and mixers with MIDI features are either equipped with a USB port or a FireWire interface, which serve as the MIDI IN and the MIDI OUT port at the same time.

◻ **DIN**   The "classic" MIDI port is the 5-pin DIN plug. The corresponding sockets on MIDI devices are labelled as MIDI IN, MIDI OUT and, if applicable, MIDI THRU. The following figure shows the front of the Traktor Scratch TA10 audio interface, which, like the Traktor Kontrol S4, is equipped with a MIDI OUT and a MIDI IN port. You can use these MIDI ports to integrate additional MIDI controllers into your setup (like MIDI keyboards) without using one of the USB ports of your laptop.

The MIDI IN port receives data only and the MIDI OUT port is only used to transmit data. All data coming in on the MIDI IN port is forwarded to the MIDI THRU port (if your device is equipped with one).

◻ **Virtual MIDI Ports**   As well as the "physical" MIDI ports there are also virtual MIDI ports, these are implemented within the software only. Their purpose is to offer an invisible MIDI cable inside a computer (with a MIDI IN port on one, and a MIDI OUT port on the other side of the virtual cable). Virtual MIDI ports are used if software, running on the same computer as Traktor, is to send MIDI data to Traktor.

The OS X version of Traktor already provides a virtual MIDI input port and one virtual MIDI output port. On Windows you need separate tools. We will cover the use of virtual MIDI ports in chapter 8 when we explain how to synchronise Traktor with other music software.

◻ **MIDI over Ethernet** MIDI data can be sent over an Ethernet network as well. This is a good way to synchronise several Traktor systems. The only thing required is a MIDI network driver that provides virtual MIDI ports and which can send and receive MIDI data via a network. (You can find Mac OS X and Windows drivers at *www.nerds.de*.) Chapter 8 contains step-by-step instructions on how to synchronise several Traktor systems.

Once the hardware and/or drivers are installed Traktor shows all available MIDI IN and MIDI OUT ports in the *In-Port* and *Out-Port* lists in the dialog *Controller Manager*.

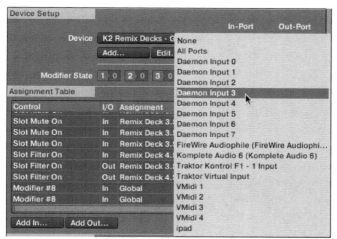

5.6 MIDI Messages: Quick Reference

The following tables can be useful while analysing the incoming MIDI data. They contain all important information about the structure of the MIDI messages explained in this chapter and which are supported by Traktor.

System messages

Byte 1	Byte 2	Byte 3	Message
0xF8	–	–	MIDI Clock Tick
0xFA	–	–	MIDI Clock Start
0xFC	–	–	MIDI Clock Stop

Channel related Messages

Byte 1, Nibble 1	Byte 1, Nibble 2	Byte 2	Byte 3	Message
0x9	Channel Number	Note	Velocity	Note On
0x8	Channel Number	Note	Velocity	Note Off
0xB	Channel Number	Controller Number	Value	Control Change
0xE	Channel Number	MSB Value	LSB Value	Pitch Bend

Chapter 6

Controller, Mappings, Modifier, Hotkeys, and Macros

You can use Traktor with a mouse only (this makes sense if have you downloaded the demo version to check out how Traktor works). However, for a gig you need either a good keyboard mapping or a MIDI controller. The quickest and easiest way to use Traktor is a combination of controller and keyboard.

When a key is pressed, or when one of the controls on a controller is used Traktor analyses the incoming event and checks if a Traktor function has been assigned, i.e. mapped, to the key or the control. When Traktor finds an assignment it executes the corresponding Traktor function. The process of assigning a key/a control to a Traktor function is called *keyboard mapping* and *controller mapping* respectively.

Using the Setup Wizard – covered in chapter 2 "First Steps" – is a quick way to make a usable Traktor configuration. Depending on your selection the Setup Wizard copies predefined configurations with keyboard and controller mappings into your personal Traktor settings file. The Wizard offers mappings for most of the popular DJ controllers. Traktor provides very special plug&play support for Native Instruments own controllers: As soon as Traktor detects that one of the Traktor Kontrol controllers is connected for the first time, Traktor will automatically load the default mapping for that controller.

The problem is, when it comes to controller mappings especially, the predefined mappings only contain a small fraction of the features that can be assigned to a controller. The features available in the default controller mappings are targeted to an average Traktor user. It is likely that the mapping will not provide all the features that you wish to use. To make your controller work the way you want you must either, adapt the predefined mappings or create a complete new mapping from scratch.

That's what this chapter is about.

6.1 Mapping – An Overview

Traktor offers more than 300 different "actions"; in this book they are referred to as "mapping commands" in this book. All mapping commands can either be assigned to a key on your keyboard or a control on your controller.

> **NOTE** In "Traktor language" the mapping commands are called "controls" or "controller". Because "control" and "controller" are very ambiguous terms I will use "mapping command" when referring to what Traktor calls map-able controller/control, use "controller" when referring to the physical controller, and use the term "control" for the knobs, buttons, sliders etc. that are the control elements on a controller.

In this book the available mapping commands are covered in the context where they are needed. For example, information about the mapping commands for the FX unit are explained in the chapter covering the Traktor effects, the mapping commands for looping and cue points are described in the corresponding chapters etc. This way all relevant information for a topic can be found in one place.

Additionally, you can use the interactive mapping command finder on *www.traktor-bible.com* to quickly find the command you need. The mapping command finder is simply a webpage with several screenshots showing the different sections of the Traktor user interface. Hover the mouse over a button, knob or slider to see the name of the related mapping command. Then use the index of the Traktor Bible to find the pages with detailed information about this command.

The main goal of this chapter is to help Traktor newcomers to get up and running with keyboard and controller mapping. The first tutorial sections contain some very simple examples that explain the basic steps of mapping. Here the different mapping parameters that Traktor offers are also explained. The more advanced topics are covered further down the chapter, such as macros and how to use modifiers. Promise: this isn't as complicated as it first seems once the foundation is laid.

Before we start with practical mappings, the following section provides you with important information about the architecture of controller mappings.

Logical and Physical Controllers

This section describes the mapping architecture of Traktor, it explains the differences between a logical controller and a physical controller and it shows which device classes are available when you create a new logical controller.

Admittedly, the next pages are a bit dry. However, having some background knowledge about the way controller mappings are organised is essential to make use of all the possibilities that Traktor offers. If you are already familiar with the way mappings worked in earlier Traktor versions, the following pages will help to switch to the new mapping concept. If Traktor 2 is the first version you use then read the following pages to get a good overview. Don't worry if everything makes little sense to you on first sight. Check the different tutorials, make yourself familiar with the user interface of the *Controller Manager* dialog and return to this section whenever more general information is needed.

In Traktor 2 a mapping is not created for a particular physical device, but instead for a logical device/a logical controller.

A logical controller has several specific characteristics and properties:

◻ When you create a logical controller you assign a device class to it. The current version of Traktor 2 supports the following device classes:

    ◻ **Generic Keyboard** to create keyboard mappings

    ◻ **Generic MIDI** to create mappings for controllers that use the MIDI protocol

    ◻ **Non-MIDI** to create mappings for controllers that either support a HID interface (like *Denon DN-HC 4500, Pioneer DDJ-T1, DJM-T1, CDJ-400/900/ 2000/2000 nexus)* or that use the proprietary Native Instruments protocol NHL (Native Hardware Library), currently implemented for all Traktor Kontrol controllers

◻ The device class of a logical controller determines, if only an In-Port or an In-Port and an Out-Port can be assigned to the controller

    ◻ For controllers of the class *Generic Keyboard* only an In-Port can be selected; the only In-Port that is available is the *Keyboard* port.

    ◻ Controllers of the other device classes can be assigned an In-Port and an Out-Port. When the logical controller has the class *Generic MIDI* all available MIDI-In- and MIDI-Out-Ports can be assigned. For the *Non-MIDI* controllers the corresponding USB ports of the controller are shown; the selected In-Port is automatically used as Out-Port as well; the Out-Port cannot be changed.

◻ Another characteristic of a logical controller is the type of input the controller can process and how the received input data is shown in the *Controller Manager* dialog.

Keyboard   **MIDI**   **Non-MIDI (HID/NHL)**

Shift+1   Ch01.CC.067   Play/Pause

◻ For a controller of the class *Generic Keyboard* the names of the keys are shown.

◻ For a controller of the class *Generic MIDI* the MIDI channel, the type of MIDI message and either the note name or the CC number is shown (see chapter 5 for more information about MIDI messages).

◻ For the Non-MIDI controllers the name of the button/control on the controller is shown.

◻ A logical controller is active (i.e. Traktor processes the mapped commands) if an In-Port or an In- and Out-Port of a physical controller is assigned to the logical controller.

◻ The scope of the modifiers (modifiers act as status variables to implement shift-like functionality in a mapping) is restricted to the logical controller. An example: When the value of modifier M1 has been set with the keyboard to 4, then this value can be accessed only from mapping commands that reside on the same logical controller. This means that the modifier from the keyboard mapping cannot be accessed from the mapping of a CDJ-400, because this mapping needs a different device class and therefore resides in another logical controller.

This concept makes sense when you use two identical MIDI or HID devices, for example two Pioneer CDJ-400s. Let's assume you created a mapping for one CDJ-400 and that this mapping controls deck A. You can duplicate the complete mapping for this controller, including all modifier assignments and modifier conditions. Once you have created the duplicate, open the list *Device Target* in section *Device Setup* and set deck B as target for the second logical controller. Now you are ready. This is an example of when it is desirable that the mapping for one CDJ cannot access the modifiers of the other one; this would result in chaos regarding the modifier values.

◻ A logical controller has the property *Device Target*. This property is set in the list box *Device Target* in section *Device Setup*. The device target is valid for the complete logical controller. Together with the *Assignment* selected in section *Mapping Details* this property controls whichever deck a mapping command is sent to. More about this can be found onwards.

The following figure illustrates the architecture of the controller manager by using some examples. The box on the left side symbolises the controller manager that currently contains five logical controllers and their mappings.

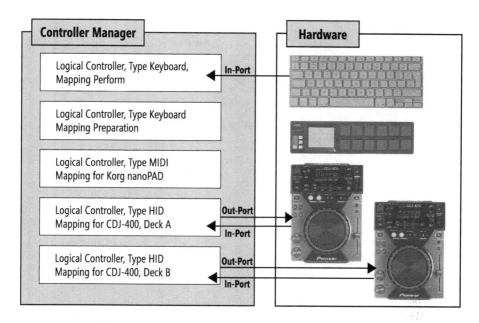

The two logical controllers in the upper part of the image are of type *Keyboard*. For example, one controller could hold the keyboard mapping *Perform* and the other one a *Preparation* mapping. The In-Port *Keyboard* has been assigned to the controller that holds the mapping *Perform*, i.e. only this keyboard mapping is currently activated. To switch from keyboard mapping *Perform* to mapping *Preparation*, the only thing you need to do is deactivate the In-Port *Keyboard* for mapping *Perform* and to activate the In-Port for mapping *Preparation*.

The logical controller in the middle contains a MIDI mapping for a Korg nanoPAD. Here no MIDI In-Port is assigned; i.e. this mapping is currently inactive.

The two logical controllers at the bottom each contain one HID mapping for a Pioneer CDJ-400. The commands used in both mappings are identical. Each of the two logical controllers is connected via the In-/Out-Port assignment to a different physical CDJ. The first CDJ-400 controls Traktor deck A; the second one controls Traktor deck B.

The Logical and Physical Controllers in the Controller Manager

Ok, the theory about the architecture of the controller management maybe a little dry, but this background information will help you to handle your controller mappings in a much smarter way. All three mapping types (Keyboard, MIDI, and Non-MIDI) are created and edited in the *Preferences/Controller Manager* dialog.

The upper section, *Device Setup*, is used to manage the logical controllers and to assign an *In-Port/Out-Port* to them.

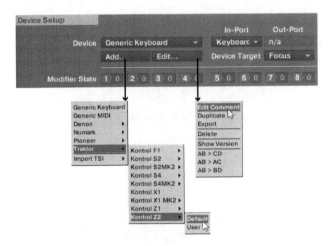

If you wish to see which logical controllers are currently available, open the list *Device*. Next to the name of the device the assigned In- and Out-Ports are shown.

ATTENTION   Sometimes the entry *None* in the list *Device* leads to confusion. On first sight it looks as if there

are no mappings at all. To check if there really is no mapping available open the list *Device*, check its entries and select the mapping you wish to see or edit. If there really is no mapping available create a new mapping (this is explained further down in this chapter) or import a pre-made mapping (see chapter 2).

You can use the list boxes *In-Port* and *Out-Port* to assign the desired ports to a controller. If your MIDI device is selected you can either select a single port or use the option *All Ports*. You can use *All Ports* if the mapped commands for *several* physical controllers (=several In-Ports) reside in *one* physical controller.

The *Add* button opens a menu to create or import new logical controllers. The *Edit* button opens another menu with commands to duplicate, export, or delete the currently selected device and where you can extend the device name with a comment (see figure above).

IMPORTANT   The *Assignment Table* always shows the commands that are mapped to the logical controller selected in the list *Device*. When you wish to map a new command you first need to select the desired logical controller in the list *Device*.

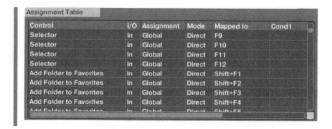

The Device Target

There are many mapping commands that control the functions of the Traktor decks, for example the *Play/Pause* or the *Filter Adjust* command. One way to inform Traktor as to which deck a command shall be sent to is by using the *Device Target* option in section *Device Setup*. The device target configured here applies to the complete controller and together with the assignment set up for one command it controls (section *Mapping Details*) where the command is sent.

The four possible combinations of the *Device Setup/Device Target* and *Mapping Details/Assignment* options are summarized in the following table.

Device Setup: Device Target	Mapping Details: Assignment	Command is sent to
Focus	Deck A–D	Deck selected in list Assignment
Deck A–D	Deck A–D	Deck selected in list Assignment
Focus	Device Target	Deck that currently has the deck focus
Deck A–D	Device Target	Deck selected in list Device Target

Despite the *Device Target* option it is still possible to hard-wire the target deck for a mapping command. This is done by selecting *Deck A* to *Deck D* in the *Assignment* list box. When a deck is selected here the command is always sent to this deck no matter what setting has been made in the *Device Target* list of section *Device Setup*.

If you wish to use the deck focus, (the letter of the deck that currently has the input focus highlighted) to set the target deck. To do this select *Focus* in list *Device Target* of section *Device Setup*. Then, for all commands that are to be sent to the deck with the input focus select the option *Device Target* in the list *Assignment* of section *Mapping Details*.

The *Device Target* option can be used for the commands that can be found in the submenus *Deck Common* and *Track Deck* of the *Add In/Add Out* buttons. Submenu Remix Deck contains a mixture of commands. Some are related to the remix deck as a whole (like *Quantize On* for example) while others can be assigned to a particular slot. For the commands targeting the remix deck you can use the Device Target option; for

163

the slot related commands however you need to specify the target slot in list Assignment and the Device Target option cannot be used.

For all commands that control an FX unit you must always select the target in List *Assignment* of section *Mapping Details*. The options available in list assignment change automatically depending on the command that is currently selected in the *Assignment Table*. The following figure shows all assignment options.

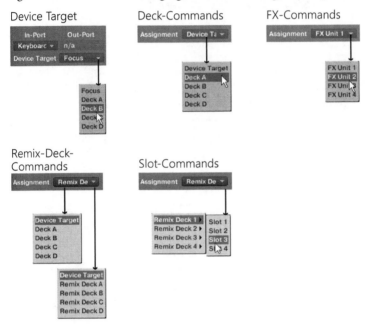

By smart usage of the *Device Target* and *Assignment* options it is very easy to create mappings for two identical controllers. Let's assume that you use two CDJ-400 in HID mode; one CD player shall control deck A, the second one deck B. Creating this mappings is done with following these steps:

1. Create a new logical controller of type CDJ-400 and add a comment to the controller name, like *CDJ-A*.

2. Open the list *Device Target* and select *Deck A*. Open the list *In-Port* and select the HID-Port of the first CDJ-400.

3. Add the mapping commands you need. Map them with the learn feature to the controls of the CDJ-400. When the command is deck specific open the list *Assignment* in section *Mapping Details* and choose *Device Target*. When this option is selected the command will be sent to the deck configured in step 2.

4. Once the mapping for the first CDJ is ready, create a duplicate. Change the comment for the duplicated mapping into CDJ-B, for example.

5. Make sure that the controller duplicate is selected in list box *Device*.

6. Use the list box *In-Port* and assign the HID port of the second CDJ player to the device.

7. Open the list box *Device Target* and select *Deck B*. Because the assignment *Device Target* was used for all deck specific commands in step 3, the mapping for the second CDJ player is already setup with this step.

The detailed steps for several actions are explained further onwards.

Creating a New Logical Controller

Follow these steps to create a new logical controller:

1. Open the *Preferences* dialog by clicking the corresponding button in the Traktor header and click on *Controller Manager*.

2. Click the *Add* button in section *Device Setup*. A menu showing the available device classes is opened.

3. Click the device class that the new controller shall have.

Traktor creates a new logical controller. For controllers of the class *Generic Keyboard* the In-Port *Keyboard* is pre-selected; for controllers of the class *Generic MIDI* the pre-selection for the In- and Out-Port is *All Ports*. For the Non-MIDI device classes the USB port found is pre-selected for the In- and for the Out-Port setting.

4. If you create a mapping for a MIDI controller open the *In-Port* and *Out-Port* list and replace *All Ports* by the port of the controller you wish to create a mapping for. Specifying the exact port avoids conflicts if you are using more than one controller.

5. To be able to distinguish controllers of the same type it makes sense to extend the device name with a comment. To do this, click *Edit* and then *Edit Comment*. Enter the comment into the dialog box and click *OK*.

6. Once these steps are done you can start to add mapping commands to the logical controller.

165

Deleting and Exporting the Mapping of One Logical Controller

To delete a logical controller select it in the list *Device*. Click on *Edit* and then on *Delete*. Traktor shows a confirmation dialog. If you are positive that the logical controller should be deleted click *OK*. This step cannot be undone.

The mapping of a logical controller can be exported into a TSI file; this TSI file can be imported when needed. Follow these steps to export a mapping:

1. Open the *Preferences* dialog by clicking the corresponding button in the Traktor header and click on *Controller Manager*.

2. Click in section *Device Setup* on *Edit* and then on *Export*.

   > **IMPORTANT** Do not use the *Export* button in the lower left of the *Preferences* dialog. This button exports **all** controller mappings and not just the mapping of one controller.

3. Navigate to the folder where the TSI file is to be stored, enter a filename and click on *Save*.

6.2 Keyboard Mapping for Newbies, Tutorials

This section contains several simple step-by-step examples of how to map a mapping command to a keyboard key.

Tutorial 1: Mapping one Command to a Key

This tutorial shows how to map the mapping command *Show Slider Values On*. This command shows the values of the different knobs in Traktors' user interface instead of the labels normally visible.

1. Open the dialog *Preferences* by clicking the corresponding button in the Traktor header.

2. Click at the left side of the dialog box on *Controller Manager*.

   After a standard installation and running the Setup Wizard the *Device* list in section *Device Setup* normally contains two entries. One entry is called *General Keyboard* with the pre-defined keyboard mapping and a second one for the controller you are using.

3. Open the list *Device* in section *Device Setup* and select *Traktor 2 default mapping* or *Traktor Scratch 2 default mapping.*

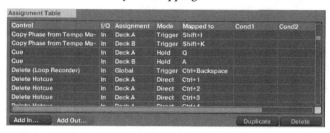

The *Assignment Table* in the upper part of the dialog shows all assignments that have been created between a mapping command (column *control*) and a key (column *Mapped to).* The other columns of the table are covered further down.

4. First you need to select the mapping command that you wish to map. Click on *Add In.* Traktor opens a submenu. Now click on *Global* and then on *Show Slider Values On.*

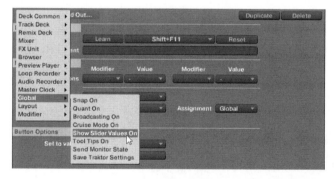

Traktor copies the name of the selected mapping command into the table column *Control,* i.e. the name of the submenu is omitted. The column *Mapped to* shows *n/a* (not assigned) indicating that the command isn't assigned to a key yet.

5. Make sure that in list *In-Port* of section *Device Setup* the option *Keyboard* is selected.

6. Click on *Learn.* The button is highlighted now indicating that learn mode is activated.

7. Now press the key you wish to map to this command. Use Ctrl+H for this example because this shortcut is not used in the predefined keyboard mappings. The key pressed is shown in the field next to the *Learn* button.

8. Click a second time on *Learn* to exit the learn mode.

   You can see if the mapping works without closing the *Preferences* dialog. Simply click the main window of Traktor so that it receives the keyboard input and press Ctrl+H. Because option *Hold* was pre-selected in list *Interaction Mode*, Traktor shows the current values of the knobs and not their labels for as long as the key is held.

   > **ATTENTION** If the values are not shown after pressing the mapped key, open the *Preferences/Global Settings* dialog and activate *Show value when over control*. This option ensures that the current knob value is shown when the mouse is on the knob. In the current Traktor version the execution of *Show Slider Values On* is coupled to this option – this is a bug in my opinion.

9. Open the list *Interaction Mode* and select *Toggle*. The shortcut Ctrl+H now behaves like an on/off switch. Give it a try.

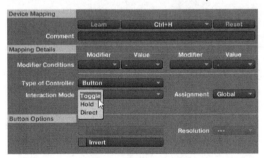

10. Open the list *Interaction Mode* and select *Direct*. Now the field *Set to value* is shown in section *Button Options*.

When using interaction mode *Direct* you can assign a certain value to the command. Traktor offers the values 1 (on) and 0 (off) for the *Show Slider Values On* command. Type 1 into the entry field *Set to value,* press Enter and try the changed mapping. Now the values of the knobs stay visible. Then type 0 into *Set to value,* press the mapped key so that the labels are shown again.

11. If you wish to delete this hotkey mapping select the entry in *Assignment Table* and click the *Delete* button below the table.

Tutorial 2: Mapping several Commands to a Key

It is quite often useful or necessary that two or more mapping commands need to be executed when one key is pressed. A mapping using more than one mapping command for one key is called a macro.

Creating a macro is in principle, not very different from creating a one command-one key mapping as explained in the previous section. When you build a macro you simply press the same key in Learn mode for all "macro-ed" commands. Here are some examples. Give this a try.

Example of a Macro with two Mapping Commands: Selecting an Effect

What the macro shall do: Switching FX unit 1 to Single Mode and then loading the *Delay* effect into the FX unit.

> **ATTENTION** In order to be able to select an effect it must be listed in the list *Pre-Selected Effects* of the *Preferences/Effects* dialog. If the effect selected in the mapping command is removed from the list *Pre-Selected Effects,* Traktor will change the effect selected in the mapping automatically to *No Effect.*

For this macro two mapping commands are needed:

- **Setting FX unit 1 to Single Mode**   Command: FX Unit | FX Unit Mode Selector; Interaction Mode: Direct; Set to Value: Single; Assignment: FX Unit 1

☐ **Loading the effect into the FX unit** Command: FX Unit | Effect 1 Selector; Interaction Mode: Direct; Set to value: Delay; Assignment: FX Unit 1

Try to create this little macro and use the $\boxed{=}$ key; this is another unused key in the predefined keyboard mappings.

When several mapping commands are assigned to the same key they are highlighted in the *Assignment Table*. For the currently active entry (that's the one whose parameters are shown in the lower part of the dialog box) bright yellow is used; for all other commands where the same key is assigned, dark yellow is used.

Column *Assignment* in the following figure shows the value selected in list *Assignment* (here *FX Unit 1*) and column *Mode* indicates the Interaction Mode selected.

Example of a Macro with three Mapping Commands: Beatjump

When two mapping commands are not enough to perform a certain action, three (and even more) mapping commands can be mapped to the same key/button. Again, here is a little example: The task of the next macro will be to perform a beatjump by 1 beat towards the end of the track. To beatjump in the Traktor user interface up to five different steps need to be carried out:

☐ The Advanced Panel in the lower section of the deck must be visible.

☐ The Advanced Panel must be switched to *Move view*.

☐ In *Move* view the *Beatjump* mode must be active.

☐ The jump length must be set to 1 beat.

☐ And finally the beatjump needs to be performed.

The first two steps ensure that the necessary panels are visible in the deck; they are not needed for the actual functionality. We then need to take care of the last three steps that correspond to the following mapping commands:

- **Activate Beatjump Mode** Command: Deck Common/Move/Mode Selector; Interaction Mode: Direct; Set to value: Beatjump; Assignment: select deck or use option Device Target, when option Device Target is set to Focus. Then the commands are sent to the deck that currently has the input focus.

- **Set Move Length** Command: Deck Common/Move/Size Selector; Interaction Mode: Direct; Set to value: 1; Assignment: select deck or use option Device Target, when option Device Target is set to Focus. Then the commands are sent to the deck that currently has the input focus.

- **Jump** Command: Deck Common/Move/Move; Interaction Mode: Direct; Set to value: Forward; Assignment: select deck or use option Device Target, when option Device Target is set to Focus. Then the commands are sent to the deck that currently has the input focus.

Try to create this macro as well. Once you know which mapping commands are needed then the remaining work is all about joining the dots. In general a good approach is to work out which steps you need to perform in the user interface and then transfer these steps to the mapping commands. For almost every action you can do in the user interface a corresponding mapping command is available.

> **NOTE** Another way to perform a beatjump is using the *Deck Common/Move/Beatjump* command. For this command the length of the jump is configured in *Set to value.*

Tutorial 3: Changing the Parameters of a mapped Command

It's quite easy to change the parameters of mapped commands. You do not need to delete the mapping and create a new one to do this. Let's assume that the jump length for the macro from the previous tutorial should not be 1 beat, but 4 beats. In order to change the parameter select the entry *Size Selector* in the *Assignment Table,* and then choose the new parameter value in list *Set to value;* in our example select 4.

6.3 Keyboard Mapping Options

There are many more options available for creating keyboard mappings that have been omitted in the tutorials. These options are explained below.

Interaction Mode

The list *Interaction Mode* offers several options to specify the action that shall be performed when a key is pressed. Which of these options are available depends on the mapping command.

◻ Some of the mapping commands simply trigger an action (then *Trigger* is used).

◻ Other mapping commands behave like a switch and support two different states (on/off) as we have seen in the example of *Show Slider Values On*. For those types of commands you can either toggle the status by using interaction mode *Toggle*. Or you can use interaction mode *Direct* to select a certain value/status.

◻ When you select interaction mode *Direct* the field *Set to value* is shown in section *Button Options*. Use *Set to value* to either select one of the available options (as seen for *Set Move Length)* or type the desired value (as for the command *Master Clock | Set Master Tempo* that is used to set the BPM value of the Master Clock).

The following table explains all interaction modes that are available.

Interaction Mode	Description
Hold	Function is activated as long as the key is pressed.
Toggle	Behaves like a switch. The first key press activates the function; the second press deactivates it, or vice versa.
Trigger	Activates the functionality of the command immediately when the key is pressed. This mode is used for actions that simply need to be initiated.
	Examples: One example of a mapping command that provides interaction mode Trigger only is Deck Common	Load Selected. This command loads the track selected in the tracklist into a deck. Another example is Deck Common	Set As Tempo Master that can be used to select the deck that shall be the tempo master.
Direct	Use this interaction mode to specify a value directly. When this mode is selected the value to set can either be selected from a list of the field Set to value or you can type it in.
	◻ Mapping commands acting like a switch offer two options 1=On and 0=Off in interaction mode Direct (like the command Layout | Fullscreen On that is used to toggle between window and full-screen view).
	◻ For commands that offer several options those are shown in the list Set to value. One example is the command Master Clock	Clock Ext/Int that is used to set the master clock mode. The options available for this command are Int and Ext).
	◻ The last group are commands where a certain numeric value can be specified. Here the field Set to value behaves like a text box. For example, FX Unit	Knob 1 is used to set the amount knob of the FX units to a certain value.

Interaction Mode	Description
Dec, Inc	These two interaction modes are used for commands ☐ that allow the stepwise change of a value (example: command Filter Adjust, to change the deck filter setting) ☐ that are used to move something (example: Move Grid Marker, that is used to move a beatmarker to the left or right) ☐ that offer a list of options in the field Set to value; here Dec and Inc are used to select the previous/next option (example: Loop Size Selector, which is used to select the loop length) For all commands where a value can be changed stepwise by using the interaction modes Inc and Dec, select the desired resolution in list Resolution. An example for this mode can be found in the section immediately after this table.
Reset	This command resets a value to its default value. The default value of a command is hard-wired and cannot be changed. Example: The command Deck Common | Loop | Loop Size Selector that selects the loop-length supports the interaction mode Set Default. This mode resets the loop-length to 4 beats/1 bar. When a command offers this interaction mode, then the default value is specified in the mapping command tables in the other chapters of this book.

Resolution

The interaction modes *Dec* (decrease) and *Inc* (increase) can be used to decrease or increase a value stepwise. This action corresponds to a click on either the *Plus* or the *Minus* button that Traktor displays when the mouse pointer rests on a knob. Right-clicking the *Plus* button opens a popup menu where you can select the resolution, i.e. the interval, by which the value is changed.

The popup menu offers the following five resolutions: *Min, Fine, Default, Coarse* and *Switch*. *Min* always selects the smallest step-size and *Switch* the largest. The same options can be found in the list box *Resolution* for all mapping commands supporting the modes *Inc* and *Dec*.

The exact intervals that are hidden behind the options depend on the particular command. This is illustrated in the following table that shows the intervals for three different mapping commands. Some of the values are only approximate. There is no official documentation explaining the resolutions. I did my best to find out the real values and it was simply by a lot of trial and error.

Resolution	Mixer | Master Volume Adjust	Mixer | EQ | High Adjust	Master Clock | Master Tempo
Min	± 0.15625 dB	± 0.78125%	± 0.00390625 BPM
Fine	± 0.625 dB	± 3.125%	± 0.015625 BPM
Default	± 2.5 dB	± 12.5%	± 0.0625 BPM
Coarse	± 5.0 dB	± 25%	± 0.125 BPM
Switch	± 50 dB	± 50%	± 0.50 BPM

The tables in this book documenting the mapping commands contain information about the resolution and intervals that Inc and Dec provide.

Assignment

The selection in the list *Assignment* specifies where a command shall be sent. Many of the commands are either deck-related (like *Deck Common | Load Selected* which loads a track into a deck) or the target is one of the FX units (like the command *FX Unit | Effect x Selector* that loads an effect into the specified FX unit). The following table describes the different *Assignment* options that are available. The selection made for *Assignment* is shown in column *Assignment* of the assignment table.

Assignment	Description
Global	This is the default and also at the same time the only value for mapping commands that are neither deck nor FX unit related.
Device Target, Deck A – Deck D	These options are available for all track deck related mapping commands. The deck can either be a track deck or a remix deck.
Remix Deck 1 – Remix Deck 4 Remix Deck A – Remix Deck D	These options are available for the commands that control a remix deck. Traktor counts the remix decks sometimes numerically and sometimes alphabetically.
Device Target, Deck A&B, Deck C&D	Those three options are available for the two mapping commands that affect two neighbouring decks. The first command is Deck Common | Deck Size Selector, that changes the deck size. The second one is Deck Common | Advanced Panel Toggle; it can be used to show/hide the Advanced Panel in the decks.
FX Unit 1 – FX Unit 4	These four options are available for all mapping commands that change settings of one of the FX units.

Assignment	Description
Remix Deck *x* Slot *y*	These options will be shown for commands that control a single slot of a remix deck.

When the option *Device Target* is selected for deck related commands as *Assignment,* the command is sent to the deck that was chosen in list *Device Target* of section *Device Setup*. This list contains the deck option *Focus*. When *Focus* is chosen as device target then selecting *Device Target* as assignment means the command is sent to the deck that currently has the input focus (the deck letter is highlighted). Please check page 163 as well for a more detailed description of how these settings work.

Setting the Deck Focus

One of the important aspects when designing a keyboard or controller mapping is the question, how to handle the deck focus for the deck related mapping commands. Generally two different approaches are possible:

▣ Commands are always mapped to a particular deck. In this case select the desired deck in the list *Assignment*.

▣ Commands are always sent to the deck that has the input focus. In this case select in list *Assignment* the option Device Target and choose *Focus* in list *Device Target*.

In most cases the best way is to use a combination of the two approaches (because the number of keyboard keys and controller controls is finite). For example, it makes sense to assign the command for loading tracks and playing decks to separate keys/button for each deck. However, for other Traktor functions, like jumping to hotcues or setting the loop-length), it could be an option to first set the focus and then using a focus oriented mapping for the actual commands.

A general recommendation cannot be made here because the best concept is very individual and it depends on which Traktor functions you need most often and on how many controls your controller provides.

By using the modifiers that are explained further down, it is possible to create "button combinations", similar to the ones used on a keyboard. This offers a great range of new mapping possibilities.

With the release of the Kontrol S4 controller the handling of the deck focus in Traktor has been changed. This change was necessary as the Kontrol S4 can control two different decks at the same time by using the sections to the left and to the right of the mixer section. This means that two decks can have the focus at the same time. This design change is reflected by the new option *Deck Focus* (can be found on *Preferences/Global Settings* dialog).

☐ **Hardware** The deck focus can only be changed by special hardware and, more than one deck can have the focus at the same time. Currently this is possible with Kontrol S4 only. As this option is named *Hardware* and not *Kontrol S4* it can be assumed that there will be more controllers in the future that will support this deck focus mode. If you use the S4 controller you should make sure that this option is enabled.

☐ **Software** With this option only one deck can have the deck focus. The deck letter of the deck that has the focus is highlighted. You can change the deck focus in a mapping by clicking on the deck letter of the deck that you want to set the focus to.

☐ **None** The deck focus can be set with a mapping command, with the S4 controller and in the Traktor user interface. However the deck letter of the focus deck is not highlighted.

To change the focus in a mapping, use the command *Layout | Deck Focus Selector*. To set the focus to a particular deck select *Direct* as interaction mode and then choose the desired deck in the list *Set to value* (and not in list *Assignment*).

Auto Repeat

There are several mapping commands where it makes sense, that the command is executed more than once. One possible example is the mapping command *Browser | List | Select Up/Down* that selects the next or previous track in the track list. Here it can be preferable that the command is executed for as long as the mapped key/button is pressed. To instruct Traktor to repeat the commands for as long as the key is pressed, simply activate the *AutoRepeat* check box.

Faster Mapping by Duplicating

Quite often you will find that you need to map the same command several times but that one of the parameters is different. Let's take the command *Deck Common | Play/Pause*, which corresponds to the Play button in the deck, as an example. Let's assume you wish to map this command to four different keys and that each key shall control one of the four decks (A–D). The optimal practice would be to insert this command once into the Assignment Table by using the standard procedure (using the *Add In* menu, setting the *Assignment* to *Deck A* and using *Learn* to specify the key). Then make sure that the new entry is selected in the *Assignment Table* and click the *Duplicate* button below the table. Traktor now creates a 1:1 copy of the selected entry. The only things you need to do are change the *Assignment* and learn the new keys. Then repeat these steps for decks C and D and the mapping is ready.

6.4 Controller Mapping for Newbies, Tutorials

The basic steps for the mapping of different controller types, are actually the same as the ones explained for keyboard mapping. For several reasons mapping a controller is a bit more complex:

- Keyboards contain one simple type of control, the keys. However, controllers are equipped with different control elements. As well as buttons that behave similarly to keyboard keys, i.e. supporting the states pressed/not pressed, most of the DJ controllers contain sliders, faders, rotary potentiometers, endless encoders, jogwheels and so on. The last group of controls transmit either their current position or information about a change in position.

- Traktor can convert or adapt the data it receives about the controller event.

> NOTE   The explanations in this and the following sections cover controller mapping from a practical point of view. More detailed theoretical information about the aspects of MIDI that are important in Traktor can be found in chapter 5, "MIDI Background".

Tutorial 1: Mapping a Controller Button

Controller buttons behave largely as the keys of a computer keyboard. To show how to map a command to a controller button the command *Filter On* is used. *Filter On* activates/deactivates the deck filter. The steps for mapping a button are almost identical to those for mapping a key.

1. Open the *Preferences* dialog by clicking the button in the header and then click on *Controller Manager*.

2. Open the list *Device* in section *Device Setup* and select the device that the new command shall be added to.

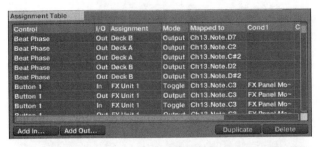

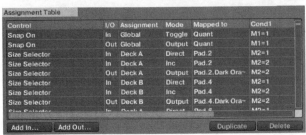

The list *Assignment Table* is organised as the table for keyboard mapping. For MIDI controllers column *Mapped to* shows information about the MIDI message; for HID/NHL controllers the name of the control on the controller is shown.

If you wish to create a completely new mapping add a new logical controller to the *Controller Manager* and select the device class you wish to use. Step-by-step instructions for adding a new logical controller can be found on page 165.

3. First select the mapping command (control) that you wish to assign to your button. Click on *Add In,* then click in the submenu on *Mixer* and finally click on *Filter On.*

4. Click the button *Learn* in section *Device Mapping* to activate the learn mode, then press the button on your controller that you wish to assign this command to.

For MIDI controllers Traktor displays information about the MIDI message the controller has sent next to the *Learn* button. For a button it is a Note-message; the note sent by the controller is *E2* and the message was sent via channel 14 *(Ch14).* (More information about the different MIDI messages can be found in chapter 5.)

For HID/NHL controllers the name of the control is shown.

5. Click *Learn* again to exit learn mode.

6. Enter a comment into the *Comment* field. This could be a note about the button that this command is mapped to or something similar. When you are creating a lot of assignments this is especially useful so you can keep a better overview.

7. The section *Mapping Details* is similar to the corresponding section for keyboard mapping. Open the list *Interaction Mode* and select *Toggle*. Then, you can use the button to switch the filter on and off.

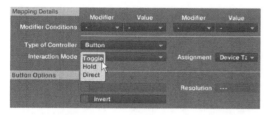

8. Open the list *Assignment* and select the deck Traktor is to send the mapping command to. Or use Device Target in combination with option *Focus* in list *Device Target* if you wish to control the deck that currently has the input focus.

9. If the mapped button is an LED button you can show the current status of the filter on the button. Make sure that in *Assignment Table* the *Filter On* command is selected, click on *Add Out* and then on *Filter On*. Traktor always shows the Out command for the selected In command at the very top of the *Add Out* menu.

10. Traktor copies the "Mapped To" setting from the In command to the Out command. Perform one of the following actions:

   ☐ If the LED button of a MIDI controller can be changed by the same MIDI message the button sends, you can use the value copied by Traktor.

   ☐ If the color of the button can be changed by sending some specific MIDI message enter the values in section MIDI Range (see also section 6.11 on page 225 and onwards). One example of such a controller is Behringer CMD-LC1; an excerpt from the MIDI map of this controller can be found in chapter 5 on page 152.

   ☐ If you need to send a different message to the button than it sends, click next to *Learn* on the *n/a* field. Then select the MIDI channel, the message type and finally the controller number or note. This approach must be used for controllers like the Allen & Heath Xone:K2 which uses different notes for the different colours it supports (see also page 151 in chapter 5).

> **TIP**   You can resize the *Preferences* window by dragging the right or the lower window frame. The selection list for the MIDI message automatically adapts to the size of the *Preferences* window; this makes selecting the MIDI message much easier.

▫ For the single colour buttons of the NI controllers you can use the *Learn* function to assign the Out command.

▫ For the multi-colour buttons of the NI controllers you need to select the colour manually. Click the text *n/a* next to the *Learn* button. Then select the button and finally one of the sixteen predefined colours.

The following figure shows the colour choices you have for the *Hotcue* buttons on the Kontrol X1 MK2.

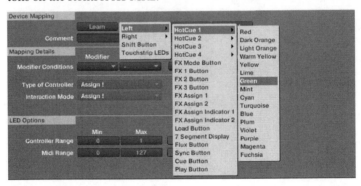

This ends the mapping for the command *Mixer | Filter On*. Press the mapped button to see if Traktor recognises the command. When you press the button on your controller the controller messages indicator in the Traktor header should become blue.

Tutorial 2: Mapping several Commands to one Button

The keyboard mapping tutorial on page 169 and onwards shows how to map more than one command to a keyboard key to create a macro. This can also be done when creating the mapping for a controller. Here are some small examples that show how useful the creation of controller macros can be.

If you have a smaller screen resolution and are using four decks, the space for the track browser can be very small and this can make searching for the next track a bit cumbersome. The Traktor header contains the *Maximize Browser* button; a corresponding mapping command is available too. If you wish to use this feature assign a second command to the button that loads a track; use the command *Layout | Only Browser On* to restore the Traktor window.

To maximize the browser you need one button. Map the following command to that button:

◻ Layout | Only Browser On, Interaction Mode: Direct, Set to value: Browser Only

Then map the following two commands to the button that shall load the track and reset the browser size:

◻ Deck Common | Load Selected, Interaction Mode: Trigger, Assignment: Select deck or use the combination of Device Target and Device Setup/Device Target = Focus.

◻ Layout | Only Browser On, Interaction Mode: Direct, Set to value: Browser Default

Tutorial 3: Mapping Faders, Slider and Knobs

What faders, slider, and knobs all have in common is that they have a defined start and end point and that they transmit the current position in their messages. In this way they correspond to the knobs and faders in the Traktor user interface.

This tutorial uses the Filter knob from the deck section as an example. (More detailed information about the deck filter can be found in chapter 12, "Equalizer, Key and Harmonic Mixing".) How to switch the deck filter on and off is explained in the tutorial on page 177. This is how to map the knob in the panel to a knob or fader of your controller.

1. Open the *Preferences* dialog by clicking the button in the header and then click on *Controller Manager.* Open the list *Device* in section *Device Setup* and select the device the new command shall be added to.

2. Click on *Add In,* then click on *Mixer* and finally on *Filter Adjust.*

3. Click the *Learn* button; then move/turn the knob of fader of your MIDI controller.

Traktor shows the received MIDI message in the field next to *Learn. CC* is the abbreviation for *Control Change.* This message type informs Traktor that the value of the control (i.e. a control element on the MIDI controller) identified by the number *12* has been changed. This message was received via MIDI channel 1 *(Ch01).*

Normally the value range of a knob fader is between 0 and 127. The Control Change message informs Traktor about the new value of this control. Then, Traktor sets the position of the mapped fader/knob according to the new value.

For HID/NHL controllers the name of the control is shown.

4. Click *Learn* again to exit learn mode.

5. The section *Fader/Knob* contains two check boxes that affect how Traktor processes the received value. Use the check box *Soft Takeover* to tell Traktor not to change the position of the Traktor knob until the value contained in the message matches to the value of the Traktor knob. This option avoids sudden jumps.

Let's assume that the Traktor knob is currently in its centre position (corresponds to the value 64) and that the controller knob is turned completely anti-clockwise (corresponds to the value 0). If the check box *Soft Takeover* is not activated when the knob is turned, the Traktor knob will immediately jump from position 64 to position 1. However, when *Soft Takeover* is enabled Traktor will ignore all incoming messages until the value they contain matches the current knob position; i.e. the Traktor knob will only change when the received value is larger than 64.

6. When check box *Invert* is enabled Traktor will invert the values received by the control. You can use this option to swap the upper and lower position of a fader, i.e. which position corresponds to the minimum/maximum value. For a knob this option swaps the left and the right side.

7. Use the list *Assignment* in section *Mapping Details* to select the target deck or use the option *Device Target*.

8. Traktor selected two options automatically when this command was added: *Interaction Mode* was set to *Direct* and *Type of Controller* was set to *Fader/Knob*. If this combination is used then the value change of the control exactly matches the change carried out by the mapped knob/fader in Traktor.

An alternative is using the controller type *Fader/Knob* in interaction mode Relative; this is covered in the next tutorial.

Tutorial 4: Controller Type Fader/Knob in Relative Mode

The easiest way to understand the differences between the interaction modes *Direct* and *Relative* offered by controller type *Fader/Knob* is to change the mapping you created for the *Filter Adjust* command in the last tutorial.

1. Open the dialog *Preferences/Controller Manager* if it isn't open. Select the entry *Filter Adjust* in the *Assignment Table*.

2. Open the list *Interaction Mode* and select *Relative*. Traktor displays two sliders in section *Rotary Encoder*.

3. Drag the slider *Rotary Sensitivity* to *50%* or click the field next to the slider, type *50* and press Enter.

4. Now move the knob/fader on your controller and watch how the position of the *Filter* knob in Traktor changes. The sensitivity is reduced. Even when you turn the control of the controller to its outermost positions, the *Filter* knob in Traktor only changes by a quarter of the possible value range.

5. Set the *Rotary Sensitivity* to *100%*. The knob now behaves as controller type *Fader/Knob* in interaction mode *Direct*.

6. Set the *Rotary Sensitivity* to *100%*. The knob in Traktor now reacts more quickly to changes of the MIDI knob.

7. Set the *Rotary Sensitivity* to *70%* and the *Rotary Acceleration* to *10%*. These settings reduce the range of allowed value changes but turning the controller knob faster, result in faster changes of the filter setting.

Tutorial 5: Using the Controller Type Encoder

Most MIDI DJ controllers or CDJs are equipped with endless encoders or jogwheels or both. These controls do not have a defined start or endpoint and they can be turned endlessly in both directions. Traktor supports this type of MIDI control with the controller type *Encoder*.

From a MIDI point of view the main difference between "normal" knobs and faders and endless encoders lies in the content of the messages they send. Endless encoders only send two different values. Traktor uses these two values to distinguish between a right turn and a left turn of the encoder. (Chapter 5, "MIDI Background", contains more detailed information about the format of the MIDI messages.) Endless encoders are very useful for commands like *Browser | List | Select Up/Down* that is used to scroll in the browser window. Or for *Master Clock | Set Master Tempo* which can be used to change the tempo of the Master Clock.

If your controller has either an endless encoder or a jog wheel, try this controller type with the two commands mentioned above. Select the option *Relative* as *Interaction Mode* and open the list *Enc.-Mode*. Then choose one of the available encoder modes. The hexadecimal numbers show the values that the control sends to distinguish between a turn to the left and a turn to the right. If you do not know which values your MIDI controller is sending or if the controller manual does not specify them, the only thing you can do is try them out and see which controller type works.

NOTE   The encoding mode is a MIDI feature, i.e. it is only available for MIDI controllers or if you are using one of the NI controllers in MIDI mode. i.e. not in NHL mode.

As for the controller type *Fader/Knob* in interaction Mode *Relative* you can use the sliders *Rotary Sensitivity* and *Rotary Acceleration* to configure the sensitivity and the acceleration of an *Encoder*.

Use the check box *Invert* if Traktor is to interpret a left turn as a right turn and vice versa.

6.5 MIDI Mapping Options

When you create a controller mapping and use controller type *Button*, the available options are identical to those available for keyboard mapping. The different interaction modes and the options for *Assignment* and *Resolution* are previously explained on page 171 and onward.

The following table summarises the information about the other controller types that are available for controller mappings.

Controller Type	Description
Fader/Knob in Interaction Mode Direct	Use this controller type in combination with interaction Mode Direct for knobs and faders with a defined start and end point and when Traktor shall convert the position of the knob 1by1 to the Traktor knob. This controller type is useful for the Filter, Key or EQ knobs.
Fader/Knob in Interaction Mode Relative	This controller type can as well be used for faders and knobs with a defined start and end point. Additionally, you can reduce the action range of the control. If you do so then the knob in Traktor will not move completely clockwise and anti-clockwise anymore. Moreover, you can configure the acceleration for this controller type. If the knob/fader is moved quickly, this results in a greater value change.
Encoder	The controller type Encoder corresponds to the endless knobs and jogwheels of the controller. This control does not have a defined start and end point; instead they inform Traktor about the direction of the movement. The two different modes in list Enc.-Mode differ in the values they send for a left or a right turn of the control.

6.6 Mappings and the Traktor Kontrol Controllers

When it comes to mapping, the various Traktor Kontrol controllers made by Native Instruments behave slightly differently to the controllers not made by NI. This section explains the most important differences.

Embedded Default Mapping

Traktor detects and configures all Traktor Kontrol controllers via Plug&Play when they are plugged in. Traktor automatically loads the default mapping for the connected device in case the mapping is not already present.

If you open Controller Manager once your Kontrol device is connected and select your controller in list device the dialog looks as shown in the following figure (except for Kontrol X1 MK1). The Assignment table is completely empty, nevertheless the controller is working. The secret: the default mappings of the Traktor Kontrol controllers live in the program code of Traktor and not in editable mappings as is the case for the other controllers. Embedding the mappings has the advantage that Native Instruments can realize a better integration between its own controllers and Traktor and they can use this to give a competitive edge against the controllers of other manufacturers. Furthermore embedding the mappings protects them against accidental changes.

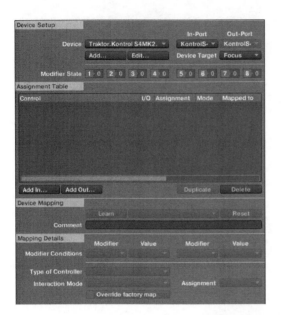

The embedded mappings of the NI controllers can be recognized at the name postfix .Default if you open the list Device. The default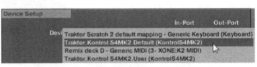
mapping can also be added manually by clicking the *Add* button, pointing to Traktor and then on the name of your controller and finally clicking on *Default*.

> **DOUBELD DEFAULT MAPPING** It is very important that the default mapping for the NI controllers is only activated once. If the mapping is added twice then every action on the controller is triggered twice in Traktor and this may cause some to function incorrectly.
>
> Let's take the Play/Pause button as an example, which uses Interaction Mode Toggle in the embedded mapping. It the mapping is loaded twice, Traktor will toggle Play/Pause twice when you press the Play/Pause button on your controller. The first toggling sets the deck from paused to play and the second toggling sets it from play to pause. Having the same embedded mapping active twice in fact will neutralize the button press. For all commands that do not use interaction mode Toggle, like the channel faders and the knobs for the deck filter, having the mapping active twice does not result into a malfunction. If your NI controller suddenly stops behaving as expected, check whether the Device list contains the same mapping twice.

Even though the embedded mapping cannot be edited directly Traktor provides several methods to change or extend the mappings for the NI controllers.

Creating Your Own User Mapping in NHL Mode

One method to change the default mapping of a NI controller is not to use the embedded mapping at all and to create a complete custom made user mappings. This is very often the preferred method of experienced Traktor users that wish to use a mapping that really fits to their individual work flow.

If you want to create a custom made user mapping it's a best practice to deactivate the default mapping. To deactivate the default mapping:

☐ Select it in list *Device* and then set the *In-Port* to *None*, or

☐ Select it in list *Device*, click on the *Edit* button and then on *Delete*.

To add a new empty user mapping click on the *Add* button, point on Traktor and then on the name of your controller and then click on *User*. Finally open the list *In-Port* and select the port of your controller.

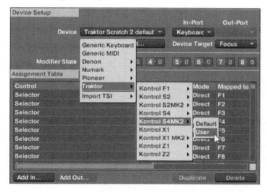

The further steps for creating a user mapping are actually the same as for creating a MIDI mapping. The main difference between the creation of a MIDI mapping and a custom NHL mapping for a NI controller is that Controller Manager shows the name of the controls instead of MIDI messages. Furthermore, for the Out commands you can select the colour of multi-coloured LED buttons as shown in the tutorial on page 177.

You can have the default mapping and a user mapping loaded and activated (i.e., an In-Port has been selected) at the same time. In this case Traktor triggers all functions mapped to a knob/button from both mappings if that control is used.

Using Two Mapping Layers: Switching between NHL and MIDI

The NI controllers lead a double life. On one hand they can use the proprietary NHL mode, on the other hand they can act as a normal MIDI controller. To switch the controller to MIDI mode each controller provides its own button combination (see the overview on page 127 in chapter 5). The two different modes allow switching between NHL mode and MIDI mode while using Traktor; the MIDI mode layer then provides a second mapping layer which you can shape completely to your own needs.

To create a MIDI mapping for a NI controller first add a new device of type Generic MIDI to the Controller Manager (as explained on page 165). Then open the *In-Port* and *Out-Port* lists and select your NI controller. The further steps to create the mapping are identical to the steps you would perform with any other MIDI controller.

Special Case Kontrol F1: User Map instead of MIDI Mode

Traktor Kontrol F1 differs from the other NI controllers regarding switching between the default and a custom mapping. The related setting can be found in the *Preferences* Kontrol F1:

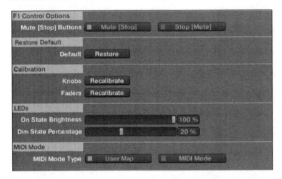

The two checkboxes in section *MIDI Mode* control the behavior of the SHIFT+MIDI button combination of Kontrol F1. Let's have a look at how they work:

◻ **User Map**   When option *User Map* is selected (the default setting), pressing SHIFT+MIDI deactivates the default mapping of F1. The 7 segment display no longer shows the remix set page numbers (P1 – P4), instead only a number.

Then Traktor looks in Controller Manager if there is a user mapping for Kontrol F1. If Traktor finds one, the In-Port of this mapping is set to the port of Kontrol F1. If there is more than one user mapping, Traktor will activate only the first one it could find.

If Traktor could not find an F1 user mapping, Traktor will load the track deck mapping for F1 from the *AutoConfig* folder (see chapter 2). This track deck mapping is a user mapping. The box of F1 contains a printed overlay that shows how the different controls are mapped to deck A and B (hotcues, beatjump, loading tracks, controlling FX units 1 and 2).

If you press SHIFT+MIDI again, Traktor will set the *In-Port* of the user mapping to *None* and the *In-Port* of the default mapping to the port of your Kontrol F1. This deactivates the user mapping and reactivates the default mapping: Kontrol F1 will control the remix decks again.

As long as option *User Map* is active you can also switch between the default mapping and the user mapping in Controller Manager by changing the In-Port setting. If you select an *In-Port* for a user mapping, Traktor will activate this user mapping and automatically disable the default mapping. If you set the *In-Port* of the user mapping to *None*, Traktor will reactivate the default mapping.

◻ **MIDI Mode** If you press SHIFT+MIDI when option MIDI Mode is enabled, Kontrol F1 will no longer send NHL messages but normal MIDI messages. If Kontrol F1 is switched to MIDI mode, all mappings of type *Generic MIDI* become automatically activated, providing that in *Device Setup* the *In-Port* (and *Out-Port*) is set to Kontrol F1.

If you press SHIFT+MIDI to switch back from MIDI mode to NHL mode, Kontrol F1 will send NHL messages again. This enables the default mapping and all NHL user mappings, where Kontrol F1 is selected as In-Port.

What does this mean for the practical usage?

◻ If you wish to use the **alternative track deck mapping** for Kontrol F1, you only need to make sure that in *Preferences/Traktor Kontrol F1* option *User Map* is enabled. Pressing SHIFT+MIDI makes Traktor load and activate the alternative mapping automatically. Make sure that no other F1 user mapping is available in Controller Manager if you wish to use this configuration.

◻ IF you wish to create and use your **custom user mapping**, use *Add/Traktor/ Kontrol F1/User* to add an empty user mapping. If the alternative track deck mapping is already present, delete it.

Make sure that in *Preferences/Traktor Kontrol F1* option *User Map* is enabled and press SHIFT+MIDI to activate the user mapping. Then add the mapping commands you wish to use.

◻ If you want to use **Kontrol F1 with Traktor in MIDI mode**, make sure that in *Preferences/Traktor Kontrol F1* option *MIDI Mode* is enabled. Then Press SHIFT+MIDI to switch F1 to MIDI mode. Go to Controller Manager and use *Add/Generic MIDI* to add a new MIDI device mapping. Set the In-Port and the Out-Port of that device to your Kontrol F1 and add the mapping commands you wish to use.

Tutorial: Overwriting Several Features of the Default Mapping

Even though the mappings of the NI controllers are embedded in the program code of Traktor and cannot be edited in a direct manner, it is possible to edit the default mapping indirectly. One variation of this approach is to assign a completely new feature to one of the controls of your controllers.

Let's assume you wish to use the Gain knobs in the middle section of Kontrol S2 or S4 to change the key of the track manually and not to set the channel gain anymore. Perform the following steps to make the required changes to the default mapping:

1. Open the *Preferences/Controller Manager* dialog, open the list *Device* and select the default mapping of your Kontrol S2/S4. It is important to select the default mapping as this is the only way to overwrite existing features.

2. Select *Add In/Track Deck/Key Adjust* and use the *Learn* button to learn the Gain encoder in the channel strip of deck A.

   Once the encoder is learned, Traktor activates the checkbox *Override factory map* in section *Mapping Details*. If this checkbox is enabled the new command that was assigned to the Gain encoder replaces the command in the embedded mapping (=factory map). And this is exactly what we want to achieve in this tutorial.

3. Open list *Assignment* and select *Deck A*.

4. Set the slider *Rotary Sensitivity* to 65%. With this setting you can set the key in semitone steps (the last section in chapter 12 contains more information about the *Key Adjust* command).

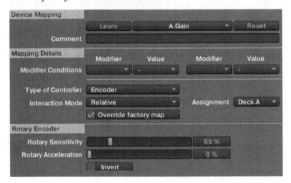

5. Create duplicates of the new command and assign them to deck B to D and the corresponding Gain encoders. (Of course, for Kontrol S2, one duplicate for deck B is sufficient).

6. Select *Add In/Track Deck/Keylock On (Preserve Pitch)* and use *Learn*, to assign pushing of Gain encoder of deck A to this command. Make sure that *Interaction Mode* is set to *Toggle* and select *Deck A* in list *Assignment*.

7. Create duplicates of the new command and assign them to decks B to D and learn the corresponding push actions of the Gain encoders (for Kontrol S2 one duplicate for deck B is sufficient).

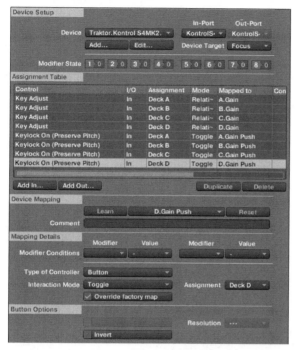

Once you are done the window of Controller Manager should look as shown in the previous figure.

Tutorial: Adding Features and Keeping the Default Mapping

This tutorial uses the mapping from the previous tutorial as a base. The previous tutorial showed how to overwrite the default function of the Gain encoders of Kontrol S2/S4 and how these encoders can be used to change the pitch of a track. The disadvantage of this approach is that the Gain functionality is lost: The newly mapped feature replaces the one from the default mapping.

It does not have to such. In the default mapping of Kontrol S4 and S2 some of the controls behave the same, no matter if the SHIFT button on the controller is held or not. For example, this is the case for the Gain encoders of Kontrol S4 and for the EQ knobs of Kontrol S2. Controls that behave the same can be remapped in a way that the embedded feature remains available when the control is used without holding SHIFT and that a new feature can be added that is only available when you hold SHIFT.

This tutorial shows how to extend the Kontrol S4 mapping from the previous example and get access to the following features:

☐   Without pressing SHIFT you can set the channel gain (this is the feature from the default mapping).

☐   While holding the left SHIFT button you will be able to change the pitch (the feature from the previous tutorial).

☐   Whole holding the right SHIFT button Traktor will show the Autogain value and you can use the Gain encoders to change it.

This approach will retain the embedded features and does allow to add new ones.

> **MODIFIER**   The mapping explained in this tutorial will use the so called modifiers. On the following pages we will show the steps to get the modifiers and this mapping up and running. More comprehensive information about modifiers can be found in section 6.7, "Modifier Basics", on page 198 and onwards.

1. Open *Preferences/Controller Manager* and select in list *Device* the default mapping for the S4 including the changes we made in the previous tutorial.

2. Select *Add In/Modifier/Modifier #1* and use *Learn* to learn the left SHIFT button of your S4.

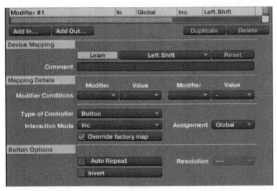

After the "Learn" Traktor uses some default values for the Modifier command that are not suited to what we wish to achieve.

3. Open list *Interaction Mode* and select *Hold* as we wish to know whether the left SHIFT button is pressed or not. Once you select *Hold* Traktor shows the list *Set to Value*.

4. Open the list Set to Value and select 1. Through this the modifier will contain a value of 1 as long as the left SHIFT button is pressed. We will use this value in a moment.

5. Disable the checkbox *Override factory map*.

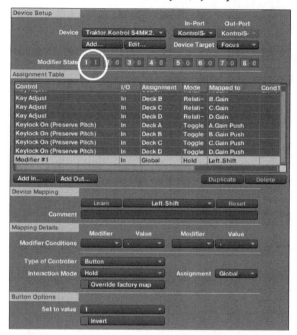

This step is very important as we do not wish to overwrite the default feature of the left SHIFT button; instead we wish to extend it. If option *Override factory map* remains enabled, then all features of the default mapping that use the SHIFT button will be gone.

6. Disable *Learn*. Now press and hold the left SHIFT button and take a look at section *Modifier State* in the upper area of Controller Manager.

   As long as the left SHIFT button is held, Traktor will show the value 1 next to the field of Modifier 1. If you release the SHIFT button the value jumps back to 0. By adding the *Modifier* command we now have inside our mapping access to the current state of the left SHIFT button.

7. Select in *Assignment Table* the command *Key Adjust* for deck A.

8. Open in section *Mapping Details* the first *Modifier* list and select *M1* (short for Modifier #1). Then open list *Value* and select *1*.

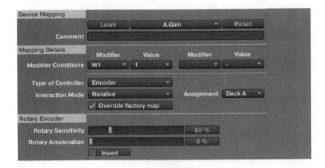

Now the execution of *Key Adjust* depends on the state of the left SHIFT button. At the same time adding the modifier condition re-activates the original feature of the Gain encoder from the default mapping, as the embedded mapping does not contain a modifier condition.

Give it a try: Turning the Gain encoder of deck A now allows you to control the channel gain; holding SHIFT and turning the Gain encoder changes the pitch.

9. Add as explained in the previous step the modifier condition for all entries of *Key Adjust* and *Keylock On (Preserve Pitch)* in the Assignment Table.

Let's now take care of showing and changing the Autogain values.

10. Select *Add In/Mixer/Autogain View On* and use *Learn* to learn the right SHIFT button of your Kontrol S4. Open list *Assignment* and select *Deck A*. Disable the *Override factory* map checkbox to make sure that the right SHIFT button is still available for the default mapping. Keep *Interaction Mode* to *Hold*.

Autogain View On switches the Gain knob of the track decks between display of channel gain and display of the Autogain value. If you press the right SHIFT button now the Gain knob of deck A shows the Autogain value (assuming that the track loaded in deck A is not locked for analysis).

11. Repeat the last step and add *Mixer/Autogain View On* for the other decks. Map these commands to the right SHIFT button as well. Controller Manager should now look like this:

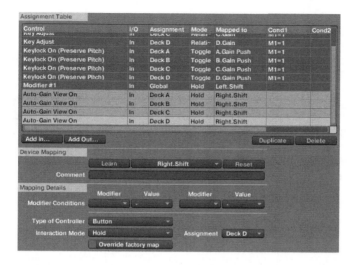

In order to be able to change the Autogain value with the Gain encoders while the right SHIFT button is pressed we need to know – similar as with *Key Adjust* – whether the right SHIFT button is currently held or not. We add a second modifier condition:

12. Select *Add In/Modifier/Modifier #1* and use *Learn* to learn the right SHIFT button of your S4.

13. Configure the following options:

   ▢ Interaction Mode = Hold

   ▢ Override factory map = disabled

   ▢ Set to value = 2

14. Select *Add In/Mixer/Autogain Adjust* and use *Learn* to learn the Gain encoder of your S4. Configure the following options for this command:

   ▢ Modifier Conditions: Modifier M1 = Value 2

   ▢ Assignment = Deck A

   ▢ Override factory map = enabled

   ▢ Rotary Sensitivity = 20%

15. Create duplicates of the command from the previous step and assign them to decks B to D.

The mapping extension is ready. The *Assignment Table* should now look as shown in the following figure:

Assignment Table							
Control	I/O	Assignment	Mode	Mapped to	Cond1	Cond2	Comment
Key Adjust	In	Deck A	Relati~	A.Gain	M1=1		
Key Adjust	In	Deck B	Relati~	B.Gain	M1=1		
Key Adjust	In	Deck C	Relati~	C.Gain	M1=1		
Key Adjust	In	Deck D	Relati~	D.Gain	M1=1		
Keylock On (Preserve Pitch)	In	Deck A	Toggle	A.Gain Push	M1=1		
Keylock On (Preserve Pitch)	In	Deck B	Toggle	B.Gain Push	M1=1		
Keylock On (Preserve Pitch)	In	Deck C	Toggle	C.Gain Push	M1=1		
Keylock On (Preserve Pitch)	In	Deck D	Toggle	D.Gain Push	M1=1		
Modifier #1	In	Global	Hold	Left.Shift			Set M1 to 1
Auto-Gain View On	In	Deck A	Hold	Right.Shift			
Auto-Gain View On	In	Deck B	Hold	Right.Shift			
Auto-Gain View On	In	Deck C	Hold	Right.Shift			
Auto-Gain View On	In	Deck D	Hold	Right.Shift			
Modifier #1	In	Global	Hold	Right.Shift			Set M1 to 2
Auto-Gain Adjust	In	Deck A	Relati~	A.Gain	M1=2		
Auto-Gain Adjust	In	Deck B	Relati~	B.Gain	M1=2		
Auto-Gain Adjust	In	Deck C	Relati~	C.Gain	M1=2		
Auto-Gain Adjust	In	Deck D	Relati~	D.Gain	M1=2		

Tutorial: Using the eight unused Pads of Kontrol F1

You can use your Kontrol F1 to set the quantize value of a remix deck by holding the QUANT button and then either using the encoder or pressing one of the eight pads on the left side of the controller. While the QUANT button is held, the eight pads on the right side of the F1 are not assigned to any function.

This makes it easy to add some new features to the F1 without overwriting any existing function. This tutorial shows as an example how two of the pads can be used to scroll through the favorites.

We will add the required commands to the default mapping of Kontrol F1:

1. Open the *Preferences/Controller Manager* dialog and select the default mapping of Kontrol F1 in the list *Device*. It is important to select the default mapping and not a user mapping, because Traktor treats the Kontrol F1 user mappings slightly different than the ones made for the other NI controllers (see page 188).

2. Select *Add In/Modifier/Modifier #1* and use *Learn* to assign the QUANT button of F1 to this command.

3. Make sure that the added command is selected and configure the following options:

   ▢ Interaction Mode = Hold

   ▢ Override factory map = disabled

   ▢ Set to value = 1

   Make sure that option *Override factory map* is disabled, as we wish to extend the functionality of the QUANT button and not replace the functionality of the default mapping.

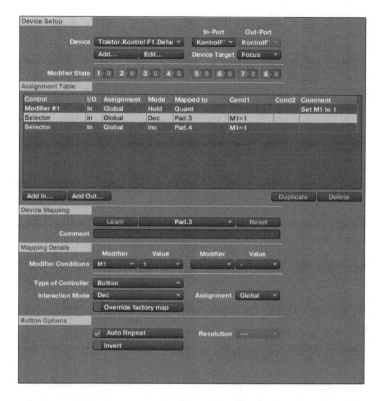

4. Select *Add In/Browser/Favorites/Selector* and use *Learn* to assign the third pad in the first row.

5. Configure the following options for this command:

   □ Modifier Conditions: Modifier M1 = Value 1

   □ Interaction Mode = Dec

   □ Auto Repeat = enabled

   With this settings you can browse backwards (=Dec) through the favourites. By enabling Auto Repeat you can keep the pad pressed and Traktor will then open bit by bit the available favourites until the first is reached.

   As the button combination QUANT+PAD3 is not assigned in the default mapping, it is irrelevant here whether option *Override factory map* is enabled or not.

6. Create a duplicate of the command added in the last step, learn the fourth pad in the first row and set *Interaction Mode* to *Inc*.

   With these settings you can scroll forwards through your favourites.

The complete mapping extension in Controller Manager appears as shown in the figure on the previous page.

> **TIP**   If you assigned one of the favourites to the browser filter "All Remix Sets", you can add another Selector command, use *Interaction Mode Direct* and select the favourite in list *Set to value*. Learn this command to another pad and use the same modifier condition as in the tutorial. This allows you to show open all remix sets in the browser and makes loading a remix set easier and quicker.

6.7 Modifier Basics

Traktor uses so called modifiers to allow you to create something similar to keyboard shortcuts (a function is only triggered when two keys are pressed at the same time) for your mappings.

The easiest way to understand a modifier is to look at it from a programming perspective. In short, modifiers are variables to which a value can be assigned. The value of the variable can be queried and it is possible to instruct Traktor that the execution of a mapped command depends on a particular value of a modifier.

Modifiers are Variables

In programming, variables are named memory locations where values can be stored. Traktor provides eight variables in total; here they are called "modifiers". The name of the modifier starts with the letter M and a digit between 1 and 8 is appended, as in M1, M2 etc. You can store a value in the range from 0 to 7 in a modifier. The default value is 0.

Assigning Values to Modifiers

To store a value in a modifier use one of the mapping commands *Modifier #1* to *Modifier #8*. These commands can be found in the submenu *Modifier* of the *Add In* button. Once you have added one of the *Modifier* commands the lower section of the dialog looks like the following figure (here interaction mode *Hold* is selected):

◻ In list *Interaction Mode* the option *Hold* has been selected. This means that the modifier contains the value selected in the list *Set to value* for as long as the mapped button is pressed.

If you use interaction mode *Direct* instead, then the value is stored when the mapped button is pressed. The value is retained even when the button is released.

◻ In list *Type of Controller* the option *Button* is selected. This does not mean that the only way of storing a value in a modifier is by using a button on your controller. You can select the controller type Button in the dialog and use any of the controls on your controller.

◻ Finally, the section *Button Options* contains the list box *Set to value*. Select the value here that you want to store in the modifier.

Let's continue with a simple example that uses five buttons in total:

◻ One button (called button A) shall be used to set and activate a 4-beat-loop.

◻ Four other buttons (called buttons 1–4) shall control whether the loop must be set in deck A, B, C or D, when one of these buttons is pressed at the same time as button A.

In this example we would use one modifier, let's say Modifier #1. The modifier value would represent the four decks. Deck A corresponds to value 1, deck B will be 2, deck C will be 3 and deck D will be 4.

First thing we need to do is create the mappings for the buttons 1 to 4. When button 1 is pressed the modifier value shall be 1, value 2 for button 2 etc. Once all four mappings are added to the assignment table the mapping dialog will look like the following figure. Note the column *Comment* in the figure; here I entered the stored values because otherwise they cannot be seen in the *Assignment Table*.

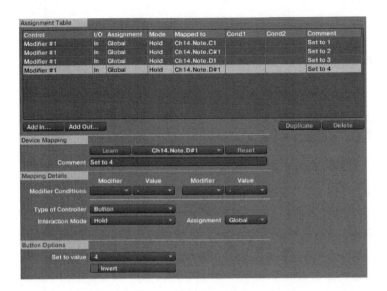

The values of all eight modifiers of the currently selected logical controller are shown next to *Modifier State*. Try it out with the four mapped buttons. As long as the mapped button is held the related value is displayed next to the field for modifier #1. The *Modifier State* display is an excellent tool to find bugs in a mapping.

Querying Modifier Values

One thing you can do with modifiers is assign a value to them. The other thing is querying their current value and then making the execution of mapped commands dependent on that value. In programmers terms this is called an, if-then-clause.

Let's return to the example of activating a 4 beat loop for one of the decks. Strictly speaking we need four more commands that use the following, if-then logic:

◻   If Modifier #1 has value 1, then set the loop in deck A.

◻   If Modifier #1 has value 2, then set the loop in deck B.

◻   If Modifier #1 has value 3, then set the loop in deck C.

◻   If Modifier #1 has value 4, then set the loop in deck D.

Let's start the implementation with deck A.

1. Click on *Add In*, then on *Deck Common/Loop* and finally on *Loop Size Select + Set*. This is the command for setting the loop-length and activating the loop at the same time.

2. Open the list *Interaction Mode* and select Direct; then open the list *Type of Controller* and select *Button*.

3. Open the list *Set to value* and click on *4*; we want to set a 4 beat loop here.

4. Open the list *Assignment* and select *Deck A*.

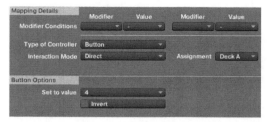

So far the steps for creating the mapping are identical to those explained earlier. Now for the exciting part and it is here in section *Modifier Conditions*

5. Open the first list labelled *Modifier* and select *M1*.

6. Open the first list labelled *Value* and select *1*.

With this, the first of the, if-then-clauses mentioned earlier is implemented. The purpose of the section *Modifier Conditions* is to make the execution of a command dependent on a certain value of a certain modifier.

7. Click *Learn* and then press the button on your MIDI controller that you wish to use for deck A. Click *Learn* again to exit learn mode.

Now the *Controller Manager* dialog should look like this:

The condition that has been defined in section *Modifier Conditions* is now displayed in column *Mod1* in the *Assignment Table* as *M1=1*.

8. To complete the mapping create three duplicates of the row *Loop Size Select +
   Set*. Change the *Assignment* in the first duplicate to *Deck B* and the value in *Value*
   to *2*; for the second duplicate use *Deck C* and the value of *3*; and for the third
   duplicate use *Deck* D and a value of *4*.

After these steps the *Assignment Table* should look like this:

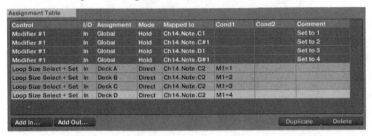

Control	I/O	Assignment	Mode	Mapped to	Cond1	Cond2	Comment
Modifier #1	In	Global	Hold	Ch14.Note.C1			Set to 1
Modifier #1	In	Global	Hold	Ch14.Note.C#1			Set to 2
Modifier #1	In	Global	Hold	Ch14.Note.D1			Set to 3
Modifier #1	In	Global	Hold	Ch14.Note.D#1			Set to 4
Loop Size Select + Set	In	Deck A	Direct	Ch14.Note.C2	M1=1		
Loop Size Select + Set	In	Deck B	Direct	Ch14.Note.C2	M1=2		
Loop Size Select + Set	In	Deck C	Direct	Ch14.Note.C2	M1=3		
Loop Size Select + Set	In	Deck D	Direct	Ch14.Note.C2	M1=4		

Add In...   Add Out...   Duplicate   Delete

Note that for all four *Loop Size Select + Set* commands the same note is shown in
column *Mapped to*. The distinction which deck shall be looped is done solely by
the conditions we defined, i.e. by the value of the modifier.

Using Modifier Buttons as Shift Keys

Another way to understand modifiers is to consider them as shift keys like those found
on a computer keyboard. Almost all common software uses the function keys of the
keyboard to enable users to choose commands quickly and without searching in the
sometimes complicated and nested menu structures. Twelve function keys isn't really
that many and so key combinations with the so called shift keys are often used like
Alt+F1, Ctrl+F5, and sometimes even shortcuts where two shift keys and one function
key are combined like Alt+Ctrl+F2, etc.

The modifiers in Traktor actually use the same concept. The control elements of a
MIDI controller can be logically divided into "shift keys", i.e. buttons activating a
modifier and "function keys". The actual Traktor functionality is assigned to the
"function keys" which may not only be a button, but an encoder, jog wheel etc. as well.

There is one important difference between the shift keys on the regular keyboard like
Ctrl, Alt, etc., which can have one of two states (pressed, not pressed) only and the
modifiers in Traktor, which can be set to one of eight different values in the range from
0 to 7. The value 0 is the default value and corresponds to the button state "not
pressed".

Although different interaction modes can be used with the modifiers the most important are *Hold* (the modifier and the assigned value are active as long as the button
is pressed) and *Direct* (pressing the button assigns the selected value to the modifier).

When using interaction mode *Hold* the button on the MIDI controller acts like the Ctrl key or the Alt key on the keyboard: you need to keep the button pressed while pressing the control a Traktor function is assigned to.

By using the Interaction Mode *Direct* you can achieve functionality similar to the Caps Lock key (for permanent capitalization) or Num Lock key on the numeric pad of a keyboard. By using *Direct* you can set the value of the modifier and the modifier retains this value (in the range from 0 to 7) even when the modifier button is released. You can use the interaction mode *Direct* to implement buttons that toggle the value of a modifier. When the button is pressed the first time the modifier is set, when the button is pressed the second time the modifier value is deleted. This can be done by using a modifier condition, i.e. the value to which the modifier is set depends on the current value of the modifier. You need to assign two MIDI mappings to the same button as shown in the following table:

Modifier #1	Interaction Mode: Direct	Set to value: 1	Modifier Condition: M1=0
Modifier #1	Interaction Mode: Direct	Set to value: 0	Modifier Condition: M1=1

The action in the first row (Set to value: 1) is executed if modifier # 1 has the value 0; the action in the second row (Set to value: 0) is executed if modifier # 1 has a value of 1.

This toggling can be done by the same control on the MIDI controller, but you can also use different controls: one control sets the modifier value and another one resets it. Section "Example 1: Crossfader for Panning – Enhanced Version" on page 219 explains how a fader is used to set the modifier value and how this value is evaluated by a button which resets the value if a certain condition is met.

Using two Modifier Conditions

The section *Modifier Conditions* contains not only one list to define modifier conditions but two. This means that the execution of a command can be based on the values of two different modifiers. Both conditions are combined by a logical AND; i.e. both conditions must be true for the mapped command to be executed.

By using two modifier conditions, one control can be mapped to several different mapping commands. This corresponds to keyboard shortcuts that use a combination of different shift keys, for example: F1, Shift+F1, Ctrl+F1, Shift+Ctrl+F1 etc. If you wish to create a similar mapping it is important to reserve the default modifier value for the state "button is not pressed". If we transfer the example of the four keyboard shortcuts mentioned above to a modifier implementation, then the conditions that must be entered into the *Modifier Conditions* are as such:

Keyboard Shortcut	"Shift" Modifier M1	"Ctrl" Modifier M2
F1	M1=0	M2=0
Shift+F1	M1=1	M2=0
Ctrl+F1	M1=0	M2=1
Shift+Ctrl+F1	M1=1	M2=1

Creating these mappings is not too difficult. What can become difficult is keeping an overview about the buttons acting as modifiers. It is helpful to first plan and design the mapping and not to do the actual implementation until the planning is done.

Using Traktor Status Values as Modifiers

As well the modifier variables that you can assign a value to and those values can be queried in a condition, Traktor provides several status values that can be used as a modifier condition as well. Those status values can be found at the end of the list with the modifier conditions.

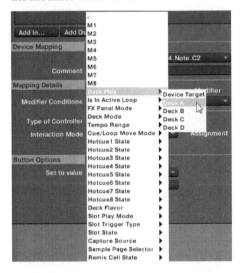

The following table explains the different conditions and the meaning of the status values available:

Condition	Description
Deck Play	Specifies if a deck is currently playing or not.
Is In Active Loop	Specifies if the playback marker is currently inside a loop or not. 0=Playback marker outside of a loop 1=Playback marker inside of a loop

Condition	Description
FX Panel Mode	Specifies the current mode of an FX unit (Single/Group).
Deck Mode	Specifies if the deck is currently set to internal playback or to scratch control.
Tempo Range	Specifies the currently selected tempo range of a deck (available options start at 2% and go up to 100%).
Cue/Loop Move Mode	Specifies the current Move mode as it can be selected in the Advanced Move Panel (Beatjump, Loop, Loop In, Loop Out).
Hotcue x State	Specifies the cue point type assigned to Hotcue x (None, Cue, Fade-In, Fade-Out, Load, Grid, Loop).
Deck Flavor	Specifies the currently selected type of a deck (Track Deck, Remix Deck, Live Input).
Slot Play Mode	Specifies whether a loop or a one-shot is currently loaded in the slot of a remix deck.
Slot Trigger Type	Specifies the current trigger mode of the sample loaded in one of the slots of a remix deck (Latched, Gated).
Slot State	Specifies the current status of a slot in a sample deck (Empty, Loaded, Playing).
Capture Source	Specifies the currently selected capture source for a remix deck (Loop Recorder, one of the track decks).
Sample Page Selector	Specifies which page of a remix set is currently selected in a remix deck (page 1 – 4).
Remix Cell State	Specifies the current state of a cell in a remix deck (Empty, Loaded, Playing, Waiting

For example, the *Deck Play* **condition** is useful if you wish to let an LED blink in time with the beat (as explained on page 235). You can let the button blink only if the deck is in play. If the deck is currently paused you can output the status of the *Play/Pause* **command** to make sure that the button is then off.

The *Deck Mode* condition is useful for a mapping that works similar to the double mapping of the buttons CUE|REL and CUP|ABS on the MK1 version of the  Kontrol X1 controller. In deck mode *Internal Playback* both buttons work as the corresponding *CUE* and *CUP* button in the transport section of the decks. If the deck mode is set to *Scratch Control* the buttons can be used to switch between relative and absolute timecode tracking mode. An excerpt of a mapping with this implementation can be seen in the following figure. Additionally the assignment table shows the usage of *Play/Pause* condition as mentioned in the previous paragraph.

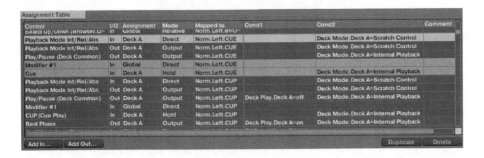

Assignment Table							
Control	I/O	Assignment	Mode	Mapped to	Cond1	Cond2	Comment
Select Up/Down (Browser.Li~	In	Global	Relative	Norm.Left.BRO~			
Playback Mode Int/Rel/Abs	In	Deck A	Direct	Norm.Left.CUE		Deck Mode.Deck A=Scratch Control	
Playback Mode Int/Rel/Abs	Out	Deck A	Output	Norm.Left.CUE		Deck Mode.Deck A=Scratch Control	
Play/Pause (Deck Common)	Out	Deck A	Output	Norm.Left.CUE		Deck Mode.Deck A=Internal Playback	
Modifier #1	In	Global	Direct	Norm.Left.CUE			
Cue	In	Deck A	Hold	Norm.Left.CUE		Deck Mode.Deck A=Internal Playback	
Playback Mode Int/Rel/Abs	In	Deck A	Direct	Norm.Left.CUP		Deck Mode.Deck A=Scratch Control	
Playback Mode Int/Rel/Abs	Out	Deck A	Output	Norm.Left.CUP		Deck Mode.Deck A=Scratch Control	
Play/Pause (Deck Common)	Out	Deck A	Output	Norm.Left.CUP	Deck Play.Deck A=off	Deck Mode.Deck A=Internal Playback	
Modifier #1	In	Global	Direct	Norm.Left.CUP			
CUP (Cue Play)	In	Deck A	Hold	Norm.Left.CUP		Deck Mode.Deck A=Internal Playback	
Beat Phase	Out	Deck A	Output	Norm.Left.CUP	Deck Play.Deck A=on	Deck Mode.Deck A=Internal Playback	

Add In...   Add Out...   Duplicate   Delete

HOW TO: Setting and Outputting the Tempo Range

All Pioneer CD players, which are supported by Traktor in HID mode, have a button to select the tempo range of the player's pitch fader. The currently selected tempo range is shown on the display of the controller. Here are two examples showing the CDJ-400 and the CDJ-2000 nexus.

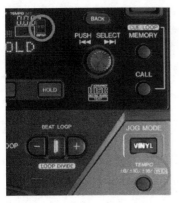

In the *Preferences/Transport* dialog you cannot change the tempo range for an individual deck but you can accomplish this by using the *Deck Common | Tempo Range Selector* command. If you map this command to a button, the *Preferences/Controller Manager* looks as shown in the next figure:

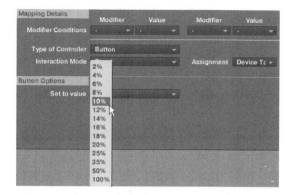

This figure uses the interaction mode *Direct*. The modes *Hold, Inc, Dec* and *Reset* are also available. Interaction mode *Reset* sets the tempo fader range to 8%. This simple example shows how to select a particular tempo range.

How can you map one button in a way that it can be used to switch between some selected pitch ranges – for example between 6%, 10%, 16%, and 100% – to simulate the functionality of the *Tempo* button of a Pioneer the CDJ. The interaction modes *Inc* and *Dec* are unsuitable, because each mode iterates through the complete list of available ranges. Instead, we need a mapping with four *Tempo Range Selector* commands and each command must activate the next desired range. For example, the button must switch to 10% if the current pitch range is 6%.

To be able to create such a mapping we need the modifier condition *Tempo Range.Deck[X]* which behaves like the "normal" modifiers containing a value: However, the value of this special modifier is read-only. It cannot be changed directly; instead it reflects one particular Traktor status. This modifier type is selected in list *Modifier* of section *Mapping Details* as with the already existing types M1 to M8. Once you click on *Tempo Range* a submenu is opened; here you select one of the decks or option *Device Target*. Then you can use the list *Values* to select the percentage value that shall be used in the condition.

To create the mapping that switches between the four desired pitch ranges we need the following four commands. The first command shall be executed if the current value of modifier Tempo Range for the selected deck is 6%; in this case the pitch range of the deck shall be set to 10%, etc.

No.	Switch from/to	Command	Condition
1	6% to 10%	Tempo Range Selector, Set to value=10% Select Deck in list Assignment	Tempo Range.Deck[x] = 6% Select Deck in Condition submenu

No.	Switch from/to	Command	Condition
2	10% to 16%	Tempo Range Selector, Set to value=16% Select Deck in list Assignment	Tempo Range.Deck[x] = 10% Select Deck in Condition sub-menu
3	16% to 100%	Tempo Range Selector, Set to value=100% Select Deck in list Assignment	Tempo Range.Deck[x] = 16%, select Deck in Condition sub-menu
4	100% to 6%	Tempo Range Selector, Set to value=6% Select Deck in list Assignment	Tempo Range.Deck[x] = 100%, select Deck in Condition sub-menu

However, the problem with this mapping is that the tempo range will only be changed if one of the defined conditions is true, i.e. if the current tempo range is either 6%, 10%, 16%, or 100%. If, for example, the tempo range for all decks has been reset to 50% in dialog *Preferences/Transport*, the tempo range cannot be changed with this mapping because neither one of the conditions in the third column of the table is true.

This issue can be solved by considering all fourteen possible Tempo Range values in the conditions of this mapping. In other words: we need to map fourteen commands with different conditions to make sure, that one of the conditions is true when the mapped button is pressed for the first time. The following table contains the complete mapping for this example:

No.	Switch Range from/to	Command	Condition
1.1	6% to 10%	Tempo Range Selector Set to value=10%	Tempo Range.Deck[x] = 6%
1.2	8% to 10%	Tempo Range Selector Set to value=10%	Tempo Range.Deck[x] = 8%
2.1	10% to 16%	Tempo Range Selector Set to value=16%	Tempo Range.Deck[x] = 10%
2.2	12% to 16%	Tempo Range Selector Set to value=16%	Tempo Range.Deck[x] = 12%
2.3	14% to 16%	Tempo Range Selector Set to value=16%	Tempo Range.Deck[x] = 14%
3.1	16% to 100%	Tempo Range Selector Set to value=100%	Tempo Range.Deck[x] = 16%
3.2	18% to 100%	Tempo Range Selector Set to value=100%	Tempo Range.Deck[x] = 18%
3.3	20% to 100%	Tempo Range Selector Set to value=100%	Tempo Range.Deck[x] = 20%
3.4	25% to 100%	Tempo Range Selector Set to value=100%	Tempo Range.Deck[x] = 25%

No.	Switch Range from/to	Command	Condition
3.5	35% to 100%	Tempo Range Selector Set to value=100%	Tempo Range.Deck[x] = 35%
3.6	50% to 100%	Tempo Range Selector Set to value=100%	Tempo Range.Deck[x] = 50%
4.1	100% to 6%	Tempo Range Selector Set to value=6%	Tempo Range.Deck[x] = 100%
4.2	2% to 6%	Tempo Range Selector Set to value=6%	Tempo Range.Deck[x] = 2%
4.3	4% to 6%	Tempo Range Selector Set to value=6%	Tempo Range.Deck[x] = 4%

Displaying the current Pitch Range on a Controller

The current tempo range can be sent to the display of the supported Pioneer CDJs or it can be sent to a normal LED. To achieve this, use the Out command *Deck Common | Tempo Range Selector* from the menu *Add Out*. If you wish to output one of the ranges to one LED or display element you need to enter the value of the Tempo Range as well in *Controller Range/Min* as in *Controller Range/Max* of section *LED Options*.

6.8 More Usage Examples for Modifiers

After this more general information and the previous simple example, the next section contains some examples of how you can use modifiers to switch the function of a control permanently or temporarily. And you will see what can be done with macros (assigning more than one mapping command to the same control).

Example 1: Using Modifiers to select Presets permanently and for choosing Decks

This example uses the Behringer controllers BCR2000 and BCF2000, both of which have a lot of encoders, buttons and faders. In the upper right corner of both controllers four buttons can be found which originally select which encoder group should be active. Depending on which encoder group is selected, the push encoders in the upper section of the controller have different functions. This way it is possible to assign 64 different mapping commands to the eight encoders: 8x4 for pushing the encoders and 8x4 for turning them.

Let's assume we want to use the first four encoders to control Traktors' 4 band equalizer: turning the encoder controls the increase or reduction of one of the frequency ranges and pushing the encoder shall be assigned to the kill function of the same frequency range. Additionally we can assume that the four buttons in the upper right shall be used to select, whether the push encoders control deck A, deck B, deck C or deck D.

This configuration can be implemented easily by using modifiers. First you need one modifier, for example modifier #1, and then assign different values to this modifier according to which of the four buttons for selecting the encoder group (in our implementation used to select a deck) has been pressed. The following table shows the mapping configuration you need to implement in Traktor:

Controller Button	Mapping Command	Interaction Mode	Type of Controller	Set to value
1	Modifier #1	Direct	Button	1
2	Modifier #1	Direct	Button	2
3	Modifier #1	Direct	Button	3
4	Modifier #1	Direct	Button	4

It is important to use the same modifier and to choose the interaction mode *Direct* so that Traktor remembers the value to which the modifier is set.

NOTE   A different approach would be to use four different modifiers and then set the four modifiers to the same value. Whichever concept you use will depend on the overall configuration of your controller.

The actual implementation of the modifier is done in the dialog box *Preferences | Controller Manager*.

1. Click on *Add In*, open the submenu *Modifier* and click the desired modifier (in our example *Modifier #1*).

2. Click on *Learn* and press the button on your controller.

3. Open the list *Interaction Mode* and select *Direct*; then open the list *Type of Controller* and select the option *Button*.

4. Open the list box *Set to value* and select 1.

5. Make sure the new line is selected and click *Duplicate*. Traktor creates a copy of the selected entry.

6. Select in the list *Assignment Table* the copy Traktor created and press the button on your controller that shall be used to activate the second preset (in our case deck B); open the list box *Set to value* and select the value 2.

7. Repeat the last two steps for the two remaining buttons and in the list box select *Set to value*, 3 for the third button value and four for the forth button value.

This completes the implementation of the modifiers. The *Controller Manager* dialog should look like the following figure:

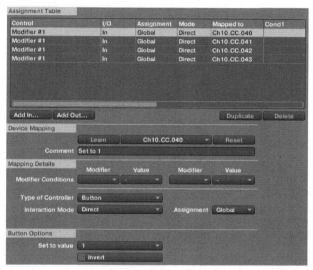

As previously mentioned, the first four push encoders shall control the equalizer:

▢ In the dialog box *Preferences | Mixer* the option *Xone* for *EQ Type* has been selected so we can use the 4 band equalizer.

▢ Turning the encoder controls the increase or decrease of the frequency range, pressing the encoder will kill it.

▢ The first encoder shall be assigned to the high frequencies, the second the middle frequencies, the third the middle low frequencies and last but not least the fourth the low frequency range.

▢ To which deck the equalizer settings will be sent depends on the value of modifier #1.

The following table shows the mapping for the commands *High Adjust* and *Mid Adjust*. The value of column *Mapped to* is important and needs to be set by using the Learn function.

Encoder on Controller	Traktor Mapping Command	Mapped to	Assign-ment	Modifier Condition
1	Mixer | EQ | High Adjust	CC 112	Deck A	M1=1
1	Mixer | EQ | High Adjust	CC 112	Deck B	M1=2
1	Mixer | EQ | High Adjust	CC 112	Deck C	M1=3
1	Mixer | EQ | High Adjust	CC 112	Deck D	M1=4
2	Mixer | EQ | Mid Adjust	CC 113	Deck A	M1=1
2	Mixer | EQ | Mid Adjust	CC 113	Deck B	M1=2
2	Mixer | EQ | Mid Adjust	CC 113	Deck C	M1=3
2	Mixer | EQ | Mid Adjust	CC 113	Deck D	M1=4
	Etc.		...	...

As explained in the section about the modifier basics the modifier acts like a condition; the condition will be evaluated by Traktor when the actual mapping command is executed: If modifier #1 is set to 1, then the mapping command is sent to deck A; if the modifier is set to 2, then the command is sent to deck B; and so forth. The following figure shows how the implementation for *High Adjust* appears in the *Controller Manager* dialog. The condition/s in columns *Mod1* and *Mod2* need to be true in order that Traktor executes the command:

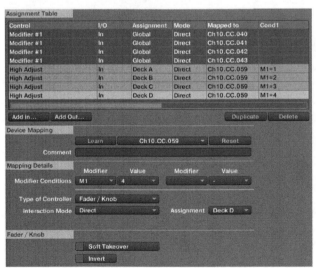

Once the overall structure is implemented, the remaining work is just about connecting the dots. If all eight push encoders are to be configured as explained it is good practice to test the implementation of each encoder so see if everything works as intended.

A similar implementation can be used for Traktor features that have a knob and a button on the user interface (like the Key or Filter feature).

If you work mainly with two decks another variation could be to use the first group of four encoders to control the equalizer of deck A and the second group of encoders to control deck B. In this case the buttons for switching the encoder groups can be used to toggle between the equalizer and the FX units. For example, if button 1 is pressed the equalizer is active. When button 2 is pressed the push encoders can be used to control the FX units. The first group of four encoders can be mapped to control FX unit 1 and the second group of four encoders to control FX unit 2.

The four buttons in the upper right corner of the controller could be configured in the same way as explained above. The only thing that would change are the conditions that control whether the pressing and turning of the encoders is sent to the equalizer or to the FX units. The following table shows an example of this mapping:

Encoder	Mapping Command	Mapped To	Assign-ment	Modifier Condition
1	Mixer | EQ | High Adjust	CC 112	Deck A	M1=1
2	Mixer | EQ | Mid Adjust	CC 113	Deck A	M1=1
3	Mixer | EQ | Mid Low Adjust	CC 114	Deck A	M1=1
4	Mixer | EQ | Low Adjust	CC 115	Deck A	M1=1
5	Mixer | EQ | High Adjust	CC 116	Deck B	M1=1
6	Mixer | EQ | Mid Adjust	CC 117	Deck B	M1=1
7	Mixer | EQ | Mid Low Adjust	CC 118	Deck B	M1=1
8	Mixer | EQ | Low Adjust	CC 119	Deck B	M1=1
1	FX Unit | Dry Wet Adjust	CC 112	FX Unit 1	M1=2
2	FX Unit | Knob 1	CC 113	FX Unit 1	M1=2
3	FX Unit | Knob 2	CC 114	FX Unit 1	M1=2
4	FX Unit | Knob 3	CC 115	FX Unit 1	M1=2
5	FX Unit | Dry Wet Adjust	CC 116	FX Unit 2	M1=2
6	FX Unit | Knob 1	CC 117	FX Unit 2	M1=2
7	FX Unit | Knob 2	CC 118	FX Unit 2	M1=2
8	FX Unit | Knob 3	CC 119	FX Unit 2	M1=2

Example 2: Using Modifiers for temporarily Switching

The second example of using modifiers shows how to use modifiers for shift buttons. As an example I will be using the Xone:3D by Allen&Heath. Even though this mixer has been replaced by the Xone:4D, the Xone:3D was ground-breaking for its time and still having it in the Traktor Bible is a tribute to this great DJing tool. The standard mapping provided by Allen&Heath used two shift buttons for each deck. The red shift button is named ALT and the blue shift button is named SHIFT, as you can see in the following figure:

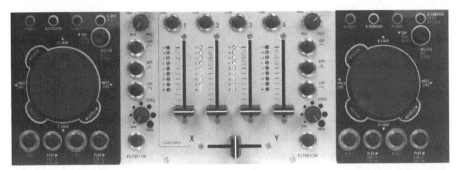

This concept allows building a controller mapping with three layers: one layer is active if none of the shift buttons is pressed, the second layer is activated with the Alt and the third layer with the Shift button. This architecture can also be used in mappings for other controllers.

The actual function of almost all other elements of the controller depends on whether the ALT or the SHIFT button is held or whether none one the buttons is held while another control is used. For such a configuration it is recommended to use four modifiers: assign each modifier to one deck (1=A, 2=B, 3=C, 4=D) and then use different modifier values for the ALT and the SHIFT function (ALT=1, SHIFT=2).

The modifier configuration for this example can be found in the following table:

Button on Controller	Modifier	Interaction Mode	Set to value
A-ALT	Modifier #1	Hold	1
A-SHIFT	Modifier #1	Hold	2
B-ALT	Modifier #2	Hold	1
B-SHIFT	Modifier #2	Hold	2
C-ALT	Modifier #3	Hold	1
C-SHIFT	Modifier #3	Hold	2
D-ALT	Modifier #4	Hold	1
D-SHIFT	Modifier #4	Hold	2

In contrast to example 1, here the interaction mode *Hold* is used, i.e. here the modifier sets the value only if the button is pressed. If the modifier button is not pressed the modifier has the standard value 0.

Once the buttons that serve as "shift keys" are mapped, the remaining work is just filling in the dots. Here the button *Duplicate* is your best friend and helps to get it done easily and quickly.

For our example the configuration of the four PLAY buttons of the controller would look like this:

Button on Controller	Mapping Command	Assignment	Modifier Condition
PLAY A	Deck Common | Play/Pause	Deck A	M1=0
PLAY A	Deck Common | Cue	Deck A	M1=1
PLAY A	Deck Common | CUP (Cue Play)	Deck A	M1=2
PLAY B	Deck Common | Play/Pause	Deck B	M2=0
PLAY B	Deck Common | Cue	Deck B	M2=1
PLAY B	Deck Common | CUP (Cue Play)	Deck B	M2=2
PLAY C	Deck Common | Play/Pause	Deck C	M3=0
Etc.			

> **IMPORTANT** It is necessary to define a modifier condition for all three cases (PLAY pressed, ALT hold + PLAY pressed, SHIFT hold + PLAY pressed). If you do not define a modifier condition for the case that only the PLAY button is pressed (i.e. the condition *M1=0* is missing) the mapped mapping command will **always** be executed, no matter what the value of the modifier is at that moment.

A variation of such a deck oriented implementation could be to assign two mapping commands (a mini macro) to the ALT and SHIFT buttons of the controller:

- ❑ The first implemented command assigns a modifier to each deck and uses different modifier values for the ALT button and the SHIFT button.

- ❑ The second command assigned to the same button is Layout | Deck Focus Selector, Interaction Mode: Direct, Set to value: Deck A – Deck D (depending on which of the buttons has been pressed).

If, in this approach one of the modifier buttons is pressed, both the modifier value is changed and the focus is set. Also when mapping the four *PLAY* buttons you can use the option *Focus* in the list box *Assignment,* because the deck you wish to control already has the focus.

Example 3: Simulating a button that has more than 2 States

You can even use modifiers to program buttons that have more than two states. A practical example can be found in section "Variation 3: Select all possible Assignments between two FX Units and one Deck with one button" in chapter 13, "FX – The Traktor Effects". The example used there shows how to program a button that allows switching between the four possible assignments between a deck and an FX unit.

Planning your MIDI Mapping

Particularly when using modifiers and more general with controller mapping a little bit of planning and a structured approach is advantageous because the *Controller Manager* dialog is a bit cumbersome and making changes later leads to a lot of effort. A few hints:

◘ Make yourself familiar with the possibilities the mapping commands offer, so that you know what can be done.

◘ Choose from the more than 300 mapping commands those you wish to use with your controller. Use keyboard shortcuts for actions that are least needed to make best use of the limited number of control elements on your controller.

◘ Become familiar with the macro possibilities and consider, which combinations of mapping commands are needed for which functionality (the following section contains some examples).

◘ Decide whether you wish to manage your mappings for one keyboard and one controller device or if it makes sense to use several logical controllers for the same physical device. When you use more than one controller it is always good practice to create a separate logical controller for each physical device. This will help you to stay in control of your mappings.

◘ Either make a little sketch of your controllers or make a copy of a suitable page from the controller manual. Use it to plan your implementation.

◘ Decide which buttons shall act as modifier buttons.

◘ Divide your controller into functional groups and assign the necessary functionality to the controls of your controller.

◘ First implement all modifiers.

◘ Then implement all necessary mapping commands.

◘ Test if everything works as intended regularly.

6.9 More Examples of using Macros

Almost all Traktor mapping commands are realised as atomic commands, i.e. one mapping command triggers exactly one action in Traktor. But, it is possible to assign several mapping commands to *one control* on the MIDI controller. This is called "macro" and opens fantastic possibilities to customise the controller mapping just the way you need it.

The following sections contain four simple examples showing what can be done by assigning two or even more mapping commands to the same control element of a controller.

Example 1: Searching for a Track, loading it into a Deck and changing the Size of the Trackbrowser

If you use cover art or work with four decks and a lower screen resolution finding a track in the track browser can be a bit difficult because the space for the track browser is limited. You can use the command *Layout | Only Browser On* (corresponds to the magnifier button in the header) to change the size of the track browser. This section explains how to implement one control on the controller to scroll in the track list and to open the track browser in maximized view and another control to load the selected track and to minimize the track browser. The example assumes that a jog wheel is used to scroll the track list and that a button is used to load the selected track.

1. Assign the command *Browser | List | Select Up/Down* to the jog wheel to implement scrolling in the tracklist.

2. Additionally assign the mapping command *Layout | Only Browser On* to the jog wheel as well and use the following parameters: *Interaction Mode=Direct, Controller Type=Button, Set to value=1 (Browser Only)*. This maximizes the trackbrowser when the jog wheel is turned.

3. Configure one button of your MIDI controller to load the selected track into a deck (command *Deck Common | Load Selected*).

4. Additionally configure the same button with the mapping command *Layout | Only browser On* and use the following parameters: *Interaction Mode=Direct, Controller Type=Button, Set to value=0 (Browser default)*. This resets the trackbrowser to its normal size when a track is loaded.

Example 2: Changing Tempo of all Decks with the Master Clock

The Master Clock tempo can only be changed when the clock is set to manual mode and when the Master Clock is designated as tempo master. Also changing the tempo of the Master Clock only affects the playing decks if synchronisation is on. To configure one encoder in a way that it can be used to change the tempo of all decks assign the following mapping commands to that encoder:

Mapping Command	Interaction Mode	Type of Controller	Assignment	Set to value
Deck Common | Sync On	Direct	Button	Deck A	1=On
Deck Common | Sync On	Direct	Button	Deck B	1=On
Deck Common | Sync On	Direct	Button	Deck C	1=On
Deck Common | Sync On	Direct	Button	Deck D	1=On
Master Clock | Set Master Tempo	Relative	Encoder	Global	–

The intervals for the tempo change can be set with the option *Rotary Sensitivity*. Because the exact behaviour always depends on the particular controller used, you need to experiment a little until the tempo adjustment will work the way you want it to.

If you use the automatic mode of the Master Clock you first need to switch the mode to manual and then assign the clock as tempo master. This can be done with the following two commands that need to be mapped to the same encoder as the other commands of this example.

Mapping Command	Interaction Mode	Type of Controller	Assignment	Set to value
Master Clock | Auto Master Mode	Direct	Button	Global	0 = Off
Master Clock | Master Tempo Selector	Direct	Button	Global	Clock

Example 3: Using the Crossfader for Panning

If you use the deck faders and not the crossfader for mixing you can use the crossfader to create interesting panning effects. Configure the following settings to:

◘ Move the balance knob of deck A to the left and the balance knob of deck B to the right when the crossfader is moved to the left, and too

◘ Move the balance knob of deck A to the right and the balance knob of deck B to the left when the crossfader is moved to the right.

Mapping Command	Interaction Mode	Type of Controller	Assignment	Modifier Condition	Options
Modifier #7	Hold	Button	Global	–	Set to value: 1
Mixer | Balance Adjust	Direct	Fader/Knob	Deck A	M7=1	Soft Takeover: On Invert: Off
Mixer | Balance Adjust	Direct	Fader/Knob	Deck B	M7=1	Soft Takeover: On Invert: On

It is advisable to configure one button on your controller as a modifier and to implement the panning in several decks, only if this button is pressed. This is why the table above contains the line for modifiers configuration; the modifier number and the value are an example only, any other modifier and/or value can also be used.

When mapping the balance of deck B you need to activate the check box *Invert*; as a result the left and the right channels are swapped.

6.10 Combining Modifier and Macros

Even more advanced configurations can be implemented by using a combination of modifiers and macros. This section contains two examples showing how to do this. The first example is an extended version of the Panning example from the previous section and explains how the balance of the decks can be reset automatically. The second example illustrates how some of the looping and beat jump features of Traktor can be implemented by means of two push encoders and one button, the latter will be used as modifier.

Example 1: Crossfader for Panning – Enhanced Version

The following example illustrates how the concept of the toggle button can be implemented to use the same button that served as "fader safeguard" for panning and resetting the balance of both decks.

Basically the principle is quite simple:

◻ When the crossfader is moved we set the value of another modifier to log that the cross deck panning feature has been used.

◻ When the original modifier button is pressed we check the value of the second modifier to see, if the cross deck panning was used. If so, both the balance settings and the value of the second modifier are reset.

The trick with this implementation is that the second modifier will be set by the crossfader and will be queried and reset by the button, which is assigned to the first modifier.

To make the configuration easier to understand I will use two tables this time. The entries in the column "Control Element on controller" always refer to the **same button** and the **same fader**. The first table describes the starting position and contains the MIDI configuration needed to implement the cross-deck panning. Here it is:

Control	Mapping Command	Parameter
Button	Modifier #7	Interaction Mode: Hold Type of Controller: Button Set to value: 1
Fader	Modifier #8	Interaction Mode: Direct Type of Controller: Button Set to value: 1 Modifier Condition: M8=0
Fader	Mixer | Balance Adjust	Interaction Mode: Direct Type of Controller: Fader/Knob Assignment: Deck A Options: Soft Takeover: On Invert: Off
Fader	Mixer | Balance Adjust	Interaction Mode: Direct Type of Controller: Fader/Knob Assignment: Deck B Options: Soft Takeover: On Invert: On

The only difference between this table and the table from the previous section can be found in row 2. When the fader is moved we check if the second modifier (in our case modifier #8) is set to the value 0. If this is true then the value of modifier #8 is set to 1.

By now all requirements are made to configure the button we already assigned to modifier #7. If this button is pressed and, if previously the cross deck panning has been used (modifier #8 then has a value of 1), pressing this button resets the balance both for deck A and deck B.

The next table contains the other mapping commands that need to be assigned to the button from the first table. These commands will reset the balance of both decks.

Control	Mapping Command	Parameter
Button	Mixer | Balance Adjust	Interaction Mode: Reset Type of Controller: Button Assignment: Deck A Modifier Condition: M8=1
Button	Mixer | Balance Adjust	Interaction Mode: Reset Type of Controller: Button Assignment: Deck B Modifier Condition: M8=1
Button	Modifier #8	Interaction Mode: Direct Type of Controller: Button Set to Value: 0 Modifier Condition: M8=1

The first two rows reset the balance of deck A and B if modifier #8 has the value 1 (this value has been set by moving the crossfader). The third row resets the value of modifier #8 to 0, but only if modifier #8 has a value of 1. This way the original situation is restored. The next time the button is held and the crossfader is moved, all actions from the first table will be executed again.

Example 2: Looping and Beatjumping

The next example shows how some of the basic features for looping and beatjumping can be implemented. The example uses two push encoders, both assigned to deck A and one button which will serve as a modifier.

The following table contains the specification for looping and beatjumping and it defines which actions are to be executed when the push encoder is turned; once when the modifier button is held as well as when it is not held. In order that this information is not too confusing, not all possible combinations of modifier button and turned/pressed push encoder are implemented.

Fea-ture No.	Control	Action	Modifier button pressed?	Behaviour
1.	Push-Encoder 1	↻ turn	no	Set the loop length. If a loop is activated then the length of this loop is changed.
2.	Push-Encoder 1	↧ press	no	Activates the loop if it is not active or deactivates the loop when it was active.
3.	Push-Encoder 1	↻ turn	yes	Moves the loop by the through Push-Encoder 2 configured length.
4.	Push-Encoder 2	↻ turn	no	Sets the move length. This feature will take care that the Advanced Panel is visible and that the Advanced Panel is set to Beatjump- and Loop Move.
5.	Push-Encoder 2	↧ press	no	Beatjump forwards by the set move length.
6.	Push-Encoder 2	↧ press	yes	Beatjump backwards by the set move length.

Let's start by implementing the modifier buttons. This approach always makes sense as it enables you to test if everything is working as intended after the mapping of the actual Traktor features has been made. The following table shows how to configure the modifier button. The modifier shall be set when the button is pressed (Interaction Mode *Hold*) and the value of the modifier is set to 5.

Control	Mapping Command	Parameter
Button	Modifier #7	Interaction Mode: Hold Type of Controller: Button Assignment: Global Set to value: 5

Feature wise we start with implementing feature 1 and 2; both can be implemented very easily. The encoder used for this example sends different MIDI control messages to Traktor, depending on whether the encoder is turned to the left or to the right. This is the reason why we need two command assignments: one, to select the previous loop length and another one to select the next loop length. The following table contains all necessary parameters as well as the commands to activate/deactivate the loop that is initiated by pressing the push encoder.

Feature No.	Control	Mapping Command	Mapped to via Learn	Parameter
1.	Push-Encoder 1	Deck Common | Loop | Loop Size Selector	Control command for turning the encoder to the left	Interaction Mode: Inc Type of Controller: Button Assignment: Deck A Modifier Condition: M7=0
1.	Push-Encoder 1	Deck Common | Loop | Loop Size Selector	Control command for turning the encoder to the left	Interaction Mode: Dec Type of Controller: Button Assignment: Deck A Modifier Condition: M7=0
2.	Push-Encoder 1	Deck Common | Loop | Loop Set	Control command for pressing the encoder	Interaction Mode: Trigger Type of Controller: Button Assignment: Deck A Modifier Condition: M7=0

Now let's take care of features 4 to 6 because feature 4 sets the move length, which is both used for moving a loop and for beatjumping. For this feature we also need to change the appearance of the decks. When push encoder 2 is turned, the following actions shall be performed:

◰ Make the Advanced Panel visible.

◰ Switch the Advanced Panel to mode Beatjump- and Loop Move.

◻   Set the Beatjump and Loop Move-Panel to the mode Beatjump.

◻   Set the length of a beat jump.

Because the push encoder sends different control commands for a left turn and a right turn we need eight different MIDI assignments which can be found in the following table. The last two rows take care of the beat jump, forward and backwards.

Mapping Command	Parameter	Description
Deck Common | Deck Size Selector	Interaction Mode: Direct Type of Controller: Button Set to value: Advanced Assignment: Deck A & B No modifier condition	Makes the Advanced Panel visible in the lower section of the deck by choosing the Deck Size option Advanced. Although the control is in fact an encoder you need to select Button in the list Type of Controller, otherwise the option Set to value cannot be used. Traktor itself does not care which kind of physical control the control message sends. Because the encoder sends different control commands for a left-turn than for a right-turn you need to configure this command twice: once for the left-turn and a second time for the right-turn.
Deck Common | Advanced Panel Tab Selector	Interaction Mode: Direct Type of Controller: Button Set to value: Move Assignment: Deck A No modifier condition	Activates the Beatjump and Loop Move Panel in the Advanced Panel. The notes for the mapping command Deck Size (Type of Controller = Button and double assignment) are valid here as well.
Deck Common | Move | Move Mode Selector	Interaction Mode: Direct Type of Controller: Button Set to value: Beatjump Assignment: Deck A No modifier condition	Set the Beatjump and Loop Move Panel to mode Beatjump. The notes for the command Deck Size Selector (Type of Controller = Button and double assignment) are valid here as well.
Deck Common | Move | Move Size Selector	Interaction Mode: Dec Type of Controller: Button Assignment: Deck A No modifier condition	Selects the previous length in the Beatjump- and Loop Move Panel. Assign this mapping command to a left-turn of the push encoders.
Deck Common | Move | Move Size Selector	Interaction Mode: Inc Type of Controller: Button Assignment: Deck A No modifier condition	Selects the next length in the Beatjump- and Loop Move Panel. Assign this mapping command to a right-turn of the push encoders.

Mapping Command	Parameter	Description
Deck Common | Move | Move	Interaction Mode: Direct Type of Controller: Button Assignment: Deck A Set to value: Forward Modifier Condition: M7=0	Performs a beat jump towards the end of the track by the length set in the Beatjump and Loop Move Panel. Assign this command via Learn to pressing the push encoder. The distinction between a backwards and a forward jump is made by setting the condition of modifier #7 (here M7=0, i.e. the modifier button is not hold).
Deck Common | Move | Move	Interaction Mode: Direct Type of Controller: Button Assignment: Deck A Set to value: Back Modifier Condition: M7=5	Performs a beat jump towards the beginning of the track by the length set in the Beatjump and Loop Move Panel. Assign this command via Learn to pressing the push encoder. The distinction between a backwards and a forward jump is made by setting the condition of modifier #7 (here M7=5, i.e. the modifier button is hold).

The feature "Loop Move" (feature no 3) is still missing. The loop shall be moved by turning push encoder 1, and holding the modifier button at the same time. For this implementation we assume that the Advanced Panel is already activated and that it has been switched to the mode Beatjump and Loop Move. Otherwise we could assign the first two rows from the table above assign to a turn of push encoder 1 as well.

To move the loop we need two mapping commands: one to set the mode of the Beatjump and Loop Move-Panel to Loop, and another one which implements the actual movement of the loop. The following table shows all commands that need to be mapped:

Mapping Command	Parameter	Description
Deck Common | Move | Move Mode Selector	Interaction Mode: Direct Type of Controller: Button Set to value: Loop Assignment: Deck A Modifier Condition: M7=5	Activates the mode Loop in the Beatjump-and Loop Move panel. Because the encoder sends different commands for a left turn and a right turn this command needs to be implemented twice.
Deck Common | Move | Move	Interaction Mode: Direct Type of Controller: Fader/Knob Assignment: Deck A Modifier Condition: M7=5	Moves the loop by the length selected in the Beatjump- and Loop Move panel.

That's it. All features specified in the table on page 221 are now implemented.

This example shows how flexible the controller mapping in Traktor is. We used the command (Deck Common/Move/Move) for the controller type button and the Interaction Mode *Direct* to implement the actual beatjump when the push encoder is pressed. The same mapping command was used for the controller Fader/Knob to move the loop when the push encoders are turned.

To be able to create these and other mappings customised to the individual needs and the personal workflow while DJing requires knowledge of the mapping commands in Traktor. This is the reason why the mapping commands are documented in detail throughout this book.

6.11 MIDI, HID and NHL Output

Traktor not only receives data from controllers via MIDI, HID or NHL, but it can also send data to the controllers. This is the method by which LED buttons, or other displays are controlled. In order that the correct controller receives the data you need to open list *Out-Port* in section *Device Setup* and select the appropriate MIDI or USB port. Additionally you can use option *All Ports* if a logical controller contains mappings for several physical controllers. For HID and NHL devices the Out-Port is always identical as the In-Port and cannot be changed.

Inserting an Out-command for an already mapped In-command is very easy in the current Traktor version. At the very top of the menu of the Add Out button Traktor shows the Out-command for the In-command currently selected in the Assignment Table. Click that command to have it inserted into you mapping. Furthermore, the Learn feature for Out-commands has returned. Learning Out-command was possible in Traktor Pro 1, but was silently removed. The tutorial on page 177 and onwards shows how to insert simple Out-commands into your mapping.

The Output Only Commands

Next to the Out-commands that are available for all In-commands, the menu of the *Add Out* button contains some special mapping commands that are only available as Out-commands. For example, you can use these output only commands to show the type of the hotcue on a multi-coloured button or to output the current state of the Flux mode. Another group of commands can be used to output the various signal level of Traktor. The following tables give an overview of the possibilities you have.

Out Command	Description
Deck Common | Extra | Post Fade-Out Marker	This command can be used to output whether the playmarker is currently behind a Fade-Out marker or not. The controller Range is 0/1.

Out Command	Description
Deck Common | Flux State	Indicates the current state of the Flux mode. The controller range is 0...2: 0 = Off, 1 = On, 2 = there was a playback action triggered that moved the playmarker away from real timeline; this state corresponds to the blinking flux button on the deck
Deck Common | Phase	This command corresponds to the phase meter as it is visible on the decks. The controller value is 0 when the phase of the deck matches the phase of the master tempo source. The value −0.5 means that the phase of the current track is half a beat behind the phase of the master tempo source; correspondingly the value +0.5 means that the phase of the current track is half a beat before the phase of the master tempo source.
Deck Common | Beat Phase	This command delivers information about the distance between the current playback position and the next gridline of the beatgrid. The controller range of this command is −0.5 to +0.5. When the value is 0 the playback marker hits a beatgrid line. The command Beat Phase Monitor can be used to make an LED button blink in rhythm with the track. The HOW TO-section on page 235 shows how to implement this feature.
Deck Common | Deck Is Loaded	This command can be used to output if a track is loaded into a track deck or not. For sample decks this information is available with Sample Deck/Slot State.
Deck Common | Is In Active Loop	This command can be used to output if the playback marker currently is inside a loop or not.
Track Deck | Track End Warning	This command can be used to send the track end warning to an LED. The command considers the time configured with the slider Track End Warning on the Preferences/Global Settings dialog. When the selected time is reached the command sends an On message to the LED; it doesn't let it blink. This is only possible if you use a controller that supports blinking buttons. In this case enter the needed values into the MIDI Range section of the dialog (more information can be found on page 238).
Track Deck | Cue | Hotcue x Type	Indicates the cue point type assigned a particular hotcue button (see the HOW TO-section on page 238)
Remix Deck | Slot State	Indicates the current state of a particular slot in a remix deck (see chapter 11).
Remix Deck | Direct Mapping | Slot X | Slot X Cell Y State	Indicates the current state of a cell in one of the four columns (slots) of a remix deck. More information can be found in chapter 11.
Loop Recorder | Playback Position	Can be used to output the current playback position of the loop recorder.
Loop Recorder | State	Indicates the current state of the loop recorder. More information about the meaning of the controller range can be found in section 10.5 on page 362.

Out Command	Description
Loop Recorder | Undo State	Indicates the current undo state of the loop recorder. More information about the meaning of the controller range can be found in section 10.5 on page 362.

The submenu *Add Out/Mixer/Meters* contains the Out-command that can be used to output the various signal levels of the Traktor mixer:

Out Command	Description
Deck Post-Fader Level (L) Deck Post-Fader Level (R) Deck Post-Fader Level (L+R) Deck Pre-Fader Level (L) Deck Pre-Fader Level (R) Deck Pre-Fader Level (L+R)	You can use these four commands to output the signal level of the left and right channel for the different decks. In Traktors' user interface the level is shown in the decks up-faders. The pre-fader commands deliver the deck level without considering the current position of the up-faders. The post-fader commands indicate the level that results from the up-fader position. The controller range for all six commands is 0.000 to 1.000.
Mixer Level (L) Mixer Level (R)	These two commands (named Monitor Mix Level in earlier versions) should output the level of the monitor signal, but they do not work as they should do. Neither changing the VOL nor the MIX knob in the Master Panel has any effect on the output shown. The other problem is that clicking the Cue button of a deck whose volume fader is down should change the monitor level; this doesn't work.
Master Out Level (L) Master Out Level (R) Master Out Level (L+R)	These three commands deliver the master level, either for the left, the right or for both stereo channels. The controller range for all three commands is 0.000 to 1.000. The HOW TO-section on page 236 shows how to create your own LED chain by sending the master level to several LED buttons
Master Out Clip (L) Master Out Clip (R) Master Out Clip (L+R)	All three commands have a controller range from 0 to 1. The value is 0 when the signal in the master level is clipped. You can use this command to activate an LED in this case.
Record Input Level (L) Record Input Level (R)	These two commands can be used to output the level of the recorded signal. This corresponds to the VU meter in the Audio Recorder Panel. The controller range of this command is 0.000 to 1.000.
Record Input Clip (L) Record Input Clip (R)	These two commands provide the controller values 0 and 1. When the value of this command is 1 then the corresponding channel is clipped. Both commands can be used to activate an LED in this case.

Three more commands in the submenu *Add Out/Remix Deck/Meters* can be used to output the signal level of the four slots of a remix deck:

Out-Command	Description
Slot Pre-Fader Level (L) Slot Pre-Fader Level (R) Slot Pre-Fader Level (L+R)	You can use these three command to output the signal level of the left and right channel of a slot in a remix deck. The pre-fader commands deliver the signal level independent of the current position of the slots' volume fader. The controller range of the commands is 0.000 to 1.000.

Tutorial: Adding and Mapping an Out-Command

To add an In-command for an already mapped Out-command proceed as explained in the tutorial on page 177 and onwards (select the In-command in Assignment Table, choose the corresponding Out-command at the top of the menu of the *Add Out* button).

The steps for adding an Out-command that has no equivalent In-command are basically the same as for adding an In-command. This tutorial explains the procedure and covers the mapping options that are available for the Out-commands only.

1. Open the *Preferences/Controller Manager* dialog box. Select in list *Device* the logical controller that shall receive the Out-command.

2. Click the button *Add Out* and select the command for the state you wish to send to the controller.

3. If the control reacts to the same message that it sends you can use the *Learn* function and proceed with step 5. If the control reacts to a different message proceed with step 4.

4. Open the list *n/a* next to the *Learn* button.

   ◻ **MIDI**   When you are adding a command for a MIDI controller you need to select the MIDI message type that shall be sent to the controller here. First select the MIDI channel and then the message type *CC* (Control Change message), *Note* (Note On/Note Off message) or *Pitch Bend* (Pitch Bend messages). Finally select the controller number for a Control Change message or the Note for a Note message respectively (left image in following figure).

   ◻ **HID**   For the HID controllers Traktor shows the names of the different controls. Buttons, knobs and jogwheels of the HID controllers can mostly be assigned by using the *Learn* feature. Because the displays are not touch screens you must select the section or label on the display you wish to use.

   ◻ **NHL**   The single-colour buttons of the Native Instruments controllers in NHL mode can be assigned by using the *Learn* feature. For multi-coloured buttons like the hotcue buttons, *Learn* cannot be used because each button supports sixteen different default colours. Here you need to select the colour in a submenu labeled with the name of the button (as shown in the right image of the following figure).

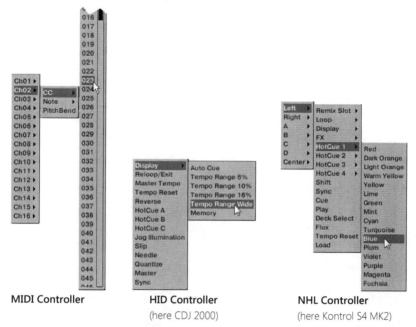

MIDI Controller

HID Controller
(here CDJ 2000)

NHL Controller
(here Kontrol S4 MK2)

5. Enter a comment into the *Comment* field.

6. The structure of the *Mapping Details* section is identical to the one found for In-commands:

   ▫ The execution of Out-commands can depend on the values of one or two modifiers. Those are selected in section *Modifier Conditions*.

   ▫ The only available *Type of Controller* for Out-commands is *LED*, and the only *Interaction Mode* is *Output*.

   ▫ Use the *Assignment* list to select the deck/FX unit/remix deck slot the command is related to. For deck-related commands the desired deck is the result of the combination of the settings *Device Setup/Device Target* and *Mapping Details/Assignment*.

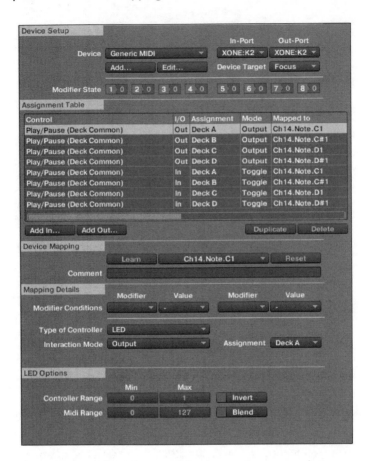

7. The interesting parameters for Out-command can be found in section *Options:*

   ◘ The values shown in section *Controller Range* are the possible values or, states that mapping commands can have. For commands representing a Traktor function that can be switched on or off (like *Deck Common | Play/Pause*), the *Min* value is 0 and the *Max* value is 1. The value 0 corresponds to the Off-status of the command; in this case the LED is off as well. The value 1 corresponds to the On-status of the command; then the LED is on.

   There are other commands offering more options than a simple on/off status, like *Loop Size Selector* or *Master Clock | Clock Int/Ext*. For these Out-commands you can change the Min and Max parameter to map one LED exactly to one loop-length or one master clock mode respectively. More information about this can be found further onwards.

□ The *Invert* checkbox does what its name implies: it inverts the status of the LED button.

□ The *Max* and *Min* fields in section *MIDI Range* are used to configure the values that the controller shall receive. These options are valid for HID devices as well; so the name *MIDI Range* is actually wrong or at least misleading; maybe *Output Range* or *Value Range* would have been a better choice. For LEDs that can either be on or off the value 0 corresponds to the Off-status of the LED and the value 1 to its On-status.

Some MIDI controllers, for example the Akai APC40 have buttons that offer different colours or that support a Blinking status as well as an Off and On status. For these types of LEDs the *MIDI Range* is used to select the colour or the Blinking-status.

□ Activate the *Blend* option when the status of a command is represented by an LED chain on the controller. When this option is activated Traktor will map the complete value range configured in *Controller Range* to the complete value range specified in the *MIDI Range* section.

8. This ends the mapping of a simple Out-command that only supports the states On and Off (which can be seen from the *Controller Range* 0/1).

The following section will dig deeper into Output mappings, explain the special Out-commands and describe all of the configuration options.

Out Commands and the Controller Range Settings

In the tutorial at the beginning of the section about MIDI and HID output I briefly mentioned that the fields *Min* and *Max* in the section *Controller Range* are used to specify which of the possible values of an Out-command the mapped LED uses.

Assuming we want to create a mapping for several LED buttons to switch between some loop lengths; when a loop length is chosen the corresponding LED shall be on.

One of these buttons shall set the loop length to 4 beats. We need the In-command *Deck Common | Loop | Loop Size Selector* to achieve this; when *Button* is selected as *Type of Controller* and *Direct* has been set as *Interaction Mode*, the desired loop length can be chosen in the list *Set to Value*. To make sure that the LED of this button is only on when the actual loop length is 4 beats, we need to enter 7 into the *Min* and the *Max* field of section *Controller Range*. 7 is the magic number representing 4 beats. Additionally, the *Blend* checkbox must be off. This way Traktor sends the value 127 inside the MIDI message when the internal value of the command *Loop Size Selector* is 7. When the command *Loop Size Selector* has another value Traktor will send the value 0 in the MIDI message and this switches the LED off.

The following table documents the "magic" controller range values for the most important Out-commands:

Out-Command	Values for Controller Range	
Deck Common | Timecode | Playback Mode Int/Rel/Abs	0 = Absolute Mode 1 = Relative Mode 2 = Internal Mode	
Deck Common | Timecode | Scratch Control On	0 = Internal Playback 1 = Scratch Control	
Deck Common | Loop | Loop Size Selector	0 = 1/32 Beat 1 = 1/16 Beat 2 = 1/8 Beat 3 = 1/4 Beat 4 = 1/2 Beat 5 = 1 Beat	6 = 2 Beats 7 = 4 Beats 8 = 8 Beats 9 = 16 Beats 10 = 32 Beats
Deck Common | Deck Size Selector	0 = Micro 1 = Small 2 = Essential	3 = Full 4 = Advanced
Deck Common | Deck Flavor Selector	0 = Track Deck 1 = Remix Deck 2 = Live Input	
Deck Common | Advanced Panel Selector	0 = Move 1 = Cue 2 = Grid	
Track Deck | Cue | Hotcue x Type	See the HOW TO section on page 238	
FX Unit | Effect 1 Selector FX Unit | Effect 2 Selector FX Unit | Effect 3 Selector	The value range is 0 to the number of effects that are pre-selected in Preferences/Effects dialog. The controller value 0 corresponds to the option "No Effect". The maximum value corresponds to the number of the pre-selected effects. The effect number itself is identical to the order that the pre-selected effects are shown	
FX Unit | FX Unit Mode Selector	0 = Group 1 = Single	
FX Unit | FX Routing Selector	0 = Send 1 = Insert 2 = Post Fader	
Master Clock | Clock Int/Ext	2 = Ext(ern) Clockmaster 3 = Int(ern) Clockmaster	
Layout | Deck Focus Selector	0 = Deck A 1 = Deck B	2 = Deck C 3 = Deck D

Out-Command	Values for Controller Range
Modifier | Modifier #1 ... #8	The controller range for modifiers is the same as the possible modifier values, i.e. the range starts at 0 and ends at 7.

Updating all LED Buttons

There is one very important In-command for MIDI and HID/NHL output you should be aware of: it is *Global/Send Monitor State*. This command is a kind of an LED update function. Whenever you issue this command Traktor sends MIDI messages for all mapped Out-commands to all connected MIDI, HID and NHL devices.

HOW TO: Changing/Showing Deck Focus and Assignment between Decks/FX Units

The following section shows another practical use case where the controller range is used to have the correct buttons light up at the right moment. This mapping shall provide the following functionality for the eight Group buttons of the Maschine controller:

☐ Buttons A to D shall be used to set the deck focus. The button of the deck that has the deck focus shall light up.

☐ Buttons E to H shall manage the assignment between the deck with the focus and the four FX units. Furthermore, the buttons shall indicate which FX units are currently assigned to the deck with the focus.

Deck A-D
FX Unit 1-4

The following description uses the Maschine controller as an example; but it is just as easy to use it with other controllers.

> **NOTE** In order to make the mapping work as described use the Controller Editor for Maschine and set the mode of all eight buttons to *Gate* and select option *For MIDI In* in section LED In. This ensures that the LED can be controlled externally by a MIDI message and that the controller itself does not make any changes to the LED status. If you use Maschine MK2 you can choose whether you wish to use one or two (one for the On state, one for the Off state) colours.

The *Assignment Table* in the following figure shows eight different commands.

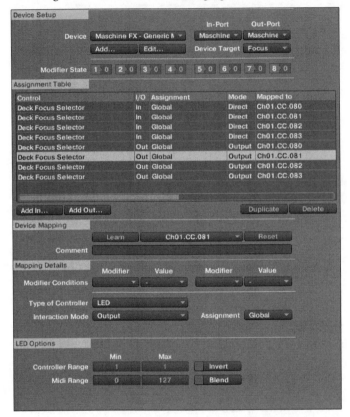

The first four commands (labelled with *In* in column *I/O*), set the deck focus to one of the four decks. The first command (mapped to MIDI message *Ch01.CC.080*) sets the focus to deck A. In order for Traktor to "know" that this button should show the status of deck A, the *Min* and the *Max* value of *Controller Range* are both set to 0. For the next command in the table (mapped to MIDI message *Ch01.CC.081*) both fields are set to 1. This tells Traktor that this LED is responsible for showing the status of Deck B. The Out-commands for the two remaining buttons are mapped in the same way.

The same model was used to map buttons E to H. The following figure shows the *Assignment Table* with the eight commands.

The first four commands are used to assign/un-assign an FX unit to the deck currently having the focus. To use the least amount of buttons as possible this mapping is focus oriented: The list *Device Target* in section *Device Setup* is set to *Focus*; the list *Assignment* in section *Mapping Details* is set to *Device Target*.

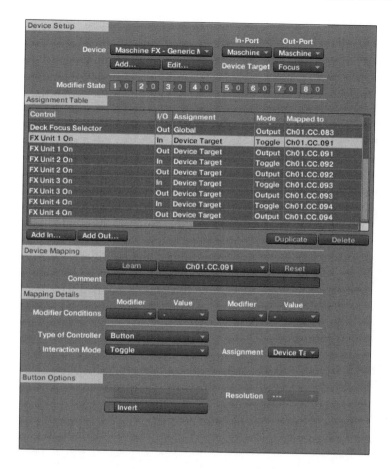

This finishes the mapping of the eight buttons: sixteen simple commands now control the deck focus and the assignment between decks and FX units.

HOW TO: LED Buttons blink in Beat

You can use the Out-command *Beat Phase Monitor* to make LEDs or pads blink when Traktor reaches a gridline of the beatgrid while playing back a track. The controller range of this command is −0.5 to +0.5. When the playback marker hits a gridline the internal value of this command is 0. To make four LED buttons blink rhythmically you need a mapping with four *Beat Phase* commands; one for each deck. If the LED button provides On/Off states only you need to reduce the controller range to make the LED blink. In our example we set *Controller Range Min* to 0.0 and *Controller Range Max* to 0.1. Activate the *Blend* checkbox for all commands: only then will Traktor map the internal value of the beat phase monitor continuously to the values of the *MIDI*

Range; and this leads to the rhythmical blinking. Here is the *Assignment Table* showing the four commands:

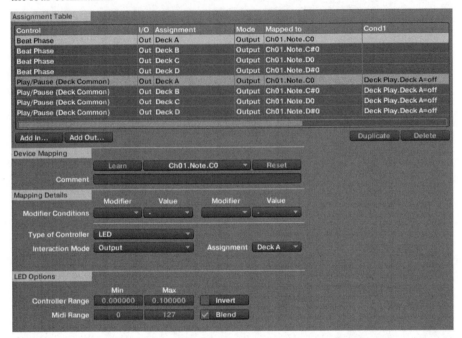

Control	I/O	Assignment	Mode	Mapped to	Cond1
Beat Phase	Out	Deck A	Output	Ch01.Note.C0	
Beat Phase	Out	Deck B	Output	Ch01.Note.C#0	
Beat Phase	Out	Deck C	Output	Ch01.Note.D0	
Beat Phase	Out	Deck D	Output	Ch01.Note.D#0	
Play/Pause (Deck Common)	Out	Deck A	Output	Ch01.Note.C0	Deck Play.Deck A=off
Play/Pause (Deck Common)	Out	Deck B	Output	Ch01.Note.C#0	Deck Play.Deck A=off
Play/Pause (Deck Common)	Out	Deck C	Output	Ch01.Note.D0	Deck Play.Deck A=off
Play/Pause (Deck Common)	Out	Deck D	Output	Ch01.Note.D#0	Deck Play.Deck A=off

The lower part of the Assignment Table shows four entries with the Out-commands *Deck Common | Play/Pause* linked to the *Deck Play* condition. If the mapped deck is currently not playing this condition makes certain that the LED is off.

HOW TO: Sending the Master Level to four LED Buttons

You can use the Out-command *Master Out Level (L+R)* to output the master level indicator (this resides in the Traktor header) on a MIDI controller. If your MIDI controller contains an LED chain where several LEDs are controlled by a single MIDI message, the only thing you need to do add is the Out-command *Master Out Level (L+R)* once, then select the MIDI message that is assigned to the LED chain in the list *n/a*.

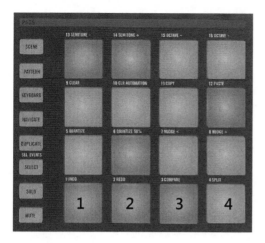

Alternatively, you can create your own LED chain by using several neighbouring LED buttons. The following figure shows the pad section of the Maschine controller. The lower button row, numbered with 1 to 4, shall display the current master level.

To do this the following trick is used: We restrict the controller range for each command to one part of the controller range that is available. As the following table shows, on pad 1 only the range – in our case the level – between 0.00 to 0.50 is shown; pad 2 displays the range between 0.50 and 0.70 and so on. Additionally, you need to activate the Blend option in order for Traktor to map the whole controller range continually to the whole MIDI range.

Pad Number	Controller Range: Min	Controller Range: Max	MIDI Message (example)
1	0.00	0.50	Ch01.Note.C0
2	0.50	0.70	Ch01.Note.C#0
3	0.70	0.85	Ch01.Note.D0
4	0.85	1.00	Ch01.Note.D#0

Of course, it is possible to use more than four buttons by simply using different *Min* and *Max* values. The same procedure can be used for all other Out-commands that output one of the signal levels, as *Deck Post-Fader Level (L, R), Deck Pre-Fader Level (L, R),* or *Record Input Level (L, R).* These commands are described in the table on page 225 and onwards.

HOW TO: LED Buttons with Several Colours/States

LED buttons on some MIDI controllers support several colours and/or several states, like a blinking status as well as on and off. The following table shows the values used by the AKAI controller APC40 to control the colour and status of the LED buttons:

MIDI Value	Colour, Status
0	On
1, 7–127	Green
2	green, blinking
3	Red
4	red, blinking
5	Amber
6	amber, blinking

To make a button light up in the desired colour enter the MIDI value from the table above into the *Min* as well as in the *Max* field of the *MIDI Range* section. Another example of how to use coloured buttons can be found in the following section.

HOW TO: Output the Current Status of the Hotcue Buttons

The submenu *Track Deck/Cue* of the *Add Out* button offers the eight commands *Hotcue1 Type* to *Hotcue 8 Type*. You can use these commands to output the status of the hotcue buttons. Combined with the In-command *Select/Set + Store Hotcue* you can create a mapping for eight LED buttons that can be used to create, select and display the status of each of the eight hotcue slots.

> **NOTE**   The In-command *Select/Set + Store Hotcue* has two purposes: If a hotcue exists in the specified hotcue slot Traktor will jump to that hotcue; if there is no hotcue set Traktor will create a new hotcue and map it on the specified hotcue button. Normally Traktor will create a Cue Point hotcue; if a loop is active Traktor will create a Loop hotcue instead.

The eight buttons need to be mapped to the In- and Out-commands shown in the following table:

Slot/Button	In-Command	Out-Command
1	Track Deck	Cue	Select/Set + Store Hotcue, Set to value: Hotcue 1	Track Deck	Cue	Hotcue1 Type Controller Range Min/Max: 0/5
2	Track Deck	Cue	Select/Set + Store Hotcue, Set to value: Hotcue 2	Track Deck	Cue	Hotcue2 Type Controller Range Min/Max: 0/5

Slot/Button	In-Command	Out-Command
3	Track Deck | Cue | Select/Set + Store Hotcue, Set to value: Hotcue 3	Track Deck | Cue | Hotcue3 Type Controller Range Min/Max: 0/5
4	Track Deck | Cue | Select/Set + Store Hotcue, Set to value: Hotcue 4	Track Deck | Cue | Hotcue4 Type Controller Range Min/Max: 0/5
5	Track Deck | Cue | Select/Set + Store Hotcue, Set to value: Hotcue 5	Track Deck | Cue | Hotcue5 Type Controller Range Min/Max: 0/5
6	Track Deck | Cue | Select/Set + Store Hotcue, Set to value: Hotcue 6	Track Deck | Cue | Hotcue6 Type Controller Range Min/Max: 0/5
7	Track Deck | Cue | Select/Set + Store Hotcue, Set to value: Hotcue 7	Track Deck | Cue | Hotcue7 Type Controller Range Min/Max: 0/5
8	Track Deck | Cue | Select/Set + Store Hotcue, Set to value: Hotcue 8	Track Deck | Cue | Hotcue8 Type Controller Range Min/Max: 0/5

When adding the Out-commands make sure to change the *Min* value of the *Controller Range* from –1 to 0. If you use the default value of –1 the mapped button is always On, even when no hotcue exists in the corresponding hotcue slot.

When you have a controller whose buttons support different colours, also change the *Min* and *Max* Value for the *Controller Range* as well as for the *MIDI Range* settings. This way the button will use a different colour depending on the hotcue type.

The hotcue type can be set by changing the *Min* and *Max* value for the *Controller Range* and by using the values from the following table:

Controller Value	Hotcue Type	Controller Value	Hotcue Type
–1	No Hotcue set		
0	Cue-Point	3	Load
1	Fade-In	4	Grid
2	Fade-Out	5	Loop

Let's assume that the buttons of a MIDI controller support four different colours. These colours are represented by the following values: 0=off, 1=green, 2 = blue, 3=red and 4 = amber. In addition we assume that no grid markers are mapped to the hotcue buttons. The LED buttons for the remaining hotcue types shall light up in the same colour that Traktor uses for the hotcue markers in the deck. To do this we need to create the following mapping for each of the buttons:

Hotcue Type	Out-Command
Cue Point (blue)	Track Deck | Cue | HotcueX Type Controller Range Min/Max: 0/0 MIDI Range Min/Max: 2/2

Hotcue Type	Out-Command
Fade In, Fade Out (red)	Track Deck | Cue | HotcueX Type Controller Range Min/Max: 1/2 MIDI Range Min/Max: 3/3
Load (amber)	Track Deck | Cue | HotcueX Type Controller Range Min/Max: 3/3 MIDI Range Min/Max: 4/4
Loop (green)	Track Deck | Cue | HotcueX Type Controller Range Min/Max: 5/5 MIDI Range Min/Max: 1/1

The values for the *Controller Range* set the hotcue type the command acts on. The values for the *MIDI Range* control which value the MIDI message contains that Traktor sends to the MIDI controller; this changes the LED colour.

HOW TO: Creating Super Buttons – Using MIDI Out as MIDI In

The MIDI out features of Traktor can not only be used to control the LEDs or other controls on a MIDI controller. Additionally, you can send the MIDI data that Traktor outputs back to Traktor in a loop back. This incoming MIDI data can then– almost magically – move a knob, fader or slider.

This tutorial shows how to program a button on MIDI controller in a way that it re-mote changes the balance knob of a deck. The rotation of the balance knob is controlled by the beatgrid and tempo of another deck. This example (and all possible variations and extensions) require that a virtual MIDI port – like LoopBe or Midi Yoke – is installed on your system (download links can be found on *www.traktorbible.com/ 2014/links.aspx*).

To implement the functionality described above we need four different commands shown in the following figure.

Control	I/O	Assignment	Mode	Mapped to	Cond1
Beat Phase	Out	Deck D	Output	Ch06.CC.027	M1=1
Modifier #1	In	Global	Hold	Ch01.Note.G#2	
Balance Adjust	In	Device Target	Direct	Ch06.CC.027	M1=1
Balance Adjust	In	Device Target	Direct	Ch01.Note.G#2	

For the sake of clarity and to avoid side effects I created a separate logical controller for this mapping (to do this click on *Add* in section *Device Setup* and then on *Generic MIDI*). Make sure that in the list *Out-Port* your virtual MIDI port is selected and that the list *In-Port* is set to *All Ports*. You need the *All Ports* option because this logical device needs to receive the input when the button on the physical MIDI controller is pressed and the incoming data is from the virtual MIDI port.

Here is the detailed information about the mapping commands needed.

Command No. 1: Setting the Modifier

The first command is needed to set Modifier #1 to value 1 as long as the button on the controller is pressed. Add the new In-command *Modifier | Modifier #1* and activate Learn mode; then press the desired button on your controller. Select *Button* for *Type of Controller*, select *Hold* as *Interaction Mode* and choose option *1* in the list *Set to value*.

Command No. 2: Changing the Deck Balance

The second mapping command is needed to change the balance knob of the deck. Add the In-command *Mixer | Balance Adjust*. Open the list *n/a* next to the *Learn* button and select a MIDI channel that is not used by any of your MIDI controllers. Then select any control change message. Finally change the settings in section *Mapping Details* as shown in the following figure:

The modifier condition M1=1 ensures that the balance knob is only changed when the button mapped as command No. 1 is held. In the list *Assignment* the option *Device Target* is used; this changes the balance of the deck that currently has the focus.

Command No. 3: Sending The Beat Phase of one Deck to The Balance Knob of another Deck

Next we need an Out-command which has data sent to the balance knob. Add the Out-command *Deck Common | Beat Phase* to the mapping (a description of its functionality can be found on page 226).

Now open the *n/a* list next to the *Learn* button and select the same MIDI channel and the same control change message you selected for command No. 2. This means that the information about the beat phase is sent to the balance knob. Then change the settings in section *Mapping Details* as shown in the following figure:

Again, the modifier condition M1=1 takes care that the beat phase information is only sent when the mapped button is pressed. In list *Assignment* select *Deck D*. This means that a track must be playing in deck D so that its beat phase information is available and that it can be sent to the balance knob. When changing the tempo of deck D, the beat phase tempo changes as well, and this changes how fast balance knob of Deck A rotates.

Command No. 4: Resetting the Balance Knob

The fourth and last mapping command we need ensures that when the mapped button is released the balance knob is reset to its middle position. Add another In-command for *Mixer | Deck Balance*. Click the *Learn* button and press the same button on your MIDI controller that sets Modifier #1 to 1. Then change the settings in section *Mapping Details* as shown in the following figure.

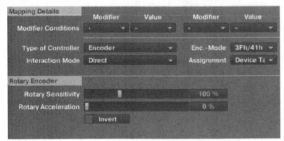

Using *Encoder* as *Type of Controller* and *3Fh/41h* as *Enc.-Mode* for a button ensures that the mapped command is reset to its default value once the button is released.

Using the Macro, Variations

Load any track into deck A and another one into deck D. Start both decks and make sure that deck A has the focus. Now press the mapped button and the balance knob should start to rotate. Pressing the button set modifier #1 to 1; now Traktor starts sending MIDI out messages containing information about the permanent changing phase of deck D via the virtual MIDI cable; this information is received by the In-command which in turn starts changing the deck balance and the knob rotates.

Make sure that the *Sync* button on deck D is off and move the tempo/pitch fader to change the playback tempo. This influences the rotation tempo of the balance knob. (To get the maximum possible tempo changes the *Tempo Fader Range* in *Preferences/Transport* must be set to 100 %.)

When creating command No. 3 we did not make any changes to the *LED Options*. For this reason the balance knob always rotates completely clockwise. To restrict the moving space of the knob only a little change is necessary. As it is now, Traktor maps the complete controller range (–0.5 to +0.5) to the complete MIDI range (0 to 127).

When we change the MIDI range, let's say to Min = 32 and Max = 100, Traktor will send only those MIDI messages that belong to the specified MIDI range. The lower and the upper parts are omitted. In turn the balance knob will no longer reach its outermost positions.

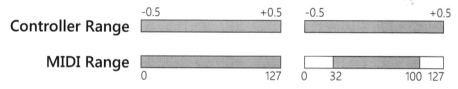

To change the direction that the balance knob rotates, activate the check box *Invert* for mapping command No. 2.

The procedure explained here can be used for all In-commands that are connected to knobs, faders or sliders in the Traktor user interface, so changing the effect parameters is also possible. You can even use the same Out-command to change two different parameters. Depending on the setting of the Invert option one of the parameter knobs (or sliders in 4 FX units mode) can move to the left and the other one to the right.

To implement different restrictions for two In-commands you need to duplicate the Out-command, use a different control change message and then set the *MIDI Range* settings to the desired value range.

Chapter 7

Organizing Tracks

The lower part of the Traktor window contains the browser. You can use the browser to access your track collection and the folders on the connected drives and to open your iTunes library. You can also create and manage playlists, search for tracks and you can assign your most frequently used folders and playlists in the favourites bar for quicker access.

The track collection is a small database in XML format that contains information about all tracks, samples and remix sets that have been imported into Traktor and about all playlists you have created. The track collection is stored in the Traktor root directory in a file named *Collection.nml.*

The default location for the root directory is the folder *Native Instruments/Traktor 2.6.7* below *MyFiles* or *Documents* respectively. Starting with Traktor 2 each version of Traktor that will be released will use its own root directory. In case you have a newer version than Traktor 2.6.7 replace the "2.6.7" in the folder name by the version number you use. The root directory can be changed in the field *Root Dir* on the dialog box *Preferences/File Management.*

7.1 Overview of the Browser

The browser area consists of several elements: the folder list (also called browser tree), the track list (also called track browser), the search field and the favourites panel.

The Folder List (Browser Tree)

The folder list at the left side of the browser shows several nodes that can be used to open the different locations where tracks can reside.

The Track Collection Node

The node *Track Collection* shows all tracks that have been imported into the Traktor track collection (more about importing tracks further on). When you open the node *Track Collection* Traktor display the subnodes *Artists, Release, Labels, Genres, All Tracks, All Samples* and *All Remix Sets.*

These nodes act like a filter and group the tracks by artist, release, label or style. Traktor extracts this data from the Meta information in the files and the collection file; therefore, in order that filtering will work the tracks need to be properly tagged.

The Playlists Node

The *Playlists* node can be used to create and manage playlist folders and playlists. After the installation of Traktor 2 this node will already contain some playlists with files from the Traktor Samples Library. More detailed information about playlists can be found further onward.

The Explorer Node

You can use the *Explorer* node to access all drives and your computer desktop. Additionally, this node contains the two subnodes *Music Folders* and *Archive*. The *Music Folders* node can be used to create shortcuts to certain folders on your drives so that they can be opened much more quickly. By default one shortcut is available; it is linked to the music folder below the folder *Documents* and *My Files*, respectively.

To create a new music folder open the dialog box *Preferences/File Management*. Click on *Add* in section *Music Folders* and navigate to the folder you wish to add. The node *Music Folders* in the folder list, lists the folders in the same sequence in which they have been created. Unfortunately it is not possible to change this order. Use the buttons *Delete* and *Change* to remove a music folder or to change its target location.

The *Archive* sub node is a shortcut to the physical folder *History* below your Traktor root folder. Traktor creates a new archive playlist after each start; it contains all tracks that are loaded/played until Traktor shuts down. The filename of the archive playlist is composed from the date and time when Traktor was shutdown and the archive playlist is saved. When you open an archive playlist you can neither move, nor delete, nor edit the tracks tags.

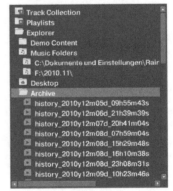

However, you can copy an archive playlist to the "normal" playlists folder by right-clicking the filename and selecting *Import to Playlists* in the context menu. This copy can be edited like any other playlist in the *Playlists* node.

The Audio Recordings Node

The *Audio Recordings* node is a special playlist where Traktor automatically stores all wave files that have been recorded with the Audio Recorder. More detailed information can be found in chapter 14 that covers the Audio Recorder.

The iTunes Node

When iTunes is installed on your computer you can use the *iTunes* node to access your iTunes Library, including all iTunes playlists. This makes it possible to use iTunes to create playlists and then use them in Traktor (more information can be found in section "7.3 Playlists" on page 261 and onwards).

When you open this node for the first time after Traktor is started Traktor will read the XML file containing the data of the iTunes Library. The location of the file is detected automatically; you can change the path in section *iTunes Music Library* on the dialog box *Preferences/File Management*.

The iTunes library is read once when you open the *iTunes* node for the first time. If you want to refresh the iTunes node right-click and select *Refresh*. Please note that this only updates the *iTunes* view, and not the tags for those audio files that are already imported into the collection. More information about how tags are handled when using both iTunes and Traktor to change them can be found on page 260.

The History Node

The *History* node contains all tracks that have been played in any of the decks after Traktor was started, and it is exactly this history that Traktor will save to the playlists archive (see page 246). This is the reason why the *History* node is empty when you start Traktor.

The minimum time a track must be played before it is added to the History can be configured with the slider *Min. Playtime* on the *Preferences/Transport* dialog. The same setting controls when the playcounter is increased and when the last played date is changed.

HOW TO: Print your Set

Traktor can export a playlist in HTML format. You can use your browser to print the HTML page. The *History* node and the playlists available in the sub node *Explorer/Archive* contain information about the start time, the duration and the deck in which a track was played.

Follow these steps to save a set as HTML and to print it with your browser:

1. Open the node *Explorer/Archive* in the browser tree.

2. Search for the playlist you wish to print. The playlists are sorted by date; the newest playlist can be found at the end of the node.

3. Right-click the desired playlist and select *Save as Webpage.*

4. Type the name of the playlist into the entry field *Playlist Title.* The entered name will be used as the filename and as the page title of the HTML file.

5. Click the ellipsis button and select the folder where the HTML file is to be saved.

6. Leave the option *Open HTML After Export* checked.

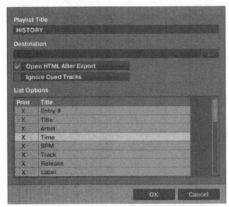

7. If you use Traktor in internal mixing mode activate the checkbox *Ignore Cued Tracks.* Traktor will then export only those tracks into the HTML page that have been played "in public". Traktor determines the play state "in public" according to which decks channel faders have been opened.

8. Leave the option *Open HTML After Export* checked.

9. Double-click the entries in the list *List Options* to select/deselect the fields that shall be exported into the HTML file.

10. Click *OK.*

Once the browser opens, the exported HTML file uses the browsers' normal *Print* command to send the page to your printer.

Unfortunately Traktor 2 forgets which fields have been selected in the list *List Options*. This means you need to re-create your field selection over and over again. It would be good if Native Instruments could improve the usability of this feature and automatically save the names of the selected info fields.

The Track List (Browser List, Track Browser)

The right side of the browser shows the track list. Here Traktor displays the content of the folder/playlist that is currently selected in the folder list.

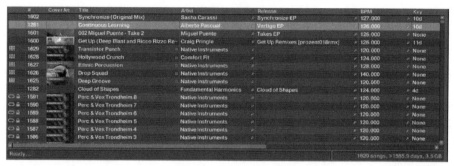

When a track contains meta information they are shown in the track list, otherwise only the filename is visible.

There are several options to configure the track list :

☐   **Sorting the List**   Click on one of the column headers to sort the list by this column. The label of the clicked column will then contain a little arrow showing the sort order (ascending/descending), as shown in the previous figure for the *Title* column.

☐   **Selecting Columns**   Right-/ctrl-click on the name of one of the columns. Traktor opens a list with all available columns. Click the name of the column you wish to show/hide.

☐   **Change Column Order**   Click on one of the column headings and drag it with the mouse to the new position. While dragging Traktor shows the new position as a vertical line.

☐   **Changing Row Height**   Open the dialog box *Preferences/Browser Details* and set the row height with the slider *List Row Height*. Selecting a larger row height is a good choice so that you see more of the track covers if you enabled the *Cover Art* column of the track list.

☐   **Changing Font**   Open the dialog box *Preferences/Browser Details* and change the font settings in the fields *Font & Font Size*. The font selected here is used in the folder list, the track list and in the deck header to display the track information.

The first column of the track list contains several icons that give some additional information about the track. All icons are explained in the following figure. Please note that the "audio file not found" icon is only visible in the *Track Collection* and *Playlists* nodes; when a track is loaded from the iTunes node Traktor displays an error message, but it does not show this icon.

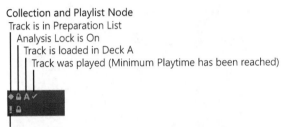

Collection and Playlist Node
Track is in Preparation List
  Analysis Lock is On
   Track is loaded in Deck A
    Track was played (Minimum Playtime has been reached)

Audio file of the track cannot be found, use Relocate

iTunes and Explorer Node
Track is in collection

The small disc icon that indicates that the audio file is already in the Traktor collection is displayed only when the *iTunes* or *Explorer* node is open.

Below the track list you will find the info bar; the first line is used to display track information, i.e. artist and title of the currently selected track; in the second row general status information and error messages are displayed. These two rows can be shown/hidden with the check boxes *Show Track Info* and *Show Status Bar/Error Messages* on the dialog box *Preferences/Browser Details*.

Navigating in Folder List and Track List with the NI Controllers

You can use the various NI controllers to browse through the folder list and track list to find the track you wish to play next. Regarding browsing Kontrol S2, Z1, and X1 behave the same. Kontrol S4 provides a special browse mode with some advanced features.

Navigating with Kontrol S2 MK2, Z2, and X1 MK2

All three controllers have a BROWSE encoder which allows you to perform the following actions:

◻ **Maximize/minimize Browser**   Press BROWSE encoder

> **X1 MK2** The BROWSE encoder of Kontrol X1 MK2 is touch-sensitive. If option *Full Browser on Touch* is enabled in *Preferences/Traktor Kontrol X1 MK2* the browser will be maximize if you touch the encoder.

◻ **Browse in Track List**   Turn the BROWSE encoder

◻ **Browser in Folder List**   Hold SHIFT and turn the BROWSE encoder

> **X1 MK2** For Kontrol X1 MK2 you can configure whether SHIFT+BROWSE browses in the folder list or through the favourites. The default setting is browsing in the folder list. Enable option *SHIFT+BROWSE to browse Favorites* if you prefer browsing through the favourites instead

◻ **Expand/Collapse the folder currently selected in the Folder List**   Hold SHIFT and press the BROWSE encoder

Once you have found the track you are looking for, use the LOAD buttons to load it.

Navigating with Kontrol S4 MK2

Traktor Kontrol S4 provides a special browse mode that makes loading of tracks and samples easier (it also allows copying samples between sample slots). Browse mode is activated by pressing the BROWSE encoder.

If browse mode is inactive, you can perform the following actions with the BROWSE encoder:

◻ **Browse in Track List**   Turn the BROWSE encoder

◻ **Browser in Folder List**   Hold SHIFT and turn the BROWSE encoder

Once you activate browse mode you can use the following controls for navigation:

◻ **Browse in Track List**   Turn the BROWSE encoder, turn the jogwheel

◻ **Browser in Folder List**   Turn the LOOP MOVE encoder

◻ **Expand/Collapse the folder currently selected in the Folder List** Press the LOOP MOVE encoder

◻ **Browse through the Favourites**   Turn the LOOP SIZE encoder

◻ **Open First Favourite**   Press the LOOP SIZE encoder

In browse mode the blinking remix slots buttons and the cue buttons indicate the decks and sample slots where you can load a track/sample into. Please note that you cannot load a remix set into a remix deck while in browse mode.

Navigating in Folder List and Track List via Mapping

The fastest way to scroll in the folder list and track list is to map the corresponding mapping commands to a jogwheel or to an endless encoder on your controller. Traktor provides the following two commands for navigating in the folder list:

Navigating in the folder list via Mapping

Browser | Tree | Select Up/Down	Interaction Mode: Relative Type of Controller: Encoder	Use this command configuration to scroll in the folder list by using a jogwheel or an endless encoder. Use the sliders Rotary Sensitivity and Rotary Acceleration to configure the scrolling speed.
	Interaction Mode: Dec/Inc Type of Controller: Button	Use this command configuration if you wish to use keys/buttons to scroll in the folder list. Using the option AutoRepeat saves you from pressing the mapped key/button multiple times.
Browser | Tree | Select Expand/Collapse	Interaction Mode: Direct Type of Controller: Button Set to value: Collapse/Expand, Expand, Collapse	This command expands/collapses the node currently selected in the folder list. When you use Collapse/Expand the state of the node is toggled and one button/key is sufficient.

The mapping commands for the track list are similar to those for the folder list. However, there are additional commands to browse page by page and to select multiple tracks. The following table documents the available commands:

Navigating in the Track List and Selecting Tracks

Browser | List | Select Up/Down	Interaction Mode: Relative Type of Controller: Encoder	Use this command configuration to scroll in the track list by using a jogwheel or an endless encoder. Use the sliders Rotary Sensitivity und Rotary Acceleration to configure the scrolling speed.
	Interaction Mode: Dec/Inc Type of Controller: Button	Use this command configuration if you wish to use keys/buttons to scroll in the folder list. Using AutoRepeat saves you from pressing the mapped key/button multiple times.
Browser | List | Select Page Up/Down	Interaction Mode: Relative Type of Controller: Rotary	Use this command to map the page by page browsing to an endless encoder
	Interaction Mode: Dec/Inc Type of Controller: Button	Browses one page up or one page down in the track list.
Browser | List | Select Top/Bottom	Interaction Mode: Dec Type of Controller: Button	Jumps to the first entry in the track list.

Navigating in the Track List and Selecting Tracks

	Interaction Mode: Inc Type of Controller: Button	Jumps to the last entry in the track list.
Browser | List | List Extend Up/Down	Interaction Mode: Dec/Inc Type of Controller: Button	Expands the selection by the previous/next track.
Browser | List | List Extend Page Up/Down	Interaction Mode: Dec/Inc Type of Controller: Button	Expands the selection by the one page up/down.
Browser | List | List Extend Top/Bottom	Interaction Mode: Dec/Inc Type of Controller: Button	Expands the selection up to the beginning or the end of the track list.
Browser | List | List Select All	Interaction Mode: Trigger	Selects all tracks in the currently open track list.

7.2 The Track Collection

The Track Collection has been mentioned several times in the previous sections. There are several actions that add a track into the Track Collection:

◻ Drag a track from the Windows Explorer or the Mac Finder onto a deck.

◻ Open the *Explorer* node in the folder list and then either, one of the drives or music folders. Then drag a track onto a deck or right-/ctrl-click the track and select *Import to Collection*.

◻ Open the *Explorer* node in the folder list and select one of the drives or folders. Right-/ctrl-click the selection and choose the command *Import to Collection* and then one of the commands in the submenu for the type of audio file you are importing (tracks, loops, one-shot samples). Depending on your selection this imports all tracks from the drive or folder respectively into the collection.

◻ Open the *iTunes* node in the folder list and then either the library or one of the playlists. Then drag a track onto a deck or right-/ctrl-click the track and select *Import to Collection*.

◻ Open the *iTunes* node in the folder list and select one of the subfolders/playlists. Right-/ctrl-click the selection and choose the command *Import to Collection*. This imports all tracks in the subfolder/playlist into the collection.

The import process can be automated by using music folders. This can be done as follows:

1. Designate one of your hard drive folders as your music folder. This is explained in section "The Explorer Node" on page 246.

2. Open the dialog box *Preferences/File Management*.

3. Activate the check box *Import Music-Folders at Startup*. When Traktor is launched it checks if any of the music folders contain new tracks and will import those tracks into the Track Collection.

4. Activate the check box *Analyze new tracks on collection load/import*. When Traktor finds new files in the music folders they will be automatically analysed.

What happens during Track Analysis?

When a track is imported into the Track collection Traktor will analyse the track (unless the analysis has been disabled by deactivating the check boxes *Analyze new tracks on collection load/import* and *Analyze new tracks when loading into deck* (dialog box *Preferences/File Management*). During analysis several steps are performed:

- **BPM Detection**   Traktor detects the BPM of the track. During the analysis the BPM value shown in the Grid view of the Advanced Panel can change. Once the analysis is done the detected tempo is written to the ID3 tag BPM. If this tag does not exist it will be added.

- **ID3 Tags are updated to Version 2.4**   During the analysis Traktor converts the ID3 tags found to version 2.4.

- **Stripe and Waveform Creation**   Traktor creates the stripe view that is shown in the lower part of the deck. The stripe is stored in the folder Stripes below the Traktor root folder.

- **Volume Analysis**   Traktor analyses the volume of the track to identify the values needed for the Autogain feature. The Autogain function is an optional feature that ensures that the volume of a loud track is decreased and the volume of a quieter track is increased, when a track is loaded. This feature can be switched on and off with the check box *Set Autogain when Loading Track* on the dialog box *Preferences/Mixer* (see section "Gain Control" in chapter 3 for more information).

- **Transients List Creation**   Traktor creates a list of the transients, i.e. the beats in the track and their position. This list is stored in the *Transients* folder below the Traktor root folder. The transients are visible in the waveform of the track as vertical lines as long as the track has **no beatmarker**.

- **Key Detection**   Since version 2.6.1 (February 2013) Traktor analyses the key of the track which then can be used for harmonic mixing. The key can either be written in musical notation or in OpenKey format into the metadata of the track. Where exactly the key is written to depends on a setting in the Preferences. More information can be found in the footnote after the table on page 258. More information about key detection and harmonic mixing can be found in chapter 12.

◻ **Thumbnails of Cover Image**   When the track contains a cover, Traktor will create thumbnails of the image; these thumbnails are used in the deck header, the track list and in the cover art panel of the track browser. Traktor does not write the thumbnails back into the file but stores them in the folder *Coverart* below the Traktor root folder.

◻ **Tag TRAKTOR4/NITR is added**   Traktor adds the proprietary tag TRAKTOR4 to the ID3 or Flac tags. For wave files the proprietary RIFF info chunk *NITR* is added. This tag is used for Traktor-specific data such as cue points and loops that have been created and saved; the position of the beatmarker is stored here as well. The data in this tag is encrypted; that's why this information about this tag is not very precise and it could be incomplete.

It is good practice to beatgrid your tracks once they imported. How beatgridding works and what to look for is extensively covered in chapter 8. As soon as the tracks have a perfect or useful beatgrid you can define cue points and loops; both topics are covered in chapter 9 and 10.

"Traktor writes into my Files without my Permission!"

As you can see Traktor is quite busy during track analysis and it write changes to the ID3 tags as well. This has caused a lot of fuss and upset in the Traktor forum since the introduction of Traktor Pro/Duo 1.0. The good news for all that do not want Traktor to make changes to their music files: Traktor double-stores the information it detects during the track analysis: They are written into the tags as explained above and also stored in the file *Collection.nml,* that contains the Track Collection.

If you wish to avoid Traktor making these changes to your music files it is sufficient to write-protect them. This produces a warning message every time Traktor tries to write to the files, but is does not affect the functionality, because Traktor will use the information from the file *Collection.nml.*

It would be even better if Traktor would provide a configurable option in the Preferences dialog and if each Traktor user could either allow or disallow Traktor to make changes to the tags. Then write protecting the files would not be necessary.

I personally think it's good that Traktor writes the information into the files because embedded data like cue points and loops move around with the file. This makes it very easy to copy the files to a USB stick, import the files into a different Traktor system and have all the necessary data immediately available.

Private ID3 Frames and Tags in WAV Files

As well as the standard tags that contain information about title, artist etc. Traktor uses a private frame to store the Traktor specific data (cue points, loops, import date etc.). The use of private frames (PRIV) is specified in ID3V2.3 as well as in the specification of ID3V2.4:

> *This frame is used to contain information from a software producer that its program uses and does not fit into the other frames. The frame consists of an 'Owner identifier' string and the binary data. The 'Owner identifier' is a null-terminated string with a URL containing an email address, or a link to a location where an email address can be found, that belongs to the organisation responsible for the frame. Questions regarding the frame should be sent to the indicated email address. The tag may contain more than one "PRIV" frame but only with different contents.*

A table that can be found further down in this chapter shows which information Traktor stores in the private ID3 frame.

The widely held belief that WAV files don't allow storing tags is wrong. WAV files use the RIFF file format. RIFF, the abbreviation of *Resource Interchange File Format,* has been jointly developed by Microsoft and IBM as a means to allow exchange of multimedia data between applications and across platforms. RIFF files consist of one or more data blocks: they are called chunks. Each block has an identifier (four characters) that describes the type of data in that block, followed by the length of the block.

The following figure shows the chunks contained in the file *Vocal Wow.wav* (one of the files in the samples library of Traktor 2):

```
File Vocal Wow.wav is a "RIFF" with a specific type of "WAVE"
WAVE (186168): Found chunk element of type "fmt " and length 16
WAVE (186144): Found chunk element of type "PAD " and length 12236
WAVE (173900): Found chunk element of type "data" and length 108798
WAVE (65094): Found chunk element of type "ID3 " and length 1412
WAVE (63674): Found list element of type "INFO" and length 63658
INFO (63658): Found chunk element of type "NITR" and length 63554
INFO (96): Found chunk element of type "INAM" and length 9
INFO (78): Found chunk element of type "IART" and length 8
INFO (62): Found chunk element of type "IGNR" and length 7
INFO (46): Found chunk element of type "ICMT" and length 38
WAVE (4):
```

WAV audio files contain at least one *fmt* chunk (the fourth character in the type identifier is a space char). The *fmt* chunk contains information about the format of the audio data. The audio data itself is stored in a *data* chunk. Beyond that the RIFF specification names some info chunks and their purpose. The type *INAM* is used to store the title and the type *IART* contains information about the artist.

As well as these and other standard info chunks, the RIFF specification allows the use of user defined types. Traktor uses the user defined type *NITR* (Native Instruments **TR**aktor), to store Traktor specific information into the wav files. User defined types should not be a problem for other applications that use the file modified by Traktor if: they are programmed solidly, they simply ignore all chunks they don't know about.

Editing Tags

The tracks tags for MP3 and FLAC files can be edited either in Traktor or with an external Tool. When you are using WAV files you should use Traktor to edit the tags. If you are using an external tag editor the tool should store the tags in ID3 version 2.3/2.4 for MP3 files and should be able to handle "Vorbis comments", the format in which tags are stored in FLAC files.

The tags can either be edited in the track list or in a separate *Edit* dialog. The check box *Allow Inline Editing in List Window* in dialog *Preferences/File Management* must be activated if you wish to edit tags in the track list.

Once the option is enabled double-click the tag field in the track list and edit its content. When you are done, press Enter; Traktor writes the changes back to the music file and into the collection. This works for files that are imported into the collection, i.e. those tracks that are accessible via the *Track Collection* and *Playlists* node as well as for files that you have changed in the *Explorer* node.

Not all tags can be edited in the track list (for example neither the release date nor the play counter can be changed). To see all fields that can be changed right-/ctrl-click a track and select *Edit*. Traktor opens the dialog box shown in the following figure:

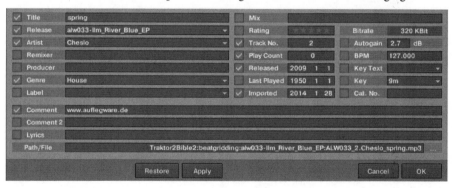

| TIP If the screen space isn't sufficient to show all tags and if you want to avoid scrolling, double-click the upper border frame of the deck to switch them temporarily to mini view.

This dialog box allows the editing of all tags. Use the *Restore* button to undo your changes or click *Apply* to save them; in both cases the *Edit* dialog stays open. The *Cancel* button undoes your changes and the *OK* button saves them; both buttons close the *Edit* dialog.

Metadata and Tags

One of the most frequently asked questions in the Traktor user forum regarding tagging is, which metadata is stored in which tags and which information moves together with the audio file when it is moved to another computer. The general answer is: All information, except the playcount and the last played date is saved inside the audio file and is immediately available when the file is moved to another system.

The track's metadata are stored in ID3 tags for MP3 files, in FLAC tags (that are actually Vorbis comments) inside FLAC files and in RIFF info chunks inside of WAV files.

The following table shows where the tags that are changed, either with the *Edit* dialog or by using inline editing of the track list, are stored. The left column shows the names as they are used in the *Edit* dialog. The column *MP3* shows the tag names for ID3 as they are defined in the ID3 specification. The column *FLAC* shows the key names used for the Vorbis comments. Finally, the WAV column shows the names of the RIFF info chunks that Traktor uses to store the meta data.

Field in Edit Dialog	MP3 ID3 Tags, Version 2.4	FLAC Vorbis Comments	WAV RIFF Info Chunks
Artist	TPE1 (Artist)	ARTIST	IART, standard
Autogain	TRAKTOR4 (Private tag)	TRAKTOR4	NITR, proprietary
BPM	TBPM (BPM)	BPM	NITR, proprietary
Cat. No.	TRAKTOR4 (Private tag)	TRAKTOR4	NITR, proprietary
Comment	COMM (Comment)	COMMENT	ICMT, standard
Comment2	TRAKTOR4 (Private tag)	TRAKTOR4	NITR, proprietary
Genre	TCON (Genre)	GENRE	IGNR, standard
Imported	TRAKTOR4 (private tag)	TRAKTOR4	NITR, proprietary
Key, Key Text*	TKEY (Initial Key) TRAKTOR4 (private tag)	INITIALKEY TRAKTOR4 (private tag)	NITR, proprietary
Label	TPUB (Publisher)	ORGANIZATION	NITR, proprietary
Last Played	–	–	–
Lyrics	USLT (Unsynchronized lyrics)	TRAKTOR4	NITR, proprietary
Mix	TRAKTOR4 (private tag)	TRAKTOR4	NITR, proprietary
Playcount	–	–	–
Producer	TIPL (Involved People)	TRAKTOR4	NITR, proprietary

Field in Edit Dialog	MP3 ID3 Tags, Version 2.4	FLAC Vorbis Comments	WAV RIFF Info Chunks
Rating	POPM (Popularimeter)	255 = 5 stars 204 = 4 stars 153 = 3 stars 102 = 2 stars 51 = 1 star 0 = 0 stars	NITR, proprietary
Release	TALB (Album)	ALBUM	IPRD, standard
Released	–	–	–
Remixer	TPE4 (Interpreted by)	MIXARTIST	NITR, proprietary
Title	TIT2 (Title)	TITLE	INAM, standard
Track No	TRCK (Track)	TRACKNUMBER	trkn, standard

* Since the introduction of key detection in Traktor 2.6.1 the new option *Written to File Tags* *(Preferences/Analyze Options)* affects in which tag the key is stored. This option has a double effect: it controls in which format the key is stored and in which tag it is stored.

If you select option *Key Text* Traktor will save the key inside the private TRAKTOR4 tag. This is the recommended setting if you use an additional key detection tool (like KeyFinder or Mixed In Key) as these tool store the key in the TKEY tag. Even if you select *Key Text* here, the key detected by Traktor will then be shown as "Key" in the track list, in the Edit and in the deck header of the track decks. If you select one of the first three options Traktor will save its key in the selected format in the MP3 tag TKEY (which is shown as INITIALKEY in many MP3 tagging tools). If the TKEY tag already contains a value Traktor will preserve it. The key detected by external tools is visible if you select option *Key Text* for the track list columns and for the track properties in the deck header.

Whenever possible, Traktor writes the metadata into one of the fields that are defined in the three different specifications. When there is no field defined for the value that Traktor needs to store, the private tag TRAKTOR4 or NITR is used instead.

Please note that the metadata is always written into the audio file and into the xml file containing the Traktor collection. Writing changed tags back into a WAV file can take a moment. Traktor first creates a temporarily copy of the original file to save the changes made to the meta tags, then deletes the original file and finally renames the temp file to the name of the original file. This whole process can take some time.

Editing Tags in iTunes and/or in Traktor?

Not all meta data fields that are either available in the tag edit dialogs of Traktor and iTunes can be used to exchange information between the two applications. (Note: The following information is based on iTunes version 11.) To make sure that the tag information is consistent only edit the following fields in iTunes:

◘ **Name** (this is the Traktor field *Title)*

◘ **Artist** (this is the Traktor field *Artist)*

◘ **Album** (this is the Traktor field *Release)*

◘ **Comment** (this is the Traktor field *Comment)*

◘ **Genre** (this is the Traktor field *Genre)*

◘ **Year** (this is the year entry in the Traktor field *Released)*

◘ **Track Number** – first entry field only (this is the Traktor field *Track No.)*

◘ **BPM** (this is the Traktor field *BPM)*

◘ **Rating** (this is the Traktor field *Rating)*

Changes made to those meta tags in Traktor are not immediately visible in the iTunes list view. When iTunes is started it doesn't re-read the tags from the file, instead the values stored inside the iTunes database are shown. You can force iTunes to update the tags by selecting all tracks, right-clicking the selection, choosing *Get Info* and clicking *Cancel* in the dialog box.

If changes you made to the tags in iTunes are not visible in Traktor, you can make Traktor to reread the tags: In the folder list right-click on the *iTunes* node and select *Refresh* from the context menu.

Saving the Collection

Every time you quit Traktor the collection will be automatically saved. During saving Traktor creates a backup of the previous version of your collection. You can use these backup files to repair the collection in case if gets damaged. The backup files are saved in the following folder:

◘ **OS X**   /Users/*[Username]*\Documents\Native Instruments\Traktor 2.x.y\Backup\Collection

◘ **Windows**   C:\Users*[Username]*\Documents\Native Instruments\Traktor 2.x.y\Backup\Collection

Replace *2.x.y* by the Traktor version you are using. (During a Traktor update Traktor imports the collection from the former version if this option is chosen. However, the collection file created in the former version and all backup files are preserved until you delete them manually. This allows you to import the collection from an earlier Traktor version.)

In case you perform extensive changes to the collection, for example by creating or editing your playlists, you can save the collection without quitting Traktor. To save the current state of your collection go to the folder list, right-click the node *Track Collection* and select *Save Collection*. Alternatively you can map the corresponding mapping command *Browser | Tree | Save Collection* to a button or your keyboard.

Restoring the Collection from a Backup or an earlier Version

In case your collection becomes damaged you can restore it from a backup files. This can be one of the backup files created in the current Traktor version, or the collection file from a previous Traktor version. Perform the following steps:

1. Go to the folder list, right-click the node Track Collection and select *Import another Collection*. Importing another collection replaces the current collection by the imported one.

2. Open the folder where the collection file resides that you wish to restore. This can be the collection backup folder of the current Traktor version or the folder *Documents\Native Instruments\Traktor 2.x.y*, if you wish to import the collection from Traktor *2.x.y*. Collection files use the file extension *.nml*.

3. Select the file with the collection you wish to restore and click *Open*.

7.3 Playlists

Playlists can be used and created in several ways:

◻ You can create new playlists directly in Traktor.

◻ You can open the *iTunes* node and use the playlists created in *iTunes*.

◻ You can import an iTunes playlists into the *Playlists* node.

Creating and Managing Playlists and Playlist Folders in Traktor

Traktor playlists are created in the *Playlists* node of the folder list. As with iTunes, this node can contain folders as well as playlists. This makes it possible to organise playlists hierarchically.

Creating Playlist Folders

To create a playlist folder, follow these steps:

1. Go to the folder list and open the *Playlists* node.

2. If you wish to create a folder at the highest level right-/ctrl-click the Playlists node. If you wish to create a folder at a lower level right-/ctrl-click the parent folder.

3. Select *Create Folder* in the context/action menu.

4. Type the name of the new folder and click *OK*.

Creating Playlists

To create a playlist, follow these steps:

1. Open the *Playlists* node in the folder list.

2. If the new playlist is to reside in *Playlists* node, right-/ctrl-click node. If you wish to create the playlist inside a playlist folder, right-/ctrl-click this folder.

3. Select *Create Playlist* in the context/action menu.

4. Type the name of the new playlist and click *OK*.

Adding, moving and deleting Tracks

Tracks can be added to a playlist by selecting them in the track list, then by dragging them onto the playlists' icon in the folder list. From Traktor 1.2 on you can also drag and drop a track from a deck either to a playlist in the browser tree or on a favourite icon that represents a playlist.

New tracks are always added at the end of the playlist. Because the folder list might scroll and dropping the tracks onto the desired playlist can be quite cumbersome it is easier to map the playlist to one of the favourite buttons. Dropping the new tracks there or using the mapping commands for adding tracks to favourites makes this easier. More information about favourites can be found on page 268 and onward.

To delete a track from a playlist, right-/ctrl-click the track and choose *Delete*. Confirm in the message box that the track is to be deleted.

To change the order of the tracks in a playlist use Drag & Drop. This only works if the playlist is currently arranged in the original sort order of the playlist. Let's assume you changed the sort order by clicking on one of the column headers. The tracks can no longer be moved around. There are two options to re-enable the sorting possibilities:

☐ Restore the default sort order by clicking on # in the column header of the track list.

☐ Right-/ctrl-click the playlist name and select *Consolidate*. This command sets the current set order as default sort order of the playlist, which makes moving tracks possible again.

Exporting a Playlist including all Tracks

If you wish to export a playlist together with all contained tracks (for example to copy them onto a USB stick for a later import on another Traktor system), perform the following steps:

1. Go to the folder list, open the *Playlists* node and right-click on the playlist you wish to export.

2. Select *Export Playlist*. Traktor displays the *Exporting Tracks* dialog. The field *Playlist Title* already contains the name of the playlist; you can change the name if you wish to.

3. If you wish to import the exported playlist including the tracks into another Traktor system, click the button in field destination and select the target. This step is important because the exported playlist will contain the path to the selected folder.

4. Open the list *Export Format* and select *M3U* if the playlist shall be created in the open playlist format. Option NML is the proprietary Traktor format for playlists.

5. Keep the check box *Copy Tracks to Destination* enabled and all tracks from the playlist shall also be copied.

6. Click on *OK*.

With the command *Import Playlist* that can be found by right-clicking the Playlists node in the older list you can import the playlist into another Traktor system.

More Actions for Playlists

The action/context menu for playlists contains some further commands that are shown in the adjoining figure. Use the command *Rename* to change the name of a playlist, or let Traktor generate a HTML file from the playlist *(Save as Webpage)*.

The command *Clear Playlist* removes all entries from the playlist and *Delete Playlist* removes the playlist itself. Use the command *Reset Played-State* to delete the check marker that indicates that a track has been played already from the icon column. Finally, the command *Analyze (Async)* triggers a track analysis for all the tracks in the playlist.

Importing iTunes Playlists into Traktor

You can import an iTunes playlist into Traktor. When importing an iTunes playlist into Traktor, Traktor will create a copy of the original list. When importing is finished there is no longer any connection between the iTunes and the Traktor playlist. Now you can use the imported list as if it was created in Traktor.

1. Go to the folder list and open the *iTunes* node and open, if necessary, the desired playlist folder.

2. Right-/ctrl-click the desired playlist and select the command *Import to Playlists*. Traktor creates a duplicate of the playlist and stores it under the same name in the *Playlists* node

3. Open the *Playlists* node, right-/ctrl-click the name of the imported playlist and select *Add to Collection*. This adds the tracks to the Track Collection and a track analysis is triggered, if necessary.

4. Beatgrid your tracks if you wish to use Traktors' sync feature and add cue points and loops.

5. Load the tracks the same way as you would do if the tracks are in the Traktor collection or in a Traktor playlist.

Using iTunes Playlists in Traktor

If you prefer to manage your playlists in iTunes only, then you can use the iTunes playlist in Traktor by following these steps:

1. Go to the folder list and open the *iTunes* node; then open the desired playlist as you would do in iTunes.

2. Select all tracks in the track list. Right-/Ctrl-click the selection and choose *Add to Collection* from the action/context menu so that the files are added to the playlist and are analysed as necessary.

3. Beatgrid your tracks if you wish to use Traktors' sync feature and add cue points and loops.

4. Load the tracks the same way as you would do if the tracks are in the Traktor collection or in a Traktor playlist.

Please note that you cannot edit an iTunes playlist in Traktor; i.e. you cannot add new tracks and you can't move tracks. What you can do, however, is change the sort order of the tracks.

> **TIP** If you wish to import a Traktor playlist into iTunes you can do this by using this little trick. Create a new iTunes playlist, and then arrange the windows of Traktor and iTunes so that both are visible. Select the tracks of the Traktor playlist and drag the selection onto the name of the iTunes playlist. When you release the mouse button all tracks are available in your iTunes playlist, even in the same order as they were in Traktor.

Playlists and Mapping Commands

Many of the actions described in the *Playlists* section can either be triggered or performed by using mapping commands.

Mapping Commands for Playlists

Browser | Tree | Create Playlist	Interaction Mode: Trigger	Creates a new playlist.
Browser | Tree | Delete Playlist	Interaction Mode: Trigger	Deletes the selected playlist.
Browser | Tree | Create Playlist Folder	Interaction Mode: Trigger	Creates a new playlist folder.
Browser | Tree | Delete Playlist Folder	Interaction Mode: Trigger	Deletes the selected playlist folder.
Browser | Tree | Analyze	Interaction Mode: Trigger	Analyses the tracks in the selected playlist/the selected folder.
Browser | List | Consolidate	Interaction Mode: Trigger	Stores the current sort order as the new default order of the selected playlist.
Browser | List | Clear	Interaction Mode: Trigger	Deletes all tracks from the playlist.
Browser | List | Reset Played-State	Interaction Mode: Trigger	Deletes the symbols from the icon column of the track list that indicates that the tracks have been played already.

Mapping Commands for Playlists

Browser | List | Select All	Interaction Mode: Trigger	Selects all tracks in the currently opened list.

7.4 The Preparation List

As well as the "normal" playlists covered in the previous section you can have one special playlist, called the preparation list. If you are familiar with earlier Traktor versions you will be aware of the concept of the preparation list already; in Traktor 3 this list was called "Current Playlist".

You can designate any playlist as preparation list. To do this right-click the desired playlist either in the *Playlists* 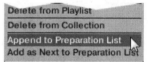 node of the browser tree or in the one of the favourite slots and select *Preparation List*. Traktor changes the icon for this playlist. Now a folder icon with a little house is used.

The playlist defined as preparation list has three features other playlists do not have and these make it easy to add new tracks either to, the end of the list or after the track that is currently selected in the list. Since Traktor 1.2 the context menu/action menu for tracks has had two new commands added to do this: One is called *Append to Prepration List*, the other one *Add as Next to Preparation List*. All tracks that are inside the Preparation List get the "diamond" in the icons column of the track list.

These two commands make it easier when preparing a playlist for a gig as well as changing a prepared playlist during a gig. In both cases you can keep the current track list opened (which can be the track collection, or the search results, or another playlist, maybe from iTunes), while adding new tracks to your preparation list (or current playlist, the name of the list is for you to choose).

Both menu commands can be mapped to a button or a key. The two mapping commands are shown in the following table:

Mapping Commands for the Preparation List

Browser | List | Append To Preparation List	Interaction Mode: Trigger	Inserts the selected track(s) at the end of the preparation list.
Browser | List | Add As Next To Preparation List	Interaction Mode: Trigger	Inserts the selected track(s) after the current selection of the preparation list.

7.5 Searching for Tracks

Traktor offers two functions to search for tracks. The first is hidden behind the magnifier icon that can be found in several columns of the track list. When you click this icon the content  of the clicked field is used as search criteria and Traktor will display the search results. For example if you click in column *Genre* on the magnifier next to *House*, Traktor will show all tracks where the *Genre* tag is set to *House*. Additionally the current query is entered into the *Search* field above the folder list. The Search field itself contains the text *HOUSE;* if you click the arrow in the *Search* field Traktor opens a list with all tag names; here the field *Genre* is checked; i.e. Traktor performs the search in the checked field only.

 To delete the search query and to make Traktor display all tracks again, click the X at the right side of the *Search* field.

Another way of searching is entering the search criteria direct into the *Search* field. This triggers a dynamic search, i.e. Traktor displays all tracks found that match the search criteria entered so far.

By default Traktor searches only in the folder/playlist that is currently shown in the track list. To extend the search to the complete Track Collection press Enter. Then the selection in the folder list jumps to the *Track Collection* node. When you click the X button in the Search field now, Traktor will select the node/folder/playlist that was selected before you pressed Enter.

When you have entered the search term you can click the arrow in the Search field to restrict the search to a certain field by clicking the field name in the popup menu. Select the entry *All* that is at the top of the list to extend the search to all available fields.

If you would like to know in which playlists a particular track has been used, right-click the track in the track list and select *Search in Playlists*. Traktor displays a dialog box with all playlists that contain the track. You can double-click one of the playlist names to open. Searching in playlists works as well if several tracks are selected.

For searching, three mapping commands are available. In the predefined keyboard mappings *Search* is mapped to Ctrl+F and Cmd+F respectively.

Searching for Tracks

Browser | List | Search	Interaction Mode: Trigger	Sets the insertion point into the Search field.
Browser | List | Search Clear	Interaction Mode: Trigger	Deletes the text in the Search field.
Browser | List | Search in Playlists	Interaction Mode: Trigger	Shows a list with all playlists that contain the selected track/s.

7.6   Favourites Panel

The Favourites Panel resides above the track browser. This panel contains twelve buttons that can be mapped to folders or playlists. Accessing one of the assigned targets by clicking a button is much faster than searching and scrolling in the folder list. You can switch the Favourites Panel on and off by using the check box *Show Playlist Favourites* on the dialog *Preferences/Browser Details* dialog box.

To assign a folder or a playlist to a favourite button simply drag the folder/playlist from the folder list onto the desired button. Traktor replaces the label "not assigned" by the name of the playlist and folder. You can open one of the favourites by clicking the corresponding button. When the buttons are mapped to a playlist you can add tracks to that playlist by dragging them from the track list or from one of the decks onto the favourite button.

You can use mapping commands to open favourites and to add tracks to favourites. In the predefined keyboard mappings these actions are mapped to the function keys F1 to F12. Pressing the function key only opens the favourite. Pressing the function key while the Shift key is pressed causes the selected track/s to be added to the corresponding playlist.

Using the Favourites Panel

Browser | Favorites | Add Folder To Favorites	Interaction Mode: Direct Set to value: Favorite 1 to Favorite 12	Adds the selected track to the favourite selected in list Set to value. The name of this command is misleading as it does not add a folder to the favourites, but a track to the specified favourite. "Add Track to Favorite" would be a much better name.
Browser | Favorites | Selector	Interaction Mode: Direct Type of Controller: Button Set to value: Favorite 1 to Favorite 12	Open the favourite selected in the list Set to value.
	Interaction Mode: Inc, Dec Type of Controller: Button	Opens the next or the previous favourite.
	Interaction Mode: Direct Type of Controller: Fader/Knob	Browses through the different favourites.

With the command *Selector* the interaction modes, *Inc* and *Dec* can be used to browse the favourites by using two buttons. In the default keyboard mappings these commands are mapped to the keys Left-Arrow and Right-Arrow.

> **TIP** You can combine the commands *Add Folder to Favorites* and *Selector* into a button macro to add a track to one of the favourite playlists and to open this playlist at the same time. This is possible because of the order the commands are executed. The *Add* command is executed first and the *Selector* command second.

HOW TO: Select Favourites from your Kontrol S2 MK2

Unfortunately the default mapping of Kontrol S2 does not allow direct access to the favourites. If you wish to use the BROWSE encoder to browse through the favourites as well, simply add two mapping commands to the default mapping.

The following mapping extension allows you to browse through the favourites by holding the right SHIFT button and turning the BROWSE encoder.

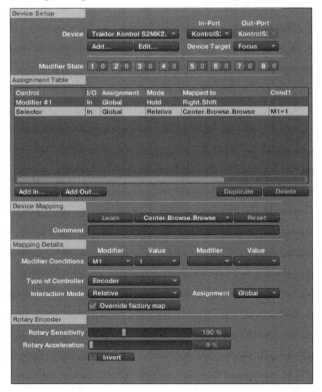

The first command creates a mapping for the right SHIFT button. While this button is held Modifier #1 shall have a value of 1. Please make sure that for this command option *Override factory map* is disabled, otherwise the integrated features will no longer work as expected.

The second command controls the functionality of the BROWSE encoder while the right SHIFT button is held (condition M1=1). Here the mapping command *Browser | Favorites | Selector* is used; this command performs the browsing. Please make sure that for this command *Override factory map* is enabled as we wish to assign a new feature to RIGHT-SHIFT+BROWSE.

Chapter 8

Staying in Sync – Beat-, Bar- and Phrase-Matching

8.1 Synchronisation – An Overview

Whether you can, should or must use the possibilities that Traktor offers regarding automatic tempo and beat synchronisation or not, is an ideological question. Chris Liebing says:

> "At the end of the day from my point of view beat-matching is a complete egoistic thing. Nobody on the dance floor has any benefit from the synchronisation process between two tracks. Clubbers realize beat-matching only then, if something goes wrong while mixing. Of course, the beat-matching advocates can come and say that they absolutely need it. Then they shall do it for heaven's sake. I don't need it at all costs and I don't need to prove it myself every night [that I'm able to manually beat-match]".[1]

One can debate it for hours without reaching any conclusion about the pros or cons. This is why I wish to end the discussion with this sentence and the quote from Chris Liebing. For the rest of the chapter I will turn to practical questions and will describe the features that Traktor provides and that everybody should use in a way that best fits their own style of spinning.

In fact, the synchronisation inside Traktor is a quite simple model: Traktor internally ticks a clock serving as a reference for synchronisation for all tracks, for beat precise jumps and last but not least as a synchronisation source for the effects, the loop recorder, and the sample slots when they contain looped samples. The currently selected Master Clock mode determines from where the Master Clock receives its tempo. The different Master Clock modes and how to use them for synchronisation purposes and their pros and cons are explained in detail on page 297 and further. If tracks are played at the same tempo as the Master Clock then those tracks are tempo synced.

However, even if the tempo of two tracks is identical it may still be that they are not running beat-synchronised. Traktor needs to know the position of a downbeat in a

---

[1] Chris Liebing (www.clr.net) in an interview with German magazine Raveline

track to be able to synchronise it. The position of a downbeat is called *beatmarker* (or *gridmarker*). In most cases Traktor is able to detect the beatmarker in a track. When the beatmarker-detection engine has detected a beatmarker, that beatmarker is called an *auto-beatmarker*. There are cases where you need to define the position of the beatmarker yourself, for example if Traktor cannot detect it due to a complex rhythmic structure in a track or if the beatmarker detection failed. When you define a beatmarker or correct the beatmarker that Traktor has detected, that beatmarker is called a *manual beatmarker*.

The beatmarker serves as a reference point for the *beatgrid*. The beatgrid, whose grid-lines have the same spacing, defines the position of the other beats on a track. Here the assumption is made that the track tempo does not change. The following rules apply to the beatgrid: The greater the spacing of the individual gridlines, the lower the track tempo. The smaller the spacing, the higher the track tempo is.

Phase Synchronous

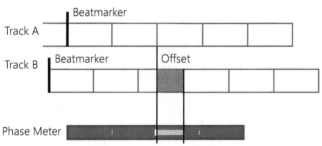

Phase Asynchronous

When two tracks are running in a way that their beatgrids exactly match, those tracks are running *phase synchronous*. When there is an offset between the beatgrids of the two tracks they will be running *phase asynchronous*. Here the down-beats will not be heard at the same time. Most of the time this sounds pretty bad.

The offset between the gridlines of a deck and the current master tempo source is shown in the *phase meter* that each deck provides. The phase meter can be displayed by activating the option *Phase Meter* (dialog *Preferences/Decks Layout*, section *Deck Header*).

Beats, Bars, and Phrases

Let's assume we have two tracks, their tempo has been defined exactly, the beatmarkers are set to the correct positions and therefore both tracks have a perfect beatgrid. Let's additionally assume that deck A is playing, that the Master Clock is running in automatic mode (in this mode Traktor decides which of the decks acts as sync master) and that Traktor has made deck A the sync master. We load another track in deck B, specify the point on the track from where we want to play the track and click the *Sync* button in deck B (the *Sync* button tells Traktor that this deck shall be synchronised with the sync master). Is everything now in perfect sync? The answer is: Well, yes and no.

Bar Synchronicity

The *Sync* button triggers two actions. First the tempo of the deck is set to the tempo of the sync master (tempo synchronisation). Second, assuming that the loaded track has a beatmarker, Traktor moves the playback marker in the track so that the beats (gridlines) in both decks match (phase synchronisation). However, the problem is that Traktor moves the playback marker simply to the next beat. Traktor doesn't care whether the first beat of a bar in deck A matches the first beat of a bar in deck B. In other words: The two tracks are running beat synchronous, but not bar synchronous. This is illustrated in the following figure:

Track A		Bar x				Bar y				Bar z				
		x.1	x.2	x.3	x.4	y.1	y.2	y.3	y.4	z.1	z.2	z.3	z.4	

Track B	Bar w				Bar x				Bar y				Bar z		
	w.1	w.2	w.3	w.4	x.1	x.2	x.3	x.4	y.1	y.2	y.3	y.4	z.1	z.2	z.3

This issue can easily be solved by combining the following techniques:

◻ When you are beatgridding a track always set the beatmarker on the first beat of a bar.

◻ Display the beatcounter in the Deck Header (this is done by opening the dialog box *Preferences/Track Decks,* and selecting the option *Beats* for one of the list boxes in section *Deck Header).*

◻ Set the playback marker in the second deck to the first beat of a bar and start this deck when the beatcounter display in the other deck shows x.1.

The beatcounter shows the current playback position as *Phrase.Bar.Beat* (the beatcounter assumes that all tracks are in a 4/4 time signature).

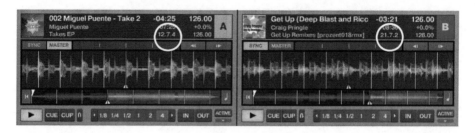

The playback position in deck A is Phrase 12, Bar 7, Beat 4 (12.7.4) and in deck B it is at Phrase 21, Bar 7, Beat 2 (21.7.2). If both decks are playing as shown here you can use the *Beatjump* view of the Advanced Panel (see chapter 3) to jump two beats forward in deck B; then both decks are playing the same beat number at the same time. Now both tracks are playing beat synchronous as well as bar synchronous.

Phrase Synchronicity

The flow of a mix gets better if, not only the synchronicity of beats and bars are considered, but also the structure of a track. For electronic dance music the different parts of a track (intro, build-up, verse, chorus, break, climax, outro), called phrases, are in most cases 8, 16, 32 or 64 bars long. If you listen to a track the transitions between the different phrases can be easily heard: a new element is added at the beginning of a new phrase, the filter is changed or effects are used, or the start of the next phrase is introduced in the last beats of the current phrase. If you start the next track at "phrase x, bar 1, beat 1" when the current track is at "phrase y, bar 1, beat 1", then the flow of the mix integrates very well into the compositional structures of 4/4 dance music. The next track will add a new element into the mix at the moment when the people on the dance floor expect it.

However: There are genres and tracks where this structure is either not present or barely noticeable. For example, one of the tutorials in the next section uses a Detroit techno track that does not follow the described phrase structure. Keep the phrase concept in mind, but don't make yourself a slave to it.

As shown earlier the field *Beats* in the deck header informs you about the current phrase, bar and beat. You can use section *Beat Counter* of the dialog box *Preferences/Transport* to configure the number of bars per phrase. The slider has a range between 0 and 64 bars. If you choose 0, then the phrase number is not shown. Normally I use a value of 8 *Bars per Phrase*, because this setting fits well with the music I play. Maybe try this setting to start with and change it later if other values better suit you.

If it is difficult to drag the slider to the desired position then type the value into the text field next to the slider and press Enter.

After you have activated the phrase number the beat counter display uses 3 digits to indicate the current beat. At the end of each phrase the bar counter is reset to 1; i.e. if you have selected 8 bars per phrase then the beat after 20.8.4 will be beat 21.1.1.

The consideration of bars and phrases applies as a general rule for DJing: What really matters is what the end result is and that your intention matches the actual result. Nevertheless it can be helpful to keep the phrase concept at the back of your mind.

The Tools in Grid View of the Advanced Panel

The tools for setting the tempo of a track and for setting beatmarkers are available in *Grid* view of the Advanced Panel.

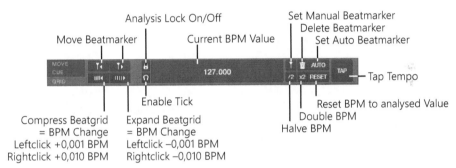

Here is a short overview of the four buttons at the right side of grid panel:

□ **AUTO** The *Auto* button removes all existing beatmarkers and sets a new automatic beatmarker at the position that was detected during the track analysis. Additionally the tempo is reset is to the BPM value that was detected during the first track analysis

□ **RESET** Resets the track tempo to the BPM value that was detected during the first track analysis. Existing beatmarkers are not affected.

□ **T** This button sets a manual beatmarker at the current position of the playback marker. Existing manual and automatic beatmarkers are not affected.

□ **T̄** This button deletes a beatmarker. When the playback marker is at the same position as a beatmarker, this beatmarker is deleted. When the playback marker is not on a beatmarker, first the beatmarkers to the left and then the ones to the right of the playback marker are deleted.

Difference between Auto-Beatmarker and Manual Beatmarker

What is the difference between auto-beatmarkers and manual beatmarkers? The essential difference is: Each track may only contain exactly one auto-beatmarker. When a track already contains a beatmarker (no matter if it is a manual beatmarker or an auto-beatmarker), clicking the *Autogrid* button initiates the following actions:

◻ All existing beatmarkers are deleted.

◻ A new auto-beatmarker is set at the position determined by the track analysis performed by Traktor.

◻ All corrections that have been made to the BPM value of the track are undone because Traktor determines the BPM value again.

If you have a track with changes in tempo it is better to use manual beatmarkers. When a track contains a second beatmarker that is not exactly on the gridlines produced by the first beatmarker, then the second beatmarker will become the new start point of the grid from that beatmarkers position onwards.

Tick – Traktors' Metronome

Another tool helpful to identify the track tempo is the internal metronome, hidden behind the *Beat Tick* button in the Grid view of the advanced deck panel. To be able to hear the tick you need to activate the *Beat Tick* button and the *Cue* (prelisten) button in the deck of which the metronome shall "tick".

When you are using the internal Traktor mixer the tick is sent to the outputs selected in section *Output Monitor* of dialog box *Preferences/Output Routing*. If you are using Traktor in external mixing mode the tick is sent to the outputs selected for the individual decks; i.e. the tick can be heard in the mix-out signal of the mixer, regardless of the cue-settings on the mixer.

8.2 Beatgridding, Tutorials

For the following tutorials I have selected some netlabel tracks (download links can be found at the beginning of each tutorial). The goal was not to find the most exciting tracks (actually, some of them are quite good) but to find tracks that can be used to exercise some of the standard scenarios you will encounter when beatgridding your tracks.

My tip for newcomers is to download the tracks and to follow the step-by-step instructions in the tutorials. You can download all tracks that I used in a single ZIP file from *www.traktorbible.com/2014/links.aspx*. All track details can be found at the beginning of each tutorial, including the URLs where I downloaded the (Creative Commons) tracks.

Once you are familiar with the basic tricks it becomes easy to beatgrid many of the standard tracks in seconds (even though you may not think so considering the length of this tutorial). A good side effect of this exercise is that you learn how to use the tools Traktor provides for beatgridding.

To be able to follow the steps as described it is important to make some changes in your Traktor configuration. Here are the settings I have used whilst writing this tutorial. Please make these changes so that Traktor behaves exactly as described:

☐ **8 Bars per Phrase** Open the dialog *Preferences/Transport* and set the slider *Bars per Phrase* in section *Beat Counter* to 8 bars.

☐ **Mouse Control: Snap** Open the dialog *Preferences/Transport* and select *Snap* in section *Mouse Control*. With Snap enabled clicking onto the waveform makes the playback marker snap on the next gridline of the beatgrid or the nearest cue point if the deck is not playing. If the deck is playing clicking the waveform triggers a beatjump.

As an alternative you can keep *Mouse Control* set to *Vinyl*. This allows you to move the waveform freely with the mouse. If you wish to set the playmarker onto a gridline of the beatgrid press the CUE button in the transport section of the deck. Activate option SNAP in the Global Section to make that work (more information about SNAP can be found in chapter 9).

☐ **Master Panel: Snap** Click in the Master Panel of the Global Section on *Snap* to activate the Snap mode. If the Snap mode is active you can use the *CUE* button to move the playback marker to the next gridline of the beatgrid.

☐ **Beatcounter display** Open the dialog *Preferences/Track Decks*. Select the option *Beats* for one of the info fields in the section *Deck Header*. Traktor then shows the beatcounter in the deck header.

☐ **Activate minute markers and highlighted beatmarkers** Open the dialog *Preferences/Decks Layout*. Activate the check box *Show Minute Markers* and set option *Grid* to *Full*. The first option shows the minute markers in the stripe and the second one makes the grid lines of the beat raster visible.

☐ **BPM Detection Range** Open the dialog *Preferences/Analyze Option* and check if the *BPM Range* in section *BPM Detection* is set at 78 to 155 BPM. This is the standard setting of Traktor and the optimal setting for detecting the BPM of 4/4 house and techno tracks.

☐ **Create automatic beatmarker** Open the dialog *Preferences/Analyze Options* and activate the option *Set Beat-Grid when detecting BPM*; if this option is enabled Traktor creates an automatic beatmarker during the tracks analysis.

◻ **Analyze Tracks when loaded into deck** Open Preferences/File Management and activate the check box *Analyze new tracks when loading into deck*. If this option is enabled Traktor will perform a tempo and beat detection when a track that has been added to the collection is loaded into a deck for the first time.

Keyboard Mapping for Beatgridding

The following tutorials explain the beatgridding techniques by using the Traktor user interface and the mouse. All beatgridding actions can be easily triggered with mapping commands with either the keyboard or a controller.

On *www.traktorbible.com/2014/links.aspx* you can download a preparation mapping that includes all commands needed for beatgridding with the keyboard. The PDF file included contains an overview of the shortcuts and it explains how to install several keyboards mappings and how to switch between them.

Beatmarker and Hotcues

Each Traktor deck offers eight hot cue buttons that can be used to jump immediately to cue points that have been stored as hotcues. (More information about cue points and hotcues can be found in chapter 9).

In older Traktor versions beatmarkers were automatically assigned to a hotcue button as long as all hotcue buttons were not occupied. In Traktor 2 there is a new option that controls whether new beatmarkers are automatically assigned as a hotcue or not. This option can be found in section *BPM Detection* of the *Preferences/Analyze Options* dialog.

The checkbox *Store Beatmarker as Hotcue* is disabled by default. Because hotcue storage is a limited resource I recommended to leave this option disabled. Changing the setting for *Store Beatmarker as Hotcue* affects new set beatmarkers only. Beatmarkers that are already stored as hotcues will not be changed if you change the checkbox state.

So far so good for the preparations, let's get started with the first tutorial.

Tutorial 1: 100% Tempo Match, Position of Auto Gridmarker is incorrect

Track: Track: Tactics, Mono.xID, CICUTA026 – Urban Warfare EP
Source: http://cicutanetlabel.com/release-026/

The little tutorial series starts with a track where the tempo has been detected correctly but where the position of the automatic beatmarker is wrong.

1. Add the track to your collection and load it into deck A. When loading and ana-lysing is finished the deck should look like this:

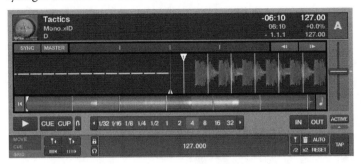

The tempo looks okay: the BPM value is an integer (which is true for most EDM tracks).

However, the automatic beatmarker that Traktor has set looks misplaced. It looks as if Traktor has set the automatic beatmarker not onto a beat, but approximately between the beginning of the track (i.e. the position with the playmarker) and the first beat.

2. Hover over the waveform to make the zoom buttons visible. Then, depending on the current zoom factor, either zoom into the waveform or zoom out until several gridlines of the beatgrid are visible (as shown in the previous figure).

3. Let's assume that the position of the auto beatmarker is wrong. Click on *Delete Gridmarker* to delete the auto beatmarker.

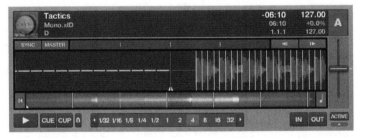

The track no longer has a beatmarker. Nevertheless we can see white vertical lines on the waveform. For a track without a beatmarker these vertical lines represent the transients Traktor has detected during the track analysis. Traktor uses the detected transients to set the BPM and to set the position of the auto beatmarker.

4. Click on the first white line indicating the first detected transient. We assume that the tracks begins here and that this is the position of the first beat. As option *Mouse Control* is set to *Snap*, the playmarker snaps to the position of the transient.

Please note the beat counter value 1.1.2 in the deck header.

5. Click on *Set Gridmarker*.

Traktor inserts a manual beatmarker at the current playback position. The beatgrid is redrawn. The intervals between the different gridlines look fine now. Additionally the beat counter value was corrected: it shows 1.1.1 now.

By default Traktor sets the playmarker on the beginning of the file (which does not necessary mean the beginning of the track). Because our sample tracks starts with one beat of silence, the playmarker would be on this empty beat when we load the track. To correct this you can set a load marker to the position of the manual beatmarker:

6. Click at the left side of the Advanced Panel on Cue to open the Cue panel.

7. Click on *Store*, to save a new cue point. Then open the list box with the cue-point-types and select *Load*. The track should now look as shown in the following figure:

8. Start playback of the track and check whether the beatmarker works well regarding the structure of the track and whether the track changes at that beat counter positions, where a new phrase starts (for example at 7.1.1, and 15.1.1).

   This looks good. Great, we are done.

9. Click on *Analysis Lock,* to lock tempo, beatgrid, the detected key and the autogain value.

Once you have finished beatgridding a track it is good practice to use the *Lock BPM* button to lock tempo, beatmarker and beatgrid to protect the track from accidental changes. Another advantage of the *Analysis Lock* button is that the track is marked with a lock symbol in the track browser. This makes it easy to see which tracks have been gridded and which ones have not.

Tutorial 2: Detected BPM is only an Integer when rounded, Silence at the Beginning of the Track

Track: Track: Convex, Victor Martinez, CICUTA013 – Fármaco EP
Source: http://cicutanetlabel.com/release-013/

1. Add the track to your collection and load it into deck A. When loading and analysing is finished the deck should look like this:

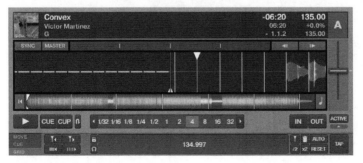

Two things attract my attention: This track also begins with some beats of silence. This leads to incorrect beat counter values in the course of the track. In our example we can see that there are four beats without audio behind the automatic beatmarker. This results in the bar value being by 1 to large.

Then we have a BPM value of 134.997. With such a slight difference from an integer I assume that the real tempo is in fact 135. We will check if this assumption becomes true.

2. First let's take care of the position of the beatmarker. Click the vertical line before the first visible beat. Click on *Delete Gridmarker* to delete the automatic beatmarker and then click on *Set Gridmarker* to set a manual beatmarker at the current playback position.

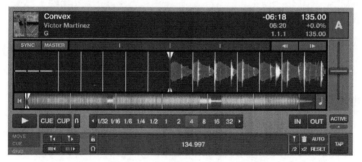

3. Now let's us take a closer look at the detected BPM value. As explained above I assume that the tempo is 135 BPM. We will now set the tempo to 135 BPM and then check, whether the beatgrid fits to this tempo.

Click the *BPM INC* button in the Advanced Grid Panel. One click will increase the tempo by 0.001 BPM. Increasing the tempo results in a slightly more compressed grid. Click again until the tempo fields shows 135.000.

4. Hover on the waveform to make the zoom buttons visible and then zoom into the waveform.

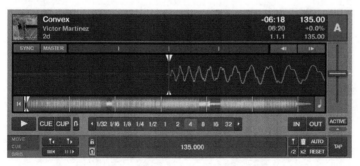

The exact position of the manual beatmarker is now easy to see. It sits exactly on the first beat. Let us check now whether the gridlines of the beatgrid are on the correct position for the rest of the track.

5. Click in the stripe at a position somewhere in the last quarter of the track.

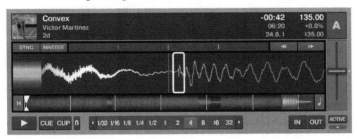

To the right of the playmarker (which corresponds to a gridline of the beatgrid as we have Snap mode on), one can see a short vertical line in the waveform. This line (marked in the figure above) represents the beginning of a beat. The grid does not sit perfectly on the beginning of the beat. Click some other positions in the track: the offset between the grid and the beat will be similar.

6. Let us revoke the changes we made to the tempo. Click twice on *BPM DEC* to decrease the tempo in steps of 0.001 BPM (which in turn widens the beatgrid).

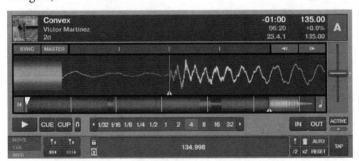

This now looks better. My working hypothesis that the tempo of the track is 135 BPM turned out to be wrong. Using 134.998 as the tempo seems to be the better choice.

7. Return to the position of the manual beatmarker and add a Load marker there (because of the silence at the beginning of the track). Then click on *Analysis Lock* to protect the track from accidental changes.

Tutorial 3: Automatic Beatmarker is slightly displaced

Track: Track: La Gota (Original Mix), Lander B & Dj Sevio, YPQN043
Source: http://ypqnrecords.com/

Finding a suitable track for the topic of this tutorial wasn't an easy task. In Traktor 2.0 there were plenty of tracks where Traktor displaced the automatic beatmarker. However, in Traktor 2.6.8 (the version these tutorials are based on) the amount of tracks that show this analysis defect is extremely small. This does reveal the improvements Native Instruments has made to the algorithms for tempo and beat detection in Traktor 2.5.

Nevertheless I found an example that shows how you can use the metronome to move the automatic beatmarker to a somewhat better position in the track.

1. Add the track to your collection, load it into deck A, and wait until Traktor has finished the track analysis. With a BPM of 126 the tempo looks pretty, pretty good and the automatic gridmarker has been set on the first beat of the track.

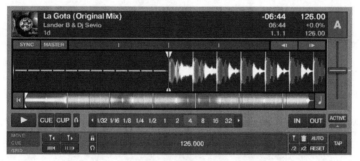

2. Click in the waveform onto the auto gridmarker. This snaps the playmarker to the gridmarker. Then zoom into the waveform.

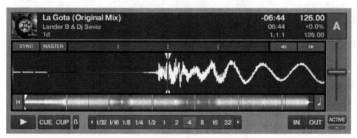

Once you zoom in you can see quite well that the automatic beatmarker does not sit exactly on the beat, but slightly behind it.

3. Click the *Beat Tick* button in the A dvanced Grid Panel. This activates the tick of Traktors' metronome.

4. If you use internal mixing mode, click the *Monitor Cue* button of deck A. This makes the metronome audible. In external mixing mode this step is not necessary.

> **TIP** Depending on the frequency range of the track, the tick can sometimes be very quiet. In most cases it helps to use the deck filter. Turn the filter knob until the ticks of the metronome, as well as the rhythm of the track, are equally audible. Another option is using the deck's gain knob to change the volume of the track.

5. Set a four beat loop and start playback of the track.

6. Use the buttons *Move Grid Backwards* and *Move Grid Forward* to move the beatmarker and the beatgrid. I have moved the beatmarker slightly to the left until tick and beat seem to match.

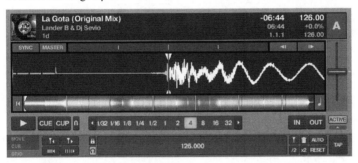

7. Stop playback of the track and check at other positions in the track whether there the beatgrid sits properly on the beginning of the beats. In case grid and case do not fit try to move the beatmarker again until you are satisfied.

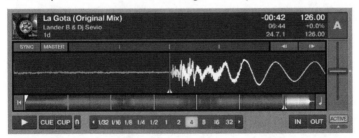

8. Finally click on *Analysis Lock* to protect the track from accidental changes.

Tutorial 4: Tempo is not an Integer

Stereophonic Sound, Kriss, no mad .e.p [unfound038]
Source: www.unfoundsoundrecords.com, click on „unreleases" to see the download links

This tutorial shows that real BPM values are not always integer numbers and that you can see from the spacing of the gridlines if the BPM value is too big or too small.

1. Add the track to your collection and load it into deck A. When loading and analysing is finished the deck should look like this:

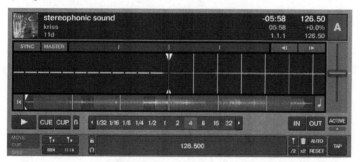

Traktor has set an automatic beatmarker (AutoGrid) but its position is at the very beginning of the track. It is quite likely that it is necessary to move the beatmarker to the first downbeat after the intro (approximately at 0:10) to get a correct value of beat/bar/phrase in the beatcounter.

2. Click in the stripe at the point where the intro ends. Then click in the waveform on the first downbeat to create a volatile cue point. The beatcounter shows the value 1.6.4.

3. Click on *Delete Gridmarker* to delete the automatic beatmarker.

4. Click on *Set Gridmarker* to insert a manual beatmarker.

   If you look at the other gridlines of the beatgrid you can see that the BPM value is almost perfect. Perform the following steps to understand the dependency between the track tempo and the spacing of the gridlines.

5. Click the *BPM* field, enter 140 and then press the Enter key. If you have a look at the waveform it is obvious that the spacing of the gridlines is too small (the second gridline is before the visible second beat).

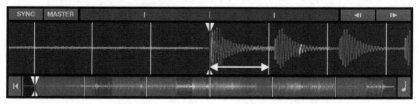

6. Click the *BPM* field again, enter 115 and press the Enter key. Look at the waveform to see that the spacing of the gridlines is now too wide (the second gridline is behind the visible second beat).

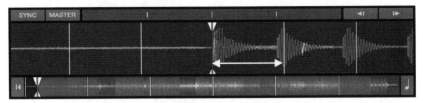

This leads to the following rules:

☐ If the spacing of the gridlines is too small then the tempo is too high; you can correct this with the button *Expand Beatgrid* (BPM DEC).

☐ If the spacing of the gridlines is too wide then the tempo is too low; you can correct this with the button *Compress Beatgrid* (BPM INC).

7. Click the *BPM* field, enter 126.5 and press the Enter key. Now the beatgrid looks much better.

8. Once you are satisfied with the position of the beatmarker check if all other phrases actually start at position x.1.1.

9. Click *Analysis Lock* to lock the track.

Tutorial 5: The analysed BPM Value is half as small or twice as big as the real Tempo

Track: Down the Drain, Cycom, Isotope [pp029md]
Source: www.plainaudio.com/dnb/releases.html

The BPM detection engine in Traktor depends heavily on the values which are configured on section *BPM Range* on the *Preferences/Analyze options* dialog.

The default value 78–155 is fine for House and Techno, if you are a Hip-Hop-DJ you will achieve better results using the 58–115 range. If your favourite style is Drum 'n' Bass then you should use 118–235.

If the configured BPM detection range does not fit the tempo of the genre, you very often get BPM values which are twice as large or half as small as the real tempo. The DnB track for this tutorial shows how the range affects the analysed tempo.

1. Add the track to your collection and load it into deck A. Let Traktor analyse the track with the default *BPM Range* (78–155).

Traktor detects the BPM as 85.004. For a Drum 'n' Bass track this is shall we say "extraordinary". The real tempo is probably around 170, this value is twice as large as the one detected by the original Traktor analysis.

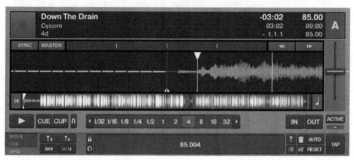

2. These kinds of errors can easily be corrected with the buttons *x2* and */2* right of the tempo field: *x2* doubles the shown BPM value; */2* halves it.

3. Make a small experiment and test what happens if you change the BPM detection range. Open the dialog *Preferences/Analyze Options* and change the BPM range to 118–235.

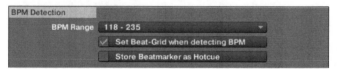

4. If you right click (Windows) or Ctrl-click on the track in the track browser Traktor opens the context menu/action menu. Then click on *Analyze (Async)* and click *OK* in the *Analyze* dialog (this dialog is covered in Tutorial 8 on page 292). When the analysis is done Traktor shows a BPM value of 170.007, this value is almost twice as large as the one detected by the original BPM detection range.

5. The further steps are the same as in the previous tutorial: check that the real BPM value is not an integer, check if the beatmarker is at the correct position etc.

Tutorial 6: Tracks with a moving Grid/changing Tempo

As well as tracks with a straight rhythm there are tracks where, after a breakdown, the beats are no longer exactly on the gridlines, maybe because the length of the breakdown is not a whole number of beats. These kinds of tracks can still be played in sync with other tracks if you know some simple tricks. I could not find a proper netlabel track for this scenario so I shall explain the procedure in a dry run.

The goal with this track is to get a stable beatgrid for mixing the track in, as well as to mix the end of the track out and into the next track. If you can create a partially stable beatgrid you will be able to use Traktors' synchronisation features.

Creating two Beatmarkers for one Track

The trick with these tracks is simply to set two beatmarkers. Set the first one, if possible on the first downbeat at the beginning of the track and then the second one on the first downbeat after the breakdown. I recommend using manual beatmarkers just to avoid clicking on the *Autogrid* button because this causes either, the manually changed tempo to be altered or it removes the already present manual beatmarkers.

Before setting the second beatmarker switch off the *Snap* option in the Master Panel of the Global Section. Open the dialog *Preferences/Transport* and activate the *Vinyl* option in the section *Mouse Control*. The first setting ensures that you are able to set cue points which are not on the gridlines of the beatgrid. By activating the Mouse Control Mode *Vinyl* you are able to move the waveform freely in its window; this is necessary if you do not wish to put the second beatmarker on the gridlines that is created by the first beatmarker.

Another variation, which is especially useful, if the overall tempo of the track is not very stable, is to find some beats at the end of the track that can be easily looped. Then, set the second beatmarker at the same position as the "Loop In point" and save the loop. When mixing in the next track just activate the loop to avoid a beat offset with the next track.

Playback of Tracks with two Beatmarkers in sync mode BeatSync

When playing back tracks that have several beatmarkers you need to switch the *Sync* button in the respective decks off, if you use BeatSync as synchronisation mode (see page 297 for more information). If the *Sync* button is on in this mode, Traktor ensures that the tempo and phase of the track are in sync with the sync tempo source. When Traktor reaches the position of the second beatmarker, which is not on a gridline of the previous beatgrid, you get a phase offset and Traktor will correct it. This leads to an audible jump in the track. To avoid this jump caused by the automatic tempo and phase synchronisation in BeatSync mode, best practice is to proceed as follows (assuming that in deck A the track with the two beatmarkers is loaded, that deck B contains a track with a stable tempo and one beatmarker and that you are using the master clock mode *Clock Master Intern):*

1. Blend deck A in with the *Sync* button activated until the channel fader of the previous track is turned completely down.

2. Let the track play for a few bars before the second beatmarker and then deactivate the *Sync* button in deck A.

3. When Traktor reaches the second beatmarker, the phase meter jumps because the phase of deck A is no longer in sync with the phase of the master tempo source. Use the tempo bend function (see section "Shifting the Phase" on page 303 and further) to get this deck back in sync with the phase of the sync master.

4. Then reactivate the *Sync* button in deck A.

5. It is now easy to create a properly beatmatched blend of the track in deck B.

Tutorial 7: Tapping the Tempo
Track: Fight Again, WAA Mike C. – YPQN041
Source: http://ypqnrecords.com/

The second to last tutorial will explain how to use the Tap button to determine a track's tempo. The idea of the Tap button is to get the tempo right by clicking the button in rhythm with the beats of the track. You can use the Tap button to tap the beats; instead of knocking on the tabletop you click the Tap button once per beat. Or, if you have mapped the corresponding mapping command to a keyboard key or a button on your controller, you can press the key/button. Traktor tries to detect the tempo using the tapping speed and displays the corresponding BPM value in the tempo field of the Grid panel. If you get a non-integer tempo you can use the other tools of the Advanced Panel's Grid view to fine tune the BPM value.

For this tutorial I've chosen a track with a clear beat; this makes it easier to understand how the *Tap* button works. After that this tutorial shows how the waveform of a track will look if you let Traktor analyse the BPM but without the automatic beatmarker.

1. Click the Preferences button in the Traktor header, select the *Analyze Options* and disable the checkbox *Set Beat-Grid when detecting BPM*. Then open the category *Transport* and set option *Mouse Control* to *Vinyl*.

2. Add the track to your collection and load it into deck A. Traktor analyses the BPM of the track. The deck should look now as shown in the following figure:

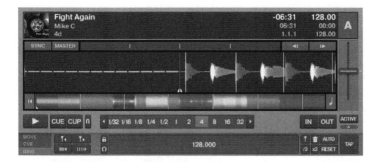

Traktor analysed the tempo as 128 BPM. This looks quite good. You can see several white vertical lines in the waveform. As Traktor did not set an automatic beatmarker these vertical lines represent the transients that Traktor has detected. (It would be nice if a colour other than white would be used for the transients. This would make it easier to distinguish between gridlines and transients.)

3. Click several times on the Plus button on the waveform to zoom into the track

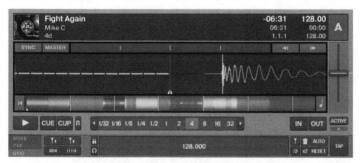

4. Drag the waveform until the playback marker and the start of the first downbeat match. Click on *Set Gridmarker* to insert a manual beatmarker.

The deck should now look as shown in the following figure:

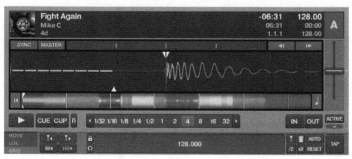

5. Make sure that the *Sync* button of the deck is off. Click the *BPM* field, type 97 and press Enter. By setting the tempo to an incorrect value it is easier to see when Traktor changes the tempo as a reaction to the tapping.

6. Click the 4 button in the *Loop* control to set a 4 beat loop.

7. Start the track, get into its rhythm, and then click the *Tap* button four times in the rhythm with the beats.

After four taps Traktor tries to detect the tempo by using the tap tempo and the analysed BPM value. Tapping with this track is quite easy and Traktor displays 128 in the *Tempo* field. When the "felt" tempo and the tempo determined by Traktor are far apart, stop tapping until the *Tap* button is no longer highlighted.

Tutorial 8: Analysing multiple Tracks, Using special options for Beat and Tempo detection

In the previous tutorials we have analyzed one track at a time and checked the detected tempo and the beatgrid. The track analysis was performed when the track was loaded into a deck for the first time.

If you add many new tracks into your track collection you can instruct Traktor to analyze all new tracks during the import. These and some other options can be found on the *Preferences/File Management* dialog.

- **Import Music Folders at Startup**   As explained in chapter 2 you can assign one or more folders as your Music Folders. If you enable Import Music Folders at Startup Traktor will check during launch whether there are new tracks inside the Music Folders. If Traktor finds new tracks they will be imported into your track collection automatically. If you also enable *Analyze new imported tracks*, the new tracks will be automatically analysed in the background.

  If you use the Analysis Lock feature it is still easy to see which tracks are new. Or you can sort the track list by *Import Date* to find the new tracks that you wish to check.

- **Analyze new imported tracks**   If this option is enabled Traktor automatically analyzes all tracks that are imported into the track collection (see also chapter 7).

If you want to analyze manually multiple tracks at a time or if you want to perform some special analysis tasks, you can trigger the analysis from the track list of the browser by performing the following steps:

1. Select in the track list of the browser the track/tracks you wish to analyse.

2. Right-click the track selection and choose *Analyze (Async)*.

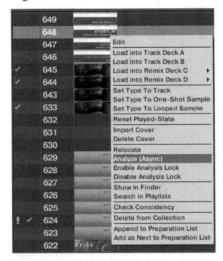

> **TIP** In this menu you can find the commands *Enable Analysis Lock* and *Disable Analysis Lock*. You can use them to activate/deactivate the lock of the analysed values (tempo, beatgrid, gain, etc.) without loading the track into a deck and without opening the Advanced Grid Panel.

Traktor opens the *Analyze* dialog.

Next to the check box *All,* which is enabled by default, Traktor displays the BPM detection range currently selected in the *Preferences/Analyze Options* dialog.

3. Perform one of the following actions:

☐ Click on *OK* to have Traktor perform all analysis tasks for the currently selected track(s). Please note that the analyzed values are only written into
these tracks, which are not locked.

☐ Activate the check box *Special* and select the analysis task Traktor shall perform. If you wish Traktor to analyze the tempo, you can overwrite the default BPM detection range by choosing one of the options in the list box
below *BPM* (the checkbox BPM needs to be active as well).

Select option *Key* if Traktor shall perform a key detection (see chapter 12);
select option *Gain* if Traktor shall detect the Autogain value of the track (see
chapter 3).

Enabling *Replace Locked Values* allows Traktor to write the new detected
values even into tracks that are currently locked. If this option is disabled,
Traktor will write the new values into unlocked tracks only.

Finally, click on *OK*.

8.3 Beatgridding: The Mapping Commands

Beatgridding your tracks by using the mouse only, is neither very easy nor, very com-
fortable. Things become easier when some of the tools you need most are mapped
either to the keyboard or your controller. The following overview documents all mapping commands available for beatgridding:

Setting, Deleting and Moving Beatmarkers

Track Deck | Grid | Autogrid	Interaction Mode: Trigger	Sets an Autogrid marker at the by Traktor ana-lyzed position. If an Autogrid marker exists then this marker and all with Set Grid Marker (or the corresponding action in Grid view of the Ad-vanced Panel) set beatmarkers are deleted.
Track Deck | Grid | Set Grid Marker	Interaction Mode: Trigger	Sets a manual beatmarker at the current position of the playmarker.
Track Deck | Grid | Delete Grid Marker	Interaction Mode: Trigger	Deletes the beatmarker at the current playback position. When there is no beatmarker at this position Traktor deletes the first beatmarker to the left of the current playback position. When there is no beatmarker to the left side of the playback position Traktor will delete the ones to the right

Setting, Deleting and Moving Beatmarkers

Track Deck | Grid | Move Grid Marker	Interaction Mode: Dec Resolution: Min, Fine	Move the beatmarker (and thus the beatgrid) to the left. The resolution Min corresponds to a left-click on the corresponding button in Grid view of the Advanced panel; the resolution Fine corresponds to a right-click. Note: When a track contains more than one beatmarkers, Move Grid Marker always moves the beatmarker to the left of the playback marker. To move the desired beatmarker position the playback marker has always to be to the right of the beatmarker that you wish to move.
	Interaction Mode: Inc Resolution: Min, Fine	Move the beatmarker (and thus the beatgrid) to the left.

Locking the BPM Value

Track Deck | Grid | BPM Lock On	Interaction Mode: Toggle Interaction Mode: Direct Set to value: 1=On/0=Off	Locks the BPM value, the beatgrid, the key, and the Autogain value of the track. This also deactivates all controls in the Grid view of the Advanced panel.
Browser | List | Analysis Lock	Interaction Mode: Trigger	Locks the BPM value, the beatgrid, the key, and the Autogain value of the currently selected track(s) in the tracklist.
Browser | List | Analysis Unlock	Interaction Mode: Trigger	Unlocks the BPM value, the beatgrid, the key, and the Autogain value of the currently selected track(s) in the tracklist.
Browser | Tree | Analysis Lock	Interaction Mode: Trigger	Locks the BPM value, the beatgrid, the key, and the Autogain value of all tracks inside the folder/playlist that is currently selected in the folder tree of the track browser.
Browser | Tree | Analysis Unlock	Interaction Mode: Trigger	Unlocks the BPM value, the beatgrid, the key, and the Autogain value of all tracks inside the folder/playlist that is currently selected in the folder tree of the track browser.

Changing and Setting the BPM Value

Track Deck | Grid | BPM Adjust	Interaction Mode: Dec, Inc Resolution: Min = ± 0.004 Fine = ± 0.016 Default = ± 0.0625 Coarse = ± 0.125 Switch = ± 0.500	Decreases (Dec) or increases (Inc) the BPM by the value selected in the list Resolution. A left-click on the corresponding button changes the value by ±0.001; a right-clock changes it by ±0.010. It would be good if the same resolutions provided by the buttons could be chosen with the Resolution list but this is currently not possible.
	Interaction Mode: Direct (Buttons, Keyboard)	Sets the BPM to the value entered in the field Set to value.
	Interaction Mode: Direct Type of Controller: Fader, Knob etc. (MIDI mapping)	This is the best command to use to assign the tempo change to a fader, knob etc.
	Interaction Mode: Reset	Sets the BPM value to 120.000.
Track Deck | Grid | Reset BPM	Interaction Mode: Trigger	Resets the tempo of the track to the BPM value detected by Traktor.
Track Deck | Grid | BPM x2	Interaction Mode: Trigger	Doubles the value shown in the field BPM.
Track Deck | Grid | BPM /2	Interaction Mode: Trigger	Divides the value shown in the field BPM by 2.

Tapping and Ticking

Track Deck | Grid | Beat Tap	Interaction Mode: Trigger	Use this mapping command to assign the tapping of the tempo to a key or a controller button.
Track Deck | Grid | Tick On	Interaction Mode: Hold, Toggle Direct: 1=On/0=Off	Inserts a tick signal into the audio output. The intervals of the ticks correspond to the current tempo of the deck which Cue button has been activated. To activate the Cue button of a deck use the mapping command Mixer | Monitor Cue.

Analyzing Multiple Tracks

Browser | List | Analyze	Interaction Mode: Trigger	Opens the Analyze dialog and allows you to analyse the tracks(s) selected in the tracklist of the Traktor browser.
Browser | Tree | Analyze	Interaction Mode: Trigger	Opens the Analyze dialog and allows you analyse all tracks currently located in the folderlist selected folder.

8.4 Syncing Decks to the Master Tempo/Phase

When tracks have the correct BPM value and if the beatmarker is at the proper position and thus the beatgrid is perfect, those tracks can be synchronised to either the Master Clock or to the deck currently assigned as the sync master. Traktor 2 provides two different synchronisation modes and various clock modes: both settings affect how the synchronisation works.

Select the Synchronisation Mode: TempoSync or BeatSync

Traktor 2 provides two different synchronisation modes. You can select the mode on the *Preferences/Transport* dialog in section *Sync Mode*.

To understand what these modes do, it helps to take a short look at the two states of a deck that Traktor can synchronise to the corresponding states of a sync master: the tempo and the phase.

☐ Tempo synchronisation ensures that the tempo of the deck and the tempo of the tempo master are identical.

☐ Phase synchronisation ensures that the beatgrid of the deck and the beatgrid of the tempo master are aligned.

☐ If the tempo as well as the phase are synchronised, Traktor calls this "beat synchronisation", or in short BeatSync.

Depending on which sync mode you select, Traktor can either ensure, that only the tempo of a synchronised deck is locked to the sync master *(TempoSync* mode) or that both phase and tempo are locked to the sync master *(BeatSync)*.

TempoSync In this mode "slaved" decks follow the tempo of the master. You can tempo bend/pitch bend on the slaved decks to move their phase. Shifting the phase does not break the synchronisation link of the tempo synchronisation.

A new addition of the TempoSync mode in Traktor 2 is that the synchronisation now works with timecode. When you use relative timecode tracking mode you can use the *Sync* button to keep the decks tempo synchronised. This is possible because Traktor uses the so called stable tempo to perform the tempo synchronisation. The stable tempo is an average value calculated by the timecode decoder and not the real tempo of the deck; the stable tempo will change once the deck uses that tempo for approximately three seconds.

When performing fast scratches on the tempo master deck, Traktor assigns the Master clock as master. The *Sync* button can be shown in a dimmed state. This indicates that currently the deck cannot be synchronised, as a user action led to a phase of tempo offset. However, when the next track is loaded into that deck, it will automatically start synchronised again.

BeatSync In this mode the "slaved" decks follow the tempo and the phase of the master. This is done during playback by constantly checking if the tempo, as well as the phase of the slaved decks are still in sync with the master. If they are off sync, Traktor then automatically triggers a re-sync action.

The difference to the sync mode in Traktor Pro 1 is, that once the *Sync* button on a deck is activated in Traktor 2, you can no longer pitch bend the deck: tempo and phase of the slaved deck are locked.

> **NOTE** To better reflect the conceptual changes introduced by the two different synchronisation modes in Traktor 2, I will use the term "sync master" for the deck or the master clock that has the Master button on. In other documentation the term "tempo master" is sometimes used instead. Even though tempo master is not completely wrong, using tempo master doesn't reflect the fact that depending on the synchronisation mode chosen, the slaved decks are phase synchronised as well. In Traktor Bible "sync master" is used as the high-level term and could mean tempo master, phase master or both, depending on the context the term is used.

The Master Clock Panel

The Master Clock panel resides at the left side of the Global Section. Click the icon with the metronome on the left side of the Global Section to make the Master Clock panel visible. (There is no direct mapping command to open the Master Clock panel; this can be done in a mapping by first defining a suitable layout and then by switching to it. More information about layouts can be found in chapter 3).

The Master Clock panel is divided in three sections:

- ☐ **OPTIONS** The button *EXT* can be used to receive external MIDI clock messages into Traktor. This allows synchronising Traktor with other applications or devices that can be configured as MIDI clock sender. Use the *TICK* button to make the tick of the master clocks metronome audible.

- ☐ **CLOCK** Section *CLOCK* can be used to enable/disable the automatic clock mode (button *AUTO)* and to designate the Master Clock itself as tempo master (button *MASTER)*. Furthermore the *BPM* field always shows the current tempo of the Master Clock. If the Master Clock acts as tempo master you can use the other buttons to change the master tempo.

☐ **SEND** The two buttons in the *SEND* section are used if Traktor is configured as MIDI clock sender. In this setup it is possible to synchronise other applications or MIDI devices that can be configured as MIDI clock slave to the Traktor clock. More about those synchronisation features can be found in a section at the end of this chapter (starting on page 312).

The different Modes of the Master Clock: Auto or Manual

Traktor provides different modes for different usage scenarios to achieve the synchro-nisation between decks. No matter which mode you use, in all modes there can only be one sync master. The sync master can either be the Master Clock, one of the track decks or one of the remix decks. The main difference between the clock modes is, ei-ther Traktor decides who acts as sync master (automatic mode), or if you assign the sync master yourself.

Automatic Selection of the Sync Master

In automatic mode Traktor decides which track deck is used as sync mas-ter. Automatic mode is enabled in Traktor Pro if the *AUTO* button in Mas-ter Clock panel is set to on.

☐ If only one deck is playing this deck will be assigned as sync master. This can be either a track deck or a remix deck, if option *Remix Decks can be Tempo Master* has been enabled. The *MASTER* button on this deck will be on.

☐ If playback of the current sync master is stopped, Traktor assigns either another deck or the Master Clock as sync master. How Traktor proceeds depends on two options that can be configured in section *Sync Mode* of the *Preferences/Transport* dialog:

☐ If no track deck is playing, only a remix deck, and if option *Remix Decks can be Tempo Master* is disabled, the Master Clock becomes the new sync mas-ter, otherwise a playing remix deck will become the sync master.

☐ In internal mixing mode the election of the Syncmaster is affected by option *Only On-Air Decks can be Tempo Master*. In internal mixing mode a deck is "On Air" if the channel fader of that deck is at least partly open. If this option is checked Traktor searches for a deck with open channel fader when the current sync master deck is stopped. This deck can be a track or a remix deck (but only if *Remix Decks can be Tempo Master* is enabled). If Traktor finds a deck with open channel fader it becomes the new syncmaster. If none was available the Master Clock becomes the new sync master.

◻   If several decks are playing, then Traktor will assign the deck with the longest playtime as sync master.

◻   In automatic mode the *MASTER* button in the Master Clock panel cannot be manually switched on and off. This can only be done by Traktor.

◻   If no other track deck or remix deck is playing then the Master Clock becomes sync master. Nominating the Master Clock as sync master ensures that a loop playing in the loop recorder and that the buffer based synchronised effects still have a synchronisation reference.

If you wish to use automatic mode and if you wish to synchronise all decks automatically to the tempo and the phase of the sync master deck, make sure, that all of your tracks are properly beatgridded. Activate the *SYNC* button in the decks. Use the tempo fader in the sync master deck to change the tempo of all the other decks.

In automatic mode the Master Clock panel always displays the BPM value of the sync master deck. Even though the sync master is selected by Traktor automatically, you can overwrite Traktors' choice by clicking the *MASTER* button in the deck that you wish to be the sync master.

Manual Selection of the Sync Master (Deck or Master Clock)

In manual mode one of the decks or the Master Clock can be the sync master, as in automatic mode. The main difference to automatic mode is that the sync master needs to be selected manually, i.e. by you. Furthermore, manual mode allows you to make Master Clock the permanent sync master; this is done by switching the *MASTER* button in Master Clock Panel to on after automatic mode has been switched off.

You can only then turn a remix deck manually into sync master if option *Remix Decks can be Tempo Master* is enabled. As long as this option is disabled the *MASTER* button in the remix decks are disabled too.

To activate manual mode click the button *AUTO* in the Master Clock panel to switch to off. If a track deck is currently playing it stays sync master. If no track deck was playing when you switched the *AUTO* button off, the *MASTER* button in the Master Clock panel remains activated.

If you wish to use manual mode to synchronise all decks automatically to the tempo/the phase of the sync master deck, make sure that, all of your tracks are properly beatgridded. Activate the *SYNC* button in the decks.

◻ If one of the track or remix decks acts as sync master, use the tempo fader in that deck to change the tempo of all "slaved" decks.

◻ If the Master Clock acts as sync master, use section *CLOCK* in the Master Clock Panel to change the tempo of all "slaved" decks. You can change the tempo of the Master Clock with one of the following actions:

◻ Type another BPM value into the *Tempo* field.

◻ Tap the desired tempo with the *TAP b*utton.

◻ Click the buttons to increase or decrease the BPM value. One click increases/decreases the tempo by 0.01 BPM.
The resolution of these buttons cannot be changed. However, you can use the corresponding mapping command and then select the desired resolution.

External Tempo Control

In external mode, the master clock receives its tempo control via MIDI

◻ from another application running on the same computer (like Ableton Live or Native Instruments Maschine)

◻ or from an external MIDI device that can send MIDI clock message (like an effect device or a mixer)

◻ or from a Traktor system running on another computer (the Traktor system has to be configure as MIDI clock sender)

To use this mode

◻ disable the *AUTO* button in the Master Clock panel

◻ activate the *MASTER button in the* Master Clock panel

◻ click in section *Options* of the Master Clock panel on the *EXT* button

In this mode the tempo of the Master Clock cannot be changed directly. You need to change the tempo in the MIDI clock master to change the BPM of the MIDI clock slave.

A section at the end of this chapter explains how to sync two Traktor systems, how to sync Traktor with Ableton Live and Maschine and how to sync an external clock or an effect device to the Traktor clock.

The Sync Button – Beat Sync, Tempo Sync, Phase Sync

The previous sections introduced the two synchronisation modes and the different clock modes of Traktor. You saw what you can achieve with the *Auto* button, and what you can do with the *Master* buttons in the Master Clock panel and in the decks. This section takes a closer look at the *Sync* buttons in the decks and the effect they have.

The *Sync* button in the decks can have one of the following three states:

- ☐ **Off**   The deck does not follow the tempo/phase of the master deck or of the master clock, i.e. Traktor will not synchronise the deck to the master deck. When you click the *Sync* button while it is off, Traktor will sync this deck to the sync master. This synchronises the tempo and the phase. Syncing the phase matches the beatgrid of the deck to the beatgrid of the master tempo; after the synchronisation-process both grids are congruent. Normally the *Sync* button stays on when it is clicked. If the button does not stay on Traktor cannot permanently sync the deck to the sync master.

- ☐ **On**   While the *Sync* button is on, it's deck is locked to the sync master. If you selected *BeatSync* mode, then tempo and phase of that deck are locked to tempo and phase of the sync master. The tempo fader and the tempo bend buttons on the slaved deck are disabled. The synced deck follows any tempo and phase changes made on the sync master. If you use the tempo bend buttons to temporarily change the tempo of the master deck, the synced deck will follow, even when the tempo change on the synced deck cannot be seen in the current tempo field of its deck header.

  If you selected *TempoSync* mode, then only the tempo is locked. The synced deck follows any tempo changes done on the sync master. The tempo fader on the deck is disabled, but you can use the tempo bend buttons to shift the phase of the deck. If the phase of the synchronised deck is off by more than 1/128 beat, then the *Sync* button is switched to the dimmed, waiting state.

- ☐ **Waiting**   The third state of the *Sync* button is officially called "intermediate", but I prefer to call it "waiting", because the deck is waiting for a state to be switched back to the *On* state.

  When the state is set to *Waiting* the deck is currently in a state that prohibits a permanent synchronisation to the sync master. This can be due to several reasons. One example has been mentioned already: the phase offset of the deck is more than 1/128 beat off the phase on the sync master. Another example is an active loop with a loop length shorter than 1 beat; loops that a shorter than 1 beat can never be played back beat synchronous.

  The *Sync* button is also dimmed if a deck with an activated *Sync* button is stopped. As soon as playback of the loaded or a newly loaded track is restarted, the Sync button switches back to On, as long as no other condition prevents the permanent synchronisation.

If the deck state changes, maybe because another deck has been selected as sync master, or because the short loop was deactivated, or because the loop length has been changed to a value greater or equal to 1 beat, or another track has been loaded, Traktor automatically changes the sync state back from *Waiting* to *On*.

You can switch from *Waiting* to *Off* state by clicking the dimmed *Sync* button.

Traktor provides three different mapping commands for deck synchronisation that correspond to the three different sync actions:

◻ **Deck Common | Sync On**   This command corresponds to the *Sync* button in the decks and triggers the same actions as clicking the button.

◻ **Deck Common | Tempo Sync**   Synchronises the tempo of the deck once, to the tempo of the tempo master.

◻ **Deck Common | Phase Sync**   Synchronises the phase of the deck once, to the phase of the tempo master.

Sync Button and Timecode Control

One of the new features of Traktor 2 is tempo synchronisation support for relative timecode tracking mode. Traktor is now able to keep a timecode controlled deck tempo synchronised to a sync master. For tempo synchronisation Traktor uses the stable deck tempo as the reference.

Automatic syncing does not (and cannot) work in absolute timecode tracking mode. In absolute timecode tracking mode the timecode signal has complete control over the playback.

If you click the *Sync* button while a deck is in absolute timecode tracking mode, then Traktor will automatically switch to relative mode because the timecode signal is no longer in complete control of the deck. Traktor synchronises the tempo and the phase to the sync master. You can then change the tempo/phase of the sync master and the slaved timecode deck will follow.

Shifting the Phase

The decks' phase meter shows whether the phase of the deck is synchronous to the phase of the sync reference. If both are asynchronous the phase meter shows the current offset as well. The width of the phase meter corresponds to 1 beat. The two red lines to the left and right of the middle position correspond to ¼ Beat. The current offset is shown as an orange bar.

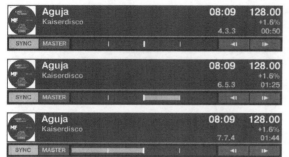

Phase of the deck is synchronous to phase of tempo reference

Phase of the deck has slipped by 1/4 beat forward

Phase of the deck has slipped backwards by 1/2 beat

When the audible beats of two tracks do not match in spite of a beatgrid or if the sound of two mixed tracks is bad even though the gridlines of their beatgrids are congruent, then you can shift the phase of one track to compensate it.

> **ATTENTION**   Please note that in *BeatSync* mode you can only shift the phase of the sync master, whereas in *TempoSync* mode you can shift the phase of the sync master and the sync slave. See page 297 for more information about the two synchronisation modes.

You can move the phase with the mouse when the phase meter is visible. You can show/hide the phase meter with the check box *Show Phase Meter* on the *Preferences/ Decks Layout* dialog (section *Deck Header*).

❑   When you click the phase meter the phase can be moved by dragging to the left or to the right. Or put the mouse pointer on the phase meter and move the phase by scrolling the mouse wheel.

❑   Double-clicking the phase meter synchronises the phase of the deck to the phase of the tempo reference.

At the right side of the phase meter are the two tempo bend buttons used to temporarily slow down (button with the left arrow) or to speed up the tempo (button with the right arrow). This moves the phase of the deck. As soon as the buttons are released the previous tempo is restored. This corresponds to nudging a spinning record on a turntable and to the two pitch bend buttons found on CDJs.

The acceleration and deceleration factor is always relative to the current tempo of the deck. The default factor is ±1.56% of the current tempo. When the current tempo is 100 BPM then the track is speeded up to 101.56 BPM or slowed down to 98.44 BPM. When the tempo is 120 BPM it is accelerated to 121.88 BMP or decelerated to 118.12.

The sensitivity of the tempo bend buttons can be configured with the slider *Tempo Bend Sensitivity* on the *Preferences/Transport* dialog. When the slider is set to 100% then factor ±1.56% is used. Changing the sensitivity to 50% changes the factor to 50% of ±1.56%, i.e. 0.78%; thus a sensitivity of 200% changes the factor to 3.12 %.

Below the slider is the check box *Tempo Bend Progressive Sensitivity*. When this option is activated you can use the *Tempo Bend* buttons on the deck to change the playback tempo in a range from 0 BPM to 250 BPM. In this case the Tempo *Bend Sensitivity* controls how fast the tempo change occurs while the *Tempo Bend* buttons are held. A smaller percentage leads to a slower tempo change, and vice versa.

Tempo Bending with Mapping Command

To map tempo bending to a jog wheel use the mapping command *Deck Common | Jog Turn*. With this mapping command you can do a nudge as you would do with a turntable or a CDJ player. If the jog wheel plate is touch sensitive map the command *Deck Common | Jog Touch On*. *Jog Touch On* stops playback of the track as long as the plate is pressed but without setting the deck to pause. If you release the plate playback continues.

The same behaviour that can be produced with the *Tempo Bend*-Buttons when the option *Tempo Bend Progressive Sensitivity* is checked, can easily be realised with a jog wheel by using the mapping command *Deck Common | Tempo Bend (stepless)*. Select the controller type *Encoder* in Interaction Mode *Relative*. Configure how quickly the tempo change should happen with the slider *Rotary Sensitivity* in section *Rotary Encoder*.

The mapping command *Deck Common | Tempo Bend* can be used for buttons but it is not suited for encoders or jog wheels; the *Tempo Bend* command does not execute a reset when the jog wheel or encoder is no longer moved; the result is that the deck tempo is not reset.

Changing the Tempo with the Tempo Faders

Use the tempo faders in the decks or the *Minus* and *Plus* button below the fader to change the decks' tempo. The range to adjust the tempo is configured in section *Tempo* on the *Preferences/Transport* dialog.

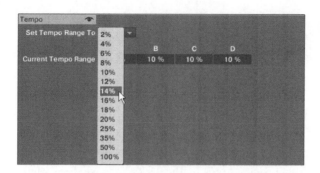

Traktor offers fourteen different ranges for the tempo fader. To set the tempo range for all decks open the list *Set Tempo Range To* and select the percentage you wish to use. It is possible to configure different tempo ranges for different decks with a few mapping commands. How this works is explained in the HOW TO section "Setting and Outputting the Tempo Range" in chapter 6 on page 206.

For example, if the 10% option is selected and if the original tempo of a deck is 124 BPM, then you can increase or reduce the tempo by 12.4 BPM. For a track with 135 BPM and with a pitch fader range of 35%, the maximum possible tempo change is 45.5 BPM.

The *Minus* and *Plus* buttons below the tempo faders of the Traktor decks can be used to change the tempo stepwise. The exact step-size depends on the selected tempo fader range and on the resolution configured for those buttons. You can select the desired resolution by right-clicking (Windows) or ctrl-clicking one of the buttons. Then select the resolution in the popup-menu. The resolution of the buttons control the number of necessary steps for changing the tempo from the original value to the maximum possible tempo change (max is defined by the selected pitch fader range). The following table shows the relation between the resolution and the number of steps.

Resolution	Number of Steps from Original Tempo to maximum possible Tempo Change
Min	256 steps
Fine	64 steps
Default	16 steps
Coarse	8 steps
Switch	2 steps

An example: Let's assume that the original tempo of a track is 130 BPM and that the tempo fader range is set to 10%. Then the maximum tempo change is ±13 BPM. If you use resolution *Default*, then the tempo can be changed in steps of ±0.8125 BPM (=13

BPM/16). If you use resolution *Min* instead, then the step-size is ±0.5078125 BPM (=13 BPM/256).

Selecting a larger pitch fader range enlarges the step-size because this does not change the number of steps. For a track with 130 BPM and a tempo fader range of 50% the maximum tempo change will be ±65 BPM. The step-size for resolution *Default* will be ±4.0625 BPM (=65 BPM/16) and for resolution *Min* it will be ±0.25390625 BPM (=65 BPM/256).

Recommendation: Which Clock Mode to use and When?

Even though it is possible to change the clock mode as often as you want it is good practice to decide which mode you wish to use and to keep to it during a set. That way you are assured that Traktor will not make unwanted changes.

☐ Use the manual clock mode and designate the Master Clock as sync master if Traktor shall be the MIDI sync master. This allows you to configure a fixed tempo value in the Master Clock panel. Other applications or devices that shall run synchronous to the Traktor clock will then receive stable clock data. This mode was called "Clock Master Intern" in Traktor Pro 1.x and it is my favourite clock mode. One of the advantages is that I only need to map tempo changes to the Master Clock and I then can use the mapped controls on my controller to keep all decks in sync once the Sync buttons in the decks are on.

☐ Use the manual clock mode, designate the Master clock as sync master and activate the EXT option if Traktor shall act as MIDI tempo slave. The tempo can be received from another Traktor system, from a mixer with a BPM counter that is able to send MIDI clock signals or from another piece of software with MIDI clock send functionality.

☐ Use the automatic mode if Traktor is to choose which deck shall act as sync master. Here it is important to assign beatmarkers to all tracks (which is valid for the other modes as well), to activate the *Sync* button in all decks and to use the master tempo deck to carry out all tempo changes.

8.5 Clock, Syncing, Pitching: Mapping Commands

Clock modes, clock tempo, pitching and nudging (tempo bend) can be configured or performed more comfortably by using mapping commands. The following tables show the commands Traktor provides.

Setting Master Clock Mode and Deck Master, Synchronising Decks

Master Clock | Auto Master Mode	Interaction Mode: Toggle	Activates/deactivates the automatic master mode (corresponds to the AUTO button on the Master Clock panel).
Master Clock | Clock Int/Ext	Interaction Mode: Inc	Activates/deactivates the external clock mode (corresponds to the EXT button on the Master Clock panel).
Deck Common | Sync On	Interaction Mode: Toggle Assignment: select deck	Toggles the status of the Sync button on the deck selected in the list Assignment. When the Sync button is set to on, a tempo and a phase synchronisation is triggered, and the deck is tempo-locked to the tempo master source. When the current deck is operating in Scratch Control mode, the tracking mode will be changed to relative mode if that mode wasn't already active.
	Interaction Mode: Direct Assignment: select deck Set to value: 1=On/0=Off	Switches the Sync button on the deck selected in list Assignment either On or Off.
Deck Common | Phase Sync	Interaction Mode: Trigger Assignment: select deck	Triggers a phase (but not a tempo) synchronisation of the deck selected in list Assignment. The tempo of the deck will not change. If the deck operation mode is set to Scratch Control and if the current tracking mode was absolute mode, than this command switches to relative mode.
Deck Common | Tempo Sync	Interaction Mode: Trigger Assignment: select deck	Triggers a tempo (but not a phase) synchronisation of the deck selected in list Assignment. The phase of the deck will not change. If the deck operation mode is set to Scratch Control and if the current tracking mode was absolute mode, this command switches to relative mode.
Deck Common | Set As Tempo Master	Interaction Mode: Trigger Assignment: select deck	Assigns the deck selected in list Assignment as master tempo deck.
Master Clock | Master Tempo Selector	Interaction Mode: Direct, Set to value: Clock	Designates the Master Clock as tempo master. This command can only be used if the AUTO button on the Master Clock panel is off (see Master Clock | Auto Master Mode). The other decks are available as option in Set to value as well, i.e. for the decks this command doubles the functionality of Set As Tempo Master.

Setting Master Clock Parameters (only available in manual mode and if the Master Clock is the tempo master)

Master Clock | Set Master Tempo	Interaction Mode: Reset	Sets the Master Clock to 120 BPM.
	Interaction Mode: Inc, Dec Resolution (BPM): Min = ca. ± 0.0039 Fine = ca. ± 0.015625 Default = ca. ± 0.0625 Coarse = ca. ± 0.126 Switch = ca. ± 0.50	Decreases/increases the tempo of the Master Clock. The intervals are configured by choosing the desired option in list Resolution.
	Interaction Mode: Direct (for controller button and keyboard) Set to Value: enter the desired BPM value	Sets the Master Clock to the tempo entered in field Set to value.
	Interaction Mode: Direct Type of Controller: Rotary	This controller type is the best choice for making tempo changes to the Master Clock. The step-size can be configured with the slider Rotary Sensitivity.
	Type of Controller: Fader/Knob Interaction Mode: Direct	This controller type allows for a very rough tempo change only. The tempo range is 40 to 300 BPM.
	Type of Controller: Fader/Knob Interaction Mode: Relative	By using this controller type/interaction mode combination you can reduce the range of the allowed tempo changes. For example, setting the Rotary Sensitivity to 20% reduces the range to approx. ±10 BPM. Use the mapping option Soft Takeover to avoid tempo jumps.
Master Clock | Tempo Bend Down	Interaction Mode: Hold	Slows the tempo of the Master Clock temporarily down; this moves the phase meter of the Master clock to the left.
Master Clock | Tempo Bend Up	Interaction Mode: Hold	Speeds the tempo of the Master Clock temporarily up; this moves the phase meter of the Master clock to the right.
Master Clock | Beat Tap	Interaction Mode: Trigger	Use this command to set the tempo of the Master Clock by repeated presses of a button or a key.
Master Clock | Tick On	Interaction Mode: Hold, Toggle	Inserts a tick signal into the audio output. The tick interval corresponds to the current tempo of the Master Clock
	Interaction Mode: Direct Set to value: On/Off	Note: Activate the Cue (pre-listen) button of the desired deck; otherwise the tick isn't audible.

Changing the Deck Phase (Tempo Bend, Pitch Bend)

Deck Common | Tempo Bend	Interaction Mode: Hold Set to value: Up	Speeds the tempo of the track up as long as the key/button is pressed. This action moves the phase meter to the right. The sensitivity can be configured with the slider Pitch Bend Sensitivity (see page 304).
	Interaction Mode: Hold Set to value: Down	Slows the tempo of the track down as long as the key/button is pressed. This action moves the phase meter to the left. The sensitivity can be configured with the slider Pitch Bend Sensitivity (see page 304).
Deck Common | Tempo Bend (stepless)	Type of Controller: Encoder Interaction Mode: Relative	This command is the optimal choice to pitch-bend with a jog wheel or an endless potentiometer over a broad tempo range. When the deck is playing and you turn the jogwheel this leads to a stepless progressive tempo change, it can also be done with the Tempo Bend commands for buttons when option Pitch Bend Progressive Sensitivity is activated. This command bends the tempo in a range from −100% to +100%. It is important to use Encoder as controller type and Relative as Interaction Mode. This combination automatically sends a reset to the deck when the "physical" jog wheel is no longer moved. This resets the deck tempo to the original value. How progressively the tempo change occurs can be configured with the slider Rotary Sensitivity. This command bends the tempo only when the deck is playing. When the deck is not playing it changes the playback position.
Deck Common | Jog Turn	Type of Controller: Encoder Interaction Mode: Relative	Jog Turn behaves in a similar way to Tempo Bend (stepless), but it does not change the tempo progressively. Furthermore, changes to the slider Rotary Sensitivity change the range of the possible tempo change. It is important to use the controller type Encoder and interaction mode Relative. Then a reset is sent to the deck when the "physical" jog wheel is no longer moved. This resets the deck tempo to the original value. This command bends the tempo, only when the deck is playing. When the deck is not playing it changes the playback position.

Changing the Deck Phase (Tempo Bend, Pitch Bend)

Deck Common | Jog Touch On	Interaction Mode: Hold Assignment: select deck	Stops playback of the track as long as jog touch is set to on, but without setting the deck to pause. Playback resumes when jog touch is set to off. Use this command in combination with Jog Turn for jog wheels with a touch sensitive plate.
Deck Common | Phase Sync	Interaction Mode: Trigger Assignment: select deck	Triggers a phase (but not a tempo) synchronisation of the deck selected in list Assignment. The tempo of the deck won't change. If the deck operation mode is set to Scratch Control and if the current tracking mode was absolute mode, then this command switches to relative mode.

Changing the Deck Tempo

Deck Common | Tempo Adjust	Interaction Mode: Reset Assignment: select deck	Sets the deck tempo to 120 BPM.
	Interaction Mode: Inc, Dec Resolution: select resolution Assignment: select deck	Increases/decreases the tempo stepwise. The step-size always is a relative value. It depends on the selected resolution, on the original tempo of the deck and on the selected pitch fader range. How to calculate the step-size is explained in the section on page 305.
	Type of Controller: Fader/Knob Interaction Mode: Direct Assignment: select deck	Use these settings to change the tempo with the fader of your controller. Make sure that Soft Takeover is activated. The maximum tempo change is defined by the value set with the slider Tempo Fader-Sensitivity (Preferences/ Transport dialog).
	Interaction Mode: Direct Set to Value: –1.000 to 1.000 Type of Controller: Button for controller or keyboard mapping	You can use this combination to set the tempo to a certain relative value that depends on the configured Tempo Fader Sensitivity. Set to value = 0.000: The deck is set to the original tempo of the track. After the command is executed the pitch fader of the deck is in its middle position. –1.000 corresponds to the maximum slow down; 1.000 to the maximum speed up.

8.6 Syncing via MIDI Clock – The Connection

Not only does Traktor Pro send MIDI clock signals but it can also act as a MIDI clock receiver as well. This makes it possible to synchronise the clock of two Traktor systems and to spin back to back. Each DJ uses his/her own computer and audio interface. If you are using a four channel mixer, each DJ can feed two stereo outs of the audio interface into the mixer. This way pre-listening is not an issue because you can either share the headphones, or each use their own if the mixer has two headphone connectors, or by using an adapter.

Syncing two Traktor systems isn't the only scenario where MIDI clock syncing is useful. For example you can sync Traktor to Ableton Live or Maschine (running either on the same or on two different computers). Or you can send the Traktor MIDI clock messages to an external effect device with the result that the effects return is tempo synced to the current Traktor beat.

In order to sync via MIDI clock two actions are required. First, a connection between the two systems needs to be established. The different possibilities are explained in this section. Second, you need to configure the MIDI clock sender and the MIDI clock receiver. Section 8.7 contains several examples of how this can be done.

Under OS X the CoreMIDI infrastructure of the operating system is used to transport the MIDI clock signals. CoreMIDI stands out because it is very stable and because the latency is very small. After many attempts to get MIDI clock synchronization working reliably on Windows I reached a point where I gave it up. This is the reason why the following sections focus solely on the usage of Macs.

Let's first have a look on the concepts of synchronisation via MIDI clock.

The Time System of the MIDI Clock

When two systems are synchronised via MIDI the MIDI clock sender does not transmit "real" time messages. Instead, per crotchet (quarter note) – i.e. for 4/4 dance music per beat – 24 MIDI clock messages are transmitted (24 ppq = pulse per quarter). That's why this signal is also called "MIDI Beat clock".

Let's assume we have a track with a tempo of 128 BPM. To transmit this tempo the MIDI clock sender needs to send 128 x 24 = 3,072 clock signals each minute, and at a constant interval of 19.53125 milliseconds. On the other side, the MIDI clock receiver needs to convert the incoming clock signals back into BPM; this is done by analysing how many clock signals were received in a certain time unit.

Therefore, the exactness of synchronisation via MIDI depends on several factors:

◻   How exact the intervals are that the MIDI clock sender is transmitting the MIDI clock messages.

- Are there any latencies (delays that either can be driver or line related) while the MIDI clock messages are transmitted?

- How good is the algorithm on the MIDI clock receivers' end, which converts the number of received clock signals back to BPM?

Generally speaking: When devices/applications are synchronised via MIDI beat clock then tempo drifts cannot be completely avoided. However, the question is: how large are those drifts? Or better put: Are the drifts small enough that clock drifts do not result in audible beat-drifts? The setups explained in the following sections have all been tested and in all setups the clock drifts are small enough.

> **ATTENTION**   When syncing via MIDI clock it is extremely important to ensure that only **one** of the participants **is sending** MIDI clock signals. In a setup with two systems (assumed that both are sending the same tempo), the number of clock signals is doubled. The conversion from clock signals to BPM causes a doubling of the analysed tempo. Another reason for incorrect BPM values can be when MIDI clock messages are sent from a MIDI enabled mixer. When the tempo shown at the receiving end is twice as high as the tempo sent then you should look for a "hidden" sender and disable its MIDI clock.

How is MIDI Clock Data transmitted?

There are several ways to transmit MIDI clock messages between a sender and a receiver:

- Inside one Mac via a virtual MIDI cable

- Between two Macs via connecting two MIDI ports

- Between two Macs via a network connection (either via Ethernet, or Thunderbolt, or FireWire)

- Between several Macs via an Ethernet connection and by using a hub or a switch

Virtual MIDI cable inside a Mac

When the applications that you wish to sync via MIDI clock are running on the same computer you can use the virtual MIDI cables Traktor provides. They are shown as "Traktor Virtual Input" and "Traktor Virtual Output" in the lists *In-Port* and *Out-Port* of the *Controller Manager* dialog.

Connecting two Macs via "classical" MIDI Ports

Another option for connecting two Macs is to use the classical MIDI ports with the 5 pole DIN connectors. Several professional audio interfaces (for example Audio 8 DJ

313

of Native Instruments or some of the FireWire audio interfaces by M-Audio) are often equipped with those MIDI ports.

As an alternative you can use one of the USB2MIDI adapters, which are connected via USB to the computer and that make MIDI ports as DIN connectors available.

Finally, a cable with two 5 pole DIN plugs is needed to make the physical connection. On the computer acting as MIDI clock master, the cable must be connected to the MIDI OUT port; on the computer that is the MIDI clock slave, the cable must be plugged into the MIDI IN port.

Connecting two Macs via MIDI over Ethernet/Thunderbolt

Not only can MIDI messages be transmitted via classical MIDI ports; it is also possible to send MIDI data over an Ethernet network connection. When only two Macs need to be connected the only thing needed is a network cable, assuming your Mac is equipped with an Ethernet port. (Although it is possible to send MIDI over a wireless network, this isn't recommended. An activated wireless network interface may be the cause of clicks and pops in the audio signal.)

The Ethernet ports on the Mac support a process called Auto MDI-X: the network interfaces can automatically detect, whether a direct connection between two computers is used (in this case the send and receive lines on one card are swapped to enable the direct data transfer) or whether the network interface is connected to a hub.

If you are using OS X 10.9.x or newer you can connect two Macs via a Thunderbolt cable instead of using Ethernet ports. This is especially useful because the newer MacBook models no longer have an Ethernet port. Furthermore, a two meter long Thunderbolt cable is cheaper than buying two Thunderbolt to Gigabit-Ethernet adapters.

To connect two Macs via Thunderbolt simply connect the cable and activate the Thunderbolt Bridge in the *Network* preferences. If you are using a Mac with more than one Thunderbolt port it is important to activate the correct port for the Thunderbolt Bridge. Open the *Network* preferences and click in the list to the right on *Settings* and then on *Manage Virtual Interfaces*. A new window is opened showing all configured interfaces. Click on *Edit* and activate the checkboxes for the Thunderbolt ports you wish to use.

No matter which type of cable you consider the best to use, you should setup the IP configuration of both PCs in a way that automatically private IP addresses are assigned. Make sure that your firewall is not blocking the data transfer between the computers.

MIDI over Ethernet Driver

When the cable connection is working you will need a driver that appears to Traktor like a "normal" MIDI port and that ensures that the MIDI data is transmitted over the network. I recommend the *ipMIDI* driver which is available for free on *www.nerds.de*. The driver supports up to 20 MIDI ports; for our usage scenario one port is enough.

Connecting several Macs/PCs via MIDI over Ethernet

If you wish to connect more than two computers you need to use a hub/switch and build a small network. You need to install a MIDI over Ethernet driver on each of the computers. It is important that only one of the Traktor systems is configured as MIDI sync master. Otherwise too many MIDI clock messages are transmitted and this will cause the problems explained in the ATTENTION box on page 313.

What about the Audio Connection?

When several Macs are used and when each computer has its own audio interface it is better to create the audio connection by using a mixer. When one, four channel mixer is used the first Traktor system can use channel 1 and 2 and the second Traktor system the remaining channels. If you wish to use more than one mixer you can feed the mix out signal of one mixer into the line input of the other mixer.

If you are using one Mac to synchronise Traktor and Live or Maschine you can use two audio interfaces as well: one for Traktor and the second one for Live/Maschine If you are using an external mixer, feed the out signal of the "Live audio interface" into one of the inputs of the mixer.

8.7 Syncing via MIDI Clock – The Configuration

This section shows the steps necessary to configure the application or – in the case of the KP3 – the device, once the physical connection is established. If you wish to sync the MIDI clock between two Macs then install *ipMIDI* first before proceeding.

Configuring Traktor as MIDI Sync Master

With the following steps you create a logical MIDI device and inform Traktor, on which port the MIDI clock messages shall be sent. These steps need to be done on the Traktor system that shall act as MIDI sync master.

1. Open *Preferences/Controller Manager*.

2. Click *Add,* then *Generic MIDI Device*. Traktor adds a new MIDI device to the device list.

3. Click *Edit,* then *Edit Comment.* Enter "Clock OUT" in the textbox and click *OK.* The new MIDI device now has a name.

4. Make sure that the MIDI Clock device you just created is selected. Open the list *In-Port* and select *None.*

5. Open the list *Out-Port* and select the port where Traktor shall send the MIDI clock messages to:

   ◻ If you are using an external effect device, like Kaoss Pad 3 for example, select the port of the device you are using.

   ◻ If you are using a second app (Ableton Live, Maschine) on the same Mac, then select the *Traktor Virtual Output* port

   ◻ If the second app (the other Traktor system, Ableton Live, or Maschine) is running on another Mac, which is connected via Ethernet/Thunderbolt, then select *ipMIDI (Port 1).*

Configuring Traktor as MIDI Sync Slave

With the following steps you create a logical MIDI device and inform Traktor, on which port the MIDI clock messages arrive. These steps need to be done on the Traktor system that shall act as MIDI tempo slave. The MIDI Sync Master could be another Traktor system running on another computer, or it could be the hardware MIDI clock available on some mixers.

1. Open *Preferences/Controller Manager.*

2. Click *Add,* then *Generic MIDI Device.* Traktor adds a new MIDI device to the device list.

3. Click *Edit,* then *Edit Comment.* Enter "Clock In" in the textbox and click *OK.* The new MIDI device now has a name.

4. Make sure that the MIDI Clock device you just created is selected in list *Device.* Open the list *Out-Port* and select *None.*

5. Open the list *In-Port* and select the port where Traktor shall receive the MIDI clock messages on:

   ◻ If the MIDI clock is coming from another networked computer select *.ip-MIDI (Port 1).*

   ◻ If the MIDI clock is coming from a mixer which is connected via USB or via a MIDI Port, select the corresponding port.

Syncing two Traktor Systems

After the physical connection is ready, the needed drivers are installed and one of the Traktor systems has a Clock-In device and the other one has a Clock-Out device you need to configure one of the Traktor systems as MIDI sync master and the other one as MIDI sync slave:

MIDI Sync Master

1. Open dialog *Preferences/MIDI Clock*.

2. Activate the check box *Send MIDI Clock* and close the *Preferences* dialog.

MIDI Sync Slave

3. Open the Master Clock Panel in the Global Section.

4. Deactivate the *AUTO* button, activate the *MASTER* button and activate the *EXT* button on the Master Clock panel.

5. Open the Master Clock Panel in the Global Section.

   Deactivate the *AUTO* button, activate the *MASTER* button and make sure that the *EXT* button on the Master Clock panel is off.

6. Click the button *Master Clock Start* in section *MIDI Clock*.

7. Click the button *Master Clock Sync* in section *MIDI Clock*.

8. Click the button *Tick* in section *Options* of the Master Clock.

9. Click the button *Tick* in section *Tempo* of the Master Clock.

10. The only thing left to do is to check, if the ticks of sync master and sync slave are congruent. If this is not the case change the clock offset in the sync master. Open dialog *Preferences/MIDI Clock* and use the *MIDI Clock Sending Offset* to configure the offset that shall be used for sending the clock messages. When both ticks are congruent, you're done.

11. Disable the "ticks" on both systems. Ready to go!

Controlling the Traktor Tempo by an external MIDI Clock

If you are using a mixer with a MIDI port and a BPM counter and, if the mixer can send MIDI clock messages, then you can send the tempo from the mixer to Traktor and change the set tempo the using the appropriate controls on your mixer.

1. First you need to configure your mixer so that it sends MIDI clock messages. Check the mixer manual for how to proceed.

2. Create a logical MIDI device in Traktor and configure the port on which Traktor shall receive the MIDI clock messages (see section "Configuring Traktor as MIDI Clock Slave" on page 316).

3. Deactivate the *AUTO* button, activate the *MASTER* button and activate the *EXT* button on the Master Clock panel.

4. As soon as the tempo display of the Master Clock Panel starts to fluctuate Traktor is receiving MIDI clock messages from the mixer. Traktor will now calculate the BPM value from the ingoing clock signals. The BPM value should stabilise after a short while; but this will never become static.

If your tracks have a proper beatgrid and if the Sync feature is activated in the decks then the tempo faders will start to move, because the deck tempo is now following the tempo of the master clock. The little tempo drifts cannot be heard because everything "is in the flow". All decks are playing with the same, slightly changing tempo.

As explained above, those small tempo drifts cannot be avoided due to reasons that are inherent in the synchronisation mechanism. Traktor Pro does a really good job when converting the clock signals into BPM values. Those little drifts have a positive side as well. The audio signal now gets a bit of the "unsteady" charm that is due to the wow and flutter that is unavoidable if you spin with analogue turntables. If this is something that you like then those drifts are actually a good reason for allowing the Traktor clock to be controlled by an external timer.

Synchronising Traktor and Ableton Live

This section explains how to synchronise Traktor Pro and Ableton Live. Both applications can run either on the same or on two different computers. The procedure is, in principle the same as if the apps were running on different computers. The only difference is that you need to select different MIDI devices in Traktor and in Live.

In this setup we will use Traktor as MIDI clock master and Ableton Live as MIDI clock slave.

1. Create a logical MIDI device in Traktor and configure the port where Traktor shall send the MIDI clock messages to (see section "Configuring Traktor as MIDI Sync Master" on page 315).

2. Open in Traktor the *Preferences/MIDI Clock* dialog. Activate the check box *Send MIDI Clock*.

3. Open the Master Clock panel. If automatic mode is currently enabled click on *AUTO*, to disable it. Then click on MASTER so that the Master Clock becomes the tempo master.

4. Click the *Master Clock Start* button in section *SEND*.

5. Switch to Ableton Live and open the *Preferences* window. Switch to the MIDI Sync page.

6. Set option *Sync* for the MIDI port that Live shall receive the clock signals on *On*. If Traktor is running on the same Mac use *Input: Traktor Virtual Output*; if Traktor is running on a second, networked Mac use *Input: ipMIDI (Port 1)*.

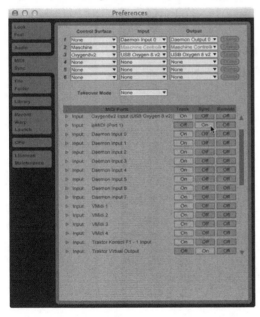

7. Now the upper box next to the *EXT* switch in the transport section should blink. This is the so called *Sync* indicator.

8. Live analyses the incoming clock signals. The converted BPM value is shown in the tempo display.

9. Switch to Traktor and click on *TICK* in the Master Clock panel to make Traktors' metronome audible.

10. Switch to Live and activate the metronome.

11. Go back to the *Preferences* window of Live and open the tab *MIDI Sync* if it is not open. Click the small triangle in front of the MIDI port that is receiving the MIDI clock signal. Live shows the advanced settings for the selected port.

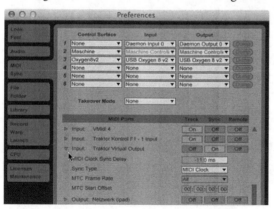

12. Click in section *SEND* of the MIDI Clock panel of Traktor on the *SYNC* button. The MIDI clock temporarily stops and will then be restarted and resynchronized.

13. Drag the slider next to MIDI Clock Sync Delay until the ticks of Live and Traktor perfectly match.

14. Disable the metronome in Traktor and in Live.

Synchronising Traktor and Maschine

This section explains how to synchronize Traktor and Maschine (if Maschine software is running stand-alone). This setup works regardless if both apps are running on the same or on different computers. The general procedure remains the same; the only difference is that you need to select the correct MIDI device in Traktor and Maschine.

1. Proceed as explained in section "Configuring Traktor as MIDI Sync Master" on page 315.

2. In Traktor, open the *Preferences/MIDI Clock* dialog and activate the check box *Send MIDI Clock*.

3. Open the Master Clock panel. If automatic mode is currently enabled click on *AUTO*, to disable it. Then click on *MASTER* so that the Master Clock becomes the tempo master.

4. Click the *Master Clock Start* button in section *SEND*.

5. Switch to Maschine. Open the *File* menu and select *Audio and MIDI Settings*.

6. Open the *MIDI* tab and click on *Inputs*.

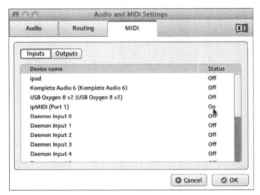

7. Click in column *Status* on the MIDI port you wish to use. A little menu is opened; select *On*. If Traktor is running on the same Mac use *Traktor Virtual Output*; if Traktor is running on a second Mac use *ipMIDI (Port 1)*. Close the dialog.

8. Open the *File* menu of Maschine and select *Sync to External MIDI Clock*.

9. Maschine analyses the incoming clock signals and displays the converted BPM value is shown in the tempo display.

10. Switch to Traktor and click on *TICK* in the Master Clock panel to make Traktors' metronome audible.

11. Switch to Maschine and open the *Preferences* window.

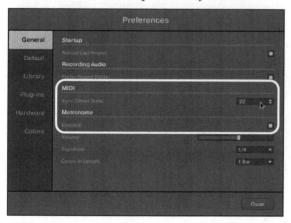

12. Enable the metronome in section *Metronome*. Then click into the *Sync Offset Slave* field in section *MIDI* and drag to change the value (shown in milliseconds) until the ticks of Maschine and Traktor perfectly match.

13. Disable the metronome in Traktor and in Maschine.

Synchronising External Devices, Example KaossPad 3

It is not only possible for Traktors MIDI clock messages to be sent to other applications, but to MIDI devices as well, as long as they are capable of receiving and processing MIDI clock messages. This section explains the necessary steps, using the Korg KaossPad 3 as an example. KP3 shall be configured as MIDI clock slave whereby the effect return is tempo synchronous to the Traktor clock.

1. Configure Traktor as MIDI Sync Master and configure the port where Traktor shall send the MIDI clock messages to (see page 315).

2. Open the *Preferences/MIDI Clock* dialog. Activate the check box *Send MIDI Clock* and close the *Preferences* dialog.

   Now the KP3 must be configured so that it acts on the received MIDI messages:

3. Press the keys *Shift+4* on the KP3. This opens the setup for the MIDI filter options. The display of the KP3 should now show CLOC (for clock).

4. Press the button *Program* on the KP3. The display now shows the currently selected clock mode (most likely *Auto*).

5. Turn the button *Program*, until the display shows EXT.

6. Press the button *Write*, to save the settings.

7. Press the button *Program* a second time. The display now shows the currently selected effect.

Finally you need to instruct Traktor to send MIDI clock messages:

8. Open the Master Clock panel by clicking the *Metronome* icon at the left side of the Traktor window.

9. Click the button *Master Clock Start*.

The button *Tap/Range* at the right side of the KP3 should now blink in the Tempo of the Traktor clock.

TIP To get a stable MIDI clock signal switch automatic clock mode off and designate the Master Clock as sync master (see page 300).

8.8 Syncing via MIDI Clock, Mapping Commands

The two buttons for MIDI sync in the Master Clock panel can be mapped either to the keyboard or the controller. This section explains the two commands available.

Syncing via MIDI Clock

Master Clock | Clock Send	Interaction Mode: Toggle, Hold	Activates/deactivates sending the MIDI clock signal to the selected devices. Traktor first sends a MIDI clock start message and then the tempo dependent MIDI clock messages.
	Interaction Mode: Direct Set to value: On/Off	
		Note: To use this function you need to activate the check box Send MIDI clock on the dialog box Preferences | MIDI Clock.
Master Clock | Clock Trigger Midi Sync	Interaction Mode: Trigger	Synchronises the external devices that receive the MIDI clock signal to the tempo of the Master Clock. Traktor first sends a MIDI clock stop message, then a MIDI clock start message and after that the tempo dependent MIDI clock messages. More information about the MIDI clock messages in general can be found in chapter 5. Please see the note for command Clock Send.

Chapter 9

Cue Points and Hot Cues

Cue points are labels that jump to a particular position in a track. Cue points can be saved and reused later to allow creative mixing as well as on-the-fly re-editing of a track. When you save a cue point Traktor automatically assigns it to one of the eight hotcue buttons, if a hotcue button is still unused and available. The hotcue buttons are visible in the *Cue* view of the advanced deck panel. If you click one of the hotcue buttons Traktor jumps to the corresponding cue point. Because Traktor provides mapping commands for the hotcue functionality you can map a hotcue to a key on a keyboard or a button on a controller.

The four NI controllers Kontrol S2, S4, X1 and Z2 allow direct to access the first four hotcues set in a track. With the exception of Kontrol S2, the other controllers can be configured to access eight hotcues with the corresponding buttons. How to use hotcues with these four controllers will be explained in section 9.4 at the end of this chapter.

9.1 Volatile Cue Points and CUE, CUP and IN

Each track loaded into a deck in Traktor contains exactly one volatile (or temporary) cue point (the cue point is volatile because it is not stored). When a track is loaded the position of the volatile cue point is at the very beginning of a track, which can even be before the actual sound if the track starts with silence. If there is a load marker in the track and if the option *Initially cue to Load Marker (Preferences/Loading)* has been activated, then the position of the load marker and the volatile cue point will be identical.

The volatile cue point is symbolised by a small white triangle and it is visible in the waveform as well as in the decks stripe.

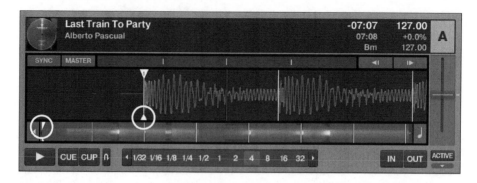

NOTE The official Traktor documentation uses the terms "current cue point" and "temporary cue point" for what I call "volatile cue point". In my opinion the term "volatile cue point" better describes this type of cue point because a "current cue point" could also be a stored cue point, either of which could be selected. To avoid this kind of confusion I will use the term "volatile cue point" consistently during this chapter.

You can use the buttons *CUE, CUP* and *IN* to start the playback at the position of the volatile cue point and to move the volatile cue point to a new position. The behaviour of these buttons depends on several conditions:

☐   Is the deck currently playing or not?

☐   Is the *SNAP* button in Master Panel of the Global Section activated or not?

☐   Is the *QUANT* button in Master Panel of the Global Section activated or not?

☐   Additionally, the behaviour of the CUP button depends on the selected *Cue Play Mode* that can be configured in the *Preferences/Transport* dialog.

You can use the two options for the CUP mode to control when the playback of the deck starts. When the *Instant* option is selected (On Press would be a better name), playback starts immediately when the *CUP* button is pressed. When the *On Release* option is selected playback starts as soon as the *CUP* button is released.

Button	Deck is on Pause	Deck is on Play
CUE	If the position of the playback marker and the volatile cue point are identical then the deck is played back for as long as the CUE button is pressed. Releasing the CUE button resets the playback marker to the position of the volatile cue point. If the position of the playback marker and the volatile cue point are different the volatile cue point is moved to the playback markers position.	Moves the playback marker to the current position of the volatile cue point and stops the deck.
CUP	Sets a volatile cue point at the current playback position. When CUP mode is set to Instant, playback starts immediately; in CUP mode On Release playback starts when the CUP button is released.	Moves the playback marker to the current position of the volatile cue point. When CUP mode is set to Instant, playback starts immediately; in CUP mode On Release playback starts when the CUP button is released.
IN	Sets a volatile cue point at the current position of the playback marker.	Sets a volatile cue point at the current position of the playback marker.

You can move the volatile cue point with the mouse if the *Snap* option is selected, in the *Mouse Control* section of the dialog *Preferences/Transport*. If the deck is paused, clicking the waveform or the stripe moves the playback marker and the volatile cue point to the clicked position. If the deck is playing clicking the stripe moves the playback marker only and not the volatile cue point.

The Effect of Snap

Activating the option *Snap* in the Master Panel of the Global Section ensures, that the cue point always snaps to the closest gridline of the beatgrid. As a result you cannot set a cue point freely in the track as long as *Snap* is on. If you wish to set a cue point at a point where there is no gridline, you first need to deactivate *Snap*.

If the track has no beatmarker (and thus no gridlines) the vertical lines represent the positions where Traktor assumes the transients of the track are. If *Snap* is activated the cue point snaps to the transient lines.

The Influence of Quant

Unfortunately the option *Quant* (button *Q* in Master Panel of Traktor Pro), which ensures that, when you jump in a track the beatgrid is considered, also has impact on the functionality of the CUP button. This is especially annoying if the Cue Play mode has been set to *On Release*. If you press CUP, Traktor triggers a quantized jump. As a result of the quantization the jump target is almost never at the exact position as the volatile cue point. The same behaviour was also seen in the later versions of Traktor 1.2.x but this defect was not corrected.

NI Controllers and volatile Cue Points

The functionality of volatile cue points can partly be used directly from Kontrol S2, S4, and X1. The CUE and the IN button behave as explained in the table on page 327.

Button	Kontrol S2 MK2	Kontrol S4 MK2	Kontrol X1 MK2
CUE	Yes	Yes	Yes
CUP	No	No	No
IN	Yes	Yes	No

If you prefer to use CUP instead of CUE with one of the controllers, you can add this feature by creating an extension of the default mapping, which overwrites the CUE functionality by CUP.

On Kontrol S2 and S4 you can use SHIFT+CUE to jump to the beginning of the track. If you do not need this feature (maybe because you can accomplish the same task by one of the hotcues in the track), you can overwrite SHIFT+CUE and map CUP to this button combination. Once you added the corresponding mapping commands, you can use CUE as CUP with your controller as well. Examples of how to overwrite features of the embedded mappings of the NI controllers can be found in chapter 6.

NI Controllers and Snap/Quant

On Kontrol S4 and Kontrol Z2 you will find two buttons to enable/disable Snap and Quant. Unfortunately Kontrol S2 and X1 are not equipped with these buttons.

Kontrol S4 MK2	Kontrol Z2

However, there is one mapping command to control Snap mode and another one for Quant mode. You can use them to map these features to any controller. The table on the next page explains these two commands.

Mapping Snap and Quant

Global	Snap On	Interaction Mode: Hold, Toggle, Direct = 0/1 (for Off/On)	Activates/deactivates the Snap option. Using Toggle mode is the easiest way to map this feature as it allows to enable and disable this option with one button.
Global	Quant On	Same as for Snap On	Activates/deactivates the Snap option.

Volatile Cue Points and Controller/Keyboard Mapping

The functionality of the buttons CUE, CUP and IN is also available for controller and keyboard mappings.

Using volatile Cue Points

Deck Common	Cue	Interaction Mode: Hold corresponds to a mouse click	The behaviour of this command depends on several factors: □ Deck paused and no cue point: sets a new volatile cue point □ Deck paused and current playback position at cue point: playback of cue point as long as button is held □ Deck playing: Current playback position is set to previous volatile cue point and deck is paused
Deck Common	Cue	Interaction Mode: Toggle	Interaction mode Toggle additionally toggles the playback mode of the deck.
Deck Common	CUP (Cue Play)	Interaction Mode: Hold corresponds to a mouse click	The behaviour of this command depends on whether the deck is paused or playing: □ Deck paused: sets a volatile cue point at the current position, playback starts when button is released □ Deck playing: jumps to the volatile cue point, playback starts when button is released
Deck Common	CUP (Cue Play)	Interaction Mode: Toggle	Interaction mode Toggle additionally toggles the playback mode of the deck.
Deck Common	Loop	Loop In/Set Cue	Interaction Mode: Trigger	Moves the volatile cue point to the current position of the playback marker. The playback status of the deck is hereby not affected.

9.2 Saved Cue Points

As well as one volatile cue point, each track can contain more than 100 saved cue points. Stored cue points can be named and you can convert up to eight cue points into hotcue points. You can immediately jump to a hotcue point by clicking the hotcue buttons in the *Cue* view of the advanced deck panel (or by using the corresponding mapping command).

You can also create, use and delete saved cue points and hotcues with the different NI controllers. This section describes the usage of cue points and hotcues from the perspective of the Traktor user interface and the corresponding mapping commands. How to use hotcues with the different NI controllers is explained in the last section towards the end of this chapter.

Cue Point Types

Traktor offers different types of cue points, each serving different purposes:

Type	Symbol and Colour	Description
Cue Point	(blue)	This is a standard cue point. Standard cue points are most often used to quickly jump to a particular position of a track.
Grid Marker	(white)	Grid markers are used to define the beatgrid in a track. Grid markers are described in detail in chapter 8, "Staying in Sync".
Load Marker	(yellow)	A load marker instructs Traktor to automatically jump to this cue point once the track is loaded, if on *Preferences/Loading* the option *Initially cue to Load Marker* is activated.
Fade Out Marker Fade In Marker	(red)	Fade in and fade out markers are used by the autoplay function (in Traktor terminology called "cruise mode") and by the automatic playback feature. If for example the playback reaches the position of a fade out marker (left figure) in deck A then Traktor starts playback in deck B. If the track loaded in deck B has a fade in marker (right figure), then Traktor does not start the playback at the beginning of the track but at the position of the fade in marker.

Type	Symbol and Colour	Description
Loop Marker	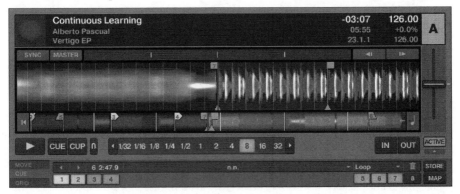(green)	Loop markers are always shown in pairs; one marker is the loop in (left in the figure) and the other is the loop out marker (right side in the figure). Loop markers show the start point and the end point of a saved loop.

A loaded track with several saved cue points looks like the one in the following figure (the different cue point types can be better seen on the screen due to the different colours used). The symbols representing the cue point type are shown in the waveform as well as in the stripe.

In the lower part of the deck you can see the *Cue* view of the advanced panel. This panel contains the tools to manage saved cue points.

HOW TO: Setting and Saving Cue Points in the Deck

The procedure to create and store a saved cue point is always the same regardless of the cue point type.

1. Set the playback marker to the desired position of the new cue point.

2. Click the *IN* button to create a volatile cue point at the current position of the playback marker.

3. Open the advanced deck panel if it is not visible and click at the left side of the panel on *Cue*. This activates the *Cue* view.

331

4. Click on *Store*. The volatile cue point is converted into a standard cue point. If all hotcue buttons are not already in use the new cue point is automatically mapped to the next free hotcue button.

5. If you wish to create a standard cue point continue to the next step. If you wish to create one of the other cue point types open the list *Cue Point Type* and click the desired type.

6. Double-click the *Cue Name* fields (new cue points are named *n.n.* by default), type a name for the new cue point and press Enter.

> **NOTE**   Please note that the playback marker always snaps to a gridline on the beat-grid if you have selected the option *Snap* in the setting *Mouse Control* (dialog *Preferences/Transport*). If you wish to create a cue point that shall not be on a gridline, you first need to change the *Mouse Control* setting to *Vinyl* and then drag the waveform until the playback marker is at the position of the desired cue point.

Selecting and Deleting Cue Points

You can select saved cue points by clicking the symbol of the desired cue point in the stripe. This can be cumbersome because it is not very easy to hit the cue point exactly. It is much easier to select a cue point in the waveform if you have activated the option *Snap* for the setting *Mouse Control*.

The *Cue* view of the advanced panel contains two controls which make it easier to select a cue point.

◻   Use the buttons *Previous Cue Point/Next Cue Point* to select the cue points in sequence. The playback marker is set to the position of the selected cue point and the name of the cue point is shown in the *Name* field.

◻   Click the arrow in the *Name* field to open the list with the cue point names. Click the name of the cue point that you wish to select.

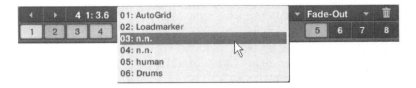

If you wish to delete a cue point you must first select it as described above. Then click the bin icon.

HOW TO: Setting, Selecting and Deleting Cue Points via Mapping

Cue points are more easily managed by mapping the corresponding mapping commands to the keyboard or the controller. Traktor provides specialized commands for setting and saving loops (see chapter 10) as well as beatmarkers (see chapter 8).

You can set all cue types directly by creating a macro of *Set Cue and Store as Next Hotcue* and *Cue Type*. The first command sets and stores a normal cue point. The second command changes the cue type to the type that is selected in field Set to value.

The following table shows the mapping commands available for cue point management.

Using Saved Cue Points

Track Deck | Cue | Store Floating Cue/Loop as Next Hotcue	Interaction Mode: Trigger	Saves the current volatile cue point and assigns it to the next free hotcue button.
Track Deck | Cue | Set Cue and Store as Next Hotcue	Interaction Mode: Trigger	Sets a cue point at the current position of the playback marker and assigns it to the next free hotcue button.
Track Deck | Cue | Cue Type Selector	Interaction Mode: Direct Set to value: Cue, Fade-In, Fade-Out, Load, Grid, Loop	Set the current cue point to the type that is selected in field Set to value.
Track Deck | Cue | Cue Type Selector	Interaction Mode: Reset	Sets the current cue point to type Cue.
Track Deck | Cue | Delete current Hotcue	Interaction Mode: Trigger	Deletes the currently selected hotcue
Track Deck | Cue | Delete Hotcue	Interaction Mode: Direct, Set to value: HotCue 1 – HotCue 8	Deletes the hotcue selected in list Set to value.
Track Deck | Cue | Jump to Next/Prev Cue/Loop	Interaction Mode: Dec Interaction Mode: Direct, Set to value: Previous	Jumps to the previous cue point/loop.

Using Saved Cue Points		
Track Deck | Cue | Jump to Next/Prev Cue/Loop	Interaction Mode: Inc Interaction Mode: Direct, Set to value: Next	Jumps to the next cue point/loop.

Using Load Cue Points

If you set a load cue point in a track you instruct Traktor to jump to this load cue point automatically when the track is loaded. To activate this function open the *Preferences/Loading* dialog and activate the option *Initially cue to Load Marker*.

This feature is useful if you do not use the beginning of a track, or if the beginning of the track contains too much silence, or if you wish to load a track and automatically start the playback of a saved loop by pressing just one button. The last scenario is explained in chapter 10 on page 357.

Using Fade In and Fade Out Cue Points

Fade in and fade out markers serve two purposes. In one instance they can be used to control the *automated playback* of two neighbouring decks (i.e. either deck A and B or deck C and D). This is explained in this section. In another instance they can be used by the autoplay feature; in this case they control when and how the automated cross fading happens. This is explained in the next section.

Automated playback with fade in and fade out cue points works like this:

☐ In order for Traktor to use the fade in and fade out markers you need to activate the option *Activate Fade In & Fade Out Markers* on the dialog *Preferences/Loading*.

☐ If the play back marker reaches a fade out marker in the currently running deck the opposite deck is started. If the track loaded in this deck contains a fade in marker the playback starts at the position of the fade in marker, otherwise playback starts at the current position of the playback marker.

☐ This process neither changes the position of the channel fader nor that of the cross fader.

Autoplay/Cruise-Mode

When the cruise mode (formerly called "autoplay") is activated Traktor can automatically playback complete playlists. When Cruise mode is active Traktor starts the adjacent deck at the end of the current track, stops this deck and loads the next track from the playlist. Cruise mode will always use two adjacent decks (i.e. either deck A and B or deck C and D). Which decks are used depends on which deck is running when the cruise mode is activated.

Follow these steps to start the Cruise Mode:

1. Open the playlist that you wish to autoplay and load the first track into deck A for example.

2. If you are in internal mixing mode check that the channel fader is up. If the channel fader is completely down cruise mode cannot be started.

3. Start playback in this deck.

4. Click the button *Cruise* in the Traktor header.

5. Traktor loads the next track from the playlist in the adjacent deck.

6. Traktor automatically performs the transition between the current and the next track:

   ◻ If the current track contains a fade out marker, and if the fade in and fade out markers are activated (dialog *Preferences/Loading*), then the adjacent deck is started when playback reaches the fade out marker; otherwise the adjacent deck is started at the end of the current track.

   ◻ If the next track contains a fade in marker and if the use of fade in and fade out markers is activated (dialog *Preferences/Loading*), then the playback of the next track starts at the fade in marker; otherwise it is started at the beginning of the track.

   ◻ If the value of *Auto Crossfade Time* (can be set in *Preferences/Mixer*) is 0, Traktor simply closes the channel fader of the current deck and opens the one of the adjacent deck. If the value of *Auto Crossfade Time* is greater than 0, then it takes half of the specified time for the channel fader of the following track to be completely open and the other half of the time for the channel fader of the current track to be closed.

7. Even in cruise mode you can affect the transition between the two tracks. Move the channel fader of the current downwards to close it. Once the channel fader is completely closed Traktor starts the next track.

Click the *Cruise* button in the header a second time to exit the autoplay mode or stop the playback in all running decks.

The main differences between automated playback and cruise mode are: In automated playback Traktor starts the track loaded in the adjacent deck; no other track is automatically loaded. You also need to take note of the channel faders in automated playback mode; Traktor will not change their position.

9.3 Hotcues

When you create a stored cue point in Traktor and if there are still unused hotcue buttons Traktor automatically assigns the cue point to the next free hotcue button. You can find the hotcue buttons in the lower part of *Cue* view in the advanced panel. The colour of the hotcue button represents the cue point type. The number shown in the cue point symbol in the waveform corresponds to the number of the hotcue button and which corresponding cue point it is mapped to. You can click a hotcue button to jump to this cue point.

The functionality of the hotcue buttons is identical to the CUE button, i.e.

▫ During playback of the deck Traktor jumps to the selected cue point and playback is resumed from there.

▫ If the deck is paused Traktor jumps to the hotcue point and plays the deck as long as the button (i.e. the mouse button) is pressed. When the button is released, Traktor jumps back to the hotcue point and stops playback.

> **NOTE** Activate the option *QUANT* in the Master Panel of the Global Section to achieve seamless jumps. If quantization is on Traktor uses the beatgrid of the master tempo source (which in turn takes care of the synchronisation) when performing a jump inside a track. The jump is then executed in a way (even when the *Sync* button in the deck is off) that the phase of the deck will stay in sync with the phase of the master tempo source. More information about synchronisation can be found in chapter 8, "Staying in Sync" and more information about quantization and hotcues can be found on page 339.

Remapping Hotcue Points

Because Traktor automatically maps each stored cue point to an unused hotcue button it can happen that hotcue buttons are used for cue points you never actually wish to jump to (like a gridmarker or a load marker) but other cue points cannot be reached via a hotcue button. Sometimes the order of the hotcue buttons is not identical to the order of the cue points in the deck, maybe because you created a new cue point between two that already exist. In these cases you can change the assignment between cue point and hotcue button.

To remap a cue point, follow these steps:

1. Select the cue point you want to remap.
2. Click the *MAP* button in *Cue* view of the advanced deck panel.
3. Click the desired hotcue button.

MAP

HOW TO: Selecting and (Re-)Mapping Hotcues via Mapping

Traktor offers two mapping commands for hotcues: one to select a hotcue, and another one to map a hotcue point to a hotcue button.

Using Hotcues

Track Deck | Cue | Select/Set + Store HotCue	Interaction Mode: Hold Set to value = HotCue 1 to HotCue 8	When the hotcue selected in the list Set to Value already exists Traktor jumps to this hotcue. Otherwise a new hotcue is created at the current position of the playback marker.
		If the deck is playing then playback is resumed at the hotcue position. If the deck is stopped it will be played until the mapped button/key is released.
Track Deck | Cue | Map HotCue	Interaction Mode: Hold	Activates the mapping mode for cue points. Before this command is used you first need to select the cue point that is to be mapped and (because of interaction mode Hold) the target hotcue button must be clicked while the button for this command is pressed.
	Interaction Mode: Direct Se to value = On/Off	Deactivates (Set to value = Off) or activates (Set to value = On) the mapping mode for hotcue points.
	Interaction Mode: Toggle	Toggles the activations state of the mapping mode for hotcue points.

In order to use the least amount of keys or buttons as possible and, in order that all eight hotcue points in all four decks can be used I recommend using Assignment *Device Target* for these commands. This is especially useful if your controller has buttons that change the deck focus.

To implement the selection and mapping of hotcues you need, depending on how many hotcues you use, between two and nine buttons. A keyboard mapping for example could be like this:

Key	Mapping Command	Description
(^)	Cue/Loops | Map HotCue Interaction Mode: Hold	Activates the hotcue mapping mode as long as the key is pressed.
(1), (2) etc.	Cue/Loops | Select/Set + Store HotCue, Interaction Mode: Hold, Set to value = HotCue 1, HotCue 2 etc.	If the key is pressed Traktor jumps to the corresponding hotcue point. If the key is pressed together with (^) the currently selected cue point is mapped to the hotcue button selected in the list Set to value.
(Cmd/Ctrl)+(1), (Cmd/Ctrl)+(2) etc.	Track Deck | Cue | Delete Hotcue, Interaction Mode: Direct, Set to value = HotCue 1, HotCue 2 etc.	Deletes the hotcues specified in list Set to value.

The same principle can be adapted to create a mapping for a controller.

> **TIP Setting the Deck Focus with the Cross Fader**   Page 81 in chapter 3 explains how you can use the cross fader of your MIDI capable mixer to change the deck focus.

HOW TO: Jump to a Hotcue Point and start Playback from there

Because the hotcue buttons act in the same way as the "normal" CUE button, the deck must be playing in order that playback continues at the hotcue position when the mapping command *Track Deck | Cue | Select/Set + Store HotCue* is used.

With a little trick the behaviour can be inverted. This is done by mapping a second command to the same button/key that *Select/Set + Store HotCue* is mapped to. Mapping *Deck Common | CUP (Cue Play)* as the second mapping command has the following effect:

◻   If the deck is paused, the deck is started at the position of the hotcue when the button/key is pressed.

◻   If the deck is playing, Traktor jumps to the hotcue position when the button/key is **pressed**; when the button/key is **released** Traktor starts playback.

A variation is to use the command *Deck Common | Play/Pause* as the second mapped in interaction mode *Direct* and by setting the list *Set to value* to *1* (=On). This macro always starts the deck at the hotcue position.

HOW TO: Jumping to the Beginning of a Track via Mapping

At the left of the stripe there is a little button you can use to jump to the beginning of the track. There are different ways to jump to the beginning of the track with a controller button or a keyboard key:

▢ If there is a beatmarker exactly at the beginning of the track and if this beatmarker is mapped to a hotcue button you can jump to the beginning of the track by using the mapping command *Track Deck | Cue | Select/Set + Store HotCue* and selecting the beatmarker hotcue in the list *Set to value.*

▢ If the beatmarker is not exactly at the beginning of the track you can set a stored cue point at this position. If you map this cue point to a hotcue button the start of the track can be quickly and easily reached (either by clicking the hotcue button or by using the corresponding mapping command). The drawback is: this consumes one of the scarce hotcue buttons. That's why in my opinion variation 3 is the best solution.

▢ The third variation uses the mapping command *Deck Common | Seek Position.* Select *Reset* as interaction mode.

Hotcue Jumps and Quantization

As mentioned above the *QUANT* button in the Master Panel ensures that jumps to hotcues are quantized. Therefore the phase of the deck stays synchronous to the phase of the master tempo source and the track will playback "in rhythm".

When making a quantized jump to a hotcue there is only one special case in which the target position of the hotcue jump is exactly the position of the hotcue. This case requires that the hotcue target position and the position where the jump is triggered are exactly on the beatgrid.

In all other cases (jump is triggered after a beat, jump is triggered before a beat) when quantization is activated Traktor can only jump to a position near the target hotcue. The result is that during the jump, audio data from before or after the hotcue position is played. Lets take a closer took at these cases.

The following figure shows a section of track as it is shown in the Traktor waveform. The white lines inside the waveform and the black lines above it represent the gridlines of beatgrid. To keep it simple I have assumed that each beat contains 1/16 notes; those are represented by the letters A to L.

Pressing Hotcue Button after a Beat

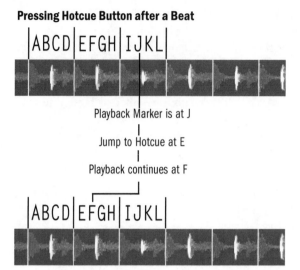

Playback Marker is at J

Jump to Hotcue at E

Playback continues at F

Audible Audio = EFGH | IJ>FGH | IJKL | ...

The current playback position of this track is the note J when the hotcue button with E as target position is pressed. Traktor calculates the jump position and executes the jump instantly. When calculating the jump position Traktor searches to a position that is closest to E and that keeps the playback in sync. Therefore in this example the actual jump position is F and not E.

In this scenario the following notes are audible: I, a part of J and a part of F, and then the notes G and H. When a hotcue jump is triggered shortly after a beat the audio data of the defined hotcue itself is not audible because Traktor shifts the target position for quantized jumps.

The second case – the hotcue button is pressed before a beat – illustrated in the following figure:

Pressing Hotcue Button before a Beat

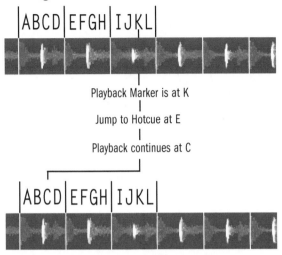

Playback Marker is at K

Jump to Hotcue at E

Playback continues at C

Audible Audio = EFGH | IJK>CD | EFGH | ...

In this example note K is played when the hotcue button is pressed that shall jump to E. Again, Traktor will search for the position closest to E when calculating the jump position. Here it is note C, a position before the position of the actual hotcue target.

In this scenario the following notes are audible: I and J, then a part of K and a part of C, then D and C not until then. This behaviour can be generalised as: If the hotcue jump is triggered before a beat then a small part of the audio data can be heard and it is always before the actual position of the hotcue.

Quantized jumps to hotcues inside a track functions at its best when the audio data at the position where the jump is triggered and the audio data at the target position are quite similar. Neither the skipped nor the additional played audio samples are audible. The more the audio differs the greater the chance that the jump will be heard. To minimize the side effect make sure that the hotcue position is well defined and that the hotcue jump is triggered at the right moment.

Cue Points and Spinning with Timecode

Standard cue points and hotcues can be used when DJing with timecode in the same way as without. The main point is that Traktor automatically switches from absolute mode into relative mode. The simple reason is that after the jump the playback position in the deck, and on the timecode are different and therefore, Traktor cannot continue in absolute mode.

Load markers are ignored if a deck is set to *Scratch Control,* if you use Timecode Vinyl and if the option *Switch to Absolute Mode when loading* is activated. If you use relative mode then Traktor jumps to the load marker position after the track is loaded.

If you use timecode CDs, the use of load markers collides with the use of the CUE buttons on your CDJ player. This leads to a load offset when load markers are used. Here is a workaround for this issue:

▢   If the CD player is still running press the button *Track Search Backward* on the player. Wait until the current track is played again from the beginning of the track. Then load the next track and it starts to playback.

▢   If the CD player is not running press the button *Track Search Backward* on the player. Then press the Play/Pause twice to move the playback marker to the beginning of the currently loaded track. Then load the next track and it starts to playback.

9.4   Hotcues and the NI Controllers

Traktor Kontrol S2, S4, Z2, and X1 provide four hotcue buttons that control each of the decks. They are labelled with the numbers 1 to 4.

Basic Hotcue Features

The basic functionality for hotcues 1 – 4 can be accessed in the same way for all four controllers:

▢   **Save Hotcue**   Press one of the free (=not lit) hotcue buttons. The hotcue button now lights up in blue. You have set and stored a normal cue point.

▢   **Save a Loop as Hotcue**   Create a loop (see chapter 10) and press one of the free (=not lit) hotcue buttons. The hotcue button now lights up in green. You have stored a loop.

▢   **Save other Hotcue Types**   First create a normal hotcue. Then use the Advanced Cue Panel and change the cue point type (see page 331). Once you changed the cue type the button will light up in the colour assigned to that cue type (red = Fade In/Fade Out, yellow = Load, white = Gridmarker).

▢   **Jump to Hotcue**   Press one of the assigned hotcue buttons to jump to that hotcue. If the deck was paused press the Play/Pause button as well if you wish that playback continues after release of the hotcue button.

▢   **Delete Hotcue**   Hold the SHIFT button and press the button of the hotcue you wish to delete.

Using Eight Hotcues with Kontrol S4 MK2

Above the four hotcue buttons of Kontrol S4 you see an area labelled as REMIX SLOTS. This section contains four buttons; in the default configuration you can use these buttons to control the four slots of the remix decks (deck C, deck D), without switching the deck focus with the deck focus buttons.

You can change the functionality of the four Sample Play buttons. This allow you to control hotcues 5–8 with these buttons. The advantage of this setting is that it allows you to control all eight hotcues of a track deck. However, the disadvantage is that you need to use the deck focus buttons (Deck C on the left side and Deck D on the right side) before you can use these buttons to control the sample slots of the remix decks.

To configure the Sample Play buttons open the *Preferences* dialog and open the category *Traktor Kontrol S4*. Open the *Sample Play Buttons* list box and select Hotcue 5–8. The four Sample Play buttons now consider the deck focus and you can use them to control hotcues 5–8 for deck A/C (left side) and deck B/D (right side of the controller). If you want to switch back to the default configuration select *Auto* in the Sample *Play Buttons list box*.

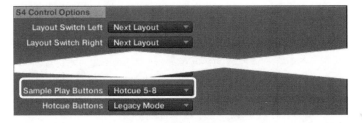

Unfortunately Native Instruments were a bit penny-pinching when choosing the Sample Play buttons hardware. These buttons are not RGB buttons that can light up in the colour assigned to the different cue point type, but are fixed to one colour.

Using Eight Hotcues with Kontrol Z2

The four hotcue buttons on each side of Kontrol Z2 have two mapping layers. When the first layer is active you can use the hotcue buttons to control hotcues 1–4 of the corresponding deck. The functionality of the second mapping layer can be configured in category *Traktor Kontrol Z2* of the *Preferences* dialog. Open in section *Secondary Cue* the list box *Track Deck* and select *HotCues 5–8* to use the second layer for more hotcues.

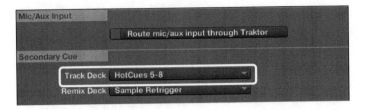

The second mapping layer is activated by holding the SHIFT button and pressing one of the deck focus buttons. If the selected deck is a track deck, you can now control hotcues 5–8 with the four hotcue buttons. The deck focus button will blink whilst the second mapping layer is active.

To return to the first mapping layer, press the blinking deck focus button.

Using Eight Hotcues with Kontrol X1 MK2

For Kontrol X1 MK2 you can configure the functionality of the two FLUX buttons. In the default configuration the FLUX button is used to enable/disable Flux mode (primary function) and by pressing SHIFT+FLUX the tempo can be tapped (secondary function).

You can change the primary and the secondary function of the FLUX buttons by opening *Preferences/Traktor Kontrol X1 MK2*:

◻   If you wish to control hotcues 5 to 8 with the FLUX button open the list box Primary in section *FLUX Button* and select *Hotcues 5–8*.

◻   If you wish to use SHIFT+FLUX to activate hotcues 5-8 with the hotcue buttons, open the list box *Secondary* and select *Hotcues 5–8*.

Using Loops

This chapter explains the looping features that are available in the track decks and with the loop recorder. The looping features of the remix decks will be explained in the next chapter.

10.1 Types of Loops

By using the loop feature in the Traktor track decks it is very easy to set and activate automatic loops to one of the predefined loop lengths. Additionally you can create loops of any desired length by using manual loops. Loops can be saved in the same way that you would do with cue points (see chapter 9). Loops can also be mapped to hotcue buttons and this also makes it possible to use them as jump targets.

Loops can be stored in Traktor Pro in the same way that you store cue points. You can store both of the loop types that Traktor offers:

- **Automatic Loops** Automatic Loops are loops in one of the default lengths Traktor provides. These are: 1/32, 1/16, 1/8, 1/4, 1/2, 1, 2, 4, 8, 16, and 32 beat(s). Automatic loops can be set and activated by one mouse click, by one key press, and with a button press on your controller.

- **Manual Loops** Manual loops are loops of random, freely selectable length. A manual loop is created by defining its loop in point and its loop out point.

10.2 Using Automatic Loops

Each deck contains the waveform with the so called "loop control" below it. You can use the loop control to set the loop length and to activate the loop at the same time. Traktor provides several default loop sizes, ranging from 1/32 beat up to 32 beats. The width of the loop control is automatically adjusted to the current screen resolution and to the size of the Traktor window. Traktor tries to display as many different loop lengths as possible. If the resolution/window size is large enough to show all available loop lengths, then the loop control looks like this:

The selected loop length is highlighted.

If you use the deck layout *Essential* the loop control is displayed in a minimized view at the right side of the transport section of the deck. Its functionality is identical to the extended loop control.

If there is not enough space available in the deck to show all available loop lengths at the same time, you can scroll the loop length list by clicking the arrow buttons at the left and right side of the control.

If the loop length list has been scrolled and if the currently select loop length is no longer visible, then the arrow button at this side of the loop control, where the loop length is hidden, starts to blink.

Setting Automatic Loops with KONTROL S2, S4, X1, and Z2

As loops are such an important and creative tool, four of the Native Instruments controllers have dedicated encoders for easy setting and activating of automatic loops. Here is a quick overview of the loop sections of the four controllers:

S2

S4

X1

Z2

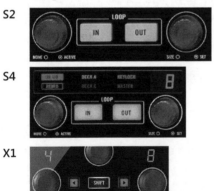

Perform the following steps to set and activate an automatic loop with any of these four controllers:

1. Press the FLUX button if playback of the track shall continue at the position where the track would have been if you had not activate a loop. When FLUX mode is active, the corresponding button in the transport section is lit.

2. If the loop in point shall be anywhere in the track (i.e. it shall not snap to the closest beat) deactivate SNAP. On KONTROL S4/Z2 you can use the button labelled with **S**.

   SNAP mode can also be set with the S button in the Global Section (below the MAIN volume knob).

   While SNAP is active, the loop always starts on a gridline of the tracks' beat grid; with other words: always on a beat.

3. Turn the LOOP SIZE encoder, until the loop length display on S4, X1, and Z2 or the loop control in the deck displays the desired loop length.

4. Perform one of the following actions when the playback marker has reached the desired start point of the loop:

   ◻ **Flux Mode is active** Press the LOOP SIZE encoder and keep it depressed. When flux mode is active. Traktor will loop the selected part of the track only while the encoder is depressed.

   ◻ **Flux Mode is inactive** Press and release the LOOP SIZE encoder. Traktor loops the selected part of the track.

5. You can change the loop length and the position of the loop while the loop is playing.

   ◻ To change the loop length turn the LOOP SIZE encoder. (Please note that when flux mode is active you need to keep the encoder depressed while turning it.)

   ◻ You can also use the controllers to move the selection that is looping.

      ◻ **S2/S4** Turn the LOOP MOVE encoder to move the loop towards the beginning or the end of the track. The loop is moved by the currently selected loop length. Or: Press and hold the SHIFT button and turn the LOOP MOVE encoder to move the loop by one beat.

      ◻ **Z2** Press and hold the SHIFT button. Turn the LOOP SIZE encoder to move the loop towards the beginning or the end of the track. The loop is moved by the currently selected loop length. Release the SHIFT button once the loop is at its correct position. Please note: When FLUX mode is active you need to make sure that the encoder is depressed all the time.

6. Perform one of the following actions to deactivate the loop:

☐ **Flux Mode is active**   Release the LOOP SIZE encoder.

☐ **Flux Mode is inactive**   Press and release the LOOP SIZE encoder.

Saving Loops as Hotcues with KONTROL S2, S4, X1, and Z2

Traktor KONTROL S2, S4, X1, and Z2 each have two groups of four LED buttons to control, to create, and to delete Hotcues. These buttons are labelled with the numbers 1 to 4.

☐ **Save a Loop as Hotcue**   Press one of the unused hotcue buttons on your controller. Buttons that are currently unused are not lit. Once you have pressed the button it will light up green indicating that you can trigger it as a saved loop.

☐ **Activate Loop Hotcue**   Activate/deactivate flux mode (see further up and chapter 9). Then press one of the green lit hotcue buttons on your controller.

☐ **Delete Loop Hotcue**   Press and hold the SHIFT button on your controller. Then press the corresponding hotcue button that you wish to delete.

Using Automatic Loops with the Mouse

Follow these steps to create an automatic loop:

1. Scroll the content of the loop control until the button with the desired loop length is visible.

2. Click the desired loop length. Traktor sets the loop at the current position of the playback marker and activates the loop. The button with the selected loop length is highlighted in green. The *Active* button at the right side is also highlighted green.

Traktor shows little green triangles in the waveform and in the stripe. These represent the loop start point and the loop end point.

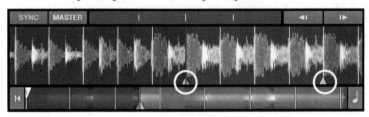

3. Click on *Store* if you wish to save the loop. After you have clicked the *Store* button Traktor adds markers symbolising the stored loop in point and loop out point. If any hotcue buttons are unassigned, Traktor assigns the loop to the next free hotcue button.

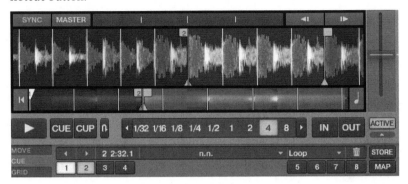

Additionally you can use the *Name* field (Advanced Panel, *Cue* view) to name the loop.

4. While the loop is active you can:

   ◻ **Change the loop length,** by clicking one of the other buttons in the loop control.

   ◻ **Deactivate the loop,** by either clicking the button *Active* or by clicking the current loop length in the loop control

   ◻ **Move the complete loop**, this is explained in section "Moving the Loop, Loop In Point and Loop Out Point" on page 351.

NOTE Loop In/Loop Out Points and the Snap Mode   If the *Snap* mode is activated in the Master Panel of the Global Section then Traktor will always set the loop in and loop out point on a gridline of the beat grid. If you do not wish the loop in and loop out points to be on a gridline, then deactivate the *Snap* mode. Additionally open the *Preferences/Transport* dialog and set option *Mouse Control* to *Vinyl*. You can now drag the waveform freely.

Looping and Beat Synchronisation

If you use one of the non integer loop lengths (1/32, 1/16 etc.) and activate the loop, the phase of the deck can no longer be in sync to the phase of the tempo master. Whether Traktor automatically syncs the phase of the deck to the tempo master when you exit the loop depends on the selected sync mode (see also chapter 8). The sync mode is configured in section *Sync Mode* of the dialog *Preferences/Transport*.

In *Beat Sync* mode Traktor always syncs the phase when you exit the loop; in *Tempo Sync* mode no synchronisation of the phase will occur.

10.3 Using Manual Loops

The length of manual loops can be set as required. Please note that FLUX mode cannot be used for manual loops.

To create a manual loop you need to define a loop in point as well as a loop out point.

1. Move the waveform until the playback marker is at the position of the desired loop in point. If the track is already playing, wait until the playback marker reaches the position where you wish the loop in point to be.

2. Click the *IN* button or press the button with the same name on your Kontrol S2/S4.

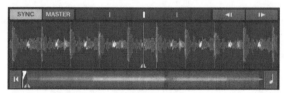

   Traktor creates a volatile cue point at the current position; this cue point serves as a loop in point as well (green triangle is shown on the waveform and on the stripe).

3. Move the waveform until the playback marker is at the position of the desired loop out point. If the track is already playing, wait until the playback marker reaches the position where you wish the loop out point to be.

4. Click the *OUT* button or press the button with the same name on your Kontrol S2/S4.

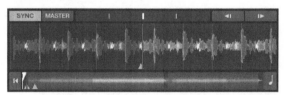

   Traktor creates a loop out point at the current playback position and activates the loop: the *Active* button is now highlighted.

Once they are created the behaviour of manual loops is the same as that of automatic loops: you can store them; you can assign a name to a stored manual loop; you can use the button *Active* to activate/deactivate the loop. To change the loop size of a manual loop you can either set a new loop out point or move the current one. This is explained in the next section.

Moving the Loop, Loop In Point and Loop Out Point

With both automatic and manual loops you can move the complete loop, the loop in point and the loop out point. Some of the move features for loops are – as explained above – also available on the NI controllers. However, much more control is available in the *Move* view of the advanced deck panel.

> **TIP** Stored loops cannot be moved. However, you can select a stored loop and move it. Traktor will then create a new loop of the same length and the new loop will be moved. Once the new loop is at the desired position and once you have the desired length you can store the new loop and delete the old one.

Follow these steps to move the loop, the loop in point or the loop out point:

1. Select the loop you wish to move.

2. Switch the advanced panel to *Move* view.

3. Open the list box at the left side of the panel. Select if you wish to move the whole *Loop*, the *Loop In* point or the *Loop Out* point.

4. Use the move length control in the middle part of the panel to select the move length. If you choose the option *Loop* Traktor will move the selected element by the current loop length. You can use the options *Fine* and *UltraFine (xFine)* to move the element by very small units.

5. Use the buttons *Move Backwards* and *Move Forward* to move either the loop, the loop in point or the loop out point.

10.4 Mapping the Loop Features

This section describes how to use the mapping command to make the loop features of S2/S4, and Z2 available on the controller of your choice. Furthermore we will explain some techniques that are by default unavailable on the NI controllers. Let's begin with the setting and activation of automatic loops.

HOW TO: Setting an Automatic Loop of a Certain Length via Mapping

If you regularly use loops of a certain length then a good practice is to map separate buttons/key for the loop lengths you require. One MIDI command is needed to set and activate the loop and a second one to deactivate the loop.

◻ *Deck Common | Loop | Loop Size Select + Set* only offers the interaction mode *Direct*. Use the list *Set to value* to select the desired loop length (in the range from 1/32 beat to 32 beats). Choose the desired deck in the list *Assignment*. The current playback position will be the Loop In point.

◻ *Deck Common | Loop | Backward Loop Size Select + Set* provides interaction mode *Direct* and you can use the list *Set to value* to set the loop length. Other than *Loop Size Select + Set* this command sets the loop backwards (i.e. towards the start of the track). The current playback position will be the Loop Out point.

◻ Use the command *Deck Common | Loop | Loop Active On* in interaction mode *Direct*. Choose *0=Off* in the list *Set to value* to deactivate the loop. Use the list *Assignment* to select the desired deck.

HOW TO: Setting Automatic Loops of Different Lengths via Mapping

In order to be able to use all available standard loop lengths more mapping commands are needed.

Keyboard Mapping/Controller Mapping with Keys/Buttons

To set the loop length and to activate/deactivate the loop you need three buttons/keys. Map them to the following mapping commands:

◻ *Deck Common | Loop | Loop Size Selector* in interaction mode *Dec;* this will select the previous loop length.

◻ *Deck Common | Loop | Loop Size Selector* in interaction mode *Inc;* this will select the next loop length.

◻ *Deck Common | Loop | Loop Set* to set a loop at the current position of the playback marker and to activate it. If a loop is currently active this MIDI command will deactivate the loop.

NOTE   Loop Backward Set Unfortunately Traktor provides no *Loop Backward Set* command that uses the current playback position as *Loop Backward Size Select + Set* does, but that uses the currently selected value in the loop control as loop length. Having this command would it make easy to replace *Loop Set* in the previous example by *Loop Backward Set*. This command would be very useful to simplify the mapping of loops. I think that *Loop Backward Set* is even more useful than *Loop Set*. Quite often you will hear some beats in a track that you like and that you wish to repeat and, that you wish to use as a loop. I have submitted a feature request for this new command and I hope that one day it will be implemented.

Mapping for Encoders sending Note On MIDI Messages when turned

Some MIDI controllers (like the Xone:4D from Allen&Heath) use push encoders which can be configured on the hardware side in a way that they do not send Control Change messages but two different Note On messages when turned to the left, and then the right. They also send a Note On message if the push encoder has been pushed.

If the push encoders send three different Note On messages then you can map the encoder as if it were three different buttons. This is explained in the previous section. When MIDI learning the command *Deck Common | Loop | Loop Size Selector*, Interaction Mode *Dec* you should turn the push encoder to the left and for Interaction Mode *Inc* turn it to the right.

Mapping for one Knob/Fader and one Button

If you have one unmapped knob/fader and one unmapped button on your controller you can use them to loop in this way:

☐ **Knob/Fader**   *Deck Common | Loop | Loop Size Selector* in interaction mode *Direct*; select the entry *Fader/Knob* from the list *Type of Controller*. Then you can set the loop length with the fader/knob.

☐ **Button**   *Deck Common | Loop | Loop Set* to set and activate a loop at the current position of the playback marker. If a loop is already active then this command deactivates the loop.

HOW TO: Activating/Deactivating Loops via Mapping

If the track already contains a loop and if you wish to activate it then you need the mapping command *Deck Common | Loop | Loop Active On*. This command switches the button *Loop Active* to *On*. If Traktor reaches the loop in point during playback, the loop is activated and repeated.

If the loop is only to be repeated whilst the button/key is pressed, then use interaction mode *Hold*; to toggle the state of the button *Loop Active* use interaction mode *Toggle* and to set the mode directly use interaction mode *Direct* and one of the options *On* or *Off.*

> **ATTENTION Flux Mode and Loop Activation**   Of all mapping commands that can be used to activate a loop, only *Deck Common | Loop | Loop Set* takes into account whether flux mode is active or not. *Hold* is the only interaction mode that *Loop Set* provides.
>
> If flux mode is activated, the buttons mapped to *Loop Set* behave as if interaction mode is set to *Hold*: the loop will only be played while the mapped button is depressed. However, if flux mode is inactive, the buttons mapped to *Loop Set* behave as if interaction mode is set to Toggle: by pressing the button the loop is activated or deactivated respectively.

HOW TO: Setting Manual Loops via Mapping

Manual loops can also be set via mapping. The mapping commands you need correspond with the steps you would perform with a mouse.

▢   Use the command *Deck Common | Loop | Loop In/Set Cue,* which has the interaction mode *Trigger* only, to set the loop in point.

▢   Use the command *Deck Common | Loop | Loop Out,* which only supports the interaction mode *Trigger,* to set the loop out point and to activate the loop.

▢   Use the command *Deck Common | Loop | Loop Active On* in interaction mode *Direct* and select option *Off* in the list *Set to value* to deactivate the loop.

HOW TO: Moving the Loop, Loop In or Loop Out Point via Mapping

All the "move actions" can also be done in a mapping. Because the move length is set in *Move* view of the advanced panel I recommend that you open the advanced panel of the deck and that you activate the *Move* view. This makes it easier to see the selected move length.

To make the necessary changes as you would in the user interface, three mapping commands are needed:

▢   First you need to use *Deck Common | Deck Size Selector,* Interaction Mode *Direct,* Set to value *Advanced.* Select the deck pair in the list Assignment. The deck needs to be in advanced size; otherwise the advanced panel will not be visible.

◻ Then switch to the *Move* view of the advanced panel. The MIDI command is: *Deck Common | Advanced Panel Deck Selector*, Interaction Mode *Direct*, Set to value *Move*.

Three more mapping commands are needed to perform the actual move:

◻ With the command *Deck Common | Move | Move Selector* you can specify if you wish to move the complete loop, the loop in point or the loop out point. Use interaction mode *Direct* and one of the following *Set to value* options: *Loop, Loop In* or *Loop Out*.

◻ Next specify the move length with *Deck Common | Move | Size Selector. Use* the interaction mode *Direct* for a button and, if you wish to pre select a particular length, select the length in the list *Set to value*. If you wish to set the move length with a fader or a knob you should also use interaction mode *Direct*, but choose *Fader/Knob* from the list *Type of Controller.*

◻ The actual move is then done with the command *Deck Common | Move | Move.* In interaction mode *Direct* Traktor offers two options for *Set to value: Back* and *Forward.*

What is the best way to assign these six mapping commands to your controller? In order to get the greatest possible flexibility for the move actions the best way is to use one fader/knob and six buttons. In this implementation the task of the fader/knob is to activate the *Move* view and to set the move length. The actual move is then done by using one of the six buttons. The following table shows all mappings and the commands for this complex mapping.

Control	Description	Required Mapping Commands
Fader/Knob	Activate Move view of advanced panel, Set move length	◻ Deck Common	Deck Size Selector, Interaction Mode = Direct, Set to value = Advanced ◻ Deck Common	Advanced Panel Deck Selector, Interaction Mode = Direct, Set to value = Move ◻ Deck Common	Move	Size Selector, Interaction Mode = Direct, Type of Controller = Fader/Knob
Button 1	Move loop backwards	◻ Deck Common	Move	Move Selector, Interaction Mode = Direct, Set to value = Loop ◻ Deck Common	Loop	Move, Interaction Mode =Direct, Set to value = Back
Button 2	Move loop forward	◻ Deck Common	Move	Move Selector, Interaction Mode = Direct, Set to value = Loop ◻ Deck Common	Move	Move, Interaction Mode = Direct, Set to value = Forward

Control	Description	Required Mapping Commands
Button 3	Move loop in point backwards	◻ Deck Common | Move | Move Selector, Interaction Mode = Direct, Set to value = Loop In ◻ Deck Common | Move | Move, Interaction Mode = Direct, Set to value = Back
Button 4	Move loop in point forward	◻ Deck Common | Move | Move Selector, Interaction Mode = Direct, Set to value = Loop In ◻ Deck Common | Move | Move, Interaction Mode = Direct, Set to value = Forward
Button 5	Move loop out point backwards	◻ Deck Common | Move | Move Selector, Interaction Mode = Direct, Set to value = Loop Out ◻ Deck Common | Move | Move, Interaction Mode = Direct, Set to value = Back
Button 6	Move loop out point forward	◻ Deck Common | Move | Move Selector, Interaction Mode=Direct, Set to value = Loop Out ◻ Deck Common | Move | Move, Interaction Mode = Direct, Set to value = Forward

HOW TO: Shortening a Loop by Moving the Loop Out Point

If a loop is active you can shorten the loop by moving its loop out point. This can be easily implemented in a controller or keyboard mapping. If you wish to use a button or key for this feature then map it with the following mapping commands:

◻ **Specify that the loop out point shall be moved:**
Deck Common | Move | Move Selector
Interaction Mode: Hold,
Set to value: Loop Out

◻ **Specify the move length:**
Deck Common | Move | Size Selector
Interaction Mode: Hold,
Set to value: select the desired length, for example *Fine*; experiment with the different values until you find the one which best suits your needs

◻ **Do the move:**
Deck Common | Move | Move
Interaction Mode: Hold,
Set to value: Previous (this moves the loop in point towards the loop in point)

HOW TO: Automatic Looping of Short Tracks

Depending on the length of a track Traktor can automatically create a loop inside it. The length is configured with the slider *Auto-Detect Size* in the *Preferences/Transport* dialog. Tracks being shorter than the specified length will be automatically looped by Traktor.

If the loaded track is shorter than the specified length Traktor will automatically set a loop in point at the beginning of the track and a loop out point a the end of the track. Traktor then activates the loop. To make this feature work properly it is important that the BPM value of the track is set correctly and that the track is neatly cut, i.e. that the end of the file does not contain silence. Otherwise the silence will also be looped (which can be a feature, if you wish to use it like that).

HOW TO: Loading a Track and Starting a Saved Loop Automatically

You can use a combination of a load cue point, the activation of one of the Traktor options and one mapping command so that after a track is loaded the stored loop automatically is played back. Follow these steps:

1. Create a loop in the track. Store the loop.

2. Select the loop in point of the stored loop, click on *Store*, open the cue point type list and select *Load*. Now you have a loop in point and a load cue point at the same position of the track.

3. Open the *Preferences/Loading* dialog and activate the check box *Initially cue to Load Marker*.

4. Create a new mapping for a controller button or a keyboard key. Use the command *Track Deck | Load, Loop, And Play*. Select the desired deck in the list *Assignment*, then click on *Learn* so that Traktor will learn the button or key respectively.

5. Done.

Now you can use the mapped button/key to load a selected track from the browser and play the stored loop.

HOW TO: Looping with the Delay Effect

An alternative to looping in the way that has been previously described is the Delay effect in Single Mode and by using its *Freeze* feature. Here a short example as a try out and as a starting point for further experiments:

1. Switch one of the FX units to Single Mode, select the Delay effect and set all four knobs to 0. This sets the Delay time (configured with the Rate knob) to four beats (4/4). Activate the effect with the first button and make sure that all other buttons are off. To begin it should look like this:

2. Start playback of the deck.
3. If playback reaches the point in the track from which the next four beats shall be looped press the *FRZ* (Freeze) button.

The next four beats that are played back are copied into the buffer of the Delay effect. If you stop the deck before the end of the fourth beat you will create silence at the end of the effect buffer.

Once the four beats are copied into the buffer you can stop the playback of the deck: the Delay effect loops the four beats from the position where you pressed the *FRZ* button.

4. Its now time to play and start being creative. See how each knob changes the *Filter* effect; the more you open the filter and the longer it is active and the more the sound fades away. The *Feedback* knob feeds the signal coming from the effect back into the effect.

5. Stop the deck and set the playback marker to the position where playback of the track is to be resumed. Wait until the delay loop finishes (i.e. after the fourth beat), deactivate the effect and start playback of the deck at the same time.

10.5 Loop Recorder

The loop recorder was introduced in Traktor Pro S4 and it is now available in both Pro flavours of Traktor 2. You can use the loop recorder to record loops with a length of 4, 8, 16 or 32 beats. The recorded loops can be saved, you can feed them into the Master Out signal and add another audio layer on top of the recorded loop (overdubbing).

You can find the loop recorder in the Master Panel of the Global Section. The following figure explains the function of the buttons and controls:

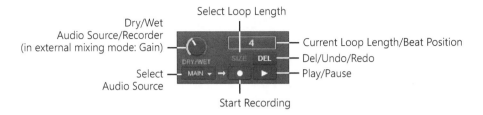

In external mixing mode the *Dry/Wet* knob is labelled with *Gain*; you can use that knob to set the gain value of the loop recorders' output signal. The actual volume can and should then be set with your mixers' channel fader where you route the loop recorder output to.

Audio Sources, Routing and Dry/Wet Control for the Loop Recorder

Before you can record a loop with the loop recorder, the audio routing needs to be configured and you need to select the audio source. The options available differ slightly for internal and external mixing mode.

Internal Mixing Mode

If Traktor is set to internal mixing mode *(Preferences/Output Routing)* you can click the button *Select Audio Source* and select one of the following options:

□ **MAIN**   Records the Main Out signal. The Main Out signal is the sum of all deck signals taking the volume faders of the decks into consideration.

□ **CUE**   Records the signal of the deck/decks where the Cue button (prelisten) is on.

□ **EXT**   Records the signal from the inputs that are routed into the Traktor inputs *Input FX Send (Ext)* *(Preferences/Input Routing* dialog).

□ **AUX**   Records the signal from the inputs that are routed into the Traktor inputs *Input Aux (Preferences/Input Routing* dialog).

In internal mixing mode the output of the loop recorder is mixed with the output of the other decks and is sent to the outputs that are configured in section *Output Master* on the *Preferences/Output Routing* dialog.

The position of the *Dry/Wet* knob in the loop recorder panel controls the ratio between the sum of the different deck signals and the audio from the loop recorder.

External Mixing Mode

When the mixing mode is set to external, the button *Recording Source* in the loop recorder panel offers very little choice. In external mixing mode you can only record the signal of the channels that are configured in section *Input FX Send (Ext)* of the *Preferences/Output Routing* dialog.

In external mixing mode the output of the loop recorder is sent to the channels that are configured in section *Output FX Return* of the *Preferences/Input Routing* dialog.

When using Traktor in external mixing mode you can probably keep the Gain knob at 0.0 dB and then control the volume of the loop recorder audio with the fader on your mixer.

Recording and Overdubbing with the Loop Recorder

To record with the loop recorder by using the controls in the Traktor interface perform the following steps. They differ slightly depending on the mixing mode that is currently active,

1. Click the button Recording Source and select the audio source you wish to use. This step can be done in internal mixing mode only.

2. Click the *Size* button until the desired loop length is shown.

   If the *Size* button does not react, then the loop recorder contains old audio material. Click on *Del* first, to delete the audio in the loop recorder and then select the loop length.

3. Click on *Record,* to start recording.

   During the recording the beat position display in the loop recorder shows the current recording position relative to the selected loop length.

   Once the selected audio length is recorded the loop recorder automatically switches to playback mode.

4. When internal mixing mode is selected use the Dry/Wet knob to feed the signal from the loop recorder into your mix. When external mixing mode is active set the Gain knob to 0.0 dB and use the channel fader of the FX return bus on your external mixer to blend the recorded audio into your mix.

As soon as the loop recorder contains audio you can click the Recording button again to record another layer of audio on top of the audio already recorded. Overdubbing ends automatically as soon as the selected loop length is reached; you can exit overdub mode any time by clicking the *Record* button.

In overdub mode the *Del* button on the loop recorder panel changes. If its label is *Undo* one click on the button undoes the last action. If its label is *Redo* the last Undo action can be made undone.

Loops that you have recorded with the loop recorder are not saved automatically. In order to save a recorded loop you need to copy it into one of the sample slots. More information can be found in chapter 11, "Remix Decks".

Mapping Commands for the Loop Recorder

With the exception of the audio source selection Traktor provides a mapping command for all controls of the loop recorder. However, the bitter pill is the functionality of the Del/Undo/Redo buttons; more about that a bit later. The following table gives an overview of the In commands that also have corresponding Out commands.

Loop Recorder		
Loop Recorder	Record	Type of Controller: Button Interaction Mode: Toggle, Hold, Direct = 0/1	Starts recording or ends recording.
Loop Recorder	Size	Type of Controller: Button Interaction Mode: Direct Set to value: select length	Set the loop length of the loop recorder to a particular value. This command can be used only if there is currently no audio in the loop recorder.
	Type of Controller: Button Interaction Mode: Inc, Dec	Select the next/previous loop length. This command can be used only if there no audio in the loop recorder.
	Type of Controller: Fader, Knob, Encoder	Browses through the loop lengths that are available for the loop recorder. This command can be used only if there is currently no audio in the loop recorder.
Loop Recorder	Play/Pause	Type of Controller: Button Interaction Mode: Toggle, Hold, Direct = 0/1	Starts or pauses playback of the loop recorder.

Loop Recorder

Loop Recorder | Dry/Wet Adjust	Type of Controller: Fader/Knob Interaction Mode: Direct	Sets the ratio of the sum of the deck signals and the signal from the loop recorder.
Loop Recorder | Delete	Type of Controller: Button Interaction Mode: Trigger	Deletes the audio in the loop recorder. You can use this command only if the loop recorder is paused.
Loop Recorder | Undo/Redo	Type of Controller: Button Interaction Mode: Trigger	Undoes the last overdubbing or undoes the last undo action.

All In commands explained in the previous table have a corresponding Out command. Additionally Traktor provides the following Out-only commands:

Out-Only Commands for the Loop Recorder

Loop Recorder | State	Provides information about the status of the loop recorder	
	Controller Range = 0	Loop recorder is empty
	Controller Range = 1	Loop recorder contains audio, paused
	Controller Range = 2	Loop recorder contains audio, playing
	Controller Range = 3	Loop recorder is recording
	Controller Range = 4	Loop recorder is recording in overdub mode
Loop Recorder | Undo State	Provides information about the status of the Undo function	
	Controller Range = 0	Neither Undo nor Redo is allowed
	Controller Range = 1	Undo is allowed
	Controller Range = 2	Redo is allowed
Loop Recorder | Playback Position	Controller Range: 0.0 bis 1.0	This command can be used to output the current recording or playback position of the loop recorder.

Cloning the Behaviour of the Embedded S4 Loop Recorder Mapping

The loop recorder section of the S4 controller mimics the loop recorder of the Traktor user interface one for one. The mapping commands Traktor provides make it quite easy to build a mapping for the loop recorder and use it either in a user mapping for the S4 or with any other controller.

However, there is a small problem with the Del/Undo/Redo functionality. The Traktor user interface and the S4 controller only offer one button for each of the three actions. But two different mapping commands are provided to map the functionality to the controller. The embedded mapping for the S4 controller allows access to all three actions by means of one button, without that the SHIFT button needs to be pressed. Is it possible to recreate the same behaviour in an S4 user mapping or in a mapping for another controller? Unfortunately not.

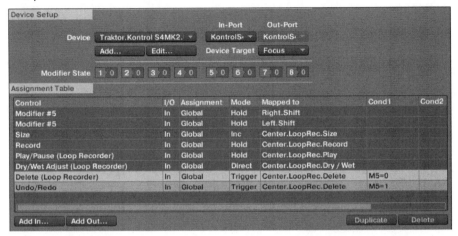

The previous image shows the mapping for the In commands for the loop recorder. The mapping is quite straight forward and contains nothing special. In order to map the delete and the undo/redo functionality to the same button, you need to use a modifier. The assignment table shows that Modifier #5 is used. The modifier value can be set to 1 either with the left or right Shift button on the S4 controller. If M5 is 0, then pressing the Delete button on the S4 triggers the delete action; if M5 is 1 then the Undo/Redo action is triggered.

The embedded S4 mapping is able to check the condition even without using a Shift button. The embedded mapping can also access the status of the loop recorder as the Undo/Redo status. Both pieces of information are available in your own mapping, but only as an Out command and not as an extended modifier condition. If Native Instruments had provided both status values as modifier conditions (similar to the state values for the sample slots), we could have mapped one button as shown in the following table:

Command	Button in User Interface	Loop Recorder Status	Undo Status
Loop Recorder | Delete	**DEL**	Loop Recorder State = 1	Undo State = 0
Loop Recorder | Undo/Redo	**UNDO**		Undo State = 1

363

Command	Button in User Interface	Loop Recorder Status	Undo Status
Loop Recorder | Undo/Redo	REDO		Undo State = 2

It would then have been very easy to map all three actions to one button. I do not understand the reason why this status information is not available as modifier conditions. This would have made creating a user mapping for the S4 and for other controllers much easier. Native Instruments should be aware that the current implementation needs to use a Shift modifier, as the S4 user mapping included with Traktor Pro S4 uses the same approach.

The second interesting question that arises with this mapping is, how to ensure that the current enabled/disabled status of the buttons in the user interface is reflected on the controller. This is easy for the buttons Record and Play as both buttons are always enabled in the Traktor user interface. However, for the Play button this makes no sense, as it should only be enabled if the loop recorder contains audio that can be played. To avoid confusion I'll close my eyes and pretend that this bug does not exist: I have mapped the out commands *Loop Recorder | Play/Pause* and *Loop Recorder | Record* to the corresponding LEDs on the S4 controller.

Let's now have a look at the buttons *Size* and *Del/Undo/Redo*. Both buttons are only enabled if certain conditions are true.

The *Size* button can only be used if the loop recorder is empty. This information can be accessed with the Out command Loop Recorder State = 0. To ensure that the *Size* button is lit only if the loop recorder does not contain audio, add the out command *Loop Recorder | State* and select the S4 button *Center.LoopRec.Size* as target for this command. Then go to the *Controller Range* section and enter a zero for *Min* as well as for *Max*. This mapped command makes certain, that the LED button is only lit if *Loop Recorder | State* has a value of 0. The *Controller Manager* dialog for this command should look like this:

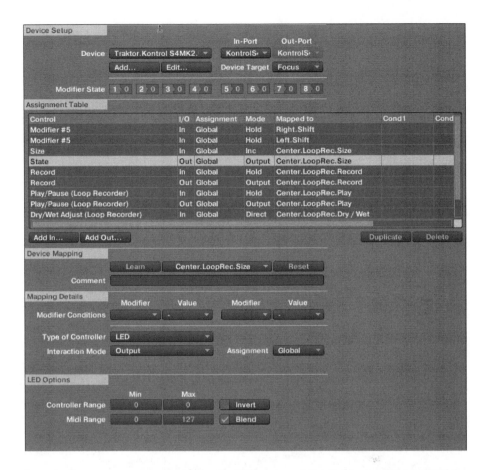

In a similar way we can control the On/Off status of the *Del* button. Because of the doubled functionality of the button for *Del* and *Undo/Redo* we need to output the *Loop Recorder | State* as well as the *Loop Recorder | Undo State* to this button:

◻ Whether *Delete* is currently possible or not depends if M5 has an output value of 0 (i.e. none of the Shift buttons are pressed). The on/off state of the LED depends on the value of the out command *Loop Recorder | State*.

◻ Whether *Undo/Redo* is currently possible or not depends if M5 has an output value of 1 (i.e. one of the Shift buttons is pressed). The on/off state of the LED depends on the value of the out command *Loop Recorder | Undo State*.

The table on the following page summarizes the information needed to implement this mapping:

LED Button	Functionality/ Button is active if	Corresponding State Values	Button mapped to	Modifier
Size	Set Loop Length Loop recorder is empty	Loop Recorder | State = 0	Loop Recorder | State Controller Range Min = 0 Controller Range Max = 0	–
Del	Delete Loop recorder is not empty and paused	Loop Recorder | State = 1	Loop Recorder | State Controller Range Min = 1 Controller Range Max = 1	M5=0
Del	Undo Undo function allowed Redo Redo function allowed	Loop Recorder | Undo State = 1 Loop Recorder | Undo State = 2	Loop Recorder | Undo State Controller Range Min = 1 Controller Range Max = 2	M5=1

The mapping for the Out command *Undo State* looks like this in the Controller Manager dialog:

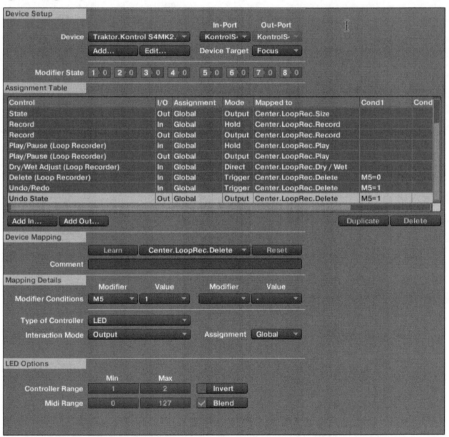

Conclusion

The loop recorder is a cool new tool introduced in Traktor 2, but the current implementation is not yet perfect and I have hope that the loop recorder will be improved in future Traktor versions. Here are some of the requests on my wish list.

☐ Level meter showing the signal strength of the loop recorder. If the loop recorder is paused the meter should show the level of the input signal; if the loop recorder is playing it should show the level of the output signal.

☐ Input Gain knob like the one in the mix recorder. This would allow the user to change the strength of the input signal where necessary.

☐ Possibility of shifting the phase of the loop recorder audio output (analogue to the Tempo Bend button found on the decks); this would compensate any eventual phasing. This should be possible in the user interface as well as with a mapping command.

☐ Possibility of manually syncing the phase of the loop recorder audio output to the phase of the current tempo master.

☐ Mapping command to select the audio source of the loop recorder.

Chapter 11

Using the Remix Decks

This chapter covers the remix decks which were introduced in May 2012 when Traktor version 2.5 and the new controller Traktor Kontrol F1 were released. At that time if you wanted to make use of the full functionality of the remix decks, you had to buy a Kontrol F1 because most of the remix decks features were not mappable to other controllers. Only a few of mapping commands for the slots which were already available for the predecessor of the remix decks, the sample decks, could be used.

Since Traktor 2.6.2, released in July 2013 Native Instruments provided more mapping commands for the extended features of the remix decks. This allowed you to map most of the remix deck feature set to the controller of your choice. Most importantly the new mapping commands allow triggering of all 64 samples of the remix deck grid.

This chapter starts with a more general overview of the architecture of the remix decks and explains how to configure some of the playback settings, how to scroll between the four pages of a remix set and how to trigger samples. We continue with the import of ready-made remix sets and then, the rest of the chapter digs deeper into the details of creating own remix set and the various properties that can be set for each sample.

All sections that explain the practical steps show, how you can use the Traktor user interface, the Kontrol F1 or the mapping commands to achieve your goal.

11.1 Overview of the Remix Decks

If we look at the remix decks from a more conceptual perspective we can distinguish three different tiers: the deck level, the slot player level and the grid level. Let's have a look at these layers and what you can do with them.

Deck Level of Remix Decks in Comparison to the Track Decks

One of the development targets for the remix deck was that they should behave in the same way as the track decks, whenever possible. This approach can be seen in the transport section of the remix decks, which is almost the same as the one we have in a track deck.

☐ **PLAY/CUE/CUP**   As in the track decks, the transport section of a remix deck contains a *PLAY*, a *CUE* and a *CUP* button. The *PLAY* button must be active in order to be able to play a sample in one of the four slot players. Traktor provides one option that can start playback of the remix deck whenever a samples is triggered in one of the slots. You can find this option in *Preferences/Remix Decks* and it is called *Auto Enable Deck Play on Sample Trigger*.

☐ **Loops**   Remix decks provide the same loop control that is available in a track deck. If you activate a loop Traktor loops all samples that are currently playing in the slots players. While a remix deck is looped the waveform of all four slots becomes green, even for the slots that are currently not playing. You can change the loop length in the same way as you would to in a track deck. Clicking the button *LOOP ACTIVE* or the currently selected loop length stops the loop and the slots return to their normal playback mode.

☐ **Timecode**   You can enable Scratch Control for a remix deck and then control playback with timecode. All actions that are performed with the timecode media (scratching, nudging) effect the playback of all playing samples in all four slot players. Switching a remix deck to scratch control works exactly as in a track deck. Either click the deck letter to open the deck menu and select *Scratch Control*, or open *Preferences/Timecode Setup,* or use the mapping commands explained in chapter 4.

☐ **Flux Mode**   The transport section contains the *Flux Mode* button that you will be familiar with from the track decks. Flux mode in a remix deck works for loops only, because you cannot set hotcues in a remix deck.

☐ **Tempo and Sync**   Remix decks contain a tempo fader (which can be made visible or hidden with the settings on *Preferences/Decks Layout*). You can use the tempo fader to adjust the tempo of all playing slots. If some nudging is needed, use the tempo bend buttons in the same way as you would do in a track deck. The tempo bend buttons are enabled as long as the *SYNC* button of the remix deck is off or if you have set the *Sync Mode* to *Tempo Sync* (*Preferences/Transport/Sync Mode).*

Remix decks can be synchronized automatically by using the *SYNC* button below the deck header. Remix decks can be the sync master, no matter whether you are using manual sync mode or automatic sync mode. So that remix decks can be the sync master, you need to enable option *Remix Decks can be Tempo Master* which can be found in section Sync Mode of the *Preferences/Transport* dialog.

If this option is disabled Traktor disables the *MASTER* button in all remix decks. If you do not control the remix decks with timecode it is advised to turn this option off and use one of the track decks or the master clock as tempo sync master.

Deck Level: Quantization for all Slot Players

One of the special features of a remix deck is the quantization feature; this is a setting applied to the complete deck. The quantization feature controls when Traktor will start the playback of a sample loaded into one of the slot players. The quantization setting is applied to slots that are currently playing and also to slots that are paused.

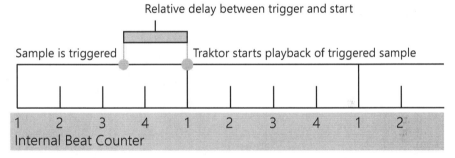

Let's assume that the quantize value is set to 4 (1 bar = 4 beats) and the playback of a sample is triggered when the internal beatcounter of the remix deck is somewhere between the start of the third and the fourth beat. If quantization is enabled Traktor will wait until the complete quantization interval has been passed before the triggered sample will start to play. The quantization results in a relative delay of the playback, where the actual delay time is the time between the triggering and the currently selected quantize interval.

Setting Quantization Options

GUI You can change the quantize value directly in the deck by clicking on the little arrow that is displayed next to the currently selected quantize value. Traktor opens a little menu, where you can select 1/4 beat (=1/16 note) up to 32 beats (=4 completer bars for songs with a 4/4 time signature. Use the small blue button shown to the right of the current quantize value to enable or disable the quantize function.

KONTROL F1 On Kontrol F1 you use the *QUANT* button to disable/enable the quantization. Hold *QUANT* for approximately one second the turn the encoder to adjust the quantization value.

MAPPING If you wish to map the quantization feature to your controller, use *Remix Deck | Quantize On* and *Remix Deck | Quantize Selector:*

Set Quantization Options

Remix Deck | Quantize On	Type of Controller: Button Interaction Mode: Toggle, Hold, Direct = 0/1	Enables/disables the quantization feature for the remix deck selected in list Assignment.
Remix Deck | Quantize Selector	Type of Controller: Button Interaction Mode: Direct Set to value: select quantization value	Sets the quantization value to the length selected in list Set to Value.
	Type of Controller: Button Interaction Mode: Inc, Dec	Selects the next/previous quantization value.
	Type of Controller: Fader, Knob, Encoder	Selects a quantization value by browsing through the available options.

Non-quantized Start of One-Shot Samples

It is often desirable that One-Shot samples that contain a sound effect (vocals, siren, white noise, hooter, etc.) should be heard immediately after they are triggered and not just when the internal beat counter of the remix deck has reached the next quantization interval. To achieve immediate start enable the setting *One-Shot Samples Ignore Quantize Mode*. This option can be found in section *Behaviors* of the *Preferences/Remix Decks* dialog.

Slot Player Level

Let's have a look at the slot player level. To playback a sample it is loaded into one of the four slot players that each remix deck provides. Each slot player is in fact a small mini deck. You can load complete tracks into a slot player. I even tried loading a recorded set with a length of two hours and Traktor could load and play that audio file in a slot player without any problems.

There are several options to change the playback of a sample in a slot player. Some of these options are quite obvious as they are visible and available in the user interface. Some other options can only be changed by mapping commands or with Kontrol F1. Let's start with the more obvious features.

Changing Slot Parameters

In the default setting Traktor shows four either grey or orange bars below the name of the sample that is currently loaded in the slot player. These four bars are the so called slot indicators that inform you about the current status of four different slot parameters. You can show or hide these slot indicators by opening open *Preferences/Remix Decks* and switch the checkbox *Permanently Show Slot Indicators* in *Remix Decks Layout* on or off.

If you hover with the mouse on one of the slot players Traktor shows the four buttons that you can use to change the playback parameters of the slot.

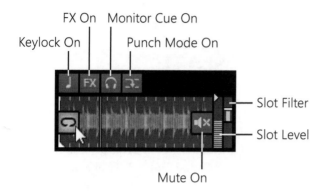

FX On   Monitor Cue On

Keylock On   Punch Mode On

— Slot Filter

— Slot Level

Mute On

▫ **Keylock On**   Use the *Keylock On* button to enable the automatic key correction of Traktor. The key correction ensures that the sample is played in its original key even if you change the playback tempo (more information about key correction can be found in section 12.6, "Traktor and the Key" on page 430 and onwards.

▫ **FX On**   Use the FX On button to assign the slot player to the FX units that are assigned to the remix deck. In other words: If you wish to use one of the Traktor effects on a sample you must assign one the available FX units to the remix deck (this is done in panel *Filter+Key+Cue+Gain+Balance)* and the *FX On* button of the slot player must be active. The separate FX On button in the slot players allows you to route individual slots only through the effect.

▫ **Monitor Cue On**   Use the *Monitor Cue On* button if you wish to pre-listen the sample in one of the slots. This button only works in internal mixing mode; it is the same behaviour that you already know from the *Monitor Cue* button of the deck. You can also use the *Monitor Cue* button of the deck if you wish to pre-listen to all four slot players. Traktor then sends the audio of the slots to the output configured as *Output Monitor* in your audio configuration.

> TIP If you have enabled Monitor Cue for several slots, you can deactivate them quickly by pressing the Monitor Cue button of the remix deck two times. Activating *Deck Monitor Cue* automatically disables all active Slot Monitor Cue buttons.

▫ **Punch Mode On**   The punch mode is a special feature of the slot players. Punch mode controls from which position the sample that is loaded into a slot players starts to play. If punch mode is disabled, the next sample will start from the beginning. If punch mode is enabled, the playback of the next sample will start where the playback of the previous sample was stopped.

Please note that Traktor accounts for the quantize settings even when punch mode is enabled. If quantize is enabled it can take a moment until the triggered sample can be heard.

You can overwrite the punch mode setting of a slot for all One-Shot samples. Open *Preferences/Remix Decks/Behaviors* and enable *One-Shot Samples Ignore Punch Mode*. Then all One-Shot samples will always be played from the beginning.

Finally each slot player has a fader to set the volume and another one to control the slot filter. You can use the small button with the speaker icon to mute or unmute the slot.

GUI To change the general playback parameters of a slot player hover on the player. Traktor will show the four buttons; click them to active/deactivate the corresponding feature. The visibility of the volume fader and the filter fader can be configured. Open *Preferences/Remix Decks* and use the check boxes *Show Volume Fader* und *Show Filter Fader* in section *Remix Deck Layout* to select whether the faders shall be visible or not.

KONTROL F1 To change the slot playback parameters with Kontrol F1 hold the *SHIFT* button. Then use the pad matrix to enable all four slot parameters for all four slots. Each column of the matrix represents one slot and each row represents one parameter (the names of the slot parameters are printed on the controller).

The slot filter is adjusted with the four knobs and the slot volume is changed with the four faders.

One specific feature shows the mute function, which can be controlled with the four smaller buttons below the pad matrix. You can use the F1 settings on *Preferences/Kontrol F1* to configure the behaviour of these buttons. If you select *Mute [Stop]* use the *MUTE* button only to mute the slot and use *SHIFT+MUTE* to stop playback. If you select *Stop [Mute]* it is the other way round.

MAPPING   All features explained above can be mapped to any controller. The following table explains the mapping commands you need to use.

Setting Parameters of the Slot Players

Remix Deck | Slot Volume Adjust	Options are the same as for Mixer | Volume Adjust (see page 79)	Sets the volume of the slot selected in the list Assignment.
Remix Deck | Slot Mute On	Hold, Toggle Direct: 1=On/0=Off	Mutes the selected slot or unmutes it.
Remix Deck | Slot Filter Adjust	see table on page 415	Sets the value of the bipolar filter.
Remix Deck | Slot Filter On	Hold, Toggle Direct: 1=On/0=Off	Activates/deactivates the bipolar filter. The filter type can be selected in the Preferences | Mixer dialog.
Remix Deck | Slot Keylock On	Hold, Toggle Direct: 1=On/0=Off	Activates/deactivates the automatic key correction for the slot selected in list Assignment.
Remix Deck | Slot FX On	Hold, Toggle Direct: 1=On/0=Off	Connects the selected slot to the FX units that are assigned to the remix deck.
Remix Deck | Slot Cue On	Hold, Toggle Direct: 1=On/0=Off	Routes the audio signal of the selected slot to the output configured as Output Monitor
Remix Deck | Slot Punch On	Hold, Toggle Direct: 1=On/0=Off	Activates/deactivates punch mode for the slot selected in list Assignment.

If you own a controller that has a 4x4 button or pad matrix (like Allen&Heath Xone:K2, one of the NI Maschine controllers or a Behringer controller CMD DC-1 and CMD LC-1), you can simulate the behaviour of the Kontrol F1 very easily. Use another button of your controller with a modifier command as a SHIFT button in Hold mode. Then use the mapping commands from the previous table, assign them to the sixteen buttons/pads and make the execution of the commands dependent on the state of your SHIFT button.

If you are using Traktor in external mixing mode there is no need to map *Remix Deck | Slot Cue On* as the cue feature is not available. Instead you can map *Remix Deck | Slot Filter On* to one of the rows of the button/pad matrix. One example of a possible button assignment can be found in the next figure for the Xone:K2. The Behringer controller shown uses the same assignment between pads and features as they can be found on Kontrol F1.

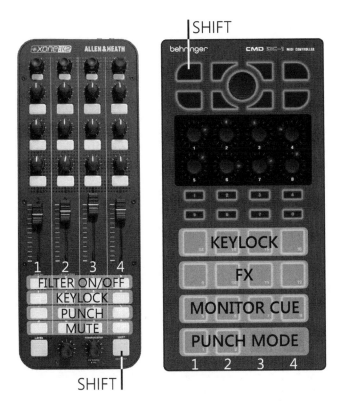

Grid Level: Triggering Samples, Switching between Grid Pages

Last, but not least a remix deck has a grid level. The sample grid of a remix deck consists of four columns and sixteen rows.

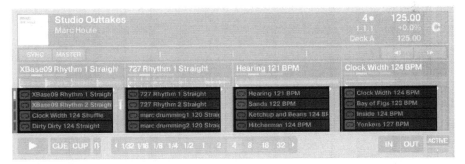

All sixteens samples in the same column can be loaded and played in the slot player above the sample cells. However, you can only see four sample cells in each column (provided that the size of the remix deck is neither set to *Micro* nor to *Small*).

The other twelve cells of each column reside on the other pages of the grid that are currently not visible. At the left side of the grid matrix you can see the "grid page control", symbolized by one white and three grey vertical bars. The white bar represents the currently visible page. Clicking on one of the grey bars opens that page of the grid matrix.

To trigger playback of a sample, click the symbol at the left side of a cell. The icon symbolizes the playback mode of that sample (Loop, One-Shot). If the quantization is enabled for that remix deck, the cell blinks until the internal beatcounter has reached a position where the sample can be started quantized.

You can stop playback of a sample by holding the SHIFT button on your keyboard and clicking the icon of the sample.

KONTROL F1   As long as none of the mode switch buttons (these are the buttons above the sixteen pads) of the F1 is hold or has been pressed, the 7 segment display of the F1 shows the letter P (for page) followed by a number indicating the currently visible page of the grid matrix. Turn the encoder to open another page of the grid matrix. Press one of the pads to trigger playback of that sample. Press the STOP/MUTE button to stop playback (please check the note on page 375 regarding the configuration of the STOP/MUTE buttons).

MAPPING   The basic feature of the sample grid can be easily mapped to any controller, although it requires some work. The following table explains the mapping commands that you need. After the table you will find some hints that you should keep in mind when creating the mapping.

Trigger and Stop Sample, Select Grid Matrix Page		
Remix Deck | Direct Mapping | Slot x | Slot x Cell y Trigger	Interaction Mode: Hold	Triggers playback of cell y (range from 1 to 16) in slot x (range from 1 to 4).
Remix Deck | Sample Page Selector	Type of Controller: Button Interaction Mode: Direct Set to value: select page	Opens a particular page of the sample grid matrix.
	Type of Controller: Button Interaction Mode: Inc, Dec	Opens the next/previous page of the sample grid matrix.
	Type of Controller: Fader, Knob, Encoder	Scrolls through the different pages of the grid matrix.

Trigger and Stop Sample, Select Grid Matrix Page

Remix Deck | Slot Stop/ Delete/Load from List	Interaction Mode: Trigger	This is one of the mapping commands that is implemented as a macro and that triggers different actions, depending on the current status of the selected slot.

- Slot is playing = Slot is paused
- Slot is paused = Sample is deleted from the slot and from the grid matrix
- Slot is empty = Sample that is currently selected in the browser is loaded into the slot

---

◻ **Sample Page Selector** Using *Sample Page Selector* is quite easy. The best approach is to map this command to an encoder.

> **TIP** For remix decks mappings it is useful to select the deck you wish to control in list *Device Target* and then use the *Assignment* option *Device Target* for the individual command, if applicable. This makes it easier to select another deck as remix deck if you wish to change your setup/configuration at a later point in time.

◻ **Slot x Cell y Trigger** Traktor offers 64 variations of this command, namely for each of the cells of the grid matrix. This allows you to trigger playback of any sample at any time even then, when the page with the sample you wish to trigger is currently not visible. The slots *(x)* are numbered from 1 to 4 and the cells *(y)* are numbered from 1 to 16.

Let's assume that you own a controller that has only 16 buttons/pads, similar to Kontrol F1. To be able to trigger all 64 samples you need to add all 64 variations of *Slot x Cell y Trigger* to your mapping. To ensure that only the samples from the currently open grid page can be triggered, use the modifier condition *Sample Page Selector* and select in list *Value* the page, where the cell resides. The following table shows the structure of the commands that needs to be added to your mapping.

Button	Mapping Command	Modifier Condition
1	Slot 1 Cell 1 Trigger	Sample Page Selector.Device Target = Page 1
2	Slot 1 Cell 2 Trigger	Sample Page Selector.Device Target = Page 1
3	Slot 1 Cell 3 Trigger	Sample Page Selector.Device Target = Page 1
4	Slot 1 Cell 4 Trigger	Sample Page Selector.Device Target = Page 1
1	Slot 1 Cell 5 Trigger	Sample Page Selector.Device Target = Page 2

Button	Mapping Command	Modifier Condition
2	Slot 1 Cell 6 Trigger	Sample Page Selector.Device Target = Page 2
	...	
4	Slot 1 Cell 16 Trigger	Sample Page Selector.Device Target = Page 4
5	Slot 2 Cell 1 Trigger	Sample Page Selector.Device Target = Page 1
	...	
16	Slot 4 Cell 16 Trigger	Sample Page Selector.Device Target = Page 4

If your controller is equipped with LED buttons you can additionally map the out command *Add Out/Remix Deck | Direct Mapping | Slot x | Slot x Cell y State* if you wish to output the current status of the cell. This out command has a controller range from 0 to 3. The meaning of the different numbers are shown in the following table:

Status Value	Description
0	Cell is empty.
1	Cell contains a sample.
2	Sample is currently playing.
3	Sample is waiting for start because the quantization of the remix deck is on.

If your controller has 16 buttons/pads you need to use the *Sample Page Selector* condition when mapping *Slot x Cell y State*. This ensures that the currently selected grid page is considered when Traktor sends the out commands to your controller. For slot 1 this mapping would look similar to the one shown in the following figure:

Control	I/O	Assignment	Mode	Mapped to	Cond 1
Slot 1 Cell 1 State	Out	Device Target	Output	Ch09.Note.C2	Sample Page Selector.Device Target=Page 1
Slot 1 Cell 1 Trigger	In	Device Target	Hold	Ch09.Note.C2	Sample Page Selector.Device Target=Page 1
Slot 1 Cell 10 State	Out	Device Target	Output	Ch09.Note.G#1	Sample Page Selector.Device Target=Page 3
Slot 1 Cell 10 Trigger	In	Device Target	Hold	Ch09.Note.G#1	Sample Page Selector.Device Target=Page 3
Slot 1 Cell 11 State	Out	Device Target	Output	Ch09.Note.E1	Sample Page Selector.Device Target=Page 3
Slot 1 Cell 11 Trigger	In	Device Target	Hold	Ch09.Note.E1	Sample Page Selector.Device Target=Page 3
Slot 1 Cell 12 State	Out	Device Target	Output	Ch09.Note.C1	Sample Page Selector.Device Target=Page 3
Slot 1 Cell 12 Trigger	In	Device Target	Hold	Ch09.Note.C1	Sample Page Selector.Device Target=Page 3
Slot 1 Cell 13 State	Out	Device Target	Output	Ch09.Note.C2	Sample Page Selector.Device Target=Page 4
Slot 1 Cell 13 Trigger	In	Device Target	Hold	Ch09.Note.C2	Sample Page Selector.Device Target=Page 4
Slot 1 Cell 14 State	Out	Device Target	Output	Ch09.Note.G#1	Sample Page Selector.Device Target=Page 4
Slot 1 Cell 14 Trigger	In	Device Target	Hold	Ch09.Note.G#1	Sample Page Selector.Device Target=Page 4
Slot 1 Cell 15 State	Out	Device Target	Output	Ch09.Note.E1	Sample Page Selector.Device Target=Page 4
Slot 1 Cell 15 Trigger	In	Device Target	Hold	Ch09.Note.E1	Sample Page Selector.Device Target=Page 4
Slot 1 Cell 16 State	Out	Device Target	Output	Ch09.Note.C1	Sample Page Selector.Device Target=Page 4
Slot 1 Cell 16 Trigger	In	Device Target	Hold	Ch09.Note.C1	Sample Page Selector.Device Target=Page 4
Slot 1 Cell 2 State	Out	Device Target	Output	Ch09.Note.G#1	Sample Page Selector.Device Target=Page 1
Slot 1 Cell 2 Trigger	In	Device Target	Hold	Ch09.Note.G#1	Sample Page Selector.Device Target=Page 1
Slot 1 Cell 3 State	Out	Device Target	Output	Ch09.Note.E1	Sample Page Selector.Device Target=Page 1
Slot 1 Cell 3 Trigger	In	Device Target	Hold	Ch09.Note.E1	Sample Page Selector.Device Target=Page 1
Slot 1 Cell 4 State	Out	Device Target	Output	Ch09.Note.C1	Sample Page Selector.Device Target=Page 1
Slot 1 Cell 4 Trigger	In	Device Target	Hold	Ch09.Note.C1	Sample Page Selector.Device Target=Page 1
Slot 1 Cell 5 State	Out	Device Target	Output	Ch09.Note.C2	Sample Page Selector.Device Target=Page 2
Slot 1 Cell 5 Trigger	In	Device Target	Hold	Ch09.Note.C2	Sample Page Selector.Device Target=Page 2
Slot 1 Cell 6 State	Out	Device Target	Output	Ch09.Note.G#1	Sample Page Selector.Device Target=Page 2
Slot 1 Cell 6 Trigger	In	Device Target	Hold	Ch09.Note.G#1	Sample Page Selector.Device Target=Page 2
Slot 1 Cell 7 State	Out	Device Target	Output	Ch09.Note.E1	Sample Page Selector.Device Target=Page 2
Slot 1 Cell 7 Trigger	In	Device Target	Hold	Ch09.Note.E1	Sample Page Selector.Device Target=Page 2
Slot 1 Cell 8 State	Out	Device Target	Output	Ch09.Note.C1	Sample Page Selector.Device Target=Page 2
Slot 1 Cell 8 Trigger	In	Device Target	Hold	Ch09.Note.C1	Sample Page Selector.Device Target=Page 2
Slot 1 Cell 9 State	Out	Device Target	Output	Ch09.Note.C2	Sample Page Selector.Device Target=Page 3
Slot 1 Cell 9 Trigger	In	Device Target	Hold	Ch09.Note.C2	Sample Page Selector.Device Target=Page 3

Another option to make the LED buttons alive is to use the deck out command *Beat Phase*. With this command you can ensure that the button blinks while the sample in the cell is playing. If you wish that the buttons corresponding to your grid matrix blink you need to add it 64 times; one command for each of the cells. Then use two modifier conditions for the *Beat Phase* command. Firstly use the *Sample Page Selector* condition to ensure that the LEDs mirror the currently selected grid page. Secondly, use the condition *Slot x Cell y State*, which offers the value *Playing*. With this approach the button will blink only if the sample is playing and if the grid page where this sample resides is currently visible. An example on page 235 in chapter 6 contains more information about using *Beat Phase*.

☐ **Slot Stop/Delete/Load from List**   As already explained in the table on page 378, this mapping command provides several actions that depend on the current state of the slot selected in list Assignment. Other than with the *Slot x Cell y* command that can be assigned to a cell, this command can only be assigned to a slot. Nevertheless, this command will delete the sample from the current cell, if the slot is paused, and it will load the sample currently selected into the current cell, if the slot is empty.

To avoid the unwanted side effect of the slot being deleted and to reduce the functionality of the command to only stop the slot, you can use modifier condition *Slot State* for this command and select option *Playing*.

11.2   Importing and Loading Remix Sets

A remix set is a container that stores information about 64 different samples. You can load a remix set into a remix deck. Loading the remix set fills the sample grid matrix of the deck. The remix set saves the different playback options that you can configure individually for each cell: is the sample a loop or a one-shot sample; shall the sample be played forward or backward; shall Traktor set a particular gain value when the sample is loaded into a slot player, etc.

There are several sources where you can find ready-made remix sets. For example, the Native Instruments website provides several remix sets for free. (You can find the download link on *www.traktorbible.com/2014/links.aspx.*) These sets are the perfect starting point if you wish to experience the remix decks. If you wish to use more remix sets have a look on the various download portals; you can find plenty of stuff there for all different genres.

Remix sets are provided as a "Traktor Pak" (this file type uses the extension .trak). A TRAK file contains all audio files, the assignment between cells and audio files, the playback parameters of each cell and the status of the four slot players.

Importing Remix Sets

Before you can use a remix set from the TRAK file in Traktor, you need to import the set into your Traktor collection by performing one of the following actions:

☐   Drag and drop the TRAK file from Finder/Explorer onto the browser list (i.e. not in the folder list at the left side of the browser).

☐   Right-click the node *Track Collection* in the folder list and select *Import Traktor Pak*. Open the folder with the TRAK file, select it and click *Open*.

Traktor imports the remix set and analyzes the individual audio files. If the status bar of the browser is visible *(Preferences/Browser Details/Show Status Bar – Error Messages)*, Traktor will inform you about the progress.

During import Traktor will copy all audio files from the TRAK file into the folder, that is configured as *Remix Sets Dir* in section *Directories* of *Preferences/File Management*. By default this is the folder *Traktor/Contentimport* below the music folder of your operating system. During the import of a remix set Traktor creates a new folder below the *Remix Sets Dir*; Traktor uses the name of the remix set as the name of the folder. Additionally all samples from the set are added to your track collection.

Loading Remix Sets

You can find all remix sets in the node *All Remix Sets* below the *Track Collection* node in the folder list. In the default configuration one of the favourites is already linked to *All Remix Sets*. Clicking on that favourite or using the encoder or button that is assigned to the mapping command *Browser | Favorites | Selector* (see chapter 7) is the quickest way to open the list with all remix sets.

> **TIP** If you are using Kontrol F1 you can assign *Browser | Favorites | Selector* in Interaction Mode *Direct* to one of the eight unused F1 pads. Then select in *Set to Value* the favourite that is linked to *All Remix Sets*. More information about the eight unused pads can be found on page 196.

Traktor shows the available remix sets if you open the node All Remix Sets (as shown in the previous figure). The parentheses behind All Remix Sets show the number of imported or created sets and the parentheses after the name of the individual remix sets indicates the number of cells used in that set. Please note that a remix set cannot be loaded from the folder list (it does not work for playlists either). The folder icon with the grid matrix picture symbolizes the "virtual folder" of the remix set. The remix set itself uses a symbol without the folder image as you can see in the tracklist of the browser.

You can only load remix sets from the track list, i.e. the right section of the browser. If you click on a remix set name in the folderlist, Traktor shows the details about the samples in that set. At the beginning of the list you will always find an entry for the remix set itself. You can use this first entry to load the remix set.

Loading Remix Sets with the Mouse

Open the *All Remix Sets* node. Drag the remix set from the track list onto a remix deck, until the mouse pointer shows a green plus icon. Then release the mouse button. Only when you see that green plus icon is the remix set loaded.

Loading Remix Sets with F1: The slightly slower variant

Perform the following steps to load a remix set with Kontrol F1:

1. Press the *BROWSE* button to enter browse mode.

2. Hold the *SHIFT* button and turn the encoder to select the node *All Remix Sets* in the folder list.

3. Release the *SHIFT* button.

4. Turn the encoder to scroll through the track list and select the remix set you wish to load.

5. Press the encoder to load the selected remix set.

6. Press the *BROWSE* button to exit browse mode.

Loading Remix Sets with F1: The slightly faster variant

Firstly map the command *Browser | Favorites | Selector* in Interaction Mode *Direct* to one of the unused pads of Kontrol F1. Select in list *Set to value* the number of the favourite that is linked to *All Remix Sets*. This only has to be done once. Then perform the following steps:

1. Hold *QUANT* and press the pad that you have assigned to the favourite *All Remix Sets*.

2. Press the *BROWSE* button to enter browse mode.

3. Turn the encoder to scroll through the track list and select the remix set you wish to load.

4. Press the encoder to load the selected remix set.

5. Press the *BROWSE* button to exit browse mode.

Loading Remix Sets via Mapping

If you have already used the mapping command explained in chapter 7, to map the basic functionality for scrolling in the browser and for loading tracks, there is no additional work to be done. The mapping command *Deck Common | Load Selected* can be used for loading tracks into track decks as well as for loading remix sets into remix decks. *Deck Common | Load Selected* shows an error message if you try to load a track into a remix deck or a remix set into a track deck.

However, Traktor provides an additional mapping command, *Remix Deck | Load Set from List*, that can only be used to load a remix set into a remix deck. Other than *Load Selected* the command *Load Set from List* does not display an error message if you try to trigger an unsupported action.

11.3 Changing Sample Properties

Section "Slot Player Level" on page 373 explains the various playback parameters for samples that can be set on the slot player level. These parameters are valid for all samples that are loaded into the slot. The status of the buttons *Keylock, FX, Monitor Cue,* and *Punch Mode* is stored with the remix set. If you load a remix set Traktor sets the four playback parameters to the saved settings.

In contrast, the playback parameters explained in this chapter, are properties that are saved for each sample/cell. The cell properties are stored in the remix set and do not change the audio file itself that is loaded into the cell. This makes it possible to use the same audio file with different playback properties multiple times in the same remix set or in different ones. Maybe you use the same sample with other key/pitch values or you use different sample lengths.

Methods for Changing Sample Properties

The properties of the samples can be changed directly in the remix deck, or with Kontrol F1, or with the provided mapping commands.

Changing Properties with the Mouse

Many of the sample properties can be changed in the *Edit* panel of the remix decks that is organized in a similar was to the advanced panel of the track decks. The *Edit* panel is only visible in deck size *Advanced*. If you have selected deck size *Full* you can use the arrow button below *Loop Active* to open the *Edit* panel. Here a first overview of the *Edit* panel and the properties that can be changed there.

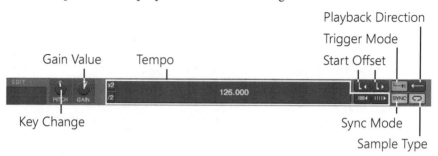

Changes that are done in the *Edit* panel apply to the currently selected cell (this does not have to be the active cell currently playing in the slot player). Click on the name and not on the trigger button (symbolized by the sample type icon) to select a cell. Traktor changes the background of the selected cell. The name of the active cell is shown in white and the names of the not active cells with a grey font.

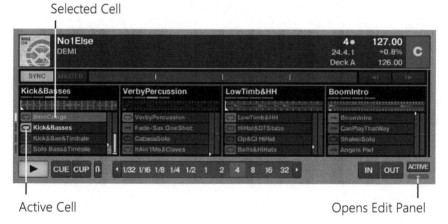

Changing Properties with Kontrol F1

With Kontrol F1 it is possible to change all playback properties of the samples. The property that is changed is selected with the eight buttons above the pad matrix. Depending on the property you wish to change you will use either the pads or the encoder. The following sections explain the steps in detail.

Changing Properties via Mapping

For a few of the sample properties Traktor provides you with mapping commands. These mapping commands use the four slot players, and not the individual cells, in option Assignment. This means that you need to load the sample into a slot player first before you can change the property.

The mapping commands are introduced in the section that explains a property; a complete overview can be found in the table on page 395.

Properties Overview

The following table shows all sample properties that can be adjusted and it shows whether you can change the property in the user interface, with Kontrol F1, or by using a mapping command.

Property	GUI	F1	Mapping
Name	X	–	–
Colour	X	X	–
Sample Type	X	X	X
Trigger Mode	X	X	X
Sample Sync Mode	X	X	–
Playback Direction	X	X	X
Start Position	X	X	–
Tempo	X	X	–
Gain	X	X	–
Pitch	X	X	–
Sample Length	–	X	X

Changing the Cell Name

The text that is visible in the cells of the grid matrix is the display name of the sample as it is used and shown in the remix set. This may not necessarily be the name of the audio file or the track name and you can freely change it. If you drop samples from the browser onto a cell or if you capture a loop from a track deck or the loop recorder,  Traktor will by default use the title tag – if available – or the file name of the audio file. Quite often the name may be too long or not very meaningful.

To change the name double-click the current name. The name is selected. Overwrite or edit the name and press the Enter key once you are done.

Changing the Cell Colour

To change the colour of a samples right-click on the sample icon in a cell. Traktor shows a colour chooser. Click the colour you wish to assign.

To change the cell colour with F1, press *SHIFT+INVERSE* and then press the pad those colour you wish to change. Wait until the pads of F1 show the sixteen available colours and finally press the pad with the colour you wish to assign. Press *SHIFT+IN-VERSE* again to exit colour mode.

Changing Sample Type, Trigger Mode and Sync Mode

The sample type – or sample playback mode – can be either loop or one-shot. Loops are normally repeated until playback is stopped and one-shot samples are played only once. Traktor shows the sample type at the left side of the cells in the grid matrix and for the selected cell in the *Edit* panel.

The trigger mode defines whether the complete sample is played after it has been triggered (this is called "latched" mode) or whether it is only played for as long as the playback button of that sample is clicked (in the user interface) or for as long as the corresponding pad is pressed (on the F1). This trigger mode is called "gated" mode.

Even in gated mode the currently selected quantize value is taken into account if quantize is enabled. Let's assume that the quantize value is set to 4 beats and that you release the pad after the first two beats of a loop haven been played. The playback of the sample will continue for another two beats because that is when the quantization interval has been reached.

There are two *SYNC* buttons in the remix deck: the *SNYC* button for the complete deck and the *SYNC* button in the Edit panel that controls the sync setting of the individual samples.

◻ The *SYNC* button of the remix decks controls whether the remix deck tempo follows the tempo of the sync master. It this *SYNC* button is on then all tempo changes done on the sync master will affect all samples currently playing in the remix deck, no matter whether the *SYNC* option of the individual samples is active or not.

◻ The *SYNC* button for the individual samples controls whether the tempo of the sample (the value that is shown in the *Edit* panel) is adjusted to the base tempo of the remix deck or not.

Sounds complicated? Let's have a look at an example:

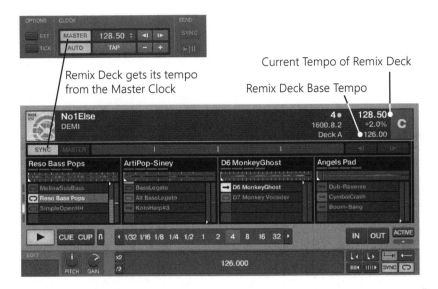

Remix Deck gets its tempo from the Master Clock

Current Tempo of Remix Deck

Remix Deck Base Tempo

In the figure above the Master Clock is used as sync master and the tempo of the Master Clock is set to 128.5 BPM. Because the SYNC button of the remix deck is on, the remix deck follows this tempo. The base tempo of the remix deck is 126 BMP and the current tempo is 128.5 BPM (same tempo as in the Master Clock).

Because the tempo of the sample currently playing in slot 1 is set to 126 BPM and because the base tempo of the remix deck is set to the same BPM, it is not necessary to perform any tempo adjustment between the sample tempo and the base tempo of the remix deck. However, because the current tempo of the remix deck is approx. 2% higher than the base tempo, the playback speed of the sample in slot 1 is 2% faster as well. This means it is played at 128.5 BPM because all samples playing in the remix deck *always* follow the current deck tempo. It does not matter whether the source of the current deck tempo is a sync master, the tempo set with the tempo fader (while deck SYNC is off) or a tempo change caused by any timecode action.

If we were to disable the *SYNC* button for the sample, this would not result in any change of the sample's playback speed. The reason is that the tempo of the sample and the remix deck base tempo are identical.

A second example is shown in the figure below. Here the *Edit* panel shows the sample properties of the one-shot sample in slot 3. The tempo of that sample is set to 90 BPM and the sample *SYNC* button is off. Because the *SYNC* button for that sample is off, the playback tempo of the sample only follows the current tempo of the remix deck and Traktor does not perform any adjustment between the sample BPM and the base tempo of the remix deck. Because the current tempo is by 2% higher than the base tempo, the playback speed of that sample is by 2% faster as well.

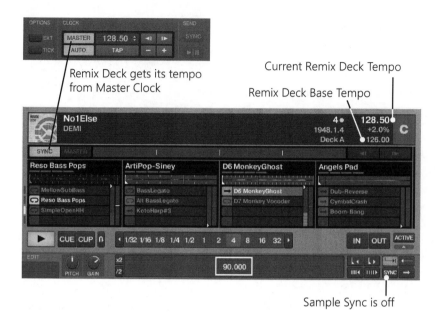

Remix Deck gets its tempo from Master Clock

Current Remix Deck Tempo

Remix Deck Base Tempo

Sample Sync is off

The situation will change if we activate *SYNC* for that sample. Then Traktor would perform a double tempo adjustment. First it would adjust the difference between the sample BPM and the remix deck base tempo (the sample would be played approx. 40% faster) and then it would adjust the tempo difference between the base tempo and the current tempo.

So that you use the smallest tempo adjustments as possible it makes sense to use loops in a remix set that have a similar tempo and then to set the base tempo of the deck to that BPM value.

If you use one-shot samples then set the BPM of that samples also to the base tempo of the deck or ensure that the *SYNC* option for those one-shot samples is off.

Changing Sample Type, Trigger Mode and Sync Mode in Edit Panel

Perform the following steps to change the sample type, the trigger mode, or the sync mode in the *Edit* panel:

1. Select the sample you wish to edit by clicking on its name in the grid matrix.

2. Click in the *Edit* panel on the button of the property you wish to change.

Changing Sample Type, Trigger Mode and Sync Mode with Kontrol F1

Perform the following steps to change the sample type, the trigger mode, or the sync mode with Kontrol F1:

1. Press the *TYPE* button and keep it held.

2. Turn the encoder and select one of the following options in the 7 segment display:

- ☐ *pl* to change the sample type
- ☐ *tr* to change the trigger mode
- ☐ *sy* to change the sync mode

Once you have selected the desired mode the sixteen pads show by their colours the current mode of the samples that are now visible in the grid:

- ☐ Sample Type: green for loops, blue for one-shots
- ☐ Trigger Mode: purple for Latched, yellow for Gated
- ☐ Sync Mode: orange for active, white for inactive

The pads of empty cells are not lit.

3. Press the pad that type or mode you wish to toggle.
4. Release the *TYPE button.*

Changing Sample Type and Trigger Mode via Mapping

The sample type can be changed with *Remix Deck | Slot Play Mode* and the trigger mode with *Remix Deck | Slot Trigger Type*. Both commands allow setting the Assignment to one of the four slots only, and not to the individual cells of the grid matrix. This means that you need to load the sample into a slot before you can change the sample type or trigger mode with the mapping commands.

Changing the Playback Direction

Traktor can playback the samples of a remix decks either forward or backward. The playback direction can be changed momentarily or permanently.

Changing the Playback Direction in Edit Panel Permanently

1. Select the cell you wish to change by clicking in its name.
2. Click in the *Edit* Panel on *SAMPLE REVERSE.*

Changing the Playback Direction via Mapping Momentarily

By default the mapping commands *Slot x Cell y Trigger* (see section 11.1) trigger the playback of the sample in that cell. Traktor provides four different Cell Modifier mapping command that allow you to overwrite and change the default behaviour of *Slot x Cell y Trigger.*

If you wish to use *Slot x Cell y Trigger* to change the playback direction, add the mapping command *Remix Deck | Direct Mapping | Cell Reverse Modifier* to your mapping. Assign that command to a button. *Cell Reverse Modifier* only supports Interaction Mode *Hold.*

Once you have made this change to your mapping, you can now hold the button where you mapped *Cell Reverse Modifier* to, and press one of the buttons/pads that are assigned to *Slot x Cell y Trigger*, to change the playback direction of that cell momentarily.

Changing the Playback Direction with Kontrol F1

Perform the following steps to change the playback direction with Kontrol F1:

1. Press the *REVERSE* button and keep it held.

2. Press the pad of the cell those playback direction you wish to change. Traktor will change the playback direction immediately.

3. Perform one of the following actions:

   □ **Change Playback Direction Permanently** First release the *REVERSE* button and then the pad.

   □ **Change Playback Direction Momentarily** First release the pad and then the *REVERSE* button.

Changing the Start Position of a Sample

In the case that a sample is not perfectly cut or if you wish to play a percussion sample slightly offbeat, you can change the start position of the sample. The start position is shown in the slot players by a vertical line plus a small triangle.

Changing the Start Position in the Edit Panel

You can change the start position in the *Edit* panel by using these two buttons. They move the start position by a 1/16th note to the left or the right.

Changing the Start Position with Kontrol F1

With the F1 you can change the start position in the same way as in the *Edit* panel by steps in the length of a 1/16th note. Additionally you can select a smaller step size where one step is 1/100 of a 1/16th note long

1. Press *SHIFT+QUANT* to enter edit mode.

2. Turn the encoder until the 7 segment display shows *OF* if you wish to use step size 1/16th note (OF=offset). Turn the encoder until the display shows *NU*, if you wish to use 1/100 of a 1/16th note as step size (NU=nudging).

3. Press the pad those start position you wish to change and keep the pad pressed. The 7 segment display now shows the current start position offset.

4. Turn the encoder to move the start position or press it, to reset the start offset.

5. Press *SHIFT+QUANT* to exit edit mode.

Changing the Sample Length

You can change the sample length to change the audible part of a sample. Shortening a sample works similar to shortening the loop length in a track deck. It moves the loop out point towards the beginning of the sample. If you shorten a sample, Traktor will reduce what is audible by the half of the current length. If you shorten the length again, only the first quarter of the sample will be audible. This makes it possible, for example to create a kind of drum roll with a sample.

If you start at the original sample length and lengthen the sample, Traktor adds silence at the end of the sample. This allows it, for example, to lengthen a one beat sample in a way that the audio is only audible on the first beat of the bar.

The first slot in the following figure shows the original length of the sample. In slot 2 the length has been doubled and in slot 3 halved.

Changing the Sample Length with Kontrol F1

Perform the following steps to change the length of a sample with the F1:

1. Press the *SIZE* button to enter size mode.

2. Keep the pad of the sample pressed those length you wish to change. The 7 segment display shows the currently set length: 1 = original length, 2 = length has been doubled up to 64. ˙2 = length has been halved, down to ˙64.

3. Perform one of the following steps:

   ◻ Turn the encoder to change the sample length.

   ◻ Press the encoder to reset the sample size to its original length.

4. Press the *SIZE* button to exit size mode.

Changing the Sample Length via Mapping

You can use the following four commands to change the length of a sample in a mapping: *Slot Size Adjust, Slot Size x2, Slot Size /2* and *Slot Size Reset.* All four commands can be found in the submenu *Remix Decks | Legacy.*

Changing the Tempo

You can use the BPM field, the buttons x2 and /2m, and the buttons *SAMPLE BMP INC* and *SAMPLE BPM DEC* to change the tempo of the selected sample in the same way as you would do in the *Grid* panel of a track deck.

Dobule BPM   Current BPM Value

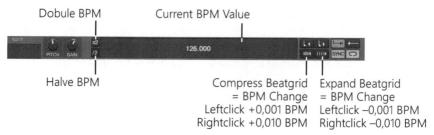

Halve BPM   Compress Beatgrid   Expand Beatgrid
                             = BPM Change   = BPM Change
                             Leftclick +0,001 BPM Leftclick –0,001 BPM
                             Rightclick +0,010 BPM Rightclick –0,010 BPM

I would assume that the function that allow you to change the tempo in the *Edit* panel are rarely used. Maybe they are useful if a sample has been loaded directly into the cell and if they have not first been analysed in a track deck. If you use samples from external sources I recommend to load them into a track deck first, change the BPM there and then load them into a remix deck.

Changing the Tempo with Kontrol F1

You can change the tempo of a sample with Kontrol F1 by performing the following steps:

1. Press *SHIFT+SIZE* to enter speed mode.

2. Press and hold the pad of the cell in which you wish to change the playback tempo.

   The 7 segment display shows the current tempo: 1 = original tempo, 2 double tempo, 4 = quadruple tempo, ˙2 = halve as fast as original, ˙4 = one quarter of the original tempo.

3. Perform one of the following steps:

   ▫   Turn the encoder to change the tempo.

   ▫   Press the encoder to reset the tempo.

4. Press *SHIFT+SIZE* to exit speed mode.

Changing the Gain

Just like with tracks you can also set a gain value for samples, to compensate a volume differences. To change the gain value select the cell you wish to edit and then use the *Gain* knob in the *Edit* panel to change the value.

To change the gain value of a sample with Kontrol F1, hold *SHIFT* and the use the volume fader of the slot where the sample is playing.

If you use samples from the browser into a remix deck Traktor can use the Autogain value that is already available in Traktors' private metadata. This is why it is recommended that you import new samples into your Traktor collection first. When you load them into a track deck you check the BPM, the grid, and the volume.

The autogain value from the metadata is used if option *Set Autogain When Loading Samples* in section *Remix Deck Layout* of the *Preferences/Remix Decks dialog is checked.*

If you capture a loop from a track deck Traktor will only copy the channel gain value of the track and not the total gain value (the sum of autogain and channel gain).

Changing the Pitch

You can use the Pitch knob in the Edit panel to change the key up or down by a maximum of twelve semitones. The pitch feature of the remix decks works in the same way as the key correction and adjustment in the track decks. You need to activate *Keylock On* in the slot player; otherwise Traktor will not perform a key change.

To change the pitch value select the cell you wish to edit and then use the *Pitch* knob in the *Edit* panel to change the value.

To change the pitch with Kontrol F1 perform the following steps:

1. Press *SHIFT+TYPE* to enter pitch mode.
2. Press and hold the pad whose pitch you wish to change. The current pitch setting is shown on the 7 segment display. Negative values are shown by a dot in the upper left corner of the display.
3. Perform one of the following steps:
   - ☐ Turn the encoder to change the pitch.
   - ☐ Press the encoder to reset the pitch to zero.
4. Press *SHIFT+TYPE* to exit pitch mode.

> **NOTE** Contrary to what is said in the F1 manual, Traktor does not automatically activate the keylock feature of the slot if you change the pitch setting. You need to activate keylock manually.

Reference: Mapping Commands to change Sample Properties

This lengthy sections ends with the information about the mapping commands you can use to change some of the sample properties.

Setting Sample Properties

Remix Deck | Slot Play Mode	Interaction Mode: Inc, Dec Type of Controller: Button	Toggles the play mode of the sample loaded the selected slot between Loop and One-Shot.
		Both interaction modes support wrap-around. This means that you need to map only of them to be able to change the sample play-back mode.
Remix Deck | Slot Trigger Type	Interaction Mode: Inc, Dec Type of Controller: Button	Toggles the trigger mode of the sample loaded in the selected slot between Gated and Latched.
		Both interaction modes support wrap-around. This means that you need to map only of them to be able to change the trigger type.
Remix Deck | Legacy | Slot Size Adjust	Interaction Mode: Direct, Relative Type of Controller: Fader/Knob, Encoder	Use this mapping command to change the sample length stepwise with a knob, fader or encoder in the same way as the size mode of Kontrol F1 is implemented.
Remix Deck | Legacy | Slot Size Reset	Interaction Mode: Trigger Type of Controller: Button	Resets the sample length to its original length.
Remix Deck | Legacy | Slot Size x2	Interaction Mode: Trigger Type of Controller: Button	Lengthens the audible area of the sample by moving the end point to the right. If the complete sample is audible Slot Size x2 adds silence at the end of the sample.
Remix Deck | Legacy | Slot Size /2	Interaction Mode: Trigger Type of Controller: Button	Shortens the audible part of the sample by one half.

11.4 Creating and Editing Remix Sets

The previous sections mainly covered how to use ready-made remix sets and how you can change the playback of the samples by changing the parameters of the slot players and the properties of the samples. This section explains how to create your own remix sets. The sample source can be audio files from your collection or loops that you capture from a track deck.

Importing New Samples into the Traktor Collection

It is easy to import new samples into your collection. You can select the type of the sample/s at the same time.

1. Go to the folder list in the Traktor browser. Open the *Explorer* node and navigate to the folder with the samples you wish to import.

2. Select the audio files you wish to import. If the folder contains loops as well as one-shot samples, only select either loops or one-shot samples.

3. Right/Ctrl-click the selection.

4. Click on *Import to Collection*.

5. Click on *as Looped Samples*, if the files you selected are loops or click on *as One-Shot-Samples* if the files you selected are one shot samples.

The imported samples now have the correct sample type. Traktor uses the sample type that was set during import when you load that sample into the remix set. Setting the type of the audio file to either loop or one-shot also makes it easier find the samples in your collection while you create your own remix sets: you will find all samples in the node *All Samples* below the *Track Collection* node of the folder list.

After you have imported the samples it is a good practice to load them into a track deck and to let Traktor analyse them. Check the autogain value and correct it if necessary; you can instruct Traktor to use the Autogain value from the audio file if you add that sample to a remix set (see also page 394).

Check the detected BPM of the sample and change it if necessary. Quite often the file name of samples that you can get from the various download portals contains information about the BPM of the file. If you use one-shot samples without a clear tempo, set the BPM for these files to the base tempo you are planning to use for the remix set (see also page 388).

Change the Sample Type of an Audio File in your Collection

Traktor 2 uses a private tag inside the audio files to be able to distinguish between tracks, looped samples and one-shot samples. You can change the audio file type on the track browser:

1. Right/ctrl-click the audio file in the track list.

2. The context/action menu opens. Click on one of the *Set Type To* commands.

Once the type is changed Traktor also changes the icon in the *Icons* column of the track list.

Creating an Empty Remix Set

The quickest way to create an empty remix set in the Traktor user interface is opening the menu of the deck letter and then switching the deck type between remix deck and track deck. Once you have set the type to remix deck again Traktor opens an empty remix set.

To create an empty set via mapping use the mapping command *Deck Common | Unload*.

To create an empty remix set with Kontrol F1 unload the current set. The steps are described in section "Deleting Samples with Kontrol F1" on page 402.

Organizing your Remix Set

Before you start added samples to a remix set it makes sense to spend some time planning the layout and structure of the grid. Most importantly you should not add samples to the same column of the grid that you wish to play at the same time.

It's a best practice to add similar samples, i.e. sample with the same instruments or similar loops, into the same column. Possible categories for such a way of structuring can be the following:

◻ Drums, Kicks, Percussion

◻ Bass

◻ Synth

◻ Lead

◻ Vocals/Acapellas

◻ Effects

Use different colours for each category. This will help you to see at a glance what kind of sample is available in which cell.

Adding Samples from your Collection

You can load samples from the collection into your remix set by using the mouse, by using the context menu of the browser, by using Kontrol F1, and by using the mapping commands Traktor provides.

Loading Samples in the User Interface

To add a sample from the browser to a remix set cell open the track collection or a playlist in the browser, drag the sample and drop it onto a cell. If the cell already contains a sample it will be replaced.

You can load a sample from the tracklist by right-clicking the sample and selecting *Load into Remix Deck x/Slot y* in the context menu. The disadvantage of this method: you can only load samples into one of the four slot players, and not a distinct cell of the grid matrix.

Loading Samples with Kontrol F1

If the samples that you wish to add are already visible in the track list, you can use the quick load feature of Kontrol F1:

1. Press the BROWSE button and hold it to enter quick load mode.

2. Turn the encoder to scroll in the tracklist and select the sample.

3. Press the pad of the cell into which the sample shall be loaded.

4. Repeat steps 2 and 3 or release the BROWSE button to exit quick load mode.

If you first need to open the folder with the samples, perform the following steps:

1. Press the BROWSE button to enter browse mode.

2. Hold *SHIFT* and turn the encoder to scroll in the browser list. If you need to open a folder in the folder list, press the encoder. Release *SHIFT* once the desired folder is open.

3. Turn the encoder to scroll in the tracklist and select the sample.

4. Press the pad of the cell into which the sample shall be loaded.

5. Repeat steps 2 to 5 or press the *BROWSE* button to exit browse mode.

Loading Samples via Mapping

By default the mapping commands *Slot x Cell y Trigger* (see section 11.1) trigger the playback of the sample in that cell. Traktor provides four different Cell Modifier mapping commands that allow you to overwrite and change the default behaviour of *Slot x Cell y Trigger*.

If you wish to use *Slot x Cell y Trigger* to load a sample from the browser, add the mapping command *Remix Deck | Direct Mapping | Cell Load Modifier* to your mapping. Assign that command to a button. *Cell Load Modifier* only supports Interaction Mode *Hold*.

Once you have made this change to your mapping, you can now hold the button where you mapped *Cell Load Modifier* to, and press one of the buttons/pads that are assigned to *Slot x Cell y Trigger*, to load the sample selected in the browser list into that cell.

A legacy function of the sample decks (the predecessor of the remix decks) is still provided with the mapping command *Remix Deck | Legacy | Slot Load from List*. As well as using *Cell Load Modifier* the command *Slot Load from List* can be used to load a sample but only into one of the four slot players but not to any particular cell of the grid matrix. Therefore it is better to use the new Modifier method.

Capture Samples from a Track Deck or from the Loop Recorder

Not only can you load samples from your track collection into a remix set, but also capture loops from a track deck or from the loop recorder.

Capturing Samples with the Mouse

Loops that you recorded in the loop recorder can be dragged and dropped onto a remix set cell or onto a slot player.

Samples can also be copied from a deck to a slot player or a cell in the remix set. The length of the sample is identical to the currently selected loop length of that deck. If there is a loop active during the copying the loop is copied; otherwise a sample starting at the current playback position is moved to the target cell.

Capturing Samples with Kontrol F1

With Kontrol F1 you will use the capture mode to grab an audio sample from the loop recorder or a loop from a track deck and copy it into one of the cells of a remix set.

1. Perform one of the following actions

   ◻   Load the track from which you wish to capture into a track deck. Set the playmarker to the start of the new sample and use the loop control of the deck to set the desired loop length. You can also create a loop with the desired length.

   ◻   Use the loop recorder and create/overdub a loop what you wish to transform into a remix set sample.

2. Press the *CAPTURE* button and keep it pressed.

3. Turn the encoder to select the capture source. The 7 segment display shows the possible sources in the following form; *ca, cb, cc, cd* und *cl*. The first four abbreviations refer to the four decks A to D and cl refers to the loop recorder.

4. Release the *CAPTURE* button.

5. If you have selected a deck in step 3, you can now use the encoder to change the loop length.

6. Press the pad of the cell where the sample shall be copied to.

7. Press the *CAPTURE* button to exit capture mode

8. Use the methods described in section 11.3 to change the various properties of the new sample: change the name, assign a colour, etc.

Capturing Samples via Mapping

To capture a sample in a mapping you will need the following three mapping commands:

- *Remix Deck | Capture Source Selector*
- *Remix Deck | Direct Mapping | Cell Capture Modifier*
- *Remix Deck | Direct Mapping | Slot x Cell y Trigger*

With *Capture Source Selector* you can select the source of the new sample. Map this command either to a knob or an encoder. *Capture Source Selector* always offers the loop recorder as a possible capture source and also all decks that are set to track deck. While you select the capture source Traktor shows the current selection in the bottom row of the deck header (assuming that the size of the remix set is set to either *Full* or *Advanced*).

The command *Remix Deck | Direct Mapping | Cell Capture Modifier* is one of the four modifier commands that overwrite the primary function of *Slot x Cell y Trigger*. Map *Cell Capture Modifier* (which only provides Interaction Mode *Hold)* to a button.

After this change you can now hold the button assigned to *Cell Capture Modifier* and then press one of the buttons that are assigned to *Slot x Cell y Trigger*. This will copy a sample from the source selected with *Capture Source Selector* into the cell of the grid matrix.

Legacy functions of the sample decks (the predecessor of the remix decks) are still provided with the mapping commands *Remix Deck | Legacy | Slot Capture from Loop Recorder* and *Slot Capture from Deck*. Both commands can capture a sample from a track deck and the loop recorder, but you can only use the four slot players as capture target. Therefore I would recommend you use the new method and not the old commands.

Moving and Duplicating Samples

Sometimes it happens that a sample is not in the correct column, maybe because you wish to play that sample at the same time as another sample in the same column of the grid. Or you wish to use the same sample more than once in the same remix set, maybe because you wish to use different pitches or different sample lengths. In those cases you can either move a sample or create a duplicate.

Moving and Duplicating with the Mouse

Moving or duplicating a sample with the mouse works not only inside a remix deck but also if the target cell is in a second remix deck.

- **MOVE** Drag the sample with the mouse to the new cell.
- **DUPLICATE** Press and hold the ALT key and drag the sample to the cell where a copy of the sample shall be placed.

> **TIP** If you have mapped the command *Remix Deck | Sample Page Selector* you can
> – as long as the mouse button is held – use the assigned encoder or knob to open
> another page of the remix set and drop the sample there.

Moving and Duplicating with Kontrol F1

Of course, you can also use Kontrol F1 to move and duplicate samples. Perform the
following steps:

1. Press *SHIFT+QUANT* to enter edit mode.

2. If you wish to move a sample turn the encoder until the 7 segment display shows
   Ct ("cut"). If you wish to duplicate a sample turn the encoder until the display
   shows *Cp* ("copy").

3. Press the pad of the sample that you wish to move or duplicate. The 7 segment
   display now shows *PA* ("paste").

4. If you wish to add the selected sample to another page of the grid turn the encoder. The display will show the selected page number for a short moment and
   will then display *PA* again.

5. Press the pad of the target cell. Traktor moves or duplicates the sample.

6. Press *SHIFT+QUANT* to exit edit mode.

Copying Samples via Mapping

Although Traktor provides the mapping command *Remix Deck | Legacy | Slot Copy
from Slot*, I would recommend to use the mouse actions for copying and duplicating
samples. Due to the limitation of the mapping architecture it is much easier using the
mouse than using the mapping command. The mouse actions are quick – maybe even
faster than using the F1 – and as these actions are needed during the preparation of a
remix set and not during a gig, there is no reason not to use the mouse.

Deleting Samples

If a sample is no longer needed you can remove it from the remix set. As usual the
following sections describe the three alternative methods.

Deleting Samples with the Mouse

To delete a sample with the mouse press Alt+Ctrl (Windows) or Alt+Cmd (Mac) and
click in the cell on the icon representing the sample playback mode

Deleting Samples with Kontrol F1

Traktor Kontrol F1 provides a distinct delete mode that allows you to delete single
cells, complete pages of the grid and even the complete remix set.

1. Press *SHIFT+CAPTURE* and hold both buttons to enter delete mode.

2. Perform one of the following actions:

   ☐ To delete a single cell press the corresponding pad.

   ☐ To delete a complete page of the loaded remix set, turn the encoder until the 7 segment display *d1, d2, d3,* or *d4. d* means "delete" and the number refers to the grid pages. Press the encoder to delete the selected page.

   ☐ To delete the complete remix set, turn the encoder until the 7 segment display shows *UL* ("unload"). Press the encoder to delete the set and to create a new, empty one.

3. Release *SHIFT+CAPTURE* to exit delete mode.

Deleting Samples via Mapping

By default the mapping commands *Slot x Cell y Trigger* (see section 11.1) trigger the playback of the sample in that cell. Traktor provides four different Cell Modifier mapping command that allow you to overwrite and change the default behaviour of *Slot x Cell y Trigger.*

If you wish to use *Slot x Cell y Trigger* to delete a sample from the grid, add the mapping command *Remix Deck | Direct Mapping | Cell Delete Modifier* to your mapping. Assign that command to a button. *Cell Load Modifier* only supports Interaction Mode *Hold.*

Once you have made this change to your mapping, you can now hold the button where you mapped *Cell Delete Modifier* to, and press one of the buttons/pads that are assigned to *Slot x Cell y Trigger,* to delete the sample.

If you wish to clear the complete remix set use the mapping command *Deck Common | Unload.* This command behaves as the UL mode of Kontrol F1.

A legacy function of the sample decks (the predecessor of the remix decks) is still provided with the mapping command *Remix Deck | Legacy | Slot Unload.* However, *Slot Unload* can only delete a sample from one of the four slot players, and not from any particular cell of the grid matrix.

11.5 Saving and Renaming a Remix Set

All changes that you make to a remix set can be automatically saved by Traktor. You can also save an edited set under a new name if you wish to keep the original, similar to the *Save as* command you find in almost any app. To change the name of the author/artist shown in the deck header of a remix deck, you can use either inline-editing from the tracklist or the Edit dialog. As with tracks you can use the tracklist context menu to set the cover of the remix set.

Setting Option for Automatic Saving

The *Preferences/Remix Decks* dialog contains a section labelled *Savings* with exactly one option: *Auto-Save Edited Remix Sets*.

If you enable this option, Traktor saves and overwrites the changed remix set,

◻   if you load another set,

◻   if you change the deck type from Remix Deck into another type,

◻   if you use the *Unload* feature of F1 or the corresponding mapping command that create an empty set,

◻   if you exit Traktor.

Whether it makes sense for you to enable this option or not depends on if you prefer to load your sets in a determined state or if you prefer that all changes you make to a remix set do not get lost accidentally (because you forgot to save them manually).

Saving Remix Sets

Perform one of the following actions to save the changes you made to a remix set:

◻   Click the deck letter to open the menu and select *Save Remix Set.*

◻   Go to the folder list and open the node All Remix Sets. Then drag the deck header of the remix set to the track list (right side of the browser).

◻   Hold the *SHIFT* button on the F1 and press the encoder.

◻   Map the command *Remix Deck | Save Remix Set* to your controller or your keyboard. Press the assigned button or key.

If the collection already contains a remix set with the same name, Traktor opens the *Save Virtual Set* dialog:

Perform one of the following actions:

▢ Click *Overwrite* if you wish to overwrite the existing remix set with the current changes.

▢ Enter a new name into the field *New Name* and click *Rename*. The current remix set will then be saved under a new name, creating a new version.

▢ Click *Cancel* if you changed your mind.

To create a new version of the set under a new name, you can also double-click the name in the deck header, enter a new name and then use one of the methods explained above to save the set.

Setting the Name and the Author of the Remix Set

To change the name of the remix set, double-click the current name shown in the deck header, edit or enter the name and then press Enter.

Unfortunately the name of the author/interpret cannot be changed directly in the deck header. To edit the author name open the node *All Remix Sets* in the folder list. Then go to the track list and double-click in column Interpret and enter the name. Changing the name in the track list only works if the inline-editing for the browser has been activated *(Preferences/Browser Details/Editing)*.

If inline-editing is disabled, go to the folder list and open the node *All Remix Sets*. Then right-click the remix set name in the track list and select *Edit*. Enter the name of the artist/author in the *Edit* dialog and click *OK*.

Set the Cover of the Remix Set

You can set the cover for a remix set in the same way as you select a cover for a track. Open the node *All Remix Sets* in the folder list. Go to the track list, right-click on the remix set name and select *Import Cover*. Use the *Open* dialog to open the folder with the image file, select it and finally click *Open*.

11.6 Exporting a Remix Set

Section 11.2 has explained how to import a remix set from a TRAK file into Traktor. It is also possible to perform the opposite: you can pack a remix set into a TRAK file if you wish to share it:

1. Go to the folder list and open the node *All Remix Sets*.

2. Right-click the name of the remix set you wish to export.

3. Select *Export Remix Set*. Traktor opens the *Save* dialog.

4. Open the folder where you wish to save the TRAK file, change the name of the file if needed and click *Save*.

Chapter 12

Equalizer, Key and Harmonic Mixing

The main topic of this chapter is the equalizer in Traktor. Next, you will find an introduction into harmonics, the concept of harmonic mixing and the tools that Traktor provides for these features. The topics harmonic mixing and equalizer have been combined into one chapter because the use of EQ settings can be an excellent way of avoiding so called key clashes.

12.1 Selecting, Displaying and Using the EQ

An equalizer (short: EQ) is a filter that can cut or boost selected frequencies inside a frequency spectrum. The most commonly used equalizers in the DJ domain are 3 band or 4 band equalizers. The term "band" means the number of frequency ranges that can be manipulated with the equalizer.

If you use Traktor in external mixing mode (see chapter 2) you will use the equalizer of your hardware mixer. In internal mixing mode where the audio from the decks is mixed inside the software mixer of Traktor, you will use the software equalizer.

Traktor offers five different 3 band EQs and one 4 band EQ. You can select the one you wish to use in section *EQ Selection* of the *Preferences/Mixer* dialog box

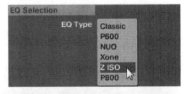

The equalizer is a deck related feature and it is shown in the *EQ+Fader* panel. This panel can be switched on and off in *Preferences/Mixer* dialog.

The EQ Types

The list box *EQ Type* contains six options; each EQ type is modelled after a different DJ mixer. *Classic* is the standard equalizer and it has been used in all earlier versions of Traktor. *P600/P800* emulate the Pioneer mixers DJM 600/DJM 800, *NUO* emulates an Ecler Nuo 4, *Z ISO* emulates a Pioneer DJM900 in isolator mode and *Xone* is an emulation of the Allen&Heath mixer Xone:92. *Xone* is the only EQ type one with four different frequency ranges.

The most important difference between the EQ types is how much they cut or boost the different frequency ranges. The following table lists the characteristic of the different equalizer types.

EQ Type	Low Cut/Boost	Mid, Mid Low Cut/Boost	Mid High Cut/Boost	High Cut/Boost
Classic	−24dB/+12dB	−24dB/+12dB	−	−24dB/+12dB
P600	−26dB/+12dB	−26dB/+12dB	−	−26dB/+12dB
P800	−26dB/+6dB	−26dB/+6dB	−	−26dB/+6dB
Nuo [1]	−30dB/+10dB	−25dB/+10dB	−	−30dB/+10dB
Xone:92 [2]	Infinite kill on High and Low; slew rate: 12dB/octave, Boost: +6dB	−30dB/+6dB	−30dB/+6dB	Infinite kill on High and Low; slew rate: 12dB/octave, Boost: +6dB
Z ISO [3]	−26dB/+6dB	−26dB/+6dB		−26dB/+6dB

[1] The cut/boost ranges in the table are taken from the original documentation of the Ecler Nuo 4. In the Traktor documentation the ranges for the mid band and high band are swapped.

[2] The EQ knobs of the Allen&Heath mixer Xone:92 allow a complete isolation of all frequency bands if the knobs are turned completely anti-clockwise. Unfortunately this is not possible with the Traktor emulation of this mixer.

[3] Early versions of Traktor 2.6.0 (this is the version from which on the NI controller/mixer Z2 was supported) the name P900 KILL was used for this EQ type. This can be seen on a photo taken by Steven James during BPM Show in October 2012 and published on his blog. (BPM Show is a music and DJ fair yearly held in Birmingham, UK.) The photo shows the EQ selection area of the *Preferences* dialog without the Z ISO type but with an EQ type named P900 KILL. This leads to the educated guess that Z ISO indeed emulates a Pioneer DJM 900, which allows to switch between an EQ and an isolator mode. While in isolator mode one can turn the EQ knobs completely anti-clockwise to kill the corresponding frequency band. The name P900 KILL is also used in the manual for Kontrol Z2. See also the pictures on the following page.

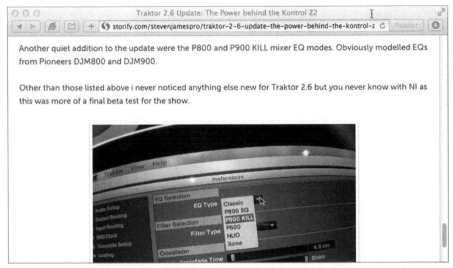

Screenshot from Traktor 2.6.0 as shown during BPM Show in Birmingham (October 2012)

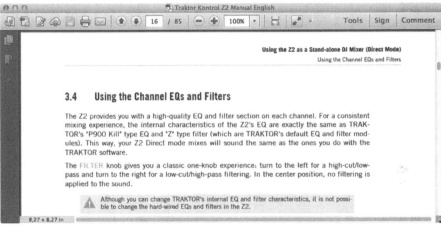

Extract from the Traktor Kontrol Z2 manual

Once the desired equalizer type has been selected and the corresponding panels have been activated they are shown in the area between the decks. The adjoining figures show the EQ panel for the 3 band and the 4 band equalizer. Because the available space for the panel is always the same, the knobs in 4 band mode are a slightly smaller.

The panel contains one knob for each frequency range that you can use to boost or cut the corresponding wave band. By using the small button next to the name of the frequency range it can be completely switched off; this is the so called kill function. Only when the EQ type *Classic* or *Z ISO* is selected do the kill buttons "kill" the corresponding frequency range completely.

> **NOTE**   Even when an equalizer is turned completely anti-clockwise it does not kill the respective frequency band. This is by design.

Let's have a look at the signal chain in Traktor. The equalizer sits almost at the end of the chain, right before the volume fader of the deck. When using Traktor in internal mixing mode the volume of a deck is controlled by its channel fader. In external mixing mode you need to use the Main knob in the Global Section; this controls the volume of all decks.

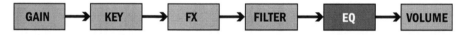

The equalizer is probably one of the most important tools for spinning. Here in short form are some examples of its use:

- ☐   One of the basic tricks is to turn down the bass for a few beats, for example during a break down (or you can use the kill button for the same purpose) and to turn the bass back up once the bassline of the track has come back in.

- ☐   The "longing for the bass to return" effect can be emphasized by lowering the level of the middle frequencies as well as the level of the bass.

- ☐   With clever use of the EQ you can combine elements of track A with elements of track B for an extended period of time. One classic example is to mash up the bassline of one track with the vocals of another. Here, one must be careful not to cut out too many frequencies because the frequency range of most instruments and vocals do not end at the wave band limits that can be controlled with the EQ knobs.

▢ The EQ is an indispensable tool to make transitions between two tracks. For the transition to be smooth leave the EQ knobs for the current track in their middle position and turn the EQ knobs for the next track completely anti-clockwise. The channel fader (and/or cross fader) of the next track should be completely open. If both tracks are well matched an almost inaudible transition can be made by slowly turning down the EQ knobs of the current track and slowly opening the EQ knobs of the next track at the same time.

Another technique is to swap the bassline. Turn the low frequencies of both tracks completely off, make the transition and then turn off the bass knob of the following track. This works more effectively if the basslines of the two tracks are similar.

▢ Most of today's music has been run through an optimizing mastering process. The sound of the track is optimal when all EQ knobs are in their middle position. This means that there is less need to mess with the EQ knobs. Also if you use older tracks (especially from the early days of CDs) you will see that the volume shown in the waveform is much quieter. Additionally there can be less bass present. In those cases the equalizer can help to adjust the sound characteristic of the two tracks

▢ Last but not least the equalizer is a great tool to attenuate key clashes (dissonances) between two tracks. Dissonances mostly occur if the keys of the two tracks differ greatly in the circle of fifths. Usually, it is the frequencies in the middle and lower band causing the key clash. If you lower the level of those frequency ranges it becomes easier to create a smooth transition between two tracks, even if the two tracks should not really be played due to the rules of harmonic mixing. (More about harmonic mixing can be found later in this chapter.)

As already said, these are only some of the capabilities of the equalizer, but as for the effects, my motto for using the equalizer is: Less can often be more.

12.2 Mapping Commands for the Equalizer

The buttons and the knobs of the *EQ+Fader* panel correspond to eight different mapping commands: four to set the level of the different wave bands and four that represent the kill buttons. The interaction modes and the further options of the groups of four are identical; they only differ in the frequency range they control.

The exact frequency range and the level cut/boost depend on the selected equalizer type.

Cutting/Boosting Frequency Ranges

Mixer | EQ | High Adjust	Interaction Mode: Direct Type of Controller: Fader, Knob, Encoder Assignment: select deck or Device Target	Increases or reduces the level of the high frequencies. The interaction mode Direct is the best choice if you wish to map this command to a knob or fader.
	Interaction Mode: Direct Type of Controller: Button Assignment: select deck or Device Target	If you chose interaction mode Direct and set Type of Controller as button you can set the knob to any value by pressing the knob. The fields Set to value allows values in the range from 0.000 to 1.000. If you enter 0 the knob is turn completely off, 1 sets it completely open and with a value of 0.5 you can set it to its middle position.
	Interaction Mode: Reset Assignment: select deck or Device Target	Resets the knob to the middle position
	Interaction Mode: Inc, Dec Assignment: select deck or Device Target Resolution: Min: ca. ±0,8% Fine: ca. ±3,1% Default: ca. ±12,5% Coarse: ca. ±25 % Switch: ca. ±50	Use these two interaction modes to change the knob stepwise. Select the desired step-size in the list Resolution. Dec turns the knob to the left and dampens the frequency range; Inc turns the knob to the right and amplifies the frequency range.
Mixer | EQ | Mid Adjust	see High Adjust	Increases or reduces the level of the middle frequencies. If the EQ type Xone has been selected this command controls the upper middle frequencies.
Mixer | EQ | Mid Low Adjust	see High Adjust	Increases or reduces the level of the lower middle frequencies (only available if the EQ type Xone has been selected).
Mixer | EQ | Low Adjust	see High Adjust	Increases or reduces the level of the low frequencies.

The following four commands correspond to the kill switches of the *EQ+Fader* panel.

Killing Frequency Bands

Mixer | EQ | High Kill	Interaction Mode: Toggle Assignment: select deck or Device Target	Kills the high frequencies. Toggle works like an On/Off switch.

Killing Frequency Bands

	Interaction Mode: Hold Assignment: select deck or Device Target	Activates the kill function as long as the mapped key or button is pressed.
	Interaction Mode: Direct Set to value: 1=On/0=Off Assignment: select deck	Use this interaction mode to either switch the kill function on or off.
Mixer | EQ | Mid Kill	Same as for High Kill	This command kills the middle frequencies (for the EQ types Classic, P600, P800, Z ISO, and NUO) and the upper middle frequencies if the EQ type Xone has been selected.
Mixer | EQ | Mid Low Kill	Same as for High Kill	This command kills the lower middle frequencies if the EQ type Xone has been selected.
Mixer | EQ | Low Kill	Same as for High Kill	This command kills the low frequencies.

12.3 Deck Filter and Sample Slot Filter

Another option to manipulate the frequency range is by using one of the *Filter* knobs that are available for each deck and each sample slot. The Filter knobs for the decks reside in the panel with the name *Filter+Key+Gain+Cue+Balance*. (You can display this panel by activating the corresponding check box on the dialog *Preferences/Mixer* in section *Mixer Layout.)*

If you use the remix decks you can find a slot filter in each of the four sample slots a remix decks provides. To make the Filter fader visible in the slots open the *Preferences/Remix Decks* dialog and enable the check box *Show Filter Fader* in section *Remix Deck Layout*. For a deck that is set to Remix Deck you still can use the *Filter* knob from the mixer section to change the filter for all slots of that deck.

If you are using the external mixing mode of Traktor, you will most likely use the filter of your mixer for your track decks. In internal mixing mode you are reliant on Traktor's software filter. However, you can also use the Traktor filter when you work in external mixing mode: in this case you can simply map the corresponding mapping command to any controller you might use.

Traktor provides three different filter types: *Ladder, Xone,* and *Z*. The filter type can be selected in the *Filter Selection* section of the dialog box *Preferences/Mixer*.

You need to choose option *Ladder* if you wish to activate a ladder type filter. The name originates from the order of the transistors/diodes that were used as a filter on the early Moog synthesizers; they were arranged similarly to a ladder. The option *Xone* activates a filter which sound characteristics and behavior is built like the filter found in the Allen&Heath mixer Xone:92. Filter type Z was introduced in Traktor 2.6.0 when the Kontrol Z2 was released: the characteristics of that software filter are identical to the hardware filter in Kontrol Z2 if you use the Z2 as a stand-alone-mixer.

The main difference between the filters is the preset resonance. The resonance circuit of the filter causes those tones that are close to the cut-off frequency of the filter to be amplified and the others to be weakened. If a high resonance setting is made the effect of the filter becomes very clear. Additionally, filters tend to create an oscillation of their own when the resonance is set to a high value; this process is called self oscillation and can lead to very interesting sound effects. The resonance (also called Q factor) is set to a high value for filter type *Ladder* and to a lower value for filter type *Xone*.

The filter is controlled with the *Filter* knob and the On/Off switch (the blue button next to the text FILTER).

When the knob is in the middle position all frequencies pass through the filter. Turning the knob to the left first cuts the high frequencies and then the low frequencies. Turning the knob to the right first cuts the low and then the high frequencies.

If you wish to have more control over the parameters of the filter you can also use the effect *Filter* (corresponds to the *Ladder* Filter) or the effect Filter:92 (corresponds to the *Xone* Filter). Set the FX units to single mode to access all available parameters. More information about these two effects can be found in chapter 13, "FX – The Traktor Effects".

Controlling the Deck Filter and Sample Slot Filter via Mapping

You can control the deck filter and the sample slot filter with two mapping commands: one command switches the filter on and off; the other controls the position of the *Filter* knob.

Controlling the Deck Filter and Sample Slot Filter

Mixer | Filter On Remix Deck | Filter On	Interaction Mode: Hold, Toggle Interaction Mode: Direct Set to value:1=On/0=Off Assignment: select deck or sample slot or Device Target	Switches the bipolar deck filter/slot filter on or off. The filter type can be selected on the dialog box Preferences | Mixer.

Controlling the Deck Filter and Sample Slot Filter

Mixer | Filter Adjust Remix Deck | Filter Adjust	Interaction Mode: Direct Type of Controller: Fader, Knob, Encoder Assignment: select deck or sample slot or Device Target	Sets the value of the filter. The Interaction Mode Direct is the best option if you wish to map this command to a knob or a fader.
	Interaction Mode: Direct Type of Controller: Button Assignment: select deck or sample slot or Device Target	If you use Button as controller type and select Interaction Mode Direct you can set the knob to a specific position. Use the field Set to value to enter a value in the range from 0.000 to 1.000. If you enter 0 the knob is turned completely anti-clockwise, 1 turns it completely clockwise and with 0.5 you set the knob to its middle position.
	Interaction Mode: Inc, Dec Type of Controller: Button Assignment: select deck or sample slot or Device Target Resolution: Min: ca. ±0,8% Fine: ca. ±3,1% Default: ca. ±12,5% Coarse: ca. ±25 % Switch: ca. ±50	You can use these interaction modes to change the value of the knob stepwise. Dec turns the knob to the left and Inc turns to the right. You can set the step-size in the list box Resolution.
	Interaction Mode: Reset Type of Controller: Button Assignment: select deck or sample slot or Device Target	Sets the filter to its middle position. Interaction Mode Reset is actually the same as using Direct for a button with a value of 0.5 in field Set to value

HOW TO: Reducing the Filter Range

If you do not wish to use the complete filter range you can reduce its frequency range by mapping the command *Mixer | Filter Adjust* or *Remix Deck | Filter Adjust* to a knob or a fader. During the mapping choose the controller type *Fader/Knob,* select *Interaction Mode Relative* and use the slider *Rotary Sensitivity* to set a value smaller than 100%. The smaller the configured value used the smaller the frequency range is cut by the filter. The larger the configured value is the more the mapped knob needs to be turned to reach the extreme positions of the knob.

12.4 Harmonics at a Glance

This section contains a short introduction into the Western musical system. The purpose of this section is to give you as much background information as necessary to understand the concept of harmonic mixing, the circle of fifths and its relation to the Camelot wheel. This helps with understanding the key adjustments features in Traktor. If you are already familiar with the theoretical basics of music continue to the next section.

Note, Octave, Half Step and Whole Step

Notes form the basis of music and they indicate the pitch/frequency of a tone. The difference in the pitch between two tones is called an interval. Of the many intervals three are of immediate interest. These are the octave, the whole step (also called major second) and the half step (also called semitone).

Almost all music cultures use the octave as an interval. An octave is characterized as such: the frequency of the higher tone is twice as high as the deeper tone. The tones between the higher and the lower tone of an octave establish a musical scale. In Western music an octave is divided into twelve semitones. Since the 19th century the so called equally tempered scale has been used. In this scale the distance between each tone is always the same.

This principle can easily be seen on a piano; the figure on the following page shows an extract. The piano in the upper image side shows the note names as they are used in the German speaking areas, in Scandinavia and in some west Slavic countries. The piano in the lower mage side is labelled with the note names as they are used in English speaking countries, in Traktor and in the tools for key detection.

As you can see the keys on a piano are arranged in groups of 12 keys each. Each group consists of 7 white and 5 black keys and each key represents one note. The interval between each note is a semitone (half step).

The white keys represent the so called naturals or white tones. Each of the white tones has one name only (C, D, E etc). This is different for the black keys. The note name of a black key – even though its frequency is always the same – depends on the perspective. Let's take the first black key as an example. If we look at it from the C, the black key is one semitone higher. In English this is expressed by adding the sign # to the original note. So we get C#, which is pronounced *C sharp*. (In German the postfix "is" is added to the original note name, so the name of the black key gets "Cis".) If we start from the second white key, the D, then the first black key to the left is one semitone lower than D. This is expressed in English by adding the postfix b to the note. So we get "Db", which is pronounced "D flat". (In German the postfix "es" is added; so the note name for the first black key gets "Des".)

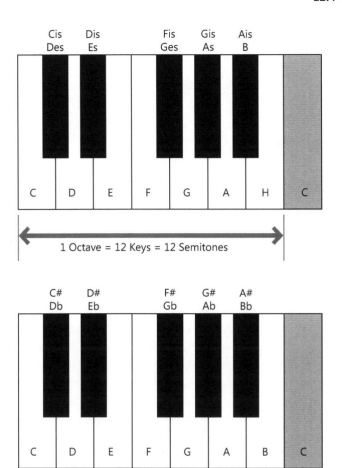

If we create a tone row from all tones of one octave we get the so called chromatic scale with the following notes (here in English notation which I will use from now on unless stated differently):

C C# D D# E F F# G G# A A# B C

The interval between all notes is one semitone. The notes C and D are one whole step apart (one semitone from C to C# and another one from C# to D).

Later, if we have a look at the Traktor features for making key changes we will come back to the fact that the smallest interval is one semitone and that 12 semitones define one octave.

417

First let's have a look at what a key is, what the differences between major scales and minor scales are and what a relative key is.

Key, Major Scale, Minor Scale and Relative Key

A musical scale is a series of notes mostly ordered in ascending order, which are musically correlated. For example, if we take the white keys from one octave on a piano then the white tones compose the following scale:

C   D   E   F   G   A   B   C

The first tone of this scale is C and is called the fundamental tone. Let's now have a look at the intervals between all tones in this scale:

No.	1	2	3	4	5	6	7	8
Tone	C	D	E	F	G	A	B	C
Interval	1	1	1/2	1	1	1	1/2	

The intervals in this scale are 'whole step/whole step/half/whole step/whole step/whole step/half'. A scale having this sequence of steps is called a major scale (in German: Dur). Because of the first tone of this scale (called tonic) is C, this scale is called C major (German: C-Dur).

> **Harmonic Mixing– Rule 1** Two tracks in the same key will sound harmonically mixed because both tracks are using the same notes of the same scale.

With this knowledge about the sequence of steps of a major scale we can create the tone rows for all major scales. If we do this for D major we have the following starting point:

No.	1	2	3	4	5	6	7	8
Tone	D							D
Interval	1	1	1/2	1	1	1	1/2	

The tonic of D major is D. All we have to do is to fill in the fields for the keys 2 to 7 and doing this in a way that conforms to the interval pattern typical of a major scale. To do this the piano figure from page 417 can help. The second tone of the tone row must be a tone with an interval of one whole step away from D. This is E. The interval between the second and the third tone must be a whole step too. We cannot use F (the interval between E and F is a semitone), so we need to use F# (in German Fis), which is one semitone higher than F.

No.	1	2	3	4	5	6	7	8
Tone	D	E	F#	G	A	B	C#	D
Interval		1	1	1/2	1	1	1	1/2

If we continue like this we get the scale which is shown in the table above. The main difference between the C major and D major scales is that D major contains two sharps (F# = Fis and C# = Cis).

The difference between a major scale and a minor scale is the pattern of the interval between the tones on the scale (Note: To keep things simple, I will only cover the natural minor and will neglect the variations, like the harmonic minor or melodic minor). The interval rules for a minor scale are: whole step/half/whole step/whole step/half/whole step. The scale of A minor (a-Moll, in German lower case letters are used for minor scales) for example looks like this:

No.	1	2	3	4	5	6	7	8
Tone	A	B	C	D	E	F	G	A
Interval		1	1/2	1	1	1/2	1	1

If you compare this scale with the scale of C major you will see that despite a different tonic, both scales use the exact same notes. If two scales use the same notes, they are called relative keys. C major is the relative major of A minor and A minor is the relative minor of C major. The relative minor of each major have both the same key signature (i.e. they use the same number of sharps or flats).

And again, with the knowledge about the interval pattern of a minor scale we now can construct the scale for any other tonic. This, for example, is the scale of B minor (German: h-Moll):

No.	1	2	3	4	5	6	7	8
Tone	B	C#	D	E	F#	G	A	B
Interval		1	1/2	1	1	1/2	1	1

If you compare this scale to the scale of D major you will see that both scales are using the same notes. As well D major and B minor use sharps (C# = Cis and F# = Fis). That's why D major is the relative major of B minor and B minor is the relative minor of D major.

If we continue like this and build the scales for all major and all minor scales we will see that there is only one major and one minor scale containing the same number of sharps and flats. The scale A major for example contains three sharps and there is no other major scale that also contains three sharps.

Let's now have a look at the interval between the keynotes of two relative keys. As we can see from the two examples explained above the interval between the keynote of a major scale and its relative minor is three semitones (this interval is called minor third).

If we combine all keys in a little table and combine the relative keys in the same column the table looks like this (first the keys in the German notation):

Major	Ces	Ges	Des	As	Es	B	F	C	G	D	A	E	H	Fis	Cis
Minor	as	es	b	f	c	g	d	a	e	h	fis	cis	gis	dis	ais

The following table contains the same information but here the English key names are used. As already said, in German lower case letters are used for minor scale; in English the letter "m" (short for minor) is added to the tonic of the scale. Instead of the musical keys the key names from the Camelot notation and the Open Key notation (more about this a bit further down in this chapter) can also be used. The keys using the same tones have been combined in the following table.

Minor			Major		
Camelot	Open Key	Scale	Camelot	Open Key	Scale
1A	6m	Abm, G#m	1B	6d	B
2A	7m	Ebm, D#m	2b	7d	Gb, F#
3A	8m	Bbm, A#m	3B	8d	Db, C#
4A	9m	Fm	4B	9d	Ab, G#
5A	10m	Cm	5B	10d	Eb, D#
6A	11m	Gm	6B	11d	Bb, A#
7A	12m	Dm	7B	12d	F
8A	1m	Am	8B	1d	C
9A	2m	Em	9B	2d	G
10A	3m	Bm	10B	3d	D
11A	4m	Gbm, F#m	11B	4d	A
12A	5m	Dbm, C#m	12B	5d	E

> **Harmonic Mixing – Rule 2** Mixing two tracks will sound harmonic if the key of one track is in the relative key of the other track. This is because the tone rows of those keys use the same note. Major scales tend to sound happier than the minor scales. Despite the fact that, the transition can sound harmonic, making a switch from a major key to a minor key or vice versa can be heard as a change of temper which can, of course be used intentionally.

The Circle of Fifths

Next let's have a look at a simplified form of the circle of fifths which shows and illustrates the harmonic relationships between the keys.

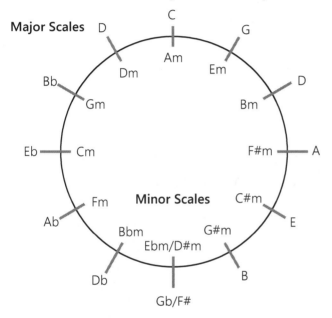

The outer circle shows the names of the major scales; the inner circle those of the minor scales. Let's first have a look at the key pairs formed by the inner and outer circle and let's begin at the noon position. The major key is C major (C) and the minor key is A minor (Am). Have a look at the table showing the relative keys on page 420. We already know the pairs being built from keys of inner and outer circle are the relative keys.

Additionally the circle of fifth shows the relationship among the different major keys and among the different minor keys. As we built the scale for D major on page 418 we needed to change two notes from C major so that the sequence of steps characteristic for a major scale was retained. This means that D major contains two notes that don't appear in the C major. It is exactly this difference that can be seen in the circle of fifths: The distance between C major and D major is two strokes (i.e. the scale D major contains two tones not appearing in C major).

This also means that the relationship between C major and G major is closer because their tone rows differ by one tone only. The interval between the fundamental tones of two adjoining scales in the circle of fifth is always a perfect fifth (this is where its name is derived).

Harmonic Mixing – Rule 3   Tracks in keys for which the interval between their tonics is a perfect fifth sound harmonic to each other because their scales differ by one tone only.

The Camelot System

Now let's have a look at the so called Camelot Wheel which was "invented" by an American company some time ago and which is often used as a tool for harmonic mixing.

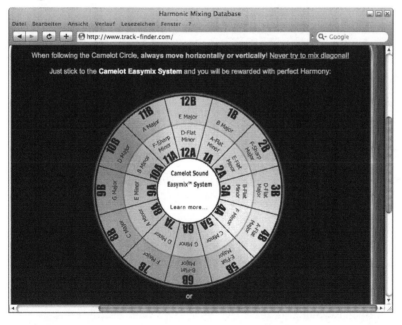

Do you see the parallel to the circle of fifths? The Camelot Wheel is nothing more than the circle of fifths; the differences between them are: The Camelot wheel has the key E major at the noon position (the circle of fifths has been rotated by 120 degrees). Additionally the wheel uses the numbers 1 to 12 for the musical keys and, the major scales are indicated by the postfix A and the minor scales by the postfix B. So, in a way the Camelot wheel isn't really a new invention, but simply another way to present the basic knowledge about harmonics (and unfortunately I couldn't find this information on their website about the Camelot system). To be honest, it is old wine in new skins but it works.

For these reasons it is not really a surprise that the rules for using the Camelot Easymix System are the same as those, which where explained in the little introduction about harmonics:

☐ When mixing use tracks with the same Camelot notation, for example use a track in 7A after a track in 7A. The tracks then have the same key.

☐ When mixing tracks use tracks with the same number from the Camelot notation (these are the relative keys), for example use a track in 7B after a track in 7A.

☐ When mixing tracks use tracks in keys with the same letter postfix (thus A or B) and tracks where the number of the Camelot notations differ by 1 only, for example after 7 A use a track in 6A or 5A. Then you stay in the same mode (major, minor) and the interval of tracks key is a perfect fifth.

☐ Make a jump by two key numbers in Camelot notation, for example from 5A to 7A, if you want to create a kind of energy boost.

The Open Key Notation

The Camelot wheel and the Camelot notation were invented by Mark Davis (you can find his website here: *http://camelotsound.com*). The rights for using the Camelot wheel and Camelot notation have been sold to the company Mixed In Key LLC. Everybody who wishes to use the Camelot wheel and the Camelot notation in other products or services (for example, using the Camelot notation in a DJ software) must obtain a license (see *http://www.harmonic-mixing.com/CommercialLicensing.aspx*). I haven't tried to obtain a license as I do not plan to use Camelot in a product or service), but I am pretty sure that obtaining a licence requires you to pay license fees.

At this point company *tagtraum industries incorporated* and their product beaTunes *(http://www.beatunes.com)* comes into play. Originally beaTunes was developed as a tool for creating playlists for iTunes and iPods and for managing, checking and maintaining the metadata for audio tracks. Since version 3 beaTunes also supports harmonic mixing and it contains algorithms for key detection. I assume that tagtraum developed the Open Key notation as they were not willing to pay licence fees for using the circle of fifth in the form of the Camelot wheel; but this is only an assumption.

Open Key notation uses the numbers 1 to 12 to indicate the key and the letters d and m to indicate the mode. The 1 is used for C major and A minor (the Camelot notation uses an 8) and the order of the keys is – unsurprisingly – the same as in the circle of fifths. For the major keys the number is followed by a d (for Dur) and for the minor keys the number is followed by an m (for Moll).

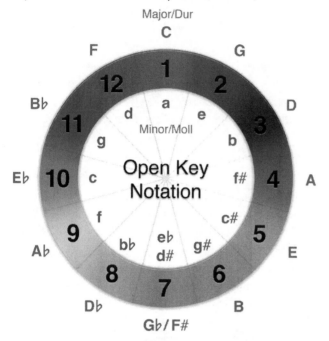

The key detection in Traktor 2.6.1 and higher can display the key either in Open Key notation or in musical notation (and here either as all flats or as all sharps).

12.5 Tools for Key Detection

The principles of harmonic mixing are mostly based on the key of a track. In order to make practical use of this knowledge you need to know which key a track is in. There are several ways to detect the key of a track.

If your hearing is musically trained you will be able to recognise the key of a track after just a few bars. In all honestly, I don't belong to this group and I need tools for key detection. This section provides an overview about the three most important tools for key detection and Traktor:

◻   the key detection integrated in Traktor

◻   the free Open Source tool KeyFinder

◻   Mixed In Key, which is commercial tool available for a fee

Traktor's integrated Key Detection

Since version 2.6.1 (February 2013) Traktor is equipped with its own key detection. The key detection is part of the track analysis Traktor performs when new tracks are added to the collection (assumed that the options that lead to automatic analysis on track imports are enabled (section 7.2, "The Track Collection" contains more information about these options).

Traktor key detection is permanently enabled; i.e. there is currently no option in the Preferences to disable it. The only way to prevent Traktor from detecting and writing the key into the metadata of the audio file is to disable the automatic analysis options. Then you can trigger an analysis manually from the tracklist of the browser: select the tracks you wish to analyse, right-click the collection and choose *Analyze (Async)* in the context menu. Then you can disable the *Key* option in the *Analyze* dialog by selecting *Special* and enable all check boxes except of *Key*. More information about the special options for the track analysis can be found in "Tutorial 8: Analysing multiple Tracks, Using special options for Beat and Tempo detection" in chapter 8 on page 292 and onwards.

The general key related options can be found in the category *Analyze Options* of the *Preferences* dialog. Use the list *Displayed in Traktor* to select which notation Traktor shall use to display the key that has been detected by its own engine. The key can be shown in the header of tracks decks and in column *Key* of the browser. The default setting is *Open Key*; Traktor will then display the key in the Open Key notation that has been explained above.

If you prefer to see the key in musical notation, you can select *Musical* (all keys are shown as flat keys), or *Musical (all sharps):* then all keys are shown as sharp keys.

Use the list *Written to File Tags* to select into which tag of the metadata and in which notation Traktor shall write the key into the audio file. If you use any other tool next to Traktor I recommend using option *Key Text* here. Traktor will then write its key into its own private tags; this will prevent collisions with tools that write the key into the M3 tag TKEY (sometimes referred to as "Initial Key"). For displaying the key inside Traktor it is irrelevant which notation the key is written in, because the key display format can be changed dynamically by using the setting *Displayed in Traktor*.

If you sort the tracklist in the browser by the *Key* column (this is the column where Traktor shows its detected key), Traktor displays the key in the color that is used in the Open Key notation wheel.

KeyFinder

KeyFinder is an open source tool that was developed by Ibrahim Sha'ath during his Master of Science study in computer science. KeyFinder is free of charge and can be downloaded from *http://www.ibrahimshaath.co.uk/keyfinder*. There you will find as a Windows version as well as one for OS X.

After downloading and installing (which means unzipping the downloaded file into a new folder) open the *Preferences* window (which can be reached in the Windows version by opening the *Edit* menu) and select, which key notation and which metadata tag you KeyFinder shall use.

The format can be selected in the list *What to write*. If you select *Keys* KeyFinder will write the key in musical notation. You can choose *Custom key codes* here and are then free to define your own custom format in the *Custom key codes* section. The custom format could be the Camelot notation. If you prefer Camelot, enter the Camelot key names as shown in the following figure:

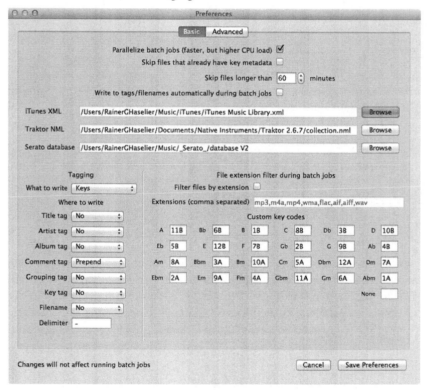

If you prefer using the Open Key notation, then enter the Open Key key names into section *Custom key codes* as shown in the following figure:

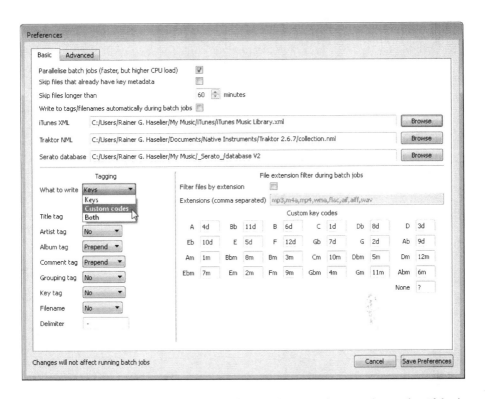

KeyFinder can also write a combination of musical keys and custom key codes. If that's what you want select option *Both* in the list *What to write*.

Use the section *Where to write* to select which tag of the metadata shall be updated by Key Kinder. You can find several of the standard tags here. If you choose one of the text tags – like title, artist, or comment –, the key can be written before or behind the already existing text. If yon select the *Key* tag, then you can only choose *Overwrite*; i.e. already existing key information will be overwritten by the key detected by KeyFinder.

In the upper area of the Preferences dialog you can click the *Browse* button next to the Traktor NML text field and then select the path to your Traktor collection file, *collection.nml*. Once you have done this KeyFinder shows the names of your Traktor playlists in the *Batch Analysis* window.

Analysis of the tracks is done in the window *Batch Analysis*; KeyFinder will open this windows automatically after launch. The list *Library* at the left side of the window contains your iTunes, Traktor, and Serato playlists. Select a playlist and click *Run Batch Analysis* to start the key detection of all tracks in the open playlist.

Clicking on *KeyFinder drag and drop* opens an empty list. Drag and drop the tracks you wish to analyse from Windows Explorer or Finder onto the list. Then click *Run Batch Analysis* to start key detection for the tracks. Using KeyFinder drag and drop allows you to analyse tracks that have not yet been imported into your Traktor collection.

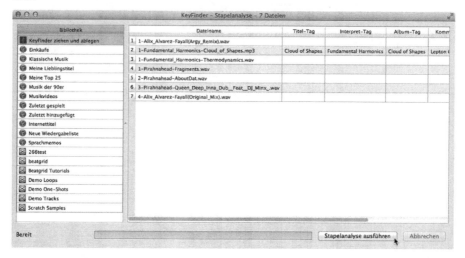

Mixed in Key

Another tool for key detection is Mixed in Key *(www.mixedinkey.com)*. This tool is available for Windows and for Mac OS X, but it is a commercial product and you need to purchase it.

After starting the tool for the first time click on *Personalize* and then on *Update Tags* to select where Mixed in Key (MIK) shall write the detected key and/or detected tempo (BPM) to. MIK can append the key and BPM information to the already available track information like title, artist or comment.

With regards to Traktor, the best way is to allow MIK to write the key information into the appropriate ID tags. To do this, enable the check box *Update custom "Initial-Key" tag*.

On the page *Analyze Songs* you can use the *Add Files* to select the tracks that Mixed in Key shall process.

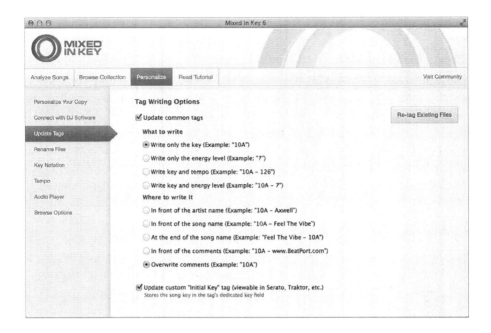

Which Tool shall I Use?

Colleagues from other DJ blogs have published comparison tests of the different tools that can be used for key detection. The results include percentage values showing the hits. The results show a tendency that the hit ratio is best for Mixed in Key, that Traktor's key detection has the least number of correct detected keys and that KeyFinder is somewhere mid-level.

However, the problem with these comparison tests may be the small number of tracks that have been used (DJ Endo used 120, DJ Tech Tools 61 tracks). From a statistical perspective the sample size may not be large enough to make statistically reliable statements.

Tools for key detection are not magical bullets and the harmonic mixing techniques are no cure-all to deliver a stirring DJ set. If you see the marketing slogans for Mixed in Key for example you might get the impression that this is the case. I do not believe it. If you use harmonic mixing as **one** tool from a larger "DJ toolbox", then the two free options (Traktor's integrated key detection and KeyFinder) could be all you need, even though both tools might not always be totally correct with the key they have detected. Find tracks with matching keys in your browser, but always use your ears to check whether they really fit.

Furthermore, the key detection engine we see in the current version of Traktor is somewhat like a version 1.0. And experience shows that Native Instruments is capable of improving technologies that might not work perfectly in early adaptions. For example, the grid and tempo detection we see in Traktor today is way better than in any earlier versions. Let's see what the future brings.

I find the modesty of Ibrahim quite refreshing. Unlike other companies he describes Keyfinder as "key *estimation* software for DJs". This is probably true for all key detection software because none of the tools works 100% correct.

Mixed In Key is used by many Traktor DJs; one reason could be that for a long time there were no usable alternatives to Mixed in Key. I assume that it is correct that the key detection of Mixed in Key is better than with other software. You should be aware that Mixed in Key needs an internet connection; otherwise tracks cannot be analysed. If it is worth paying for Mixed in Key is, at the end of the day, a question you can only answer yourself.

No matter which key detection tool you use: harmonic mixing only works if you either play the tracks in their original tempo or if you use the key correction feature of Traktor. Key correction ensures that the pitch of a track does not change, even if it is not played at its original BPM. And this is the topic of the next section.

12.6   Traktor and the Key

The focus of this section is to describe the following three Traktor controls that different functionality sometimes causes confusion:

◻   Button *Key Lock,* which is at the right side of the stripe

◻   Button *Key Switch,* which is in the *Filter+Key...* panel

◻   *Key*-Knob, which is in the *Filter+Key... panel* as well

Both the buttons and the knob can be understood better if we consider what happens if you change the tempo of a track in Traktor. Traktor helps by showing some important information in the deck header and on the *Key* knob.

◻   Traktor can show the difference between the original BPM value of the track and the current playback speed of the deck, expressed as a percentage. To see that value open the *Preferences/Track Decks* dialog and select in section *Deck Header* the option *Tempo* for one of the info fields.

The original tempo of the track can be displayed by choosing *Track BPM*; the current playback tempo can be displayed by choosing *BPM*.

☐ The little text field below the Key knob shows the current pitch shift of the track in semitones (you see an example in a bit). There are two options to read that value: either you move the mouse onto the knob, or you map the mapping command *Shows Slider Values On* to your keyboard (this is explained in section "Tutorial 1: Mapping one Command to a Key" in chapter 6 on page 166 and onwards).

The functionality of the two buttons and the knob can best be explained in a little tutorial.

Tutorial: Key Lock vs. Key Switch

Follow these steps once you have configured the deck header as explained in the previous section:

1. Load a track and make sure, that the *Key Lock* button (to the right of the stripe) is disabled. Check also if the *Key* knob in the *Filter+Key panel* is set to 0 (center position of the knob). *Otherwise* double-click the knob to reset it.

2. Play the track at it's original tempo (the quickest way to do this is by double-clicking the *Tempo Fader* in the deck). Your deck should now look similar to the following figure.

The original tempo of this track is 120 BPM. Below the BPM value you can see the deviation from the original tempo expressed as a percentage. Because the track is being played at its original speed the value shown here is 0.0%. The field below this shows the *Key* field; here the value 0.00 is shown.

3. Move the *Tempo Fader* upwards to reduce the playback tempo until the Tempo field in the deck header shows –6%. Click next to the *Key* knob on the *Key Switch* button and hover with the mouse over the knob (or hold the key that you mapped to *Show Slider Values On*).

431

The text field of the Key knob now shows a value close to –1. This means that the track is now playing in a key which is about one semitone below the original key.

From this little experiment we can derive the following rule of thumb: A tempo change of 6% leads to a key change of approximately one semitone. This formula is not completely accurate, but it can serve as a good reference point.

Furthermore, now the *Key Lock* button to the right of the stripe is on as well. This button indicates whether the pitch correction engine of Traktor is engaged or not. The *Key Lock* button became active when you clicked on *Key Switch*; the status of the *Key Lock* button and the *Key Switch* button are coupled.

4. Double-click the *Key*-Knob to bring it back to the middle position. The Key knob now shows a value of 0.00; this means that the track is now played in its original key, despite of the tempo change we made with the tempo fader.

The same state can be achieved by clicking the *Key Lock* button at the right side of the stripe. If you click this button and if the track is not played at its original BPM, this activates the automatic key correction of Traktor. If you click *Key Lock* Traktor will automatically activate *Key Switch* and in the info field the value 0.00 is displayed.

5. Hover on the *Key* knob to make its *Plus* and *Minus* buttons visible and click once on the *Plus* button.

In the default setting/resolution one click on *Minus/Plus* changes the pitch by twos semitones. That's why the info field of the *Key* knob now displays 2.00.

6. Right-click the *Plus* button to open the Resolution context menu and select *Fine*.

7. Click the *Plus* or *Minus* button several times. Traktor changes the pitch now in steps of one semitone. Having an idea of the different resolutions makes it easier to use the *Key Adjust* mapping command and to change the key from your controller (see table on page 436).

8. Turn the *Key* knob to perform more manual changes to the key. The *Key* knob has range from –12 to +12. This allows you to change the key by up to one octave downwards and upwards.

9. Set the *Key* knob to –1. This changes the pitch to one semitone below the original key. The track should now sound similar to how it did after step 3, i.e. before you clicked on *Key Switch*.

Conclusions

The conclusions from this little tutorial can be summarised as follows:

☐ The button *Key Lock* adjusts the key change which results from a tempo change. *Key Lock* ensures that the track is played at its original key, despite any tempo changes that have been made. In other words: *Key Lock* activates key correction. (While *Key Lock* is on, the *Tempo/Pitch Fader* no longer functions as a pitch fader, only as a tempo fader, because a tempo change will not affect the pitch.)

☐ If the *Key Lock* button is enabled, the *Key* knob is also enabled. You can use the *Key* knob to change the key by one octave downwards (the range from –12 to 0) or by one octave upwards (the range from 0 to 12). Each integer represents one semitone.

☐ The button *Key Switch* activates the manual key change feature. Clicking *Key Switch* does **not** activate the key correction feature. But *the* Key knob is set to a value representing the current key pitch which is caused by the current tempo change.

> NOTE The keylock feature is also available for the individual slots of a remix deck. To enable/disable keylock hover on the name of the sample in the slot to make the slot buttons visible. Then click on the *Slot Key Lock* button.

Traktors Key Features and Harmonic Mixing

The key correction, which is activated with the *Key Lock* button, is an important tool for harmonic mixing. Using key correction ensures that the track is played at its original key (if the *Key* knob is in its middle position). When searching for the next track that you wish to be in the same key as the one playing, you can be sure that they match, even when the tracks in both decks are not played at their original BPM.

Another use of the *Key* knob is to adjust the key of a track in a way that the key of the current track fits to the key of the next one. This can even be when the original keys of the tracks are different. It is important to remember, that the *Key* knob "thinks" in semitones, and not in the note names of the Camelot notation. An example: The original key of a track is F major (7B in Camelot notation). If we turn the *Key* knob from 0 to -1 then we are one semitone downwards, i.e. E major (12B in the Camelot notation). This means that if we decrease the key by one semitone we need to move seven fields anti-clockwise in the Camelot wheel.

The same is also valid for an upwards key change. Let's assume the original key of a track is E major (12B in Camelot notation). If we turn the *Key* knob from 0 to +1 we are at F major (7B) in the chromatic scale. To get from 12B to 7B in the Camelot wheel we need to move seven fields clockwise.

Selecting the Key Lock Algorithm

If *Key Lock* is enabled the audio signal needs to be converted so that a tempo change does not result in a pitch shift. Traktor uses a so called time stretching engine to get this done. Which time stretching algorithm is to be used can be selected in section *Key Lock/Quality* of the dialog box *Preferences/Transport*.

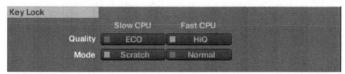

The Quality setting selects the quality of the "time-stretched" audio and it effects the CPU load:

- ☐ **ECO**   Use this option on a slower computer.
- ☐ **HiQ**   Use this option on a faster computer; even then when you use timecode control.

Use the *Mode* option to change the setting if you are scratching or if you use timecode media, but do not scratch. Internally the *Mode* option is connected to the range of tempo changes for which Traktor can correct the key. In mode *Scratch* the key is only corrected for a pitch change in the range of +50/–30%. In mode *Normal* the key is always corrected. To achieve the best results make sure that you use *Scratch* mode when scratching and set *Quality* to *HiQ*.

> **NOTE** If you cause extreme or fast tempo changes, maybe during a backspin, while scratching or by making sudden and quick changes to the *Pitch Fader*, Traktor will automatically disable the Key Lock engine. This is to make sure that the sound stays clean. This is very wise behaviour and is independent from the settings you may have made in section *Key Lock*.

More practical Tips for Key Lock and Key Changes

The most important feature for harmonic mixing is the Key Lock feature. If Key Lock is enabled tracks are played in their original key even when the deck tempo has been altered. The main use for this is to find key compatible tracks. It is still important that you continue to trust your own hearing and not rely solely on the key information, no matter if it's available in musical or Camelot notation.

Even then when you have two tracks with a perfect beatgrid and even when both tracks are genuinely in the same key, it can be, that they do not sound good when mixed together. In this case use the Tempo Bend buttons on one of the two decks to slightly shift the phase of one track. In 98% of all cases this will remove the disharmonies.

If a track which would, due to the flow of your set, fit best as the next track has a different or "incompatible" key to the current one, then play the track. You should not make yourself a slave to harmonic mixing. Use the equalizer here and, especially the mid and low bands, or the deck filter to either soften the disharmony or to amplify it in a way that the tension created by this is "screaming" for the release that is offered by the next track.

Or use the *Key* knob to transpose tracks in different keys to the same key. The *Key* knob delivers good results in the range between three and four semitones. Greater changes do not always sound good. Trust your hearing.

Independent from the harmonic mixing paradigm you can use the *Key* knob as a sort of effect. For example you can lower the key until you reach the breakdown in a track. Then, you can either turn the *Key* knob slowly back to its middle position during the breakdown or you can reset it in one go at the exact time that the breakdown ends.

This is only a small selection of the possibilities the equalizer and the key settings have to offer. If this chapter has shed some more light on the key related questions, and if you are now up for further experiments and exploration, then this chapter has served its purpose.

12.7 Key Settings via Mapping

The three buttons and the knob from the user interfaces can be mapped to your keyboard or your controller with the following three mapping commands.

Keylock and Key Adjust		
Track Deck | Keylock On (Preserve Pitch)	Interaction Mode: Hold, Toggle Interaction Mode: Direct Set to value=On/Off	Activates/deactivates the key change feature. Change the key with the command Tempo | Key. Activating the key change feature doesn't alter the current pitch of the track.
Track Deck | Keylock On Remix Deck | Slot Keylock On	Interaction Mode: Hold, Toggle Interaction Mode: Direct Set to value: 1=On/0=Off	Activates the Keylock feature of Traktor for a track deck or a slot of a remix deck. If key correction is enabled the track will continue to play in its original key even when the tempo of the deck is changed. (On a track deck the Key knob must be in position 0 to achieve the original key.)
Track Deck | Key Adjust	Interaction Mode: Direct Type of Controller: Fader, Knob, Encoder Assignment: select deck or Device Target	Changes the key of a track. You can change the key by up to one octave downwards and by up to one octave upwards
	Interaction Mode: Dec, Inc Type of Controller: Button Assignment: select deck or Device Target Resolution: see table below	Changes the key of the deck. Changing the value by 1.00 corresponds to changing the key by one semitone. If you wish to configure a key/button to change the key by one semitone use the Interaction Modes Inc and Dec and select the resolution Fine. See table below for more information about the different resolutions.
	Interaction Mode: Reset Assignment: select deck or Device Target	Sets the key knob to its middle position (0).

The following table explains the different resolutions for the *Key* command and how they are mapped to musical intervals.

Resolution	Step Size	Interval in Cent	Musical Interval
Min	0.1	10	1/10 Semitone
Fine	1.0	100	Minor Second, Half Step, Semitone
Default	2.0	200	Major Second, Whole Step, Whole Tone
Coarse	3.0	300	Minor Third
Switch	4.0	400	Major Third

Chapter 13

FX – The Traktor Effects

Traktor Pro comes with a huge amount of effects. All effects are controlled with the FX units at the left and the right side of the Global Section. If the Global Section is not visible on your screen open the *Preferences* dialog, select the category *Global Settings* and enable *Show Global Section*.

You can choose between using two or four FX units at the same time. This is how the FX units (panels) look like:

FX Unit 1, Group Mode, 2 FX Units

FX Unit 2, Single & 2 FX Units Mode

FX Units 1 & 3, Group & 4 FX Units Mode

FX Units 2 & 4, Single & 4 FX Units Mode

The left FX panel shares its space with the Master Clock Panel. The panel on the right side shares its space with the Audio Recorder. You can use the buttons at the outer left or outer right to switch between the FX panel and the Master Clock panel or the Audio Recorder respectively.

> **NOTE** There is no mapping command available to perform the view switch directly. One workaround is to define different layouts, for example one with both FX panel and another one showing the Master Clock Panel and the Audio Recorder. Then use a MIDI command to switch between the defined layouts. More information about layouts can be found in chapter 2.

The FX units can either be used in Group mode or in Single mode. In Group mode you can load up to three effects into one FX unit. There is one knob available for each effect with which we can configure the effect parameter. In Single mode you can load only one effect into the FX unit but then you get three different knobs and have more control about the various effect parameters.

All FX units contain a Dry/Wet knob. This knob controls the mixing ratio between the original audio signal (dry) and the signal that has been modified by the selected effect (wet).

13.1 Basic Effect Configuration

The basic effect settings are made in the dialog box *Preferences/Effects*. Here you can configure the effect routing (Insert, Send, Post Fader), you can select the operation mode of the units (Single or Group), the number of FX units you wish to use and you can choose which of the effects are to be available for selection.

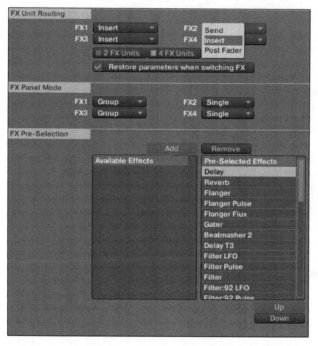

Selecting the Number of FX Units

Section *FX Unit Routing* of the *Preferences/Effects* dialog has two options to select the number of FX units that are to be used at the same time. When you select option *2 FX Units* only 2 FX units are available. When you select *4 FX Units*, then each FX panel contains two FX units; this looks like the figure as shown on page 437.

Configuring the Effect Routing: Insert/Send/Post Fader

Use section *FX Unit Routing* to configure the signal path for each FX unit individually.

Insert

The default setting for effect routing is *Insert*. If this routing option is enabled then you can assign the audio signal of each of the four decks to the FX unit. The original signal is fed into the FX unit; the FX unit modifies the signal and is then sent to the deck output. With *Insert* routing the original deck signal and the modified signal are mixed. The little "LED" in the FX unit is highlighted if the routing is set to *Insert*.

Send

The signal path for option *Send* is a bit different. The FX unit then behaves like an external effect device. An external audio signal is fed into the FX unit; the audio signal is modified here and the modified signal is sent to the "outer world". In order to use an FX unit in *Send* mode you need to configure the following four options:

☐ Open dialog *Preferences/Output Routing* and set *Mixing Mode* to *External*.

☐ Open dialog box *Preferences/Effects* and set the routing for the desired FX unit to *Send*.

☐ Open dialog box *Preferences/Input Routing*. Use section *Input FX Send (Ext)* to configure the audio interface inputs that are providing the signal that shall be sent to the FX unit. Those inputs are normally connected to the FX Send connectors of the external mixer.

☐ Open dialog box *Preferences/Output Routing*. Use section *Output FX Return* to select the outputs that shall receive the audio signal modified by the FX unit. Those outputs are normally connected to the FX Return connectors of the external mixer.

The FX unit routing can be configured in this dialog box only; there are no mapping commands available to do that.

Post Fader

The routing option *Post Fader* is only available if you use internal mixing mode. In *Post Fader* routing the deck signal and the effect signal are combined as with option Insert. However, in *Post Fader* mode the position of the channelfader and the crossfader does not affect whether the effect signal is audible or not. In other words: If you close the channelfader in *Insert* mode neither the deck signal nor the effect signal can be heard. With routing set to *Post Fader* the effect signal is still audible even if the channelfader is down.

Please note that even if routing is set to Post Fader, this setting does not have an audible effect for all Traktor effects. Post Fader works well with all delay and echo effects (Delay, Delay T3, Reverb, Reverb T3, Iceverb, etc.), with the effects that provide a feedback knob (like Mulholland Drive where the feedback knob should be very wide open) and with all macro effects, because they are using delay and or echo effects.

If you use Traktor in external mixing mode, the FX routing modes Insert and Post Fader behave identical.

FX Unit Operation Modes: Single/Group

Section *FX Panel Mode* of dialog box *Preferences/Effects* contains the list boxes to select the operation mode for each FX unit. You can choose between *Single Mode* and *Group Mode*. How do these modes differ?

Single Mode

The following figures show an FX unit in Single mode (here the *Delay* effect is loaded as an example). The left figure shows an FX panel when *2 FX Units* mode is used; the right figure shows the panel in *4 FX Units* mode. In Single mode you can only load one effect into the FX unit. To load an effect open the dropdown list box that lists all activated effects, and select the one you wish to use.

Click the *ON* button at the left side of the unit or to the left of the effect name respectively to switch the effect on. The *D/W* knob controls the ratio between the original signal (dry) and the signal modified by the effect (wet). If the knob is set to 0% only the original signal is heard; if it is set to 100% only the effect signal is fed into the audio output.

The other three knobs or sliders respectively, and the three buttons at the right side are used to configure the effect parameters. The first button, labelled RST (reset) – which is available for all effects in single mode – resets the effect parameters back to the last default values (see section "HOW TO: Storing and Loading Effect Parameters" on page 448 and onward for more information). The other knobs and buttons are effect dependent; this will be explained in section "13.4 Effects in the Detail".

The macro effects (which combine several of the "normal" Traktor effects, are all controlled by the Dry/Wet knob and the third slider/knob. If the knob is in its centre position the effect is off. Turning the knob to the left or the right changes various effect parameters at once. For the macro effects the FX panel looks in Single Mode as shown in the following figure (left image shows using two FX units, right image shows using four).

Group Mode

The following figures show the FX panels if *Group Mode* is activated. The left figure shows an FX panel when *2 FX Units* mode is used; the right figure shows the panel in *4 FX Units* mode.

In Group mode the FX unit contains three list boxes to load the effects that you wish to use. You can select three different effects and it is also possible to load the same effect several times. For each effect there is one knob/slider to change the effect parameter. Use the three buttons to switch any the effects on or off.

In Group mode there is also a *Dry/Wet* knob at the left side of the unit to control the ratio between the original and the effect signal.

Processing Order of Effects in Group Mode

When in Group mode the order of the selected effects controls how the output sounds. The audio signal "walks" through the effect chain. The original signal is first modified by the first selected effect. This modified signal is then sent as input to the second selected effect, and so on. At the end of the effect chain the *D/W* knob controls the ratio of the original and the effect signal.

Original Signal

To try out how the effect order impacts the sound the following approach is helpful:

1. Switch both FX units to Group mode.

2. Load the same effects into the first two effect slots of the FX units, but in reverse order.

3. Make sure that the parameter knobs for the identical effects and both D/W knobs are set to the same values.

4. Assign FX unit 1 to deck A and FX unit 2 to Deck B.

5. Load a track in deck A, start playback and then duplicate the track into deck B (either by using the corresponding mapping command or by dragging the track from deck A and dropping it into deck B).

6. Now you can use the channel faders of deck A and B to easily hear the differences caused by the processing order.

HOW TO: Setting the FX Unit Operation Mode via Mapping

You can configure the operation mode of the FX units either in the dialog box *Preferences/Effects* or in the context menu that opens if you click the number of the FX unit. In the context menu you can switch between Single and Group mode, you can set the routing mode, and you can save the current effect settings to your settings file.

To change the operation mode and the FX routing mode with your keyboard or MIDI controller use the mapping commands *FX Unit | FX Unit Mode Selector* and *FX Unit | Routing Selector*. Details about these commands can be found in the following table:

Setting the Operation and Routing Mode of the FX Units

FX Unit | FX Unit Mode Selector	Interaction Mode: Inc/Dec Assignment: Select FX Unit	This is actually the only interaction mode that is needed to switch the two operation modes with one button between. Both Inc and Dec act like a toggle; so it is sufficient to map only one of them.
	Interaction Mode: Reset Assignment: Select FX Unit	Activates Group Mode for the selected FX unit.
	Interaction Mode: Direct, Hold Set to value: Group, Single Assignment: Select FX Unit	With Direct and Hold the operation mode selected in the list Set to value is activated. Direct switches the mode permanently; with Hold the mode is active as long as the key/button is pressed
FX Unit | Routing Selector	Interaction Mode: Inc/Dec Assignment: Select FX Unit	Selects the previous/next routing mode for the FX unit selected in Assignment.
	Interaction Mode: Reset Assignment: Select FX Unit	Sets the routing mode of the assigned FX unit to Insert.
	Interaction Mode: Direct, Hold Set to value: Insert, Send, Post Fader Assignment: Select FX Unit	With Direct and Hold the FX routing mode selected in the list Set to value is activated. Direct switches the mode permanently; with Hold the mode is active as long as the key/button is pressed

Selecting the Effects

Let's return to the dialog box *Preferences/Effects* (see figure on page 438). The section *Effect Pre-Selection* contains two list boxes. The list *Available Effects* shows all effects Traktor provides and which haven't been selected yet. The list *Pre-Selected Effects* shows all effects that have been selected. The effect selectors in the FX units only show the effects that have been added into the list *Pre-Selected Effects*.

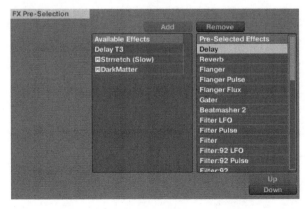

You can move an effect between the lists by double-clicking it or, by selecting an entry and then using the buttons *Add* and *Remove*. To rearrange the order of the effects use the buttons *Up* and *Down* below *Pre-Selected Effects*. The effect selectors in the FX unit list the effects in the order configured here.

> **TIP** If you move your favourite effects to the beginning of the list and, if you remove the effects you don't use, the selection list get shorter and clearer and you can select effects much faster.

Assign FX Units to Decks

The panel with the dizzying name *Filter + Key + Gain + Cue + Balance* (which can be activated in the *Preferences/Mixer)* contains two (in 2 FX units mode) or four buttons (in 4 FX units mode of Traktor Pro) to assign the deck to the FX units. Several different combinations are possible: assign a deck to none of the FX units, assign a deck to one, several or all FX units

The high degree of flexibility for the assignment makes it possible to emulate the Master effect from Traktor 3. The only thing you need to do is assign the same FX unit to all decks.

> **NOTE** The assignment buttons can only be used if the FX routing for the FX unit is set to *Insert* or *Post Fader*. In *Send* mode the button is disabled. If you are wondering why you cannot click the buttons, then check if one of the FX units is set to *Send* mode (see page 439).

HOW TO: Assigning a FX Unit to a Deck via Mapping

The two mapping commands to create assignments between FX units and decks can be found in the *Mixer* submenu.

Assigning FX Units to Decks

Mixer| FX Unit 1 On Mixer| FX Unit 2 On Mixer| FX Unit 3 On Mixer| FX Unit 4 On	Interaction Mode: Toggle Assignment: select deck or Device Target	Connects FX unit 1, 2, 3 or 4 to the deck selected in the list Assignment or removes the connection.
	Interaction Mode: Hold Assignment: select deck or Device Target	The Interaction Mode Hold can be used to create a kind of Effect-Punch-In.

Assigning FX Units to Decks

Interaction Mode: Direct Set to value: 1=On, 0=Off Assignment: select deck or Device Target	Use Interaction Mode Direct to create or remove an assignment between a FX unit and a deck directly.

These commands can be mapped in different ways. The method that is best suited for you depends on the overall concept of your mapping. The following sections describe three of the possible variations.

Variation 1: Cloning the Buttons 1:1

One possibility to map the different assignments between FX units and decks to your keyboard or MIDI controller is cloning the eight (2 FX unit mode) or sixteen buttons (4 FX units mode), i.e. you will need eight/sixteen keys/buttons for this mapping. Each mapped key/button then corresponds to one of the eight buttons in panel *Filter + Key + Gain + Cue + Balance*. This mapping looks like the following:

Key/Button No.	Mapping Command	Interaction Mode	Assignment
1.	Mixer | FX Unit 1 On	Toggle	Deck A
2.	Mixer | FX Unit 2 On	Toggle	Deck A
3.	Mixer | FX Unit 3 On	Toggle	Deck A
4.	Mixer | FX Unit 4 On	Toggle	Deck A
5.	Mixer | FX Unit 1 On	Toggle	Deck B
6.	Mixer | FX Unit 2 On	Toggle	Deck B
7.	Mixer | FX Unit 3 On	Toggle	Deck B
8.	Mixer | FX Unit 4 On	Toggle	Deck B
9.	Mixer | FX Unit 1 On	Toggle	Deck C
10.	Mixer | FX Unit 2 On	Toggle	Deck C
11.	Mixer | FX Unit 3 On	Toggle	Deck C
12.	Mixer | FX Unit 4 On	Toggle	Deck C
13.	Mixer | FX Unit 1 On	Toggle	Deck D
14.	Mixer | FX Unit 2 On	Toggle	Deck D
15.	Mixer | FX Unit 3 On	Toggle	Deck D
16.	Mixer | FX Unit 4 On	Toggle	Deck D

Variation 2: Assignment depends on Deck Focus

If you have already created a mapping to change the deck focus (mapping command *Layout | Deck Focus Selector)* you only need two or four keys/buttons to assign the FX units and the deck which currently has the focus:

Key/Button No.	Mapping Command	Interaction Mode	Device Target/ Assignment
1.	Mixer	FX Unit 1 On	Toggle	Focus/Device Target
2.	Mixer	FX Unit 2 On	Toggle	Focus/Device Target
3.	Mixer	FX Unit 3 On	Toggle	Focus/Device Target
4.	Mixer	FX Unit 4 On	Toggle	Focus/Device Target

Variation 3: Select all possible Assignments between Two FX Units and one Deck with one Button

If you use 2 FX units only the possible assignments between the FX units and the decks can be implemented completely different. The concept uses one button for each deck and to map the button in a way that it walks through the different states, which the assignment between both FX units and the deck can have. In this model we need to distinguish four different states, which are listed in the following table.

Status	FX Unit 1	FX Unit 2	User Interface Buttons
0	not assigned	not assigned	
1	assigned	not assigned	
2	not assigned	assigned	
3	assigned	assigned	

To implement this mapping one modifier is needed:

▫ The current state is stored in the modifier.

▫ When the mapping command *FX Unit x On* is used we check the current value of the modifier to see what the current status is and then switch to the next state.

The complete mapping can best be described as a form of state changes. In a way we need to implement a kind of interaction mode *Inc;* the problem is that command *FX Unit x On* doesn't offer this interaction mode and we need to emulate it. The following table shows all commands which need to be mapped. The modifier used in the table is just an example; you can use any modifier you wish (if it is available).

From	To	Required MIDI Commands		
Status 0	Status 1	□	Modifier #8, Interaction Mode: Direct, Set to value: 1 Modifier Condition M8=0
		□	FX Unit 1 On, Interaction Mode: Direct, Set to value: 1 Assignment: Select deck, Modifier Conditions: M8=0
		□	Effect Unit 2 On, Interaction Mode: Direct, Set to value: 0 Modifier Conditions: M8=0
Status 1	Status 2	□	Modifier #8, Interaction Mode: Direct, Set to value: 2 Modifier Condition M8=1
		□	FX Unit 1 On, Interaction Mode: Direct, Set to value: 0 Assignment: Select deck, Modifier Conditions: M8=1
		□	FX Unit 2 On, Interaction Mode: Direct, Set to value: 1 Modifier Conditions: M8=1
Status 2	Status 3	□	Modifier #8, Interaction Mode: Direct, Set to value: 3 Modifier Condition M8=2
		□	FX Unit 1 On, Interaction Mode: Direct, Set to value: 1 Assignment: Select deck, Modifier Conditions: M8=2
		□	FX Unit 2 On, Interaction Mode: Direct, Set to value: 1 Assignment: Select deck, Modifier Conditions: M8=2
Status 3	Status 0	□	Modifier #8, Interaction Mode: Direct, Set to value: 0 Modifier Condition M8=3
		□	FX Unit 1 On, Interaction Mode: Direct, Set to value: 0 Assignment: Select deck, Modifier Conditions: M8=3
		□	FX Unit 2 On, Interaction Mode: Direct, Set to value: 0 Assignment: Select deck, Modifier Conditions: M8=3

The advantage of this mapping is that we only need one button to use all possible combinations of assignments between both FX units and one deck. The disadvantage is that we need one modifier for each deck. And because the modifier is used to remember the current state, we cannot use the same modifier anywhere else in the complete mapping. If we did, the status memory could or would be overwritten and the implementation becomes broken

An alternative way could be to use this mapping for decks A and B only, and then we would use only two of the eight modifiers that are available.

Another alternative is to create a new logical controller and to include the commands to assign an FX unit to the decks in this mapping. In Traktor 2 each logical controller has its own set of modifiers. By using this advantage you prevent overwriting the modifier values by accident and avoid running out of modifiers.

HOW TO: Storing and Loading Effect Parameters

At the very button of the menu that Traktor opens if you click on the FX unit number you can find the *Save Snapshot* command. You can use this command to store the current parameter settings. Traktor saves the position of the four knobs (i.e. also the position of the Dry/Wet knob) and buttons in your personal configuration file as the new default values. This works in Single mode as well as in Group mode.

Traktor loads the last stored settings automatically when you load the effect. In Single mode you can use the *RST* button on the panel to restore all settings to their default values. In Group mode double-click the knob of which value you wish to be restored.

HOW TO: Storing and Loading Effect Parameters via Mapping

The effect parameters can be stored with mapping commands as well. In Single mode it is also possible to restore the default settings.

Storing and Loading Default Effect Settings		
FX Unit | FX Store Preset	Interaction Mode: Trigger Assignment: select FX unit	Stores the currently configured parameters from the selected FX unit.
FX Unit | Button 1	Interaction Mode: Trigger Assignment: select FX unit	Restores the default values for the currently in the selected FX unit loaded effect. This works only if the FX unit is set to Single Mode.

13.2 Controlling FX Units via Mapping

Some of the mapping IDI commands to control the effects have already been mentioned in the previous section. This section lists all commands that are available in Group mode and in Single mode.

You can find all commands in the submenu *FX Unit* of the *Add In* button (*Preferences/Controller Manager*). Please note that not all commands are available for both Single Mode and Group Mode. Furthermore, the effect of a command can differ between Single Mode and Group Mode.

SINGLE MODE

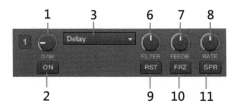

GROUP MODE

The following table pages shows the mapping commands available for Single and for Group mode. The numbering of the elements in the figure corresponds to the numbers in the table.

Nr.	FX Unit |...	Parameter	Description
1	Dry/Wet Adjust	Interaction Mode: Direct Type of Controller: Button Set to value: Decimal value in the range between 0.000 (knob position 0) and 1.000 (knob position 100)	Sets the ratio between the original signal (Dry) and the signal that has been modified by the effect (Wet). A value of 0 sends the original signal to the output and selecting 100 the sends signal affected by the FX.
		Type of Controller: Fader, Knob, Encoder	Use this option to assign the command to a fader, knob, etc.
		Interaction Mode: Dec/Inc Resolution: Min = ± ca. 0,5 Fine = ± ca. 2 Default = ± 6,25 Coarse = ± 12,5 Switch = ± 50	The ratio between the dry and wet signal can be changed stepwise. Use the list Resolution to select the desired interval.
2	Unit On	Interaction Mode: Toggle, Hold Interaction Mode: Direct 1=On/0=Off	Turns the effect on or off if the FX unit is set to Single Mode Note: The mapping command to assign a FX unit to a deck is explained on page 444 and further.

Nr.	FX Unit |...	Parameter	Description
3 4 5	Effect 1 Selector Effect 2 Selector Effect 3 Selector	Interaction Mode: Dec/Inc Interaction Mode: Hold Set to value: select effect Interaction Mode: Direct Set to value: select effect	Selects the effect you want to use in the FX Unit. You can only select the effects which are activated in the dialog box Preferences | Effects. **Tip:** The order of the effect in the list box Pre-Selected Effects (Preferences | Effects) determines which effect gets selected next when using the Interaction Modes Previous and Next. For fast switching remove the effects you don't need and put the effects you need most often at the top of the list
6 7 8	Knob 1 Knob 2 Knob 3	The parameters are almost identical to those specified for Dry/Wet. One difference: not all parameters can be set step less but some change only stepwise. An example is the parameter Rate for the delay effect, which sets the delay time.	**Single Mode:** Sets the value of the first, second or third effect parameter. These parameters differ for the various effects. **Group Mode:** Sets the intensity of the effect in one of the three effect slots. Which parameter is to be controlled depends on which effect is selected. More information about the parameters can be found in section 13.4 of this chapter.
9	Button 1	Interaction Mode: Toggle, Hold Direct: On/Off	**Single Mode:** Resets all parameters of the effect to the saved default values. **Group Mode:** Activates/deactivates the effect currently loaded in slot 1.
10 11	Button 2 Button 3	Interaction Mode: Toggle, Hold Direct: On/Off	**Single Mode:** Activates/deactivates the function of the first effect button. **Group Mode:** Activates/deactivates the effect currently loaded in slot 2/slot 3.

LFO and Mapping Command to Reset the LFO

Some of the Traktor effects, like Flanger, Filter LFO and Filter:92 LFO use a low frequency oscillator, LFO, which creates a waveform in a particular rhythm (frequency). This waveform is used to modulate/modify the audio signal. The best way to "see" how a LFO affects the sound is by using the effect *Filter LFO*. If you wish to try this out yourself load any track, set an 8 beat loop in the track, assign the deck to an FX unit running in Single mode and load the effect *Filter LFO* into this FX unit. Map the command *Effect LFO Reset* to a keyboard key or a controller button.

Resetting the LFO

FX Group| Effect LFO Reset	Interaction Mode: Trigger	Resets the LFO used for the effect creation. This resets the oscillation phase to zero, i.e. the highest point.

Then configure the knobs as seen in the following figure:

> **TIP Showing the values of knobs instead of the labels** In order to make the configured values visible in this screenshot and not the labels I used the quite useful mapping command *Global | Show Slider Values* which is often overlooked and which is mentioned in the official documentation but only shortly in one of the addendums. A better name for this command would be *Show Knob Values,* because it shows the values of all knobs in all panels instead of the normally visible labels. This command supports the interaction mode *Hold;* so you can use it to get all knob values for as long as the mapped button/mapped key is pressed.
>
> Please note that for reasons I do not understand the functionality of this mapping command is coupled to the setting *Show value when over control* on dialog *Preferences/Global Settings.* This option controls whether Traktor shows the value of a knob when you hover the mouse over it. But if you disable the setting the mapping command *Show Slider Values* doesn't work anymore either.

The *D/W* knob is set to 100, so we can hear the modified audio signal only. The first parameter knob *(SHAPE)* is used in this effect to set the waveform of the LFO. The second knob *(RES)* is used to control the resonance; the higher the resonance value (Q factor), the more intensive the effect of the filter will be heard. That's why this knob is set to 100. The third knob *(RATE)* controls the oscillation frequency (tempo) of the

LFO. I selected 2 bars (=8 beats), because this makes it very easy to hear the course of the oscillation.

That's all the preparations. Start the track and wait until the first beat of the loop is reached. Then activate the filter effect by pressing the *ON* button. We can imagine the sound modified by the filter as a sinus wave in which every point on the wave defines a different frequency range being cut out of the original signal.

There is one point in the loop where most of the high frequencies are filtered (the track sounds dull) and another one, where most of the low frequencies are filtered (the track sound very bright). Between those states the filter "swings". One filter run takes 8 beats (=2 bars); this is the frequency configured with the *RATE* knob.

Let's now check what the function of the *LFO RESET* feature. Wait until the loop reaches the point where the track sounds most dull (this is the point where most of the high frequencies are filtered). Click the key/button yon mapped to *LFO Reset* when this point has been reached. Instead of the "dark version" immediately the "extremely bright version" can be heard. To stay within the image of the curve: Resetting the LFO causes the filter process to be re-initiated at the point where least high frequencies are filtered.

The second factor influencing the filter process is the shape of the waveform that can be controlled with the *SHAPE* knob. When the knob is at position 0 a triangle wave is used to modulate the original signal. This results in a more gentle change in the frequency range. When the knob is at position 100 a sawtooth wave with short a decay time is used; this results in a harsher, more aggressive sound impression. Between those outmost points the waveform continuously changes from a triangle wave to a saw wave.

Use the *RATE* knob to change the frequency rate of the LFO to hear how this parameter affects the sound.

13.3   Controlling FX Units with the NI Controllers

The Native Instruments controllers Kontrol S2, S4, and Z2 are optimized towards different usage scenarios. As a side effect this means that not all FX features Traktor provides are equally available on these controllers. Kontrol X1, which is designed as an add-on controller takes a special position. You can use X1 to control two more FX units. Which units you are able to control depends on the deck assignment you perform on the controller after you launched Traktor.

Controlling Effects with Kontrol S2 MK2

Kontrol S2 is a controller that is optimized for using two track decks. Additionally you have some limited control of the remix decks. In the default configuration of the S2 you use decks A and B as track decks and decks C and D as remix decks.

If Kontrol S2 is the only controller you use with Traktor it is highly recommended to use just two FX units. Controlling four FX units from the S2 can be done, however it requires a huge amount of mapping work. In the Traktor setup with two FX units the left FX section on the S2 controls FX unit 1 and the FX section to the right controls FX unit 2.

Use the *FX Assign* buttons at above the channel strip of deck A and B to assign the FX units to the deck. Pressing the *FX Assign* buttons only assigns them to decks A and B. If you hold SHIFT you can assign them to decks C and D. This allows you to use the Traktor effects on the samples from the remix decks.

More FX feature that can be controlled from the S2 can be found in the overview on page 457.

Controlling Effects with Kontrol S4 MK2

Kontrol S4 is a controller optimized for using four Traktor decks. To control the FX units you use the two sections labeled *FX 1* and *FX 2* at the top of the controller. The four knobs and buttons in the FX sections correspond to the knobs and buttons from the FX units in the Traktor user interface. Additionally the controller's FX section has a button labeled *MODE*: use it to switch the FX unit between Single Mode and Group Mode. The MODE button is lit when Group Mode is active.

The buttons to assign a deck to a FX units can be found above the channel strip of the four decks.

In its default configuration Kontrol S4 allows you to use either two or four FX units.

□   **2 FX Units**   If Traktor is configured to two FX units, the FX section to the left controls FX unit 1 and the FX section on the right side controls FX unit 2. Both FX units can then be freely assigned to any of the four decks. Button *FX Assign 1* assigns FX unit 1 to the corresponding deck; button *FX Assign* 2 assigns FX unit 2 to deck.

□   **4 FX Units**   If Traktor is configured for using four FX units the tow deck focus buttons *(DECK C* and *DECK D)* control, which FX units are controlled by the knobs and buttons.

If the deck focus for the left side controller is set to deck A, then section FX 1 controls FX unit 1; of the focus is set to deck C, then section FX1 controls FX unit 2. This applies to the right side as well: here the deck focus button toggles between FX unit 2 and 4.

In the default configuration of Kontrol S4 you can assign only one FX unit to each deck: deck A uses FX unit 1, deck B uses FX unit 2, etc. This means that only one of the two FX assign button for each deck can be used. For the left side of the controller (deck A/C) you can use *FX Assign 1,* and for the right side (deck B/D) you can use *FX Assign 2.*

However, by creating a little mapping extension that needs to be inserted into the default mapping of the S4, you can set aside this restriction. The following figure shows the mapping commands that are needed if you wish to be able to use FX units 1 and 3 for decks A and B and FX units 2 and 4 with decks B and D.

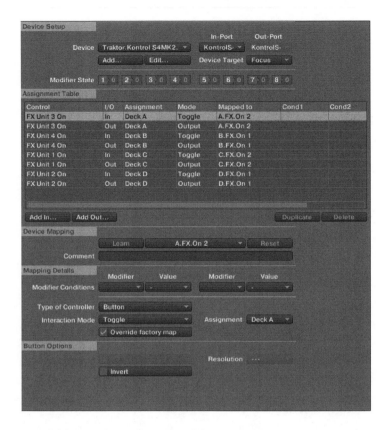

More FX feature that can be controlled from the Kontrol S4 can be found in the overview on page 457.

Kontrol S2/S4: FX Quick Load Feature

Kontrol S2 and Kontrol S4 provide a FX feature called "quick load". With quick load you can select up to three different effects which then can be loaded quickly by using some button combination of the controllers.

To select the three quick load effects open the *Preferences* dialog and click on the category *Traktor Kontrol S2* or *Traktor Kontrol S4*. Then use the list boxes *Direct FX1, Direct FX2, and Direct FX 3* to choose the effects you are using the most.

The quick effects can now be selected by using the button combinations from the following table:

FX Mode	Button	Function
Single Mode	SHIFT + FX-Button 1	Loads the effect selected in Direct FX 1
Single Mode	SHIFT + FX-Button 2	Loads the effect selected in Direct FX 2
Single Mode	SHIFT + FX-Button 3	Loads the effect selected in FX 3
Group Mode	SHIFT + FX On	Loads the three in Direct FX 1, 2, and 3 selected effects into the three effect slots of Group Mode

Controlling Effects with Kontrol Z2

At the same time as Native Instruments started to ship Kontrol Z2 Traktor version 2.6 was released. One of the new software features are the so called macro effects. Macro effects combine several of the normal Traktor effects and the sound characteristics are then controlled with a single knob.

This reduction of possible FX parameter settings is reflected in the simple MACRO FX section on the Z2 which stands out by the few controls it offers. If you use the Z2 without any add-on controller it makes sense to use two FX units only and to switch both units to Single Mode. The MACRO FX section on the left side will then control FX unit 1, and the section on the right FX unit 2.

Use the On button to activate the effect, use the D/W knob to control the dry/wet ratio and finally use the FX knob to set the parameters of the effect. The macro effects provide one settings knob only (this is the third knob of the FX panel in the Traktor user interface). For the non-macro effects the FX knob of the Z2 controls the third effect parameter as well.

The FX Assign buttons can be used to assign both FX units to all four decks. Pressing FX only assigns deck A and B; holding SHIFT and pressing FX assigns the FX units to deck C and D.

More FX feature that can be controlled from the Kontrol Z2 can be found in the overview on page 457.

Controlling Effects with Kontrol X1 MK2

Kontrol X1 was designed as an add-on controller. The main functions of the X1 are using effects and controlling hotcues and the main transport features of the decks. The upper section of the X1 is the effect section. You can use them to control two FX units.

Which FX units can be controlled depends on the deck selection you make on startup. Other than on the MK1 version of X1 you cannot change the deck assignment while Traktor is running. In order to make changes to the setup you need to disconnect and reconnect the X1 MK2 and then change your deck and FX unit selection.

The following table shows how your deck selection affects the FX units that can be controlled:

Deck Setup	Left FX Section controls	Right FX Section controls
A and B	FX-Unit 1	FX-Unit 2
C and D	FX-Unit 3	FX-Unit 4
C and A	FX-Unit 3	FX-Unit 1
B and D	FX-Unit 2	FX-Unit 4

The four knobs and four buttons on each of the two FX sections correspond to the knobs and buttons in Traktor's FX panels. The upper FX button offers another feature: if you press it while holding SHIFT you can switch the FX unit between Single Mode and Group Mode.

The four *FX Assign* buttons to the left and right of the Browse encoder connect the deck selected for this side with the FX units. Which FX units can be used depends from your deck selection.

Some additional FX features that can be controlled from X1 MK2 can be found in next section.

Overview: More FX Units Features

The following table gives you an overview of additional FX features that can be controlled directly from the controllers. The most important feature here is the effect selection.

Function	Controller	Triggered by
Switch between Single Mode/Group Mode	S2 MK2	–
	S4 MK2	MODE Button
	X1 MK2	SHIFT+FX/MODE Button
	Z2	–

Function	Controller	Triggered by
Single Mode: Select FX	S2 MK2	SHIFT + FX On
	S4 MK2	SHIFT + FX On
	X1 MK2	SHIFT + one of the FX/Dry-Wet Knobs
	Z2	SHIFT + FX Knob
Group Mode: Select FX	S2 MK2 S4 MK2	SHIFT + FX Button 1/2/3 (slots 1–3)
	X1 MK2	SHIFT + FX Button 1/2/3 (slots 1–3) or SHIFT + FX Knob 1/2/3 (slots 1–3)
	Z2	SHIFT + FX-Knob (on the Z2 you can only select the effect of the first slot when the FX unit is set to Group Mode)
Switch FX routing between Insert (Pre Fader) and Post Fader	Z2	SHIFT + FX On

13.4 Effects in the Detail

The huge number of Traktor effects opens various creative possibilities. However, the problem is that you can only use an effect spontaneously and intuitively if you know how it modifies the sound and if you are familiar with the function of the different effect parameters in Single mode. It takes some time until you really know the effects.

I recommend that you first get a rough overview of the effects and then select maybe five for a start and to dig deeper into the features and parameters of this selection. Use different tracks to see how the effect affects different genres or styles.

Sometimes it is easier to hear what an effect does, if you separate the original signal from the effect signal and then listen to either one or to the other. If you use an external mixer you can achieve this by switching one of the FX units to *Send* Mode (see page 439). This way you can listen to the original signal in the deck and to the effect signal in the FX return bus.

In both external and in internal mixing mode you can use the feature *Duplicate Deck*. This way you can listen to the original signal from one deck. Then set the *Dry/Wet* knob in the second deck to 100 to get the effect signal only (the feature *Duplicate Deck* is covered in section "Processing Order of Effects in Group Mode" on page 441 and in chapter 3 on page 65 and onward).

Delay and Delay T3

As the name implies *Delay* is a delay effect where copies of the original signal are inserted into the output, and this results in an echoic impression. There are two variations of Delay available. *Delay T3* is the same effect that was used in Traktor 3 and Traktor Scratch. *Delay* is an improved rework of this effect.

Apart from the different sound of the effect (Delay T3 sounds a bit duller; and when the *Dry/Wet* knob is set to a higher value the sound is slightly distorted or clipped), the main difference between the two effects is the delay time settings. In *Delay* the delay time can only be set to predefined intervals. However, Delay T3 supports a Free-Run-Mode that allows the delay time to be set to any value within a certain range.

On the other hand, the *Delay* effect has an additional spread button labelled *SPR* that can be used to get more spatial depth. This is done by using different delay times for the right, and the left stereo channel. When *SPR* is on, the delay time shown below the *RATE* knob is used for the left stereo channel. For the delay time 1/32 and 4/4 the effect uses the same values for both channels. For 2/4 the delay time for the right channel is shorter and for all other values the delay time for the right channel is longer than the one used for the left channel.

The delay time is configured with the *RATE* knob. Because the Delay effect is synchronised to the tempo of the Master Clock, the delay time is specified in fractions of beats and not in milliseconds. The following delay times are available: 1/32, 1/16, 1/8, 3/16, 1/4, 3/8 and 4/4 beats.

The signal path of the Delay effect looks like this:

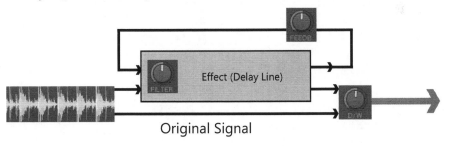

Original Signal

The *FILTER* knob for this effect controls the band-pass filter (see sidebar "The Filter Types" on page 461 and onward) that filters stepwise the low, and the high frequencies the more the filter is closed.

The *FEEDBACK* knob, which can also be found in other effects, controls if, and how much of the effect signal is fed back into the effect. By feeding the effect signal back into the filter, the intensity of the effect is increased.

> IMPORTANT   To disable the *Delay* effect signal completely you need to remove the assignment between deck and FX unit.

 In Group mode the knob controls the *RATE* parameter of both effects. The feedback parameter is set to a middle value.

Reverb and Reverb T3

These two effects simulate the acoustic echo effects in rooms of different sizes. As with the *Delay* effect there is a new version available as well as the one used in Traktor 3. The effect parameters for both effects are identical. I actually prefer the sound of the new variation more than the old one.

The most important knob for these effects is the *SIZE* knob; it is used to configure the room size. To create an echo effect which relates to the room size, the *SIZE* knob controls several timing parameters of the echo: the time until the early reflections can be heard; the time until the reflections themselves are reflected by the "walls"; and the time until the energy of the echo is sustained and the echo ebbs away. The smaller the room, the shorter the duration of the echo is. The bigger the room, the longer its duration is.

Because the *SIZE* knob controls the timing behaviour of the Reverb effect you can use it to create interesting pitching effects, for example by changing the *SIZE* parameter very quickly. Another option is to use *Deck Duplicate* to let the same track run parallel in two decks. Using the Reverb effect in one deck only, setting the *Dry/Wet* knob for this deck to 100, changing the *SIZE* knob and feeding the pitched echo only into the output.

The Reverb effect has a high-pass filter (HP) as well as a low-pass filter (LP). The low-Pass filter is open if the knob position is 0; the high-pass filter is open if the knob is at 100. You can use these two filters to configure the frequency range of the effect signal.

 In Group mode the knob is used to set the size parameter for the Reverb effects.

Sidebar: The Filter Types

Several of the Traktor effects use either one or two filter knobs that can be used to change the frequency range of the effect signal. Depending on the effect the following filter types are available:

☐ **High-Pass Filter (= Low-Cut Filter)** A high-pass-filter damps the low frequencies, i.e. the middle and the high frequencies can pass the filter.

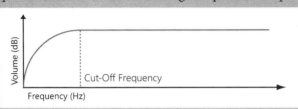

The cut-off frequency, which can be set with the knob, controls the frequency from which on the audio signal can pass.

☐ **Low-Pass Filter (= High-Cut Filter)** The low-pass filter damps the high frequencies and the low frequency can pass.

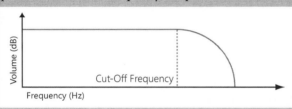

☐ **Band-Pass Filter** The band-pass filter is a combination of a high-pass and a low-pass filter. The band-pass filter uses two cut-off frequencies that define the frequency range that can pass the filter. The *Delay* effect offers one knob to set both cut-off frequencies; the *Filter* effect has separate knob to set the cut-off frequency for the high-pass and the low-pass filter.

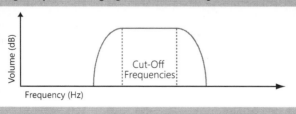

> ☐ **Band-Reject Filter, Notch Filter** Like the band-pass filter the band-reject fil-
> ter uses two cut-off frequencies. Unlike the band-pass filter the cut-off frequen-
> cies for band-reject define the frequency range which is cut from the audio sig-
> nal. This means that the lower and the upper part of the frequency spectrum
> are not altered but that the selected range in the middle of the spectrum is fil-
> tered out. The Traktor effect Filter for example has a button labelled BRJ (=
> Band Reject) that can be used to switch between a band-pass and a band-reject
> filter.
>
>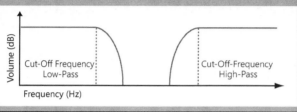

Iceverb

The *Iceverb* effect is another type of echo effect. It doesn't simulate the acoustics of a
room but those of an ice cave, resulting in a cooler, more metallic effect. As with the
Reverb effect you use the *SIZE* knob to select the "cave size" which in turn configures
the timing behaviour of the reflections.

The *COLOR* knob is used to select the cut-off frequency of the filter. The more the
filter is opened, the more of the lower and middle frequencies are cut. Use the *ICING*
knob to configure the resonance of the effect; when the resonance is increased the frequencies close and the cut-off frequencies are amplified.

 In Group mode the knob controls the *SIZE*-Parameter.

Freeze for Delay, Delay 3, Reverb and Iceverb

The effects Delay, Reverb and Iceverb all have a Freeze button *(FRZ)* but the behaviour
of the button is slightly different for each of the effects. In all cases pressing the Freeze
button suspends the input of the original signal and only the effect signal is sent to the
output. This means that the *D/W* knob does not function once *FRZ* has been pressed.

Freezing with Delay

The new *Delay* effect uses an audio buffer and the size is set with the *RATE* knob; the buffer is filled when the *ON* button is pressed. After pressing *FRZ* the content of the audio buffer is looped and neither the D/W nor the *FEEDB* have any more effect. However, the *FILTER* knob stays active. If you wish to loop the content of the audio buffer infinitely then the *FILTER* knob should be at position 0. To let the looping fade away slowly turn the *FILTER* knob clockwise towards its position 100.

The *RATE* knob is also still active in freeze mode and you can use it to shorten the loop length. You need to be careful not to leave the *RATE* knob on the smaller values for too long; otherwise the audio buffer looses its content.

ATTENTION If you switch the *ON* button as well as the *FRZ* button off after freezing the delay and, if the channel fader is still up, the effect signal can still be heard (although at low volume only). To disable the effect signal completely you need to remove the assignment between deck and FX unit.

Freeze with Delay T3

I am of the opinion that the behaviour of the Freeze feature of the Delay T3 effect is unpredictable. Quite often, but not always, the sound disappears after only a few beats have been repeated. I couldn't find a reproducible scenario for this effect. My advice: Use the Freeze feature of the Delay effect

Freezing with Reverb, Reverb T 3 and Iceverb

For these three effects the result of the Freeze button depends a lot on the value that the SIZE knob is set at. Here the freezing causes a kind of added echoing of the audio signal that depends on the room size. The smaller the room the fewer echoes are added and vice versa. To get an echo with a long duration set the *SIZE* knob to a high value before pressing *FRZ*.

TIP The Iceverb effect especially creates very interesting sounds if you change the *SIZE* knob **after** *FRZ* is pressed.

Bouncer

The Bouncer effect belongs to the group of effects that use granular synthesis to modify the audio that has been copied from the assigned deck into a buffer. Bouncer allows you to change the playback tempo and the pitch; the sampled grains are constantly repeated.

The grains that are modulated by the effect can either be static or dynamic. This option is controlled by the *AUT* button.

- If the *AUT* button is deactivated, the audio buffer of the effect is filled with samples as you switch the effect to *ON*. The assigned deck needs to be playing; otherwise there is no audio available to be copied. Once the samples are inside the buffer, their playback can be changed with the effect knobs.

- If the *AUT* button is activated, the effect audio buffer is constantly updated with material around the current playback position of the assigned deck.

The *TRANSPOSE* knob transposes the playback tempo of the samples that, at the same time leads to a pitch change. The *SPEED* knob controls the speed by which the samples are "reflected" between two walls. Pressing the *X2* button doubles the currently selected *SPEED* value.

The *FILTER* knob for this effect controls the cut-off frequency of the integrated low-pass filter. The low-pass filter is open when the *FILTER* knob is turned completely anti-clockwise.

 In Group Mode the knob controls the *SPEED* parameter of the effect.

Auto Bouncer

Auto Bouncer is based on the same principle as the Bouncer effect; they differ in how the samples are repeated. Auto Bouncer does not use a fixed speed but ten different patterns that can be selected with the *PATTERN* knob and the *ALT* button. The *PATTERN* knob has a value range from 0 to 4. If the *ALT* button is off, the *PATTERN* knob selects patterns 1 to 5; if the *ALT* button is on you can choose from patterns 6 to 10.

Auto Bouncer continuously copies new audio from the assigned deck into the effect buffer, which corresponds to the activated *AUT* button of the Bouncer effect.

The *TRANSPOSE* and *BEND* knobs can be used to modify the patterns and the sampled audio. Using *TRANSPOSE* leads to a pitch change. The *BEND* knob controls the tempo and the tempo change by which the samples are repeated. In the centre position of the knob the audio snippets are repeated steadily at the same interval. If you turn the knob from its centre position clockwise, the samples are repeated first fast and then the repeat tempo decreases. If you turn the knob anti-clockwise from its centre position, the audio is first repeated at a slow rate which then constantly increases. You can press the *X2* button to double the number of repetitions.

Please note that unlike with the Bouncer effect the dry signal stays slightly audible even if the *D/W* knob is at its outermost right position.

 In Group Mode the knob controls the *BEND* parameter of Single Mode.

Tape Delay

Tape Delay emulates the echo effect, as it was produced with tape recorders before digital signal processing was invented. The simplest tape machine that was used for an echo effect had one record head and one play head. The incoming audio signal was recorded onto the tape and then played back by the playback head. The delay between the input signal and the effect signal was the result of the physical distance between record head and the play head. Additionally the delay time could be modified by changing the playback speed. Besides these simple machines there were other more sophisticated systems that use several play heads, which can be individually activated or used combined.

Another effect that Traktors' Tape Delay emulates is the tape saturation. Tape saturation can be achieved by raising the input signal until a slight overdrive occurs. Because the possible magnetisation of a magnetic tape is endless, a signal that cannot be recorded because the tape is "full", is cut. The saturation effect leads to a small almost inaudible compression, which makes the sounds softer and warmer. The tape saturation is enabled by default and has no parameters that can be changed.

The most important knob for Tape Delay is the *SPEED* knob that controls the "tape speed": the more this knob is turned clockwise the faster the tape is playing which results in a shorter delay. You can activate the *ACCL* button which intensifies the audible speed-up and slowing down of the tape. The tempo change is then no longer almost linear, but more unsteady, as if the tape speed is being changed by hand.

The *FILTER* knob controls the cut-off frequency of the effects internal high-pass filter. The filter is open if the knob is at its outermost left position. The more the knob is turned clock-wise, the more the low frequencies are damped.

As with other effects the *FEEDBACK* knob controls if and at which amount the effect signal is fed back into the effect engine. The higher the feedback value the more intense the effect. Furthermore the *FEEDBACK* knob allows you to create a nice trail: Turn the *FEEDBACK* knob wide open, then stop playback of the assigned deck or start playback only for a short time, to get some audio into the effect buffer.

Use the *FRZ* button to freeze the effect. The nice thing with the freeze feature of Tape Delay is, that the frozen audio can be played back endlessly, because the echo of Tape Delay does not emulate a "real room" where the echo reflections fade away over time. Once the audio is frozen you can continue to change the sound with the *SPEED* knob and the *FILTER* knob; the *FEEDBACK* knob has no functionality as long as *FRZ* is on.

 In Group Mode the knob corresponds to the *SPEED* knob of Single Mode.

Ramp Delay

Ramp Delay works like the normal Delay effect if the delay time *(RATE* knob) is not being changed when the effect is on. The interesting dynamic sound of Ramp Delay is achieved by the configurable duration it shall take to make the transition from one delay time to another one. The duration can be set with the *DURATION* knob. If you change the *RATE,* the effect will need the configured time to change the rate, i.e. the rate doesn't change instantly as with the standard Delay.

The possible values for Ramp Delay *RATE* are identical to those available for Delay: 1/32, 1/16, 1/8, 3/16, 1/4, 3/8, and 4/4. For the "length of the ramp" the *DURATION* knob provides the fol1/4, 2/4, 4/4, 2 bars, 4 bars, 8 bars, 16 bars.

The *FILTER* knob controls a combination of low-pass filter and high-pass filter. When the knob is in the middle position all frequencies pass through the filter. Turning the knob to the left first cuts the high frequencies and then the low frequencies. Turning the knob to the right first cuts the low and then the high frequencies.

You can use the *FRZ* button to freeze the effect. Because the filter is still active in freeze mode you wish to make sure that the *FILTER* knob is close to the middle position. Otherwise the effect signal will decay.

Pressing the *FB+* button set the feedback amount to 90%.

 In Group Mode the knob controls the *RATE* parameter of Single Mode; the *DURATION* parameter is set to 2 bars by default and cannot be changed.

Beatmasher 2

Beatmasher 2 is, like the Delay effect, a buffer based effect. Samples of the playing track are copied into the audio buffer and the buffer content can be manipulated afterwards. Beatmasher 2 can therefore be used like a sampler to playback loops.

The size of the audio buffer is always 1 bar (4 beats). The size in seconds depends on the current tempo of the Master Clock and is automatically adjusted. If you press the *ON* button the sampling is started and the next four beats are copied into the buffer. If the *D/W* knob is set to 0 when *ON* is pressed the sample cannot be heard. You can feed the sampled audio at any time into the deck signal by opening the *D/W* knob.

The four beats sample can either contain a copy of 4 adjacent beats of the tracks or a short snippet only that has been copied several times into the buffer. The easiest way to get a snippet multiple times into the buffer is by setting a cue point at the desired playback position and then pressing the *CUE* button several times

Once the sample is in the buffer you can manipulate it:

☐ Use the *LEN* knob (Length) to select the length of the snippet that shall be taken from the buffer and played. This does not change the buffers' content; i.e. the length can be changed as often as wanted. The length is adjustable in a range between 4/4 and 1/32; if you use 4/4 the complete sample is looped.

☐ The *GATE* knob is a bipolar encoder; i.e. it causes different effects depending on if its current position is to the left or to the right of the centre position. If the knob is turned completely anti-clockwise (the value shown is 0) than the gate effect is disabled. From 0 towards the centre position (value shown is 100) the snippet size is increased. If the knob is at its middle position the complete sample is audible.

If you further turn the knob from the centre position to the right the knob creates an effect similar to the Gater effect. At the middle position (G100) the gate is completely open, i.e. the audio signal can pass through all the time. Turning the knob clockwise (towards the value G0) the gate is closed more and more.

☐ The *ROT* knob (Rotate) moves the start point where the audio is taken from in the buffer towards the end of the buffer; the step size is 1/8 note. Using the ROT knob together with the LEN knob allows you to play back different snippets from the buffer.

☐ The *REV* button (Reverse) plays the audio snippet backwards.

- ☐ The *WRP* button (Warp) synchronises the effect signal to the Master Clock once per bar. This better integrates the effect signal into the overall rhythm of the mix in a better way and also if other decks are also following the Master Clock.

 In Group mode the knob controls the *LEN*-Parameter.

Flanger, Phaser and their Variations

Flanger and Phase belong to the same effect family, because both set the overtones of the audio signal in motion. For this an LFO is used (see section on page 451 and onwards) to modulate the audio signal and this causes the audible sweeps.

In short, the difference between Flanger and Phaser is: The Flanger effect adds a *time delayed copy* of the original signal and the delay time is continuously changing (mostly between 1 and 10 milliseconds). Because the delay time is very short this isn't perceived as an echo. Instead the delay creates kind of a filter effect producing notches in the frequency spectrum. The result is that groups of frequencies are filtered. And because the delay time is changing those notches in the frequency spectrum change as well. This in turn creates the typical dynamic swirl effect of the Flanger.

The Phaser, which is actually a Phase Shifter, uses a *phase-shifted copy* of the input and mixes it with the original signal. When the original and the phase shifted signal are combined this again creates one or several notches in the frequency spectrum; those frequencies are eliminated in the output signal. This creates the typical frequency sweep of the Phaser. To get the phase shifted copy the signal is sent through an all-pass filter; this filter type lets all frequencies pass through, but it changes the phase response.

Flanger and Phaser

The effect parameters for Flanger and Phaser are identical:

- ☐ The *RATE* knob controls the duration of the oscillation cycle. The following options are available: 16, 8, 4, 2 bars, 1 bars and 2/4, 3/8, 1/4, 3/16, 1/18 and 1/16 note. If you switch the *FR.R* (=Free Run) button on, then the duration can be set within a range between 30 seconds and 1/30 second.

- ☐ Use the *FEEDB* knob (FEEDBACK) to change the sound characteristics of the effect. When you select a higher value the sound of the Flanger becomes more metallic and the sound of the Phaser becomes more bell-shaped.

☐ The *SPRD* knob (SPREAD) can be used to get more spatial depth. If the knob is set to 0 then this feature is disabled; a value of 100 delivers the most intense stereophonic effect.

☐ The *UP* button reverses the direction of the oscillation of the LFO. If you press the button the oscillation starts with the low frequencies and moves upwards in the frequency range.

 In Group mode the knob controls the duration of the oscillation cycle for both effects *(RATE* knob in free run mode).

Flanger Flux and Phaser Flux

Flanger Flux and Phaser Flux are variations of the Flanger and Phaser effect respectively. They differ from their effect "fathers" in offering a *PITCH* knob that can be used to configure the frequency range that in turn creates different notches in the frequency spectrum and thus other sounds.

Again, the *FEEDB* knob controls how much of the effect signal is fed back into the engine; use the knob to alter the intensity and the sound characteristics.

The panel of Flanger Flux displays the button *FB–* that controls which tones are passed through in the feedback signal. If the button is switched on then only the uneven harmonics are passed (Uneven harmonics are those overtones of a fundamental tone. Those frequencies are non integer multiplies of the fundamental frequency). This emphasizes the lower frequencies and the sound is softer, deeper.

On the other hand Phaser Flux offers the button *8PL*. This button switches the all-pass filter from a 6 pole to an 8 pole filter. That changes the phase shifting occurring as the signal is run through the filter and it makes the effect more noticeable.

 In Group mode the knob corresponds to the *PITCH* knob of Single mode.

Flanger Pulse and Phaser Pulse

Flanger Pulse and Phaser Pulse are variations of the Flanger and Phaser effect as well. They differ from their effect "mothers" by the fact, that the effect creation is triggered by the signal peaks in the audio signal. Thus, both effects are impulse triggered.

The sound produced by both effects is the result of the three different parameter settings. When all three knobs are in the centre position the audio signal flows almost unchanged through the effect. The most important parameter is controlled with the *AMNT* knob (amount); its setting controls the intensity of the modulation of the flanger frequency. The *SHAPE* knob controls the form of the effect and, the *FEEDB* knob controls, as usual, how much of the effect signal is fed back into the effect and it allows us to change the intensity and the sound characteristics of the effect.

The button *FB–* in Flanger Pulse has the same function as the corresponding button in Flanger Flux. When the button is switched on only the uneven harmonics can pass. The button *8 PL* of Phaser Pulse switches the all-pass filter from a 6-pole to an 8-pole filter. This affects the phase shifting that occurs when the signal is running through the filter and makes the effect stronger.

The *SPR* button (SPREAD) creates more spatial depth. This effect is only audible if the *FEEDB* as well as the *AMNT* knob are opened widely.

 For both effects the *AMNT* knob is the same in Group mode and in Single mode.

Filter, Filter:92 and their Variations

The base of the six different filter effects are, the effects Filter and Filter:92. Filters, in general change the sound by damping selected frequencies. The *Filter* effect is a so called ladder filter (the name derives from the arrangement of the transistors/diodes use in Moog synthesizers as filters; they looked similar to a ladder). The sound characteristics and the behaviour of *Filter:92* are built after the filters that are used in the Allen&Heath mixer Xone:92.

More general information about basic filter types can be found in the sidebar "The Filter Types" on page 461 and further.

Filter and Filter:92 – Configuring Low-Pass and High-Pass Filter separately

In the default mode of both filters effects the cut-off frequencies for the high-pass and the low-pass filter can be set separately with the knobs *HP* and *LP*. The high-pass filter is open when the knob is turned completely anti-clockwise; the low-pass filter is open when the knob is turned completely clockwise.

The *RES* knob can be used to change the resonance (Q Factor) of the effect. The resonance circuit causes those tones near the cut-off frequency to be emphasized and the other tones to be attenuated. When you select a high resonance the effect of the filter is more prominent. Furthermore, with higher resonance values filters tend to produce an oscillation by themselves; this effect is called self-oscillation and creates interesting sounds.

Filter and Filter:92 – Band Reject Mode

The button *BRJ* switches the filter into band-reject mode, i.e. the filter acts like a band-reject filter. In band-reject mode the knobs *HP* and *LP* control the frequency range that is cut out from the middle of the frequency spectrum.

Please note that the knobs for the low-pass and the high-pass filter are swapped when the effect is switched to band-reject mode.

Filter and Filter:92 – DJ Mode (1 Knob Mode)

The effect is switched to 1 knob mode when the button *DJM* (DJ Mode) is pressed. In this mode only one button is available to configure the cut-off frequencies; the button is labelled *LP-HP*.

When the knob is in its middle position all frequencies can pass the filter. When the knob is turned anti-clockwise first, the high frequencies and then the low frequencies are filtered. When the knob is turned clockwise from its middle position the effect is reversed: first the low frequencies are filtered and then the high frequencies.

 In Group mode both filter effects behave as the *LP-HP* knob in DJ mode of the FX mode Single. The result you get is actually the same as that of the Key knob from the panel *Filter-, Key-, Gain* next to the decks. The effect *Filter* corresponds to the filter selection *Ladder* and the effect *Filter:92* corresponds to filter selection *Xone* (dialog *Preferences/Mixer*, section *Filter Selection*).

Filter LFO and Filter:92 LFO

Filter LFO is a filter that uses the ladder architecture and Filter:92 LFO is an emulation of the filters found in the Allen&Heath-Mixer Xone:92. Both filters are driven by a LFO that causes a cyclic change of the filter that results in cutting out different frequency ranges.

Specific to both filters is that the *D/W* knob is here labelled *D/RNG* (Dry/Wet/Range), because it not only controls the ratio between the dry and the wet signal but also the frequency range that shall be filtered. The more the *D/RNG* knob is turned clockwise the duller the sound gets because more of the high frequencies are filtered out.

The *SHAPE* knob is used to set the shape of the LFOs' waveform. When the knob is at position 0 a triangle wave is used to modulate the original signal. This results in smoother changes of the frequency spectrum. At the knob position 100 a sawtooth wave with short decay time is used resulting in a sharper, more aggressive sound. Between this two extreme points the triangle wave is slowly transformed into a saw wave.

The *RES* knob can be used to change the resonance (Q Factor) of the effect. When a high resonance is selected the effect of the filter is more prominent.

Click the *UP* button to reverse the direction of the oscillation of the LFO. The oscillation then begins at the low frequencies and moves towards the high frequencies in the spectrum. If the button was ON and is switched off the oscillation starts at the high frequencies and moves towards the low frequencies in the spectrum.

 In Group mode the knob controls the rate of the oscillation cycle (*RATE* knob) and in a way similar to the pressing of the Free Run button of Single mode.

Filter Pulse and Filter:92 Pulse

These two effects respond to the signal peaks like the other effects of the "Pulse" family in the input signal. In these two filter effects the signal peaks cause filter events. Because these effects are triggered by signal peaks they are best suited for tracks that have short interval volume changes in (like for example, a drum loop in a track).

The *D/W* knob is called *D/RNG* (Dry/Wet/Range) here as well because it not only controls the ratio of the dry and wet signal but is also used to configure the cut-off frequency: The more the *D/RNG* knob is turned clockwise the duller the effect signal becomes because increasingly more and more high frequencies are filtered out.

The result of the effects depends mostly on the positions of the *D/RNG* and the *AMNT* knobs. The *AMNT* knob mainly controls the direction of the modulation. In the middle position the modulation is neutral. When the knob is turned clockwise the modulation runs upwards, i.e. the pitch goes up. When the knob is turned anti-clockwise off its middle position the modulation runs downwards, i.e. the pitch drops.

The *RES* knob controls the resonance (Q Factor) of the filter. When a high resonance is selected then the effect of the filter is more prominent because the resonance circuit emphasizes the tones near the cut-off frequency and it damps the other tones.

Finally, the *SOFT* knob can be used to control the smoothness of the filter envelope that controls the cut-off frequency of the filter. The more the knob is turned clockwise the smother the filter sweeps become.

 In Group mode the knob mainly controls the same parameter as the *AMNT* knob of Single mode.

Gater

The Gater effect "shoots" audio holes into the original signal. In other words: It acts like a gate that is opened and closed at particular intervals and at a particular tempo. The audio signal can only be heard when the gate is open.

The interval used to open and close the gate can be set with the *RATE* knob. The following intervals (expressed as fractions of bars) are available: 1/4, 1/8, 1/16 and 1/32. If you activate the button *STT* (Stutter) the interval is set to 3/16; because of the shortness this leads to a kind if stutter effect.

You can use the *NOISE* knob to add white noise to the effect signal; this amplifies the rhythm of the effect. The more the knob is opened the more intense the noise. The sound of the noise is not only controlled by the *NOISE* knob but by the *RATE* and also the *SHAPE* knob. You can use the Mute button *(MTE)* to mute the effect signal of the "gated" tracks; this results in only the noise being audible (assuming that the *NOISE* knob is not at position 0).

Thanks to the *MTE* button the rhythmic noise can be used in three different ways:

☐   **As a part of the Gater effect signal for the playing track**   For this usage the *MTE* button may not be switched on and the NOISE knob must be open (i.e. it may not be at position 0). Then the effect produces as well the noise as the modified audio signal by using the configured parameters. Then the effect signal is mixed with the original signal using the configured *D/W* ratio.

☐   **As the only output of the Gater effect signal for the playing track**   For this scenario the *MTE* button must be enabled and the *NOISE* knob must be open. The effect produces the rhythmic noise by using the configured parameters and mixes it with the original signal by means of the configured *D/W* value.

☐   **As an effect in a deck with no track playing**   For the last scenario the FX unit must be assigned to the deck, and the *Dry/Wet* and the *NOISE* knob also need to be set to 100. Additionally, press the *MTE* button. This makes the white noise louder. Now you can use the SHAPE knob and the *RATE* knob to configure the sound characteristic of the noise. It's interesting that the interval of the noise can be set almost steplessly; it is not restricted to the values shown beneath the *RATE* knob. Use the channel fader of the deck to feed the noise into the mix out signal.

The rhythm of the effect is controlled with the *SHAPE* knob. The *SHAPE* knob controls the hold and the decay value (in percentage) of the envelope that produces the characteristic sound of the Gater effect. The x-axis in the following graph shows the possible values of the *SHAPE* knob. The two lines represent the hold and decay value corresponding to the different positions of the *SHAPE* knob.

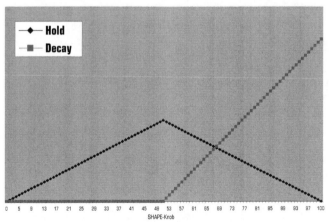

The hold value controls the time the gate should at least be open. The larger this value is the less abrupt changes (i.e. fast opening and closing of the gate) will occur. The decay value controls the time it takes for the volume to decline from the Attack level to the Sustain Level. The larger this value is set for the Gater effect, the longer the original signal can be heard.

When the *SHAPE* knob is at position 0 and also the decay and the hold value are set to 0 percent creates a kind of wobbling sound is created. The more the knob is turned clockwise towards its middle position the longer the gate stays open and the intensity of the wobbling decreases. The more the *SHAPE* knob is turned further clockwise starting from the middle position, the longer the original signal is audible in the effect signal: the duration that the gate is closed is getting shorter.

TIP One example showing the possibilities of the Gater effect can be seen in a YouTube video with James Zabiela: *www.youtube.com/watch?v=K17OU5cAbBc*

 In Group mode the effect knob behaves like the *RATE* knob in Single mode. Additionally the *NOISE* knob is opened in Group mode. Try this: Load the Gater effect in two effect slots of the same FX unit and then play with the knobs.

Digital LoFi

Digital LoFi (which could be called Bitcrusher as well) is one of Traktors' distortion effects. It can be used to change the sampling rate as well as the bit depth of the audio signal.

The bit depth is set with the *BIT* knob; 0 corresponds to the original bit depth; when the knob is set to 100 the bit depth is slightly above 1 bit. The sampling rate is controlled with the knob *SRTE* (Sample Rate). The position 0 corresponds to the original sample rate; by turning the knob towards 100 the sample rate is continuously reduced down to 00 Hz. You can use the Smooth knob *(SMTH)* to lessen the effect that is produced by reducing the sample rate; this results in a less harsh and much softer sound.

Finally, the Spread button (SPR) can be used to create more spatial depth.

 In Group mode the knob controls the sample rate as well as the bit depth. But even when in Group mode and when the knob is set to 100% the sound is less obvious than in Single mode.

Reverse Grain

Reverse Grain is a buffer based effect using granular synthesis. The audio buffer of the effect is filled with audio samples as you press the *ON* button. This means the assigned deck must be playing; otherwise there will not be any samples in the buffer. The audio data in the buffer is portioned into little snippets, called grains. The size of the grains, i.e. their time length is controlled with the *GRAIN* knob.

Once the audio data is in the buffer it can be manipulated in several ways:

☐ The grains can either be played forward or backwards. The default playback direction is backwards; the button *FWD* can be used to change the playback direction.

☐ The playback sequence of the grains can be inverted by using the *INV* button.

☐ The playback tempo is controlled with the *SPEED* knob. When the knob is at position 100 the grains are played at their original tempo. By turning the knob anti-clockwise towards the 0 position the tempo is reduced.

☐ You can use the *PITCH* knob to change the pitch steplessly. When the knob is at position 100 the playback is at the original pitch. The more the knob is turned towards 0 the more the pitch is decreased.

 In Group mode you can use the knob to change the size of the grains. Playback always happens backwards; the original tempo and the original pitch are used.

Turntable FX

Turntable FX simulates different sound effects that are normally produced by using a turntable. Unlike the other effects, Turntable FX actually has three different *ON* buttons *(BRK, RCK* and *REW)*; each of them activates one of the three different sound effects that Turntable FX can produce. Even though more than one button can be set to *ON,* only the last activated effect is used.

Turntable FX belongs to the group of buffer based effects. This means the assigned deck must be set to *Play* before the effect is activated so that the buffer can be filled with audio data.

The four different sounds of the effect can be used as follows:

□ **Turntable Brake** To simulate switching off the turntable motor proceed like this: The deck whose motor is to be switched off must be set to Play. Configure the following parameters: set *D/W* to 100 so that only the effect signal is audible. Use the *B.SPD* (Brake Speed) knob to configure the brake speed. My recommendation is to use the value 0; that way the brake takes as long as possible. Now click *BRK* to switch the motor off.

□ **Turntable Start** This effect can also be used to emulate the turntable start. To start the turntable motor proceed like this: Set the D/W knob to 100 so that only the effect signal can be heard. Use the B.SPD (Brake Speed) knob to configure the start-up pitch. I recommend using a value of 0; this causes the start-up time to be as long as possible. Click the BRK button to activate the brake effect; i.e. the "motor" is now switched off. Start the deck and wait approximately 8 to 10 beats; this time is needed so that the audio buffer can be filled with samples. Then click the *BRK* button a second time; this deactivates the brake and starts the motor.

□ **Rocking Motion** The button *RCK* and the knobs *AMNT* (Amount) and *R.SPD* (Rocking Speed) can be used to emulate the torsional vibration that happens during the power transmission between the motor and the platter and thus to the vinyl. Those vibrations can cause distortions in the audio. The tempo of this effect is set with the *R.SPD* knob and its intensity with the *AMNT* knob.

To better hear what the effect does set the D/W knob to 100 and then click the *RCK* button to activate the effect (this should be done when a track is playing). Traktor samples a short audio snippet and plays it continuously. The more the *R.SPD* knob is turned clockwise, the more the playback stutters because this knob controls the repetition rate.

□ **Backspin** The last trick that can be created with this effect is a backspin. You need the *REW* button (Rewind), which switches the effect on. The *B.SPD* knob can be used to configure the acceleration of the backspin. The smaller the configured value the slower the backspin will start and the longer it will take until the backspin speed is raised. When using the rewind effect the *B.SPD* knob is very sensitive. A value of 25 can make the acceleration happen very quickly.

 In Group mode Turntable FX can be used to simulate turning the turntable on or off. The *ON* button of Group mode corresponds to the *BRK* button of Single mode; you can use the knob to configure the brake and start-up tempo. Even in Group mode it is important to set the *D/W* knob of the assigned FX unit to 100 so that only the effect signal is audible.

Ringmodulator

Amplitude modulation is a technique where two different signals are multiplied. This creates two new signals. The frequency range of one signal contains the sum of the input frequencies and the second one, their difference. Amplitude modulation changes the harmonic proportions of sounds.

The Traktor effect Ringmodulator uses the playing track as one input signal; the second input signal can be controlled by the *RAW* and *PITCH* knob. The PITCH knob is used to control the frequency of this signal (called carrier frequency) in a range between 100 Hz and 8731 Hz. The characteristic of this signal – its wave form – is set with the *RAW* knob. If the *RAW* knob is at position 0 then a sinus wave is used (which leads to softer sounds). The more the knob is opened, the more the wave form is changed to a filtered square wave, which makes the sounds harder.

The Ring modulator effect offers two different modulation methods: amplitude modulation and ring modulation. The difference between those methods is that with amplitude modulation the output signal contains the carrier frequency; this is not the case with ring modulation. This makes the sound of a signal modified by amplitude modulation softer. You can emphasis this soft impression by setting the *RAW* knob to 0 (= sinus wave) and by setting the *PITCH* knob to a high frequency.

The knob *AM-RM* can be used to change the modulation method continuously from amplitude to ring modulation.

 In Group mode the knob behaves like a combination of the *RAW* and the *PITCH* knob. The modulation method used in Group mode has more of the sound characteristics of the ring modulation.

Transpose Stretch

The effect Transpose Stretch is a combination of a Pitch-Shifter and a Time-Stretcher. A Pitch-Shifter creates a signal whose pitch has been changed (transposition = pitch shifting). A Time-Stretcher changes the playback speed of the audio without affecting its pitch. (The key lock functionality of Traktor is based on a time stretcher. More information can be found in chapter 11, "Equalizer, Key and Harmonic Mixing".)

Both features of the effect can either be used separately or in combination.

Pitch-Shifting

Pitch-Shifting changes the pitch (key) of the original signal without affecting the audio length. If only the playback tempo is increased this will change the pitch, but this process changes the audio length as well. To solve this problem a pitch shifter uses granular synthesis to split the audio signal into small snippets that are called grains. Those grains are then played at different tempo. If the pitch is increased eventually some grains are looped. If the pitch drops it possible that some of the grains are not completely used.

The desired pitch can be configured with the *KEY* knob. When the *KEY* knob is in its centre position then the playback happens at the original pitch. When the knob is turned clockwise the pitch increases by one octave maximum. Turning the knob anticlockwise declines the pitch up to a maximum of five octaves.

When the *GRN* button is disabled Traktor will control the grain size automatically to achieve an optimal pitch effect. You can turn the Grain button on to be able to control the grain size with the *GRNSZ* knob (Grain Size). At position 0 the grain size is 333 milliseconds; the more the knob is turned clockwise the shorter the grains get. The shortest grain size is 5 milliseconds.

Time-Stretching

The Time-Stretcher effect is one of the buffer based effects in Traktor. Here the buffer is filled when the *STRCH* button (Stretch) is turned clockwise starting at its 0 position (i.e. not by pressing the *ON* button). If the Stretch knob is not at position 0 when the *ON* button is pressed then activation of the effect and the filling of the buffer will happen at the same time. By separating the sampling and the effect use you can fill the buffer at any time (for example with some vocals) and then play it time stretched at a later moment.

◻ To fill the buffer set the *D/W* and the *STRCH* knob to 0. Activate the effect by pressing the *ON* button. When playback reaches the point from where the audio is to be sampled turn the *STRCH* knob clockwise. This will copy the next 4 or 8 beats into the effect buffer.

◻ To playback the buffer, open the *D/W* knob at the right moment and set the playback tempo with the *STRCH* knob. Additionally you can use the *KEY* knob to change the pitch.

The default buffer size is 1 bar (4 beats in the current tempo of the master tempo source. The buffer size can be doubled by clicking the button *ST.2* (stretching of 2 bars = 8 beats).

Time-Stretching as well as Pitch-Shifting are based on granular synthesis. As with the Pitch-Shifter you can use the *GRNSZ* knob to configure the grain size after the GRN button is enabled (see section "Pitch-Shifting" for more information about the grain size parameter).

 In Group mode this effect behaves like a Pitch-Shifter. The knob then corresponds to the *KEY* knob of Single mode.

Mulholland Drive

The Mulholland Drive effect belongs to the group of so called overdrive effects (the name refers to the movie with the same name, directed by David Lynch, in which a Los Angeles highway with the same name plays an important role).

Mulholland Drive simulates the overdrive of the final stage of a guitar amplifier that creates the typical distortion of this effect.

The effect uses two different overdrive units that can produce different sounds. Which overdrive unit is used gets controlled with the DRIVE knob. When this knob is either at the outer left or at the outer right position only one of the both units is used. At all positions in between the effect both units create the signal. Here the knobs' position specifies the ratio between which effect signal from the two overdrive units is used.

The *FEEDB* knob (Feedback) is used to feed the effect signal back into the effect unit. When this knob is at position 0 (=no feed-back) then the effect sound is similar to an overdriven valve amplifier. The more the knob is opened the more intensive the effect gets. IF you enable the button *FB–* then only the uneven harmonics are fed back into the effect generator. (Uneven harmonics are those overtones of a fundamental tone whose frequencies are non integer multiples of the fundamental frequency).

The *TONE* knob can be used to change the sound colour of the feedback signal. The effect of this knob is best heard when the *FEEDB* knob is opened quite a lot and when the position of the *DRIVE* knob is in the range between 0 and 50. When the *TONE* knob is near position 0 the feedback signal is harsher; the more the knob is turned clockwise the smoother and the less harsh the sound gets.

 In Group mode the knob controls the distortion intensity. Unlike in Single mode in Group mode the portion of the original signal is larger, even when the *D/W* knob is set to 100.

Beatslicer

The Beatslicer is one of the buffer based Traktor effects. When you activate the effect with the *ON* button Traktor samples 2 bars (8 beats) of audio and cuts it into small slices. Those slices are played back in a different sequence. Traktor takes care that playback occurs in the rhythm of the currently selected master tempo source. In the default setting only the slices from the first four beats are played. When you activate the button *2 BAR* Traktor will use slices from the complete audio buffer.

Use the knobs *STYLE* and *PAT* (=PATTERN) to select the pattern and the sequence in which the slices are to be played back. The range of the STYLE knob is *S1* to *S5*. After selecting the style group use the *PAT* knob to select one of four patterns (*P2* to *P5; P1* sends the input signal unchanged to the effect's output path). Generally speaking, patterns with a higher numbers use smaller slices that are repeated more often.

The button *GTE* (which is incorrectly labelled as *GO)* also sends the audio signal trough a gate that in turn is controlled by another pattern. This results in a similar sound to the one produced by the Gater effect.

The *BUZZ* knob finally creates a beat-roll effect by increasing the repetition rate of one beat. You can use the *BUZZ* knob by itself as well by selecting the pattern *P1*. When you activate the *GTE* button the *BUZZ* effect is automatically disabled.

When you use this effect in Group mode you can select one of the four patterns of style *S2*.

Formant Filter

Despite all the differences between the sounds of human voices there are similarities in the way we "produce" letters with our mouth. In this way we are able to identify the different letters. The so called formants are important for the perception of vowels. To put it simply, formants can be thought as areas inside the frequency spectrum. When speaking different vowels different frequency areas are emphasised. This way we are able to distinguish between a "u", that is more a "dark" vowel and an "i", which is a "brighter" vowel.

The following figure shows a spectrogram where the frequency ranges typical for the vowels "i,", " u" and "a" are marked with little arrows.

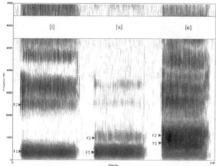

Image by Wikipedia user Ishwar

The Formant filter uses the frequency ranges that are typical for vowels as filter frequencies. To do this the audio signal is sent through several band pass filters (the Traktor effect uses three). After the audio signal has been processed only those frequency ranges that correspond to the formant regions of the different vowels are still audible. You can use the *TALK* knob to select which vowel shall be used. When the knob is at its outer left position, the dark "u" is used; when the knob is turned completely clockwise the brighter "i" is used.

Because the formant regions of the vowels also depend on the language you can use the *TYP* button to switch between "English spoken" (button activated) and "German spoken" (button disabled).

The *SIZE* knob controls the size of the virtual mouth that speaks the vowels which, affects the sound colour. When the knob is turned anti-clockwise the effects sounds damper; the more the knob is turned to the right the brighter the effect signal gets.

Finally the *SHARP* knob makes the effect more intense and emphasises the vowels; but its effect on the overall sound impression seems to be weak.

In Group mode the knob controls the *TALK* parameter, i.e. the frequency range that is still audible after the audio is run through the filter.

Peak Filter

The Peak filter is a variation of a band pass filter; but here the frequencies below and above the band pass are not attenuated, instead the selected frequency range is amplified.

Use the *FREQ* knob to select the frequency range that is to be amplified. When the knob is turned completely anti-clockwise the low frequencies are emphasised; the more the knob is turned clockwise the more the high frequencies are emphasised.

When you activate the *KILL* button the effect is switched to band-rejection mode. When this mode is active and when the FREQ knob is at its outmost clockwise position the audio can pass through the filter almost unchanged. The more the knob is turned towards its middle position, the more low and middle frequencies are emphasised. When the knob is turned from its middle position anti-clockwise, the more low and middle frequencies disappear the more high frequencies are audible.

The *PUMP* knob has two functions: First you can use it to configure how strong the selected frequency range is emphasised. The more the knob is opened the stronger the frequencies are amplified. At the same time the knob activates the brick wall limiter of the effect which makes sure, that the output level of the effect signal is 0 dB at its maximum.

The *EDGE* knob functions like a resonance knob, which is also available in several of the other effects. It emphasises the frequency range that is amplified by the filter.

 In Group mode the knob controls the *FREQ* parameter, i.e. you can configure the frequency range that is amplified by the filter.

Macro Effects

Since version 2.6 Traktor has had the so-called macro effects as well as the normal effects that we have become accustomed too. A macro effect glues several of the normal effects into one new effect. For the macro effects all effect parameters are controlled by one knob. If you use the FX unit in Single mode, use the third knob.

If the knob is in the centre position, the effect is off. Depending on whether you turn the knob to the left or to the right, different settings are applied to the effects that are bundled in the macro effect.

Actually, macro effects are not a new invention of Traktor 2.6. Even in previous Traktor versions (and of course also in the current version) you can use some clever mapping tricks to create your own macro effects. You can use either Group mode for one FX unit and one deck and create a macro effect that is a combination of the three selected effects. To have more control of the parameter settings, you can use maybe two FX units in Single mode, assign them to the same deck, and then tweak several effect settings with one knob or button on your mapped controller.

A great example of how to create your own macro effects can be found in the following video: *www.youtube.com/watch?v=lMbsAIBs3uE*. The video uses Traktor Pro 1.x, but the procedures that are shown can also be used for the current Traktor version. The only thing you need to change are the names of the mapping commands, as they have changed.

If you prefer to use the macro effects that Traktor provides, check them and see which ones you like. The fantasy names of the macro effects do not really describe what they do or how they sound: Bass-o-matic, DarkMatter, EventHorizon, FlightTest, Granu-Phase, LaserSlicer, PolarWind, Strretch Fast, Strrretch Slow, Wormhole, and Zzzurp.

Chapter 14

Recording

The audio recorder that is integrated into Traktor makes it easy to record your own sets. Traktor saves your recordings in wave format in the default folder for recordings. Alternatively you can route the recording signal in internal mixing mode to an external output. This setup allows you to record your mix with an external recording device. This chapter contains all information needed to make recording your mix a success.

If you use one of the Traktor Kontrol controllers S2, S4, or Z2, that are equipped with a microphone input, you can record the mic input as well. You will most likely need to tweak your input routing slightly before this will work. The section on page 493 and onwards explains all the steps required to make this work.

14.1 Setting up the Audio Recorder

Before you can record your mixes in Traktor you need to configure the audio routing and in some cases you even have to setup the hardware. The following sections explain how it works.

Audio Routing for Internal Mixing Mode and recording in Traktor

Traktor Kontrol S2/S4, and Z2 use the internal mixing mode of Traktor. All three controllers are equipped with a soundcard having two stereo outputs. These specifications are valid for many of the various other DJ controllers that you can use with Traktor.

If you use internal mixing mode and if you wish to use the integrated mix recorder, you only need to do a minimal amount of configuration work:

1. Open the dialog *Preferences/Output Routing*. Check if *Mixing Mode* is set to *Internal*.

2. Open the category *Mix Recorder*. The setting *Source* must be set to *Internal*.

3. Close the *Preferences* dialog.

4. Click the cassette icon on the right side of the Global Section to open the Audio Recorder panel.

> **NOTE** If the cassette icon is not visible open the *Preferences* dialog and switch to the category *Global Settings*. Activate the checkbox *Show Global Section*.

5. Play a track and check if the level meter in the audio recorder panel shows some activity. Finally, use the Gain knob in the recorder panel to change the signal strength. Make sure that the level meter does not clip.

In this configuration Traktor will record the same signal, which is sent to the *Output Master*, in a wave file.

Direct Thru and Recording with Kontrol Z2

The Direct-Thru mode of Traktor Kontrol Z2 (see also chapter 4) allows it, to use Z2 as a stand-alone mixer. If you switch both input channels of the Z2 to Direct-Thru you can use both channels for normal vinyl or audio CDs. You can also use a mixed setup and use one channel for normal vinyl/audio CD and control the other channel via timecode.

As in Direct-Thru mode the signal coming from the phono or line input remains inside the soundcard/mixer of the Z2 you cannot use the internal source for Traktors' mix recorder.

Perform the following steps to record you mix if one or both input channels are set to Direct-Thru:

1. Open the *Preferences/Input Routing* dialog and select *Master Left* and *Master Right* in section *Input FX Send (Ext)*.

2. Open the category *Mix Recorder* and set *Source* to *External*.
3. Open the list *External Input* and select *Input FX Send (Ext)*.

Audio Routing for Internal Mixing Mode; recording is done by an External Recorder or by another Application on a different Computer

Using the integrated recorder isn't the only way to record your mix. Another option is using an external recording device or to record with another application running on a different computer. In this case you need to configure Traktor in a way that the master output signal, which is routed to the channels selected as *Output Master,* will be additionally routed to the two channels which are selected in the section *Output Record.* For this configuration you need an audio interface with at least three stereo channels (= six channels).

1. Open the dialog *Preferences/Output Routing* and check if *Mixing Mode* is set to *Internal.*

2. Open the category *Mix Recorder.* The setting *Source* must be set to *Internal.*

3. Open the category *Output Routing.* Use the section *Output Record* and select the two channels of your audio interface to which Traktor shall send the mix out signal.

4. Connect your external recorder to the two outputs selected in step 3. Or connect the outputs selected in step 3 with the second computer and configure the recording software on this computer to use the connected inputs.

In this configuration you start and stop the recording on the second computer or on the external recording device, respectively.

> **NOTE** In this setup it is possible to record your mix in other file formats than .wav if the recording software supports the desired format.

Audio Routing for External Mixing Mode and a Mixer with Integrated Audio Interface

If you use one of the Traktor certified mixers (they always have an integrated audio interface) the signal path is a bit different. The reason is that the master output signal is not generated by Traktor but by the external mixer. The mixer sends the master output signal via the USB or FireWire port back to Traktor. Traktor catches this audio signal and saves it in a file.

For this to work you must first configure the mixer. You need to specify to which audio channels the signal is to be sent from the mixer to Traktor. Before this will work you need to configure Traktor accordingly and select the audio channels, on which Traktor receives the signal that the mixer is sending.

The mixer Xone:4D for example is equipped with four stereo inputs. Channel 4, inputs 7 and 8, are internally connected in a way that this channel receives the mix out signal. To activate this configuration you need to make sure that the upper red button above channel fader no. 4 is **not** pressed.

Once the mixer is properly configured you can setup the recording settings in Traktor.

1. Open the dialog *Preferences/Output Routing*. Make sure that in Section *Mixing Mode* the option *External* is selected.

2. Open the *Input Routing* dialog. Assign the two mixer channels that the mix out signal is being sent on to one of the four *Channels A to D*. For a Xone:4D for example you should use Inputs 7 and 8; in this screenshot I have routed those two inputs to *Input Deck D*.

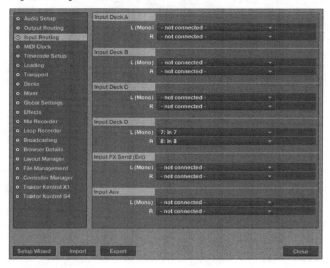

3. Open the category *Mix Recorder*. The settings *Source* must be set to *External*.

4. Open the list *External Input* and select the channels to which you assigned the two mixer channels in step 2. For this example you want to use *Input Deck D*.

5. Close the *Preferences* dialog.

Once these settings have been made you can record the mix out signal of your mixer with the internal Traktor recorder.

> **TIP** Check the weblink page on *www.traktorbible.com/2014/links.aspx* for a tutorial explaining how to record your mix with Xone:DB4 and Traktor Pro.

Audio Routing for an External Mixer and an External Audio Interface

The fourth and the last configuration is an external mixer without an integrated audio interface. To be able to record your mixes in this setup you need to physically connect the mixer outputs, to which the mix out signal is sent, to one of the inputs of your audio interface. Once the physical connection is made you can configure Traktor accordingly.

The following shows this using the example of the Traktor Audio 10:

1. Open the *Preferences/Output Routing* dialog and check if *Mixing Mode* is set to *External*.

2. Open the category *Input Routing*. Assign the channels of your audio interface to which, you connected the cable coming from your mixer, to one of the *Input Channels A to D*.

   There is a level meter at the right side of the list boxes for the channel selection. Here you can check if the selected inputs are receiving the audio signal.

3. Open the category *Mix Recorder*. The setting *Source* must be set to *External*.

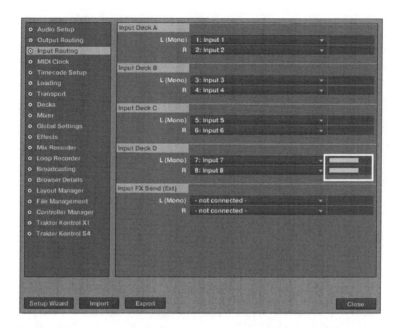

4. Open the list *External Input* and select the channels that you assigned the two mixer channels to in step 2.

5. Close the *Preferences* dialog.

Once those settings have been made you can record the mix out signal of your mixer with the integrated Traktor audio recorder.

More Recording Settings

As well as the settings for the audio routing Traktor offers three further options regarding audio recording. Those three options can be found in the section *File* of the *Preferences/Mix Recorder* dialog.

Directory   Here you can configure the folder where Traktor shall save the recorded wave files. The default setting depends on your operating system:

◘   **Windows 7/Windows 8**   C:\Users*[Username]*\Music\Traktor\Recordings

◘   **OS X**   Macintosh HD/Users/*[Username]*/Music/Traktor/Recordings

The folder list in the Traktor browser contains a node named *Audio Recordings*. If you click this icon Traktor opens a special playlist inside the Traktor collection named *Audio Recordings;* it does *not* open the physical folder with your recordings. Every time you create a new Traktor recording Traktor will add a new entry with this recording to the special playlist.

If you use the *Browse* button for the *Directory* option and if the new folder already contains wave files Traktor does not add them automatically to the *Audio Recordings* playlist. Unfortunately it is not possible to add new entries to this playlist via drag and drop. This means if you change the location of the *Audio Recordings* folder after you have already made some recordings you can only load the old recordings by searching for them in the *Track Collection* node.

Prefix The default format of the file names of your audio recordings *Year-Month-Day_TimeOfRecording*, for example *2014-03-01_11h28m32.wav*. The filenames can be extended by a prefix which you can enter in the *Prefix* field.

> **ATTENTION** Make sure that you only use characters in your *Prefix* setting that are valid in a filename for your operating system. If you should enter "Techno :)" here, the audio recording cannot be started because the colon is an invalid character in a filename.

Split File at Size The list *Split File at Size* offers several file size options. If the recorded file becomes larger than the selected file size Traktor automatically creates a new file. The *700 MB* option is useful if you wish to burn the wave file onto an audio CD. The 2048 MB (= 2 gigabyte) option makes it possible that the created wave file can be opened in any audio editor application.

File Size of Audio Recordings

Traktor always saves the audio recordings in wave format. The required file space depends on the bit depth (in Traktor always 16 bit), the number of channels (in Traktor always 2 = stereo) and the sample rate of the audio interface. The sample rate is the only parameter which can be configured in Traktor. The wave file created by Traktor always uses the same sample rate as configured in the dialog *Preferences/Audio Setup*.

The following table shows the space requirements for some standard sampling rates. The third column shows how many minutes of uncompressed audio fit into a 2 gigabyte wave file.

Sample Rate	Space Requirement per Minute	Audio Duration in a 2 GB File
44.100 Hz	10.09 MB	approx. 202 minutes
48.000 Hz	10.90 MB	approx. 186 minutes
88.200 Hz	20.18 MB	approx. 101 minutes
96.000 Hz	21.97 MB	approx. 93 minutes

The maximum size of a wave file is four gigabytes. Each wave file contains a header at the very beginning of the file. This header contains information about the file content and about the file size (to be precise: here the file size minus 8 bytes is stored). The field for storing the file size is actually 4 bytes (=32 bits) long. This means that the value range for the file size is between 0 and 4.294.967.295.

Sony developed an extension to the classic wave format, called Wave64 format. Wave64 is a 64 bit wave format which means that the maximum file size restriction of 4 gigabytes no longer exists. Unfortunately the current Traktor version does not support the Wave64 format.

14.2   The Audio Recorder in the Global Section

Once the necessary configuration is done, the recording itself is just a matter of a few mouse clicks in the Audio Recorder panel of the Global Section. To open the Audio Recorder  panel click the icon with the cassette on the right side of the Global Section.

While recording Traktor shows the current file size and audio length in the Audio Recorder panel. The level meter displays the signal strength of the audio signal that Traktor is sending to the internal recorder. If the level meter shows no activity check the audio routing. The previous sections contain detailed information about setting up the audio routing for different configurations.

Button/Knob	Description
●	This button starts and stops the recording. You can use the mapping command Audio Recorder | Record/Stop instead.
GAIN	Use the Gain knob to set the signal strength of the recorded audio signal. You can use the mapping command Audio Recorder | Gain Adjust for this as well.
CUT	The CUT button can be used to save the current recording into a file and to seamlessly create a new file. If you use the CUT button Traktor automatically appends the length of the file to the filename. You can use the mapping command Audio Recorder | Cut instead.

14.3 Recording the Mic with Kontrol S2/S4/Z2

Traktor Kontrol S2, S4, and Z2 are equipped with a microphone input. When and whether the mic gets recording is slightly different with the three devices. This section describes how you get it working with all three controllers.

Kontrol S2 MK2: Recording and Using the Microphone

In the default configuration the mic signal from Kontrol S2 remains in the internal soundcard of the S2. When you press the *MIC ENGAGE* button at the front of the controller, the mic audio is fed directly into the main output. As a result the mic input is not recorded. In internal mixing mode, which is used by Kontrol S2, only the audio signals that are available to the software mixer of Traktor are recorded.

However, a little trick will allow you to record the mic. You need to route the microphone signal back into the software mixer to Traktor. Perform the following steps:

1. Make sure that the *MIC GAIN* knob at the rear of S2 is turned completely to the left and then connect your microphone to the *MIC* input.

   If you are using a condenser microphone you need to connect a phantom power adapter between your microphone and the S2 because the S2 cannot supply the phantom power needed to drive the mic.

2. Open the *Preferences/Input Routing* dialog. Select the microphone input of the S2 in section *Input Aux*.

   As the microphone signal is only mono it is sufficient to select an entry in list *L (Mono)* only.

   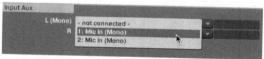

3. Keep the *Preferences/Input Routing* dialog open and press the *MIC ENGAGE* button at the front of Kontrol S2.

   The Microphone LED in the middle section of the controller should now be on.

4. Speak or sing into your mic and open the *MIC GAIN* knob at the rear of Kontrol S2 until the level meter in section *Input Aux* shows a sufficient level.

5. Once you have made these changes to the *Input Routing* you need to control the microphone level with the *AUX* knob at the very right of the crossfader panel. If this panel isn't visible activate the checkbox *Crossfader* (*Preferences/Mixer/Mixer Layout*). In order for the microphone to work, the *MIC ENGAGE* button at the front of S2 must also be on.

6. You may find it a bit cumbersome to use the mouse to get the microphone level right. An easy way to solve this is adding the following mapping commands to the default mapping of the S2:

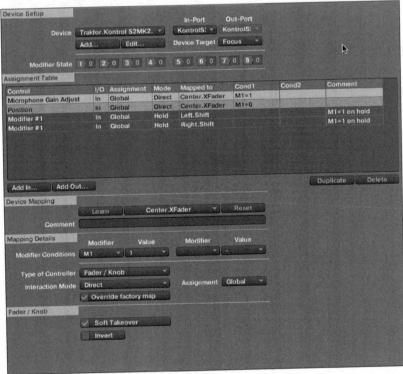

The first two commands are assigned to the crossfader of the S2. Which one of the two mapped commands gets executed when you move the crossfader, depends on the value of modifier #1. This modifier is set to value 1 while one of the two *SHIFT* buttons is hold (mapping commands 3 and 4).

If no *SHIFT* buttons is pressed the crossfader works as in the default mapping. If one of the *SHIFT* buttons is pressed, the crossfader controls the level of the microphone by using the mapping command

Please make sure that option *Override factory map* is disabled for both modifier conditions. This ensures that the *SHIFT* button keeps working in a normal way for all other controls of the S2.

For both mapping commands assigned to *Center.XFader* you **must** activate *Override factory map*. Only then the crossfader has its new functionality which is now dependent on the state of the *SHIFT* buttons.

Kontrol S4 MK2: Recording and Using the Mic without EQ and Effects

On the rear you will find a microphone connector and a gain knob for the mic. The volume of the mic can be set with the *MIC VOL* knob on the front of the S4.

Perform the following steps to use a microphone with Kontrol S4 MK2. Once you are done the mic signal will be automatically recorded together with your mix:

1. Make sure that the *MIC GAIN* knob at the rear of S4 is turned completely to the left and then connect your microphone to the *MIC* input.

    If you are using a condenser microphone you need to connect a phantom power adapter between your microphone and the S4 because the S4 cannot supply phantom power needed to drive the mic.

2. Open the *Preferences/Input Routing* dialog. Please check if the microphone input is selected in section *Input Aux;* if not, select it.

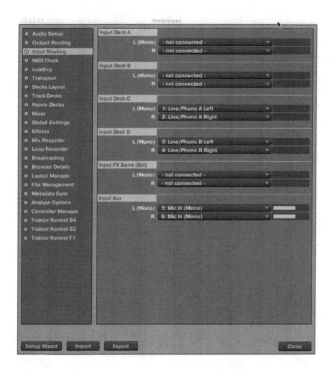

3. Keep the dialog open and then speak or sing into your mic and open the *MIC GAIN* knob at the rear of Kontrol S4 until the level meter in section *Input Aux* shows a sufficient level.

4. Close the *Preferences* window.

The microphone is now ready to use. Use the knob *MIC VOL* at the front of the S4 to set the volume level. While the microphone is open it will be recorded together with your mix.

Kontrol S4 MK2: Recording and Using the Mic with EQ, FX, and Filter

With the setup explained in the previous section you can record the microphone input, but you cannot modify it with a filter, with the EQ, or with a Traktor effect. There is a way to achieve this: you need to route the microphone input not only into *Input Aux* but also into one of the decks and then set the input mode for that deck to *Live Input*. The following examples shows how to proceed if you wish to use deck D; however, you can use any of the four decks.

1. Make sure that the *MIC GAIN* knob at the rear of S4 is turned completely to the left and then connect your mic to the *MIC* input.

If you are using a condenser microphone you need to connect a phantom power adapter between your microphone and the S4 because the S4 cannot supply phantom power needed to drive the mic.

2. Open the *Preferences/Input Routing* dialog. Please check if the microphone input is selected in section *Input Aux;* if not, select it.

3. Go to section *Input Deck D* and select the microphone input here as well.

4. Keep the dialog open and then speak or sing into your mic and open the *MIC GAIN* knob at the rear of Kontrol S4 until the level meter in section *Input Aux* shows a sufficient level.

5. Close the *Preferences* window.

6. Click the letter D on deck D to open the context menu and select *Live Input.*

Now you can use your microphone in two different ways: If you do not need a filter, the EQ or a Traktor effect for the microphone signal use the *MIC VOL* knob at the front of Kontrol S4 to open and close the microphone.

If you wish to modify the microphone signal by a filter, by the equalizer, or by a Traktor effect switch the deck to Live Input. Then you can control the volume as for track decks with the channelfader and you can use the deck filter, the EQ, and the FX in the same way as you would for a track deck. In this setup the position of the *MIC VOL* knob no longer affects the volume.

Kontrol Z2: Recording the Microphone

Traktor Kontrol Z2 also provides a microphone input. The level of the microphone is controlled with the VOLUME knob that you can find in section AUX/MIC of the Z2. You can use the TONE knob to change the frequencies of the signal. Turning the knob anti-clockwise emphasizes the higher and turning it clockwise emphasizes the lower frequencies.

As long as the MIC ENGAGE button is active, the microphone signal is added to the master output of the internal soundcard of the Z2. Because in the default configuration the mic signal is not routed back into the internal software mixer of Traktor, the mic signal does not get recorded.

If you wish to record the microphone together with your mix, route the microphone as Live Input into deck C or deck D. Then open the volume knob of the deck you use completely and keep it open. You can then control the microphone with the button and the knobs in section *AUX/MIC*.

Perform the following steps if you wish to be able to recording the microphone connected to your Kontrol Z2:

1. Open the *Preferences/Input Routing* dialog. *Select either in section Input Deck C* or *Input Deck D* the microphone/aux input.

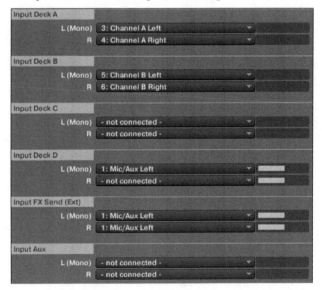

2. Open the category *Decks Layout* and select in section *Deck Flavor* either for Deck C or for Deck D option *Live Input*.

3. Close the *Preferences window*.

4. Set the level knob for deck C or deck D to the maximum level.

   As long as you use this deck for your microphone only, you do not need to change this setting because the microphone is only active if the mic button is pressed and if the *VOLUME* knob in section *AUX/MIC* is open.

14.4 Splitting the Wave File into Tracks

If you wish to create an audio CD with individual tracks from your mix you first need to split the recorded wave into the desired tracks. Once this is done use your CD burning software and configure it so that there are no pauses between the tracks.

Using Audacity

One way to split the wave file is using the free tool Audacity, which is available for Windows as well as for Mac OS X *(http://audacity.sourceforge.net/)*.

Download and install Audacity and then follow these steps:

1. Choose *File/Open* to load the wave file created by Traktor. Depending on the file size this can take some time.

2. Please make sure that the playmarker is at the begging of the track. Use the command *Tracks/Add Label at Selection* (Shortcut: Cmd+B/Ctrl+B). Audacity inserts a label track into the project. At the same time a new label is inserted at the very beginning of the file. Audacity uses those labels to split the loaded wave file into individual tracks.

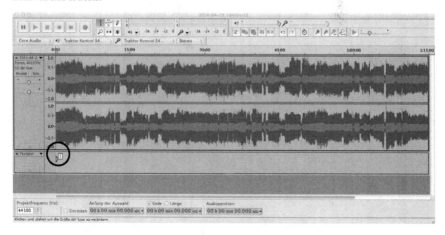

3. Click in the waveform at the position where the next label is to be inserted or start the playback of the file. Use the command *Tracks/Add Label at Selection*) to insert another label.

> **NOTE** Labels can only be inserted during the playback of the file or if playback is paused. You can start playback with the Space key (it toggles between Play and Stop). Use the hotkey P to pause playback. To move the playback marker you need to pause the playback, then click the waveform and then resume playback.

4. Labels cannot be moved. To move a label you first need to delete the old one and then create a new label at the desired position. To delete a label select it in the track and then press then Del key.

5. Once all desired labels are inserted you can let Audacity split the wave file. Click on *Stop* to stop playback. Files can only be exported when playback is stopped.

6. Choose the menu command *File/Export Multiple*.

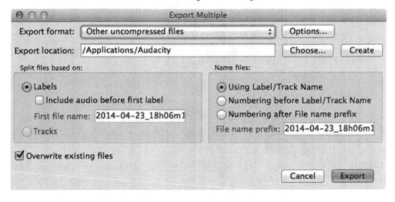

7. Enter the name of the folder where Audacity is to save the exported files into *Export location*.

8. Activate the option *Labels* in the section *Split files based on*.

9. Check the option *Numbering after File name prefix* in section *Name files* and enter the prefix into field *File name prefix*. Audacity will then automatically append a track number to the file names.

10. Click on *Options* to select the file format of the exported audio files. The OS X version of Audacity uses AIFF as default and the Windows version uses WAVE.

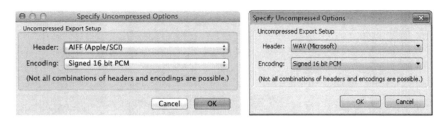

11. Click on *Export*. When export is finished you can use your CD burning application to create an audio CD. Make sure that the CD burning application removes the default pause between the tracks. The following figure shows a screenshot from the application Nero with the appropriate setting,

Using CD Wave Editor

An alternative to Audacity is the tool CD Wave Editor, a Windows application that you can download from *www.milosoftware.com*. The handling is slightly better than in Audacity. CD Wave Editor shows the complete waveform and a zoomed view at the same time.

1. Use the command *File/Open to load the recorded wave file*. Depending on the file size this can take some time.

2. Use the *Split* button below the waveform to insert a split marker or use the shortcut Alt+S. The split list in the lower part of the window shows all tracks which result from the inserted split markers.

3. To change the track name (which will be used as the filename for the exported file) click the desired entry in the Split list to select it. Press F2, enter the track name and press Enter.

4. To remove an incorrectly placed split marker click the entry in the Split list to select it. Then press the key combination Ctrl+Del to delete the split marker.

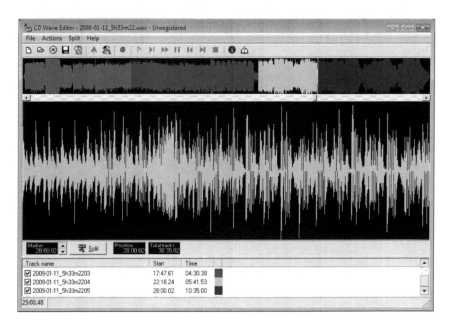

5. Once all split markers are inserted use the menu command *File/Save* to export the individual tracks.

6. The dialog *Select Output* is shown. Enter the folder where CDF Wave Editor is to save the individual tracks in the field *Output Location*.

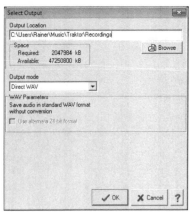

7. Select the option *Direct WAV* in the list *Output Mode*. This creates standard wave files which can be burned onto an audio CD.

8. Click *OK* to export the individual tracks.

14.5 Recording and Mapping Commands

There are only a few mapping commands for the audio recorder. The following table shows which commands are available.

Recording		
Audio Recorder | Record/Stop	Interaction Mode: Hold, Toggle Interaction Mode: Direct Set to value: 1=On/0=Off	Starts/stops the recording with the internal Traktor recorder.
Audio Recorder | Cut	Interaction Mode: Trigger	Saves the current recording into a file and seamlessly creates a new file.
Audio Recorder | Gain Adjust	Interaction Mode: Direct Type of Controller: Fader, Knob, Encoder	Set the signal strength of the audio signal sent to the audio recorder
Audio Recorder | Load Last Recording	Interaction Mode: Trigger Assignment: select desired deck	Loads the last recording into the deck selected in the list Assignment.
Mixer | Meters | Record Input Level (L) Mixer | Meters | Record Input Level (R)	Interaction Mode: Output	Can be used to display the level of the recorded signal on a controller. See chapter 6 for more information about LED output.
Mixer | Meters | Record Input Clip (L) Mixer | Meters | Record Input Clip (R)	Interaction Mode: Output	Can be used to display the level of the clipped part of the recorded signal on a controller. See chapter 6 for more information about LED output.

You can use these commands together with one modifier to configure a button like this: the first press of the button will start the recording, pressing the same button again stops the recording and loads the recorded file into the selected deck. The initial condition for the modifier (the following example uses modifier #1) is the value 0.

The following five commands need to be mapped to the same button/the same key:

First button/key-press

◻ Modifier | Modifier #1, Interaction Mode: Direct, Set to value = 1,
Modifier Conditions: M1 has Value 0

◻ Audio Recorder | Record/Stop, Interaction Mode: Direct, Set to value = 1,
Modifier Conditions: M1 has Value 0

Second button/key-press

◻ Modifier | Modifier #1, Interaction Mode: Direct, Set to value = 0,
Modifier Conditions: M1 has Value 1

◻ Audio Recorder | Record/Stop, Interaction Mode: Direct, Set to value = 0,
Modifier Conditions: M1 has Value 1

◻ Audio Recorder | Load Last Recording, Interaction Mode: Trigger,
Assignment: select the desired deck,
Modifier Conditions: M1 has Value 1

Index

Index

Index

Index

Index

Index

Index

Index

X

Z

Made in the USA
Middletown, DE
02 November 2015